Performance Management

Performance Management

Multidisciplinary Perspectives

Edited by

Richard Thorpe
University of Leeds, UK

Jacky Holloway
Open University Business School, UK

First published 2008 by
PALGRAVE MACMILLAN
Houndmills, Basingstoke, Hampshire RG21 6XS and
175 Fifth Avenue, New York, N.Y. 10010
Companies and representatives throughout the world

PALGRAVE MACMILLAN is the global academic imprint of the Palgrave
Macmillan division of St. Martin's Press, LLC and of Palgrave Macmillan Ltd.
Macmillan® is a registered trademark in the United States, United Kingdom
and other countries. Palgrave is a registered trademark in the European
Union and other countries.

ISBN-13: 978-1-4039-4761-1 hardback
ISBN-10: 1-4039-4761-9 hardback

This book is printed on paper suitable for recycling and made from fully
managed and sustained forest sources. Logging, pulping and manufacturing
processes are expected to conform to the environmental regulations of the
country of origin.

A catalogue record for this book is available from the British Library.

A catalog record for this book is available from the Library of Congress.

10   9   8   7   6   5   4   3   2   1
17   16   15   14   13   12   11   10   09   08

Printed and bound in Great Britain by
CPI Antony Rowe, Chippenham and Eastbourne

This book is dedicated to Tony Beasley, a valued friend and colleague. As a founder member of the British Academy of Management Performance Management Special Interest Group, Tony was the inspiration both for this book and the associated ESRC seminar series. The editors both worked closely with Tony over a number of years, first as an ESRC Teaching Fellow and later as an officer of BAM and researcher with an interest in performance and performance management. Many of the contributors in the book have similarly worked with him and he has been an inspiration to us all.

Contents

List of Figures and Tables

Figures

Tables

Preface

This book builds on the activities of the British Academy of Management Performance Management Special Interest Group, and the ESRC Seminar Series 'Perspectives on performance' that has provided a structure and impetus for the book.

The seminar series was designed to explore the way performance management is researched and practised from the perspective of a range of fields of study and disciplinary domains. Between 2004 and 2006, seminars were held at the Open University Business School, Warwick Business School, Cranfield School of Management, Leeds University Business School, Henley Management College and the University of East Anglia. For their support in helping both plan and mount these seminars and for their continued enthusiasm for the project, we would like especially to thank Mike Kennerley, Zoe Radnor, Liz Houldsworth, Jean Clarke, David Barnes, Vinh Chau and Barry Witcher. All the seminars were ably supported administratively by Rebecca Davies and would not have happened at all without funding from the Economic and Social Research Council.

Between the conferences and the Special Interest Group meetings and the completion of this book the bulk of the secretarial work has fallen to Carol Reeves. Carol has quietly and expertly organized the formal paperwork and manuscript as well as completing the bibliography. We are most grateful for her continued patience and enthusiasm without which the project would not have been completed.

RICHARD THORPE
JACKY HOLLOWAY

Acknowledgements

The editors and publishers are grateful to the following for permission to reproduce copyright material:

Palgrave Macmillan, for Chapter 3, originally published as 'Performance management: a framework for analysis', by David Otley, in Berry, A. J., Broadbent, J. and Otley, D., *Management Control: Theories, Issues and Performance*, 2nd edn (Palgrave Macmillan, 2005). (Ch. 6, pp. 79–95); Chapter 9, originally published as 'Performance management and operational research: a marriage made in heaven?', by Smith, P. C. and Goddard, M., in *Journal of the Operational Research Society*, Vol. 53, pp. 247–55; Figure 7.3, forthcoming in Van Dooren, W. and Van de Walle, S. (eds), *Utilising Public Sector Performance Information*, Kernaghan, K. and van der Donk, W. (series eds) *Governance and Public Management*; and for Chapter 19, Table 19.1, which includes concepts and ideas drawn from previous research contained in Bowey, A. M. and Thorpe, R., with Hellier, P., *Payment Systems and Productivity* (Basingstoke: Macmillan, 1986).

The Hay Group, for Figure 6.1 Performance management continuum.

Blackwell Publishing, for Figure 6.2, Storey's evolution of HRM, taken from *Developments in the Management of Human Resources: An Analytical Review*, 1st edn (London: Blackwell, 1992) p. 168.

FT Prentice Hall, for Figure 7.1, originally published as Figure 1.3 in Slack, N., Chambers, S., Johnston, R. and Betts, A., *Operations and Process Management* (FT Prentice Hall, 2005); Chapter 10, adapted from the Executive Summary of *Marketing and the Bottom Line*, by Tim Ambler (FT Prentice Hall/Pearson Ltd., 2003); Figure 18.1, originally in Thorpe, R. and Homan, G. (eds), *Strategic Reward Systems*; and for Chapter 7 in Thorpe, R. *Designing and Implementation of Remuneration Systems* (Prentice Hall/Financial Times, 2000).

The President and Fellows of Harvard College for permission to adapt and reprint an Exhibit in 'Using the Balanced Scorecard as a Strategic Management System' by Kaplan, R. S. and Norton, P., *Harvard Business Review*, January–February 1996, 77, all rights reserved, as Figure 15.1, 'Kaplan and Norton's description of the balanced-scorecard process'.

European Foundation for Quality Management for permission to adapt and reprint Figure 15.2, 'The measurement model of the EFQM', from *EFQM Self-assessment Guidelines* (2001).

Bernard Marr and Butterworth-Heinemann for Chapter 13 which is based on parts of *Strategic Performance Management: Leveraging and Measuring Your Intangible Value Drivers* (Oxford: Butterworth Heinemann, 2006); David Wise and ICSA Information and Training Ltd. for Chapter 17, Figure 17.1, 'Figure-of-eight model for value for money', originally published as Figure 4.2 in Wise, D., *Performance Measurement for Charities* (ICSA Publishing, 1995).

Chapter 2 was first published as 'The characteristics of performance management research: implications and challenges', by Thorpe, R. and Beasley, T., in *International Journal of Productivity and Performance Management*, Vol. 53, No. 4 (2004) 334–44, Emerald Pubs.; Figure 15.3 was first published in 'It's all action, it's all learning: action learning in SMEs', by Clarke, J., Thorpe, R., Anderson, L. and Gold, J., in *Journal of European Industrial Training*, Vol. 30, No. 6 (2006) 441–55, Emerald Pubs.

Acknowledgement of unpublished work

Figure 7.2, 'The three E's Model (Radnor, 2005)' is taken from unpublished teaching material, Warwick University.

Chapter 8, Figure 8.1 is taken from Wickes, M., *An Explorative Study into the Utility of Visual Reporting Systems in Project and Programme Management Environments* (Cranfield University, PhD Thesis, 2005).

Every effort has been made to contact all the copyright-holders, but if any have been inadvertently omitted the publishers will be pleased to make the necessary arrangements as quickly as possible.

List of Abbreviations and Acronyms

APEC	Asia Pacific Economic Cooperation
APM	Association for Project Management
BAM	British Academy of Management
BPR	Business Process Re-engineering
BSC	Balanced Scorecard
BSI	British Standards Institution
CBA	Cost-Benefit Analysis
C/SCSC	Cost/Schedule Control Systems Criteria
CDC	Centers for Disease Control
CEO	Chief Executive Officer
CFO	Chief Financial Officer
CLV	Customer Lifetime Value
CPA	Comprehensive Performance Assessment
CPA	Critical Path Analysis or Critical Path Method
CSF	Critical Success Factor
CSFs	Critical Success Factors
DEA	Data Envelopment Analysis
DETR	Department of Environment, Transport and the Regions
DGEISR	Defense Global Emerging Infections Surveillance and Response System
EFQM	European Foundation for Quality Management
EIS	Executive Information System
EPS	Earnings Per Share
ERP	Enterprise Resource Planning
ESRC	Economic and Social Research Council
EVA®	Economic Value Added
EVM	Earned Value Method
FMI	Financial Management Initiative
GAAP	Generally Accepted Accounting Practice
GSK	GlaxoSmithKline
GVA	Gross Value Added
HBR	Harvard Business Review
HR	Human Resource
HRM	Human Resource Management
ICTs	Information and Communication Technologies

IFRS	International Financial Reporting Standards
IiP	Investors in People
INFORMS	Operations Research and the Management Sciences
IPPD	Improving Programme and Project Delivery
IT	Information Technology
KPI	Key Performance Indicator
KPIs	Key Performance Indicators
MBO	Management by Objectives
MHN	Markets, Hierarchies and Networks
MIS	Management Information Systems
MPAF	Major Projects Agreement Forum
nAch	Need To Achieve
nAff	Need For Affiliation
NCVO	National Council for Voluntary Organisations
NHS	National Health Service
NPM	New Public Management
nPow	Need For Power
NVQs	National Vocational Qualifications
OB	Organizational Behaviour
OECD	Organisation for Economic Co-operation and Development
OGC	Office of Government and Commerce
OM	Operations Management
OP	Occupational Psychology
OP & OB	Occupational Psychology and Organizational Behaviour
OPSR	Office of Public Services Reform
OR	Operational Research
PAR	Programme Analysis and Review
PERT	Programme Evaluation and Review Technique
PI	Performance Indicators
PM	Performance Management
PMM	Performance Measurement And Management
POW	Production of Welfare
PPBS	Planning, Programming and Budgeting Systems
PRP	Performance-Related Pay
PSA	Public Service Agreements
PSPP	Public Services Productivity Panel
R&D	Research and Development
ROI	Return on Investment
SARS	Severe Acute Respiratory Syndrome
SEMSs	Strategic Enterprise Management Systems

SMA	Strategic Management Accounting
SME	Small and Medium-sized Enterprises
SSCs	Shared Service Centres
SSRIs	Selective Serotonin Re-Uptake Inhibitors
TQM	Total Quality Management
TRIPS	Trade Related Aspects of Intellectual Property and Public Health
UK	United Kingdom
US	United States
VCOs	Voluntary and Community Organizations
VCS	Voluntary and Community Sector
WTO	World Trade Organisation

Notes on the Contributors

Tim Ambler is a Senior Fellow at London Business School. His main research covers dynamic marketing capabilities, how advertising works and the evaluation of marketing performance. He is currently also researching narrative disclosures in company annual reports as well as regulation and deregulation by the EU and UK governments. His books include *Marketing and the Bottom Line* (2000, 2003), *Doing Business in China* (2000, 2003), *The SILK Road to International Marketing* (2000) and *Marketing from Advertising to Zen* (1996). He has published in the *Journal of Marketing, Journal of Marketing Research, International Journal of Research in Marketing, Psychology & Marketing, Journal of Advertising Research* and *International Journal of Advertising*. A member of the *Journal of Marketing, International Journal of Advertising* and *Psychology & Marketing* Editorial Review Boards and Economics Committee of the Advertising Association, he is a Fellow of the Institute of Chartered Accountants in England and Wales and previously Joint Managing Director of International Distillers and Vintners (IDV), now part of Diageo plc. During his various marketing roles in IDV, in the UK and internationally, he was involved in the launch of Baileys, Malibu and Archers and the development of Smirnoff vodka worldwide.

David Barnes is a Senior Lecturer at Royal Holloway, University of London. He has held lecturing posts with the Open University and Thames Valley University. Prior to academia, he worked for over 15 years in industry. His research interests include the strategic management of operations, performance management and e-business. He has written extensively in these fields.

Tony Bovaird is Professor of Public Management and Policy at the Institute of Local Government Studies (INLOGOV) at Birmingham University. He worked as an economist at the Department of the Environment before joining Birmingham University in 1972 and he returned to INLOGOV in 2006 following spells at Aston and Bristol Business Schools. Tony is a prolific author and researcher in the fields of performance management in the public sector; assessment frameworks for public and local governance; evaluation and monitoring of public programmes; strategic management of public organizations; marketing and quality management for public services. He is Director of the Long-term Meta-evaluation of the Local Government Modernisation Agenda (2002–2007), commissioned by the Office of the Deputy Prime Minister (ODPM). He has been a Specialist Advisor to House of Commons Select Committee on the Environment, a consultant to the European Commission, the World Bank and OECD and has advised many central government departments, regional and statutory bodies, national and international NGOs and arts and media organizations.

Stan Brignall started his career at the Boots Co., where he worked for 10 years, latterly as their factory accountant. He was appointed Lecturer in Accounting and Finance in Warwick Business School in 1979. In 1998 he joined Aston Business School as Senior Lecturer in Management Accounting. He was then promoted to Professor of Accounting in 2003. In 2004 Stan was appointed Adjunct Professor at Copenhagen Business School. Stan sits on the advisory board of the Performance Measurement Association and is a member of the research board of the Chartered Institute of Management Accounting. His published research includes planning and closure decisions in the UK coal and steel industries, inflation accounting and industrial policy. In recent years, his research has focused on performance measurement and product costing in services, with theoretical and empirical work in both the private and the public sectors. He has published in the refereed research journals of all the main UK professional accounting bodies, as well as a wide range of other journals reflecting his interdisciplinary approach to research.

David Bryde is a Reader in Operations Management at Liverpool John Moores University, which he joined in 1991 after a career in project management at Metier Management Systems and ICI. His research interests focus on performance management in programme and project environments. David is widely published in peer-reviewed journals and conference proceedings.

Sue Burkinshaw is Academic Practice and Staff Development Coordinator at the University of Bolton. Sue has led an academic career in Higher Education for over 20 years and was a University Learning and Teaching Fellow and a Senior Lecturer in Human Resource Management. Sue has previously undertaken research in performance-related pay for academics in the higher education sector.

Jean S Clarke has recently been awarded her PhD by Leeds University Business School, The University of Leeds, United Kingdom. Her research and publications focus mainly on small firms and entrepreneurship. She is particularly interested in the visual aspects of the entrepreneurship process and visual methodologies in the wider field of management.

Gail P Clarkson earned her PhD at Leeds University Business School, The University of Leeds, United Kingdom, where she is currently employed as a Research Fellow of the (UK) Advanced Institute of Management Research (AIM). Her research centres on the factors that are associated with, shape and better explain the employee's relationship with the organization and how these drive motivation, performance and well-being.

Carmel de Nahlik is a Senior Lecturer at Coventry Business School. Prior to this she held a number of academic and other posts at British and European universities and has published articles and conference papers. Her previous career was as a troubleshooter in the project finance area after completing her MBA at Manchester Business School, becoming first a commercial and then an investment banker, working in the UK, the USA, Australia and the Middle East. She has been an adviser, financier and negotiator for projects around the world including several politically sensitive ones. She teaches strategy and finance to MBA students, teaches bespoke specialist in-house finance programmes and has consulted to sponsors, banks and to the oil industry. Carmel has worked for Bank of America, several other large international commercial banks, a European investment bank and a major US insurance company, as a Director of their UK investment arm. She has recently completed her doctorate at Cranfield – her research interests are firm survival and inter-firm partnering. She is a Fellow of the Royal Society of Arts, a former Council Member of the Institute of Petroleum and a Member of the Association of Project Managers.

Anne Fearfull holds a PhD from UMIST and is a Lecturer in Management at the University of St Andrews, School of Management. Her research interests, which are explored through a qualitative methodology, encompass the inter-related areas of gender, race and ethnicity, structure and agency and personal identity.

Maria Goddard is the Assistant Director of the Centre for Health Economics at the University of York. She leads a research team that provides an economic perspective on health-policy issues. Her research interests include performance management and the regulation of public services, areas in which she has published widely. Maria Goddard has previously worked as an economic adviser in the English Department of Health. She has undertaken work for a number of organizations such as Dr Foster, the Healthcare Commission, WHO and the World Bank. She is on the editorial board of two international health policy/research journals.

Jacky Holloway is a Senior Lecturer at the Open University Business School, and Head of the Centre for Public Leadership and Social Enterprise. A graduate of the LSE and the Open University, she spent some years working for a large trade union and then as an NHS administrator before completing her PhD with the Open University Systems Group. Her doctoral and subsequent research has focused on the design and impact of organizational performance management systems. She has published book chapters and journal papers particularly in the areas of public sector performance and benchmarking and is on the editorial boards of *International Journal of Productivity and Performance Management* and *Systems Research and Behavioral Science*. She was the co-editor of *Performance Measurement and Evaluation* (Sage Publications, 1995). Active in the British Academy of Management (BAM), she has been a member of Council and was a founder member of the BAM Performance Management Special Interest Group.

Elizabeth Houldsworth is Subject Area Leader for Managing People and Performance at Henley Management College. She has a background in Human Resource Consultancy as well as in teaching. Her individual research interests include aspects of HR, particularly performance management, adult/management learning and also the application of technology within the learning process.

Richard Kerley is Professor of Management and Dean of the Faculty of Business and Arts at Queen Margaret University College. He has previously worked at the Universities of Edinburgh and Strathclyde. Prior to an academic career he worked in various settings including four different councils and also served eight years as a councillor in Edinburgh. He has researched, consulted and published in different aspects of local government and public service management. In 2000 he chaired the Working Party on Renewing Local Democracy, the report of which led to the establishment of salaries for councillors in Scotland and the introduction (in 2007) of the Single Transferable Vote for the election of councillors.

Fiona Lettice joined University of East Anglia in 2005, having previously been a Senior Lecturer at Cranfield University and a Senior Project Manager for Centrica. Her research interests include new product development, innovation management and performance management. Fiona has over 50 peer-reviewed journal and conference papers, of which three have received awards.

Stephen Little is Head of the Centre for Innovation, Knowledge and Enterprise within the Open University Business School and a Co-Director of the University's Centre for Innovation, Knowledge and Development (www.open.ac.uk/ikd). He is also Chairman of the Asia Pacific Technology Network (www.aptn.org). Previously, he has worked at Manchester Metropolitan University and Griffith and Wollongong Universities, Australia. He has co-edited books and journal issues covering the influence of the Asian economies in the twenty-first century, intelligent urban development and meta-governance. His book *Design and Determination*, which examines the role of information technology in redressing regional inequities in the development process, was published in 2004.

Bernard Marr is recognized as one of the world's leading experts on strategic performance management. He is the Chief Executive and Director of Research of the Advanced Performance Institute, UK. Prior to that, he worked in consulting, manufacturing and international trading, before he started his academic work at the Judge Institute of Management Studies, the University of Cambridge and later at the Cranfield School of Management. He has produced and contributed to over 100 books, reports and articles including: *Strategic Performance Management: Leveraging and Measuring Your Intangible Value Drivers*, *Perspectives on Intellectual Capital: Managing, Measuring and Reporting Intangibles*, *Weighing the Options: BSC Software* and *Automating Your Scorecard*.

S Andrew Morton is Senior Lecturer in Human Resource Management at London South Bank University and Associate Course Director for its Masters in Public Administration programme. Previously HRM Programme Director at Bromley Business School, Andrew worked the previous 17 years in the voluntary sector in management, public education, communications and personnel. He is one of the writers for the Chartered Institute of Personnel and Development's Flexible Learning programme, specializing in pay and reward, and maintains a research interest in using IT in professional education.

David Otley is Professor of Accounting & Management and Associate Dean at Lancaster University Management School, Lancaster. He has conducted research into the behavioural aspects of accounting and budgetary control systems for over three decades, publishing widely in major international journals. He is currently developing theoretical approaches for the study of the design and use of performance management systems in practice.

Zoe Radnor is a Senior Lecturer in Operations Management at Warwick Business School. Her research and publications are in the areas of performance measurement and management, improvement and innovation for both private and public sectors. She is Deputy Director of a 3-year research project evaluating the Beacon Council Scheme, and was Project Manager of a research project for the Scottish Executive which evaluated how 'lean' techniques are and can be used in the public sector. In 2005 she won the Warwick University Award for Teaching Excellence. She is a member of BAM Council and co-editor of the *International Journal of Productivity and Performance Management*.

Peter C Smith is Director of the Centre for Health Economics at the University of York. His research interests include financing, efficiency and performance management of the public services, topics on which he has published widely. He has advised numerous government departments, and is a board member at the Audit Commission. Professor Smith has also acted as consultant to many international agencies, including the Organization for Economic Cooperation and Development (OECD), the International Monetary Fund (IMF), the World Health Organization and the World Bank.

Richard Thorpe is Professor of Management Development and Deputy Director of the Keyworth Institute at Leeds University Business School. After spending a number of years in industry culminating in managing a small manufacturing company in the highlands of Scotland, Richard joined the Pay and Reward Research centre at Strathclyde University. This is where he gained initial interest in the way pay can affect performance. Richard has published in the areas of remuneration and reward, management and organizational development and research methods. He has served as a member of the ESRC training and development board, is currently President of the British Academy of Management and was a founder member of the BAM Performance Management Special Interest Group.

Martin Wickes is a Project Manager at Barclays Bank and is currently delivering a project to implement a standard approach to project management across Barclay's emerging markets in Africa, the Middle East and India. Martin has consulting experience across public, telecommunications and financial sectors in project and programme management, and holds a PhD from Cranfield University in project portfolio management.

Part I

A Multidisciplinary Approach to Performance Management

Part I

A Multidisciplinary Approach to
Performance Management

1

Introduction and Overview

Jacky Holloway and Richard Thorpe

Aims of this book

The overall aim of this book is to assemble a number of reviews of how the key disciplines of management define and understand performance management. Our purpose is to strengthen the development of theory and through our collective efforts make a contribution to management practice.

The case for such a publication is neatly summed up by Smith and Goddard (in Chapter 9, below):

> The literature on performance management is eclectic, diffuse and confused. The definitive 'general theory' of performance management remains elusive, and is unlikely ever to emerge. Important contributions can be found in fields as diverse as strategy, organizational behaviour, operations management, industrial economics and accountancy.
>
> (2002, p. 253)

It will become clear from the large number of discipline and domain-based chapters we present here (and yet more could have been included), that 'performance management' is a phenomenon that is collectively 'owned' by the management research community. Before commencing the project of producing this book, most authors intuitively made a disproportionate claim for their discipline to have credit for our understanding of the nature and effects of performance management. We believed that such claims were at best unhelpful, and at worst highly destructive. The end product has validated this belief, as what have been revealed are shared theories, models and tools, as well as multidisciplinary perspectives that serve together in addressing organisational problems. The project has elicited accounts of the evolution of performance management within disciplines that show many common roots (often originating in other social science disciplines that go back many decades).

The contributions to the book also reveal a wide range of research methods in use, with potential for greater benefit to be gained from awareness of developments elsewhere in the broad domain of social science. Apart from a limited number of theoreticians, for the foreseeable future most management research will be judged against very explicit expectations, for example, 'relevance to user communities', as well as for high standards of academic rigour. What this book demonstrates is the potential for all disciplines to benefit from an awareness of 'what is going on over the fence' and for us to share useful theories and good methodological practices with our nearest neighbours, for the collective advantage of 'management studies' in general and as part of an evolving social science.

Much of the popular literature that is aimed at practising managers (generalists and functional specialists, senior and junior) is normative and prescriptive. Often, it can be difficult for management research to avoid exacerbating such tendencies, as many academics are genuinely concerned to identify 'what works' and why. There is pressure to translate contingent findings into recommendations for practice; and in so doing, weak causal explanations and the logical or ethical critiques that perhaps should form part of an accompanying discussion are often consigned to footnotes or for papers published in the more obscure journals. Although the majority of the authors are realistic about the fact that there is a need for performance management within our organizations for quite pragmatic reasons, most of us realize that on occasions we have a duty to stand back and reflect on the wider implications that our work suggests. A further aim of this book then, has been to enable the authors to express doubts and concerns about any of its dysfunctional effects and embrace an understanding of a wider set of stakeholders. Also, assembling contributions from so many disciplines can lead to a shared agenda for addressing some of these concerns more effectively.

Scope of the book

As will now be becoming clear, this book covers a very wide territory. Not content with seeking out analyses of performance management applied from micro to macro and operational to strategic levels, views from research traditions across the spectrum from positivist to inter-pretive, with theoretical influences ranging from deterministic to highly contingent, have also been encouraged. The level of eclecticism (or frag-mentation) varies between disciplines, at least from the perspectives of the present authors as they reflect on the state-of-the-art of performance management knowledge within their fields.

As well as identifying predominant values and world views (where they are discernible!), a number of authors have indicated how knowledge about performance and its management is obtained in their field. Space constraints have precluded detailed coverage of research methods but there are many references to explanatory as well as empirical literature.

The authors included offer examples from empirical research as well as from secondary sources in order to illustrate approaches to the practice of performance measurement and management in widespread use today. Even 'new' academic disciplines and management functions have a his-tory, and most chapters include accounts of the evolution of the theory in which the apparatus and views are based and locate these in terms of their genesis.

The relationship between research and professional practice is often mediated by consultancy, and is one of the main areas of diversity we found between the disciplines as the chapters in Part II reveal. What surprised us, and may also surprise readers, is the amount of common ground the disciplines share – not simply through the use of performance management tools that integrate different perspectives, but also in terms of the theoretical influences and historical turning points and responses to environmental pressures that they reveal. This understanding forms the overall picture that we attempt to synthesize and conceptualize in Part III. Assembling such a wide-ranging account of practice, research and theory in a single volume (complemented by wide-ranging dis-cussions through an ESRC-supported seminar series 'Perspectives on performance') has provided the opportunity to identify priorities for multidisciplinary research and critical analysis. It also suggests to us some new directions for management education and organisational development that are revealed in the final two chapters.

In order to compile a book which is both authoritative and accessible inevitably means that the chapters do vary in terms of their style and their breadth of coverage. Several contributions have been published pre-viously in relatively specialized journals or books but have been chosen because we feel they are ideally suited as vehicles for the audience we are writing for – to explain performance management issues and innov-ations as well as discipline-specific processes and systems. The majority of chapters reflect the authors' UK and North American origins, because to introduce wider European and Asian-Pacific traditions and emerging trends would necessitate the inclusion of large amounts of contextual, historical and theoretical background material. Another tendency on the part of many authors has also been to concentrate on commercial practice, principally due to the constraints of space, but we do include several chapters that focus on significant economic sectors outside the 'mainstream' (small firms, the public sector and voluntary organizations) and these serve to challenge the robustness of performance management theories and practices. As we have indicated, a larger book would be needed if we were to do justice to the diversity of practice that is rapidly emerging – and cross-fertilising – beyond the territory of the medium to large firms on which most management literatures continue to be focused.

On the other hand as editors we have deliberately retained some degree of 'duplication' particularly in terms of the role models and theoretical influences play, not only because it would be misleading to imply that only one or two disciplines should lay claim to these insights, but more importantly it reveals the common ground that might not previously have been acknowledged if all overlapping content had been edited out. It also serves to indicate the multidisciplinary research agenda and potentially holds considerable promise for future effective and inclusive performance management practice.

What follows is an introduction to the main topics addressed in each chapter.

Section and chapter overviews

The remaining part of this section provides contextual foundations for the relatively bounded perspectives presented in Part II. In Chapter 2 Richard Thorpe and Tony Beasley locate the territory of performance management research within the continent of management research and the world of social science more generally. The paper on which this chapter is based was originally written as a contribution to an ongoing debate being propagated with the British Academy of Management about the nature, social organisation and impacts of knowledge production through management research. 'Performance management' is self-evidently highly relevant to management practice, and the authors explore the implications of normative and objectivist preferences, and the under-developed theoretical and critical tendencies that continue to dominate performance management research.

Chapter 3 is also based on a pre-existing contribution, this time from a book that reviews the theories, issues and contributions to performance management from a 'sister' field, Management Control. Although the author, David Otley, has an accounting background, his concerns here are with how both financial and non-financial performance measures are applied to manage performance. He introduces a generic framework for analysing how organizations seek to manage their performance, incorporating critical success factors, performance targets, incentives and rewards and information requirements. Otley then explores the relationship between performance management and strategic management, and considers in detail the role of the performance management model most frequently mentioned by later authors – the Balanced Scorecard.

Otley and Thorpe and Beasley acknowledge that there are normative tendencies within performance management, which the last chapter in this opening section seeks to address particularly through the identification of more critical contributions from a range of organisational theories. In Chapter 4 Carmel de Nahlik identifies a number of tensions that surround performance management systems, for example, between their official purposes and how they appear to stakeholders; between intended and unintended outcomes; between competing explanations for comparative strategic success; and arising from the complexity of operating across boundaries within and between organizations. The 'currents and controversies' identified in Chapter 4 pose questions for the assumptions underlying each of the discipline's understanding of performance management, to which we return in the final section.

Turning to Part II of the book, the reader will find that the majority of the chapters are written from the perspectives of 'conventional' disciplines within the broad field of management – some mapping tidily on to management functions (operations management, marketing etc.), others more readily recognized in university departments and scholarly groupings (information management and political economy, for example). All of the disciplines fall within the purview of social science when it comes to research paradigms; and none are exclusive in terms of the types of organizations they study. With respect to the order in which they appear, we have attempted to reflect their prevailing levels of focus where this is easy to establish – from micro, intra-organisational to macro, inter-organisational or wider. However, by classifying in this way we in no way intend to imply a hierarchy of 'scientific contributions' or 'building blocks'.

The last three chapters in Part II are defined in scope by the 'domains' which they investigate (small firms, the public and voluntary sectors), and in so doing provide examples of the way disciplinary approaches can be synthesized as well as illustrating the need to incorporate theories and research methods from other social sciences such as policy analysis. We recognize that there could have been many more domain-based chapters had space allowed but have chosen some examples of what we consider are the most significant. In addition to their role of illustrating multidisciplinary analysis and contingency factors in performance management, these three chapters reflect the formation of new fields of study within management (as evidenced by the emergence of dedicated university departments and research programmes, Masters degrees and specialized consultancy organizations). The tendency of most of the 'discipline based' chapters to draw their evidence and theories derived from larger, for-profit organizations has already been noted; the last three chapters of Part II convey a flavour of the challenges and limitations of applying, adapting and enhancing tools and theories originating in a different organisational milieu.

Turning to the first discipline-based chapter, in Chapter 5 Anne Fearfull and Gail Clarkson introduce performance management as viewed from the perspective of occupational psychology and organisational behaviour (OP and OB). They outline how these two tightly knit disciplines seek to examine and explain important relationships between individual behaviours, management practices and organisational outcomes. The application of influential theories about the effects of human motivation and individual differences on work performance, by OP and OB specialists, is also critically evaluated.

The management discipline most directly related to OP and OB is human resource management (HRM), the focus of Chapter 6. Here Liz Houldsworth and Sue Burkinshaw describe the evolution of HRM as a profession, and the interplay between theory and practice. They show how competing philosophies about the purpose of the employment relationship are played out through the management of employee performance.

While the main beneficiaries of effective HRM are still commonly regarded as being individual organisational employers and/or their employees, David Barnes and Zoe Radnor argue that their discipline – operations management – has come to represent the driving force for the productivity of national economies. Poorly performing operations are frequently cited as the root causes of wider economic malaise and Barnes and Radnor chart how a widening of focus during the twentieth century continues to be accompanied by increasing complexity of performance measurement models and performance management systems.

Chapter 7 also demonstrates how a combination of policy and research influences have enabled the service sector – including public services – to adopt tools and techniques today that were originally conceived for manufacturing, to an extent that would have been unimaginable to operations managers before the 1980s.

A similar broadening has taken place in terms of the domains within which 'project management' can be found, as David Bryde, Fiona Lettice and Martin Wickes explain in Chapter 8. The authors focus on what is arguably one of the most important (and often least clearly articulated) components of performance management: the often-competing dimensions of performance valued by project stakeholders. They integrate a diverse set of empirical research findings to show how project performance can only be fully understood when projects are located in their strategic contexts and evaluated systemically in terms of qualitative as well as quantitative criteria.

Although Chapter 9, 'Performance Management and Operational Research: A Marriage Made in Heaven?' was written for a special issue of the Journal of the Operational Research Society on performance management, the case made by Peter Smith and Maria Goddard is fully compatible with the theme of this book. As in the previous chapter, the critical importance of designing holistic performance management systems that link strategy formulation, performance measurement tools and information and 'second order' feedback is demonstrated. The prominence given to individual and organisational behavioural responses – including the kinds of unwanted effects that give performance management a bad name – may surprise those who only associate operational research (OR) with computer modelling and number-crunching. This chapter illustrates both the broad scope of contemporary OR and the additional power it is gaining through links to accounting, strategic management, HRM and other disciplines featured in this book.

Whereas Smith and Goddard were unlikely to upset many in the OR community by articulating the case for the discipline's contribution to 'the performance management movement' in a leading OR journal, in some disciplines this kind of argument may be more sceptically received. Chapter 10 is based on the executive summary of the second edition of *Marketing and the Bottom Line*, by Tim Ambler, a book which provides a critical guide for marketers to make marketing fully accountable. The chapter captures the essence of the key messages in Ambler's book, which incorporates a framework for evaluation, numerous examples and recommendations for management action. Many marketing professionals seem unaware of the impact of their work on overall organisational performance, and academic literature giving a marketing perspective on performance management is still relatively scarce. Ambler's book is a wake-up call to the profession, and the extract in Chapter 10 vividly illustrates the often-untapped potential contribution from marketing particularly when working with other disciplines.

The critical role played by information in performance management is a recurring theme in this book, and in Chapter 11 it takes centre stage. Focusing on the changing scope of the production value chain in the global economy, Steve Little highlights the impact of the Internet in enabling organisational performance to be exposed to the scrutiny of an ever-widening number of stakeholder interests. He uses a series of case studies to illustrate economic, social and political benefits and risks of performance information being communicated to places and by people beyond the control of the organizations and industries under scrutiny.

In Chapter 12, Stan Brignall presents an accounting and finance perspective on performance management. Financial performance measures are often taken for granted as the basic, and largely neutral, building blocks of management control and accountability, transparent and highly regulated. However, Brignall introduces a number of critiques relating to the relationships between financial performance measurement systems (especially at divisional level) and organisational structures, strategies and stakeholders. In doing so he explores the potential offered through the integration of accounting and financial information within multidimensional performance management systems.

While Chapter 12 alerts us to complexities in accounting for tangible assets and liabilities as part of the evaluation of organisational performance that persist even after decades of experience, in Chapter 13 Bernard Marr highlights emerging challenges posed by the search for ways of valuing intangible assets. While intangible resources play a crucial part in determining organizations' capabilities and competencies, Marr argues that understanding and managing them needs to go beyond 'quantifying the unquantifiable'. Innovative approaches to measurement are vital to organisational learning and improved strategic decision making.

'Last but by no means least' is an apt way to introduce Chapter 14, 'Political Economy Perspectives'. In this final discipline-led perspective, Tony Bovaird picks up a strand that cunningly weaves itself through the book: the effects of the economic environment on performance management at all levels from the firm or public service down to the individual. Bovaird focuses on how different schools of economic thought seek to define appropriate objectives especially for public services, and the implications for policy makers, managers and other stakeholders in terms of logically relevant performance measurement systems. As well as technical considerations, political, behavioural and social factors are examined and it becomes clear that a 'good' performance measurement system in the eyes of a political economist is just as contingent on value-based assumptions as we saw in the 'softer' disciplines.

Three domains in which the economic and preceding perspectives can be tested follow in the remaining chapters of Part II, starting with Richard Thorpe and Jean Clarke's exploration in Chapter 15 of what 'performance' means to small and medium-sized enterprises (SMEs). This vividly demonstrates Bovaird's point about the need to ask first what the organisation exists to do, before developing appropriate approaches to measuring and managing its performance. Small firms are not just embryonic large firms, and entrepreneurial owner-managers do not all dream of becoming tycoons. At the same time, Thorpe and Clarke argue, SMEs remain critical to the competitiveness of all modern economies and those who advise them must avoid making patronising assumptions; they need clear strategies as well as effective operational control. Drawing on a recent action learning programme, the chapter concludes with an evaluation of the potential benefits to SMEs of three multidimensional performance management tools (the EFQM Excellence Model, Balanced Scorecard and Gross Value Added technique). Of overriding importance is the need to recognize the heterogeneity of the small firms sector when academics, consultants and policy makers seek to support practitioners in enhancing their firms' performance.

The focus of Chapter 16 returns to the public sector (in the USA and Australia as well as the UK), as Richard Kerley examines contributions from management and economic theories to our understanding of attempts over recent decades to plan and manage the use of public resources in the service of citizens. A selection of policy initiatives illustrate the dilemmas faced by public sector managers as they juggle conflicting stakeholder demands and search for performance information that is genuinely useful to service improvement, rather than merely easy to obtain.

As if life were not complicated enough, in Chapter 17 Andrew Morton rounds off Part II by examining what performance management looks and feels like in the voluntary sector. Even defining the sector is contentious, although claims about its distinctiveness may have been exaggerated. As well as the complex interests that volunteers, managers, donors and beneficiaries contribute to the picture, governments increasingly treat the voluntary sector like any other service provider in their supply chain and the potential to adapt 'standard' performance management tools is considerable. Morton uses the framework introduced by Thorpe and Beasley in Chapter 2 to classify current and potential performance management research in this sector and discuss some key tensions underlying the research agenda, as well as unresolved issues for practitioners.

To complete the book, the two chapters in Part III draw out points of comparison and contrast from the pictures painted by our discipline specialists and sector-focused contributors. We (Thorpe and Holloway) reflect on how a relatively small number of social science theories have informed the field to date, revealing enormous scope for theory-testing and adaptation as well as innovation. We comment on the research approaches most frequently used and discuss the opportunities for use of a wider range of methods and mixed-mode studies.

Having assembled a multitude of empirically informed disciplinary viewpoints about the strengths and limitations of some widely-applied performance management tools, we also synthesize some recommendations for performance management practice. Finally we acknowledge the implications for management educators working in the rapidly evolving field of performance management, and suggest priorities for a multidisciplinary research agenda that reflects the interests of key stakeholders.

2
The Characteristics of Performance Management Research – Implications and Challenges

Richard Thorpe and Tony Beasley

Introduction

There is now a growing interdisciplinary interest in organizational performance in all its manifestations (Neely and Waggoner, 1998). To date this interest has been sustained by the considerable attention the subject has been given by practitioners but more recently there has been a developing focus on the academic contributions that might be made to the field. [. . .] [I]ncreasingly the notion of performance is being used as an integrating theme on postgraduate programmes to reflect 'real world relevance' and as way of integrating and balancing practically useful techniques (as used by managers and consultants), with theoretical constructs. This has moved the focus of study away from simply practice and more towards theory. We see this shift in emphasis as inevitable as academics will need to take a critical stance so that they can better understand and explore the theoretical and empirical bases on which many of the principles on which notions of performance rest – the ideas themselves, how they arose, how they might be developed and how they might be changed. This [chapter] attempts to locate the study of performance by using the same constructs used by researchers who have been attempting to categorize management. Having set out the results of this exercise we speculate on the ways the study of performance might change as interest increases.

Management research – the double hurdle

The debate about whether management can be called an applied discipline is a long running one. As Bain (Economic and Social Research Council, 1994) pointed out, the idea of a discipline that sets out solely to produce prescriptive outcomes fits uneasily with a research agenda, where curiosity and discovery are important. An even greater concern would be the danger felt that too strong an identification with a focus on 'who are the customers of management research' might unintentionally encourage the production of spurious certainty in research (Economic and Social Research Council, 1994, p. 2). However, without some notion of end users, academics may well be tempted to 'perform research of marginal importance to management'.

Notwithstanding, few would disagree that there must be close links between theory and practice and a demonstration of the link at some stage in the research process lies at the heart of how management might be thought of as maintaining its relevance. Even so management researchers haven't always taken the link relationship for granted and the different sub-disciplines that make up management have often placed different emphases in this respect. This [chapter] seeks to examine the evolution of performance management research. We do not claim disciplinary status for those works in this field but suggest it is distinct in that, in contrast to management researchers operating from one of its sub-disciplines, research in the field of performance management is characterized by an applied focus. We have also defined performance management in such a way as to subsume the fields of performance measurement concentrating our focus of analysis on performance management at an organizational level.

The emergence of performance management

The growth in academic interest in performance management has mirrored the development of actual performance management practice. The 2001 Bain & Co. survey of the use of, and satisfaction with, management tools and techniques (Bain & Co., 2001), reports that over 80 per cent of companies make use of Benchmarking, over 50 per cent have some form of 'pay for performance', and over 40 per cent utilize some form of Balanced Scorecard application. Whether the definitions of terms have been applied equally across all the organizations surveyed or not is a questionable issue but perhaps of more interest is the fact that Bain found that senior executive satisfaction and subsequent 'defection' rates from using these tools were significantly better than the average across the 25 management tools and techniques Bain & Co. (2001) surveyed. As well as the tremendous growth in the number of organizations practising some form of formal performance management, all of the large consultancy firms have significant performance management 'offers' in

their portfolios and there is a plethora of commercial performance management software/IT applications available to those who wish to avail
themselves of it.

Performance management as an identifiable subject for academic
study and research arguably began in the mid-1990s (see, for example,
Eccles, 1991; Kaplan and Norton, 1992; European Foundation for Quality Management, 1998). However, the study of the narrower fields of
performance improvement, such as industrial engineering, work study
and management services have had a much longer tradition (see, for
example, Hicks, 1977). Since this time, the academic research in the
field has [grown exponentially] [. . .] (Neely and Waggoner, 1998; Neely,
2000). To support this, a review of the key reference works in the 1980s
shows that many of the contributions are accounting related. The establishment of the Performance Measurement Association and the British
Academy of Management's Performance Management Special Interest
Group [. . .] [is] indicative of the emergence and growth of interest in
forming academic networks to focus study around new topics relating
to performance whereas the Management Control Association (with a
focus on accounting) has been active for many years.

The nature of an academic contribution in performance management

This growth in interest in performance management research, unlike
research in other disciplines poses some interesting challenges and as
a consequence the perspectives taken need careful analysis. There are
perhaps three main issues that make performance management distinctive as a focus for research. These challenges reflect the challenges facing
business and management research more generally.

The first is that despite the development of distinct disciplines within
management, the practice of management is largely eclectic: managers
need to be able to work across technical, cultural and functional boundaries; they need to be able to draw on knowledge developed by other
disciplines such as sociology, anthropology, economics, statistics and
mathematics and they need to have a view of what their findings mean
for practice. Secondly, the issue with regard to a research agenda in
performance management then, is whether to examine performance
management from the perspective of one discipline, or whether to adopt
a cross-disciplinary approach and to what extent can practitioners bring
insights to our understanding of this domain. Thirdly, for academics the
safest course of action is to seek respectability from academic peers, but to

produce findings that are useful the involvement of practising managers is essential. Heron and Reason (2001) suggest that theories of organization have little relevance to the practical concerns of those actually managing organizations. Other observers believe that the lack of 'real world' relevance can be attributed to the emphasis on under-theorized, quantitative approaches to research (Mintzberg, 1976).

Discipline is a concept borrowed from the church and suggests someone who entertains a particular belief or argues for a particular interpretation of the scriptures. In the context of our academic frames of reference a discipline dictates the boundaries of what counts for knowledge – even the research processes that should be adopted. This not only means that the discipline dictates the research networks and the research processes that should be used, but also gives legitimacy to the questions asked and defines the problematics of the day. The practical implications of this, for a field of study such as performance management is that many disciplines stake a legitimate claim on the subject, and each has a different perspective on not only what counts as useful and valid knowledge but also how that knowledge should be collected, interpreted and valued.

A multidisciplinary perspective might be one solution, but the question then is, which discipline should predominate? Those committed to multidisciplinary research will need to ask themselves whether such a venture is even practically possible, as one paradigm or perspective or schema will always be in danger of attempting to subsume others as they compete for supremacy. This reality is perhaps born out by the fact that there are very few examples of genuine multidisciplinary research to be found within the field of management in general and performance management in particular. An alternative approach would be either to pursue a uni-disciplinary research design or to attempt inter-disciplinary research in order to see where the gaps in knowledge and perspectives exist. Inter-disciplinary studies might attempt to examine performance management from different disciplinary perspectives, and observe where they touch, with the purpose of giving insights into situations or phenomena currently unexplained. [...]

Methodology adopted

The methodology adopted to locate performance management and to explore the directions in which it might move as a field of study are those employed by researchers in their attempts to conceptualize the

nature of management research. The following section offers a mapping of performance management research along the same 'cognitive'
and 'social organizational' dimensions that Tranfield and Starkey (1998)
used for their British Academy of Management study into the nature and
organization of management research. [. . .]

Tranfield and Starkey (1998) adopted a framework from the sociology of knowledge, originated by Biglan (1973a, b) and extended by
Becher (1989). We adopt that framework here to analyse the current
level of development of performance management research and to discuss some possible implications for the evolution of the domain. Biglan
identifies two substantive dimensions on which to map academic fields
(hard versus soft, and pure versus applied); these Becher suggests reflect
the 'cognitive dimensions of disciplines'. In addition Becher extends
Biglan's original schema to include the 'social organization' dimensions of disciplines, which also includes two substantive dimensions
(convergent versus divergent, and urban versus rural). The following discussion attempts to map performance management onto each of these
dimensions in order to assess the extent to which the field has been
conceptualized and to assess the types of methods being adopted by
researchers in the field and whether or not there is unanimity about
the research questions that need to be asked.

The 'cognitive' dimension of disciplines

Hard versus soft

[. . .] the degree to which a paradigm exists.

(Biglan, 1973a, p. 201)

This distinction is closely related to the notion of paradigmatic agreement (Kuhn, 1962). Biglan (1973a, p. 201) argues that the degree to
which 'a body of theory is subscribed to by all members of the field',
reflects the degree of 'hardness' of a discipline. The paradigmatic agreement of much of the natural sciences serves an important coordinating
role in that it helps define key research questions; specifies the appropriate epistemological orientations; provides consistent accounts of the
field of interest; unites discipline; develops consensus; and defines the
disciplinary boundaries. In contrast, domains of knowledge without
unitary paradigms, such as the humanities, education and the social
sciences (including management and business research) are essentially
'pre-paradigmatic' in both their content and method. With regard to
the location of performance management on this spectrum, we suggest

that a relatively 'hard' core area of activity can be identified. This core is dominated by a hard systems approach, with systems design being perceived as an essentially technical problem, often incorporating quantitative performance measurement and information technology design solutions.

Pure versus applied

> [...] the content of the area with application to practical problems.
>
> (Biglan, 1973a, p. 202)

In his original analysis Biglan contrasts education, engineering and agriculture from other sciences, humanities and the social sciences by the

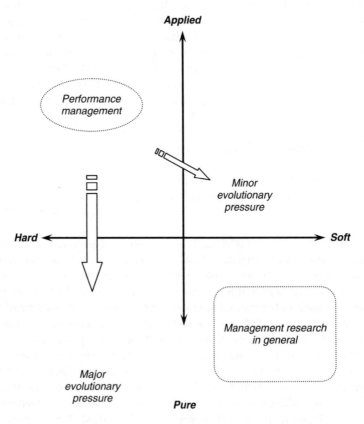

Figure 2.1   The cognitive dimensions of performance management research

formers' relative focus on largely practical problems. An important aspect of this distinction between pure and applied approaches is the way in which disciplines progress. In more pure areas, progress is often cumulative, with systematic development according to an internal logic of the emerging discipline. In contrast, applied areas are exposed to a wide range of environmental influences, such as changes in users' needs and/or government policy. Such a distinction is important because 'progress' in the academic sense of an accumulation of knowledge is often more difficult to identify, with such disciplines 'often building high level theoretical and conceptual material "bottom-up" from case law' (Tranfield and Starkey, 1998, p. 345).

Perhaps one of the most striking characteristics of the performance management literature is its very applied nature. The large majority of studies involve the application of a particular performance management tool or technique and the case-study method is common. The combination of 'hard' and 'applied' locates performance management in the upper-left quadrant of the Cognitive dimension in Figure 2.1. But in contrast to this Tranfield and Starkey appear to imply that management research should be located more towards the right hand quadrant again as indicated in Figure 2.1.

The social organization of disciplines dimension

Convergent versus divergent

> [...] convergent...tightly knit disciplinary configurations...and those which are divergent and loosely knit.
>
> (Becher, 1989)

Convergent disciplines share similar ideologies and values, which are often reflected in commonly expressed views of quality, and a sense of community, with shared purpose. Although such convergence may lead to a low tolerance of deviation, it also serves in the identification of well-defined boundaries that are more easily defended. For divergent disciplines the converse to the above is true, and whilst the fragmented ideologies might lead to a greater tolerance of deviation, it may also lead to diverse quality judgements, a lower level of intellectual debate and discipline boundaries which are difficult to defend. We suggest that using this framework to locate work in the field of performance management means placing it as relatively convergent. The rapid growth of performance management practice and consultancy provides a common point of interest, and understanding of the phenomena under investigation. In addition, the concern with application provides a common sense of purpose.

Urban versus rural

[...] the people to problem ratio.

(Becher, 1989)

An 'urban' discipline is characterized by a relatively narrow field of study, with a limited number of discrete and separable research problems. The relatively small intellectual space and high people-to-problem

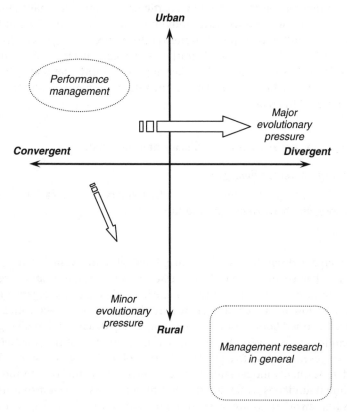

Figure 2.2 The social organization dimensions of performance management research

ratio lead to intense research environments, with close communication between research groups. In contrast, rural disciplines cover a wide, but sparsely populated field of inquiry. The lack of sharp demarcation in disciplinary boundary and low level of communication between research groups means that they are often perceived to be unfashionable, risky and unattractive to funding agencies when compared to urban environments.

Performance management as a specific field is a relatively new area of academic interest, which appears to be expanding quite quickly. Despite this our contention is that it is a relatively 'crowded' field of academic endeavour. Its 'popularity' and 'topicality' means that it is generating a lot of academic interest, and this combined with its hard, applied and convergent characteristics means that it is a relatively 'urban' domain. The combination of convergent and urban characteristics of performance management suggest that it occupies a position in the social organization dimension of the upper-left quadrant of Figure 2.2.

Again, considering the field of study of performance management there is a contrast to the tone of Tranfield and Starkey's (1998) analysis of the management domain more generally as can be seen in Figure 2.2. Tranfield and Starkey's analysis of the position of management research leads them to suggest that a solution is the adoption of a transdisciplinary approach to management research. Whilst for many researchers this suggestion is relatively radical, thinking about the current state of performance management research in this way does make this option appear particularly appropriate.

Future evolutionary pressures for performance management research

From convergent to divergent?

We see an analogy here between the evolution of accounting research through the 1970s and 1980s which saw a shift away from normative thinking and theorizing (paramount in the 1970s) towards more empirically based research in order to have more impact on practice (Laughlin, 1995). Much of the current performance management literature (Olve and Wetter, 2000; Eccles, 1991) is implicitly normative (in a prescriptive sense). It may be argued that one of the developing trends might be increased divergence in the research agenda, particularly between the more economics-based domains of knowledge which make up the field of inquiry to include stakeholder-sensitive approaches and an increasing use of policy evaluation-led research.

From applied to pure?

In terms of the major evolutionary pressures on the cognitive dimensions perhaps the greatest pressure on researchers will be more of a move towards the pure and theoretical ends of the continuum. Academics recognize the value of different kinds of theories but do not always value the contributions they make in equal measures. Burgoyne (2000) suggests that perhaps a stereotypical view of the value of theory is that practitioners value normative theory over descriptive theory over analytical theory over critical theory. Academics on the other hand, appear to have the opposite priorities with critical theory being the most valued and normative theory being the least valued – except he suggests as material for the critical theorists! This trend unfortunately produces a dynamic that takes the performance management agenda away from one of its greatest strengths, that is practical usefulness and application.

Given these dilemmas one way forward might be the formal adoption what Tranfield and Starkey (1998) refer to as the adoption of a mode 2 or transdisciplinary approach to the way research is conducted.

Gibbons et al. (1994) distinguished between two modes of knowledge production. [...] Mode 1 characterizes the 'traditional' approach in which knowledge generation occurs within the context of existing institutions and academic disciplines. This approach is driven by an academic agenda – one that distinguishes between fundamental and applied knowledge. The dissemination of this knowledge occurs downstream of its production with little concern for its practical relevance. In contrast, mode 2 is characterized as being of a transdisciplinary nature when (as we have discussed) it is created in a particular context, a context that values those involved in practice. This form combines tacit/practitioner understandings with those of academics. This approach emphasizes teamwork rather than 'heroic individualism' and recognizes the transitory nature of knowledge. It creates knowledge that is produced and exploited almost simultaneously. As a consequence, a particular knowledge becomes shared more widely between a variety of stakeholders.

The key aspect of mode 2 knowledge production is that it occurs as a result of the interaction that takes place between theory and practice. This is the antithesis of the more traditional mode 1 form in which theoretical knowledge generally precedes application and where a distance is usually maintained between knowledge production and application as well as between academics and users. It is argued that if this kind of system is to work effectively then there must be a rapid inter-play between management theory and practice (Tranfield and Starkey, 1998). [...]

Conclusions

This [chapter] began by arguing that the rapid growth in performance management research has led to a need to evaluate the current theoretical and methodological drivers behind this field of study.

Our analysis began by comparing and contrasting the field of perform-ance management research with management research in general. Its strength we saw as its relatively hard/applied nature, its weakness as the absence of explicit links to underpinning theoretical constructs. [...]

Our conclusions suggest that there are likely to be a number of evolutionary pressures at work within the field of performance man-agement research that will, over time increasingly move its focus away from application and more towards a critical position that embraces an understanding of a range of theoretical underpinnings. In other words, the pressure for academics to publish within their discipline will move them away from the current 'convergent' tendencies towards being more divergent in character. Our argument is, that as academics engage in the study of performance from an increasingly broad range of disciplines, they will need to locate the knowledge they gain within the context of their own disciplines and fields of study. In addition, they will need to seek academic credibility for the work they do which will mean far less focus on practice and the perspectives of practition-ers (mode 2). In addition they are likely to reject the current implicit normative agenda, finding the current explanations and approaches inappropriate.

Whatever the case we suggest there is a need for the field of perform-ance management to address the growing criticisms which are attached to the current implicit normative research agenda.

Further reading

Performance Measurement Association, *Perspectives on Performance*, Vol. 1, No. 4 (2001).

Bain, G. *Summary Statements of Evidence Submitted to the Commission on Management Research* (Swindon: ESRC, 1993).

Griffiths, P. and Murry, M. *Whose Business? Radical Proposals For The Reform of British Business Schools*, Hobart Paper No. 102 (London: Institute of Economic Affairs, 1985).

3

Performance Management: A Framework for Analysis

David Otley

Introduction

Performance management systems, which tend to be taken for granted by organizations, consist of several interrelated but often loosely coupled parts. The design of these separate parts is often the responsibility of different business functions, such as management information systems, operations management, human resources and finance. When there is a degree of integration, this tends to be focused on budgeting and management accounting-based performance measures. [...] More recently some attention has been paid to the development of non-financial performance measures, but this has been done on an *ad hoc* basis using frameworks that have little theoretical underpinning, such as the balanced scorecard. In this chapter we shall broaden this perspective by looking beyond the measurement of performance to the management of performance. Management accounting systems provide information that is intended to be useful to managers, so any assessment of the part played by such information therefore requires us to consider how managers will make use of it. The traditional framework for considering these issues was developed in the 1960s by Robert Anthony of the Harvard Business School, under the title of management control systems (Anthony, 1965).

Anthony classified managerial decision making and control activities into three major types – strategic planning, management control and operational control – and argued that most managers are usually concerned with only one of these. As the nature of the control process is very different in each case, it is important that a manager's task is correctly identified. Strategic planning is defined as the setting and changing of overall corporate strategies and objectives; management control involves monitoring activities and taking action to ensure that resources are effectively and efficiently used to accomplish organizational objectives; and operational control is concerned with carrying out specific tasks on a day-to-day basis.

Management control is seen as the mediating activity between strategic planning (objectives setting) and task control (the carrying out of specific tasks). It is integrative because it involves the whole organization and is concerned with effective management of the interrelationships between disparate parts. Unlike strategic planning and operational control, Anthony sees management control as routine reporting on the performance of all areas of the organization on a regular basis, so that all areas are systematically reviewed. He also concentrates on techniques that have universal applicability across all types of business and organization. The principal tool for achieving management control is management accounting information. Such information is collected in a standard manner from all parts of the organization. Because it is in a quantitative (monetary) form it can easily be aggregated into summaries for higher levels of management, and it is routinely collected and disseminated. Research into the behavioural aspects of management accounting generally, and budgetary control in particular fits neatly into this viewpoint as it emphasizes the social, psychological and motivational aspects of control.

Although this can usefully serve as an initial framework, it would be erroneous to assume that management accounting is the only or even the main means of management control. Anthony's classification assumes away too many problems. Strategic planning cannot be divorced from control, for effective control involves changing plans and objectives. Nor can operational control be kept separate from management control as its technological complexities impinge directly on the control process. [...] As Machin (1983) argues, Anthony himself specified social psychology as the principal source discipline for the study of management control, and it is perhaps surprising that accounting continued to dominate his thinking. [...] The aim of this chapter is to develop a more comprehensive framework for the study of management control systems.

The performance management framework

Four main questions have to be answered when developing a framework for managing organizational performance. The questions remain the same, but organizations need continually to find new answers to them. [...] In an organizational context the answers are different because the context in which the organization is set is constantly changing and new strategies have to be developed to cope with the new operating environment. The questions are as follows:

1. What factors does an organization see as crucial to its continued success, and how does it measure and monitor its performance in each of these areas?
2. What level of performance does the organization wish to achieve in each of these areas, and how does it go about setting appropriate performance targets?
3. What rewards (both monetary and non-monetary) will managers gain by achieving these performance targets (or conversely, what penalties will they suffer by failing to achieve them)?
4. What information flows are necessary for the organization to be able to monitor its performance on these dimensions, to learn from its past experiences and to adapt its behaviour in the light of those experiences?

These questions relate very closely to some of the central issues in modern management accounting practice. The first is concerned with performance measurement, not just in financial terms but also in operational terms. It is closely connected to strategy formulation and deployment, and also to the very practical areas of business process management and operations management. The second question is more traditional and has a long pedigree of research on the subject, but it remains important, as reflected in current practices such as benchmarking. The third question has tended to be neglected by those who view performance measurement as being in the purview of human resource management. However, the interconnections between the two fields must be recognized to avoid the many counterproductive examples of short-termism driven by financial incentive schemes we see in practice. The final question has been considered by management information systems (MIS) specialists but still needs to be better linked to issues such as the 'learning organization', employee empowerment and emergent strategy.

The following sections will consider each of these questions in turn in order to clarify their meaning. (See Otley, 1999, for a fuller outline of the application of the questions.) [...] [I]t is first necessary to consider the question of organizational strategy, as this forms the basis of the whole structure of control being developed.

Strategy

Numerous texts have been written on the topic of corporate strategy, and it is not our intention to duplicate those here. [...] Before we can discuss corporate strategy we need to consider the mission, goals and objectives of an organization. Mintzberg (1983) provides some useful definitions, although his terminology is not universally accepted.

1. *Mission*: An organisation's mission is its basic function in society, and is reflected in the products and services that it provides for its customers or clients. [...]
2. *Goals*: An organisation's goals are the intentions behind its decisions or actions. Goals will frequently never be achieved and may be incapable of being measured. [...] [A]lthough goals are more specific than a mission statement and tend to have a shorter timescale, they are not precise measures of performance.
3. *Objectives*: Objectives are goals expressed [in] a form in which they can be measured. [...]

However, a strategy is more than a statement of desired outcomes, whether expressed in terms of mission, goals or objectives. It is essentially a plan of action to achieve those outcomes. Unfortunately, as Coad (1995) succinctly points out, the term strategy is probably one of the most ill-defined in the business vocabulary, having a wide range of connotations. Published definitions vary, with each writer adding his or her own ideas and emphases. For some, strategy refers to a plan as the end product of strategy formulation. Some include objectives as part of the strategy, while others see objectives as what the strategy should achieve. Many mention the allocation of resources as a crucial aspect of strategy. Some prescribe a review of the market and specifically mention competitive position. To complicate matters further, some writers suggest that strategy is a formal logic, explicitly stated, that links together the activities of a business, whilst others suggest that a strategy can emerge from a set of decisions and need not be explicitly stated.

Whilst recognizing the importance of emergent strategy, it is clear that performance cannot be managed unless there is some agreement on the plans the organization is intending to implement and the desired results of those plans. We shall go down an explicitly hierarchical route whereby strategies become codified in performance measures that are used to motivate and monitor performance at lower organizational levels. However, when so doing we shall not lose sight of two major issues that stand outside this framework. First, strategies are not solely developed by senior managers; some strategies emerge from what has been found to work at the grass-roots level. The ways in which such emergent strategies can be incorporated into the subsequent strategy re-formulation process is an important aspect of organizational learning. Second, the explicit specification of performance measures is only one means of strategy implementation. Ideas such as 'visioning', whereby employees at all levels are given an insight into the strategic position of an organization and have the values of the organization inculcated into their thinking, are also important. [In addition,] Simons' (1995, 2000) 'levers of control' framework makes an important contribution here. [. . .]

[. . .] The formal specification of performance measures and the development of measurement and monitoring systems are major means of performance management in a wide range of organizations, and it is this process that we shall now consider in more detail.

Performance measurement

The starting point when designing a performance measurement system to assist performance management is the business strategy. This specifies the key factors that the organization must attend to in order to be successful. So, the performance measurement system has to be concerned with measures of outcomes or results, and the means by which such results can be achieved. For example, a company may wish to achieve a certain return on investment; to realize that aim its strategy is to offer its customers a level of service that is sufficiently high to justify its relatively high prices, and hope that this strategy will enable the business to grow in a profitable manner. Here the overall objective is return on investment, and the means of its achievement is customer service, which may be further refined into more detailed measures of service levels, such as speed of response, the value added to services and customer satisfaction ratings. [. . .]

The process of setting up the set of performance measures may well stimulate the further development and articulation of strategy. Only when we try to measure performance do we fully understand what achieving it will require. It is tempting to be satisfied with specifying performance indicators, defined here as aspects of performance that are relatively easy to measure but do not capture the underlying dimensions of performance. Many efficiency measures fall into this category, such as measures of idle or non-productive time. Clearly we do not wish our workforce to be unnecessarily idle, but it is also necessary that they work on useful tasks. [...]

It is also very easy to set up measures that are inappropriate or easily manipulated. We are suggesting here a top-down approach to the design and specification of performance measures, but it is also important rigorously to test every measure developed to ensure that it is appropriate. Some of our engineering colleagues (Neely, 1998) have referred to this process as 'destructive testing' of performance measures. This involves examining each performance measure through the eyes of the manager who is accountable for its achievement, and testing whether it might be possible to make the measure look good whilst actually engaging in inappropriate behaviour. [...]

One major framework for developing a set of performance measures for an activity or a business unit has been developed by Kaplan and Norton (1992, 1996b, 2001). Their balanced scorecard approach, which is discussed in the following section, provides a structured way of developing an appropriate set of performance measures for the chosen business strategy. It demonstrates that a logical, cohesive system can be devised to integrate both financial and non-financial performance measures. However, the choice of which measures to use, avoiding of conflict between them and keeping their number to an adequate minimum are issues for individual companies to address.

The balanced scorecard

The balanced scorecard was the product of a research project conducted by the Harvard Business School and involving 12 leading companies in the United States. It allows managers to look at a business from four important perspectives and provides answers to the following questions:

1. How do we look to shareholders? (Financial perspective.)
2. How do customers see us? (Customer perspective.)
3. What must we excel at? (Internal business perspective.)
4. Can we continue to improve and create value? (Innovation and learning perspective.)

As well as defining the four perspectives the balanced scorecard approach suggests that no more than four measures of performance should be defined, although more recently the internal business perspective has been allowed between five to eight measures. This is to focus senior managers' attention on crucial factors rather than being distracted by unnecessary detail. It is said that companies rarely have too few measures. The justification for the four 'boxes' on the scorecard is as follows.

Financial perspective

This is the most traditional perspective and most organizations will already have some measures of financial performance. Most commonly, at the divisional level the overall measure of financial performance is likely to be return on capital employed. However, this may be replaced by a less manipulable measure such as residual income, or its more modern counterpart, Economic Value Added®. This may be supplemented by measures of sales revenue growth, asset utilization, liquidity and budget achievement. Companies may also wish to include a measure of shareholder value added, as this is ultimately the benefit that shareholders gain from their investment in the company. The measures used here are likely to represent desired results rather than the means by which such results can be obtained.

Customer perspective

In order to be successful it is necessary to keep customers happy. Thus measuring how a company is responding to its customers' requirements has become a top priority for most organizations. Customers' concerns tend to fall into one of four categories: time, quality, service and cost. The balanced scorecard requires managers to translate their general customer service goals into specific objectives and measures. For example, the cycle time from receiving a customer's order to delivering the completed order is a commonly used measure. But it is vital to ensure that the performance measure targets exactly what the customer requires. [...] It may also be important to clarify exactly what the organization's position is in terms of competitive strategy: does it emphasize cost competitiveness or added value products that will be priced at a premium? Developing balanced scorecard measures may require a strategy to be articulated more precisely.

Internal business perspective

Customer-based measures are important but they should be supplemented with measures of exactly what the company must do to deliver the level of service expected by its customers. Thus the internal business perspective box will generally contain measures that relate to the means by which the business objectives will be achieved. To achieve goals on cycle time, quality, productivity and cost, managers must devise measures that are clearly related to employees' actions. This linkage is the most important thread in the process of strategy deployment. That is, a clear link must be maintained between hierarchical levels (and between organizational units) to ensure that the means targeted at one level lead to the results required at the next level. Information systems can play a vital part in helping managers to disaggregate the summary measures. This 'drill-down' capacity is seen as an essential component of an effective information system for use in performance management.

Innovation and learning

All the performance measures in the three areas discussed above are necessarily short term in orientation. They are reported frequently and represent actual achievement over a relatively short period of time (generally weekly and monthly). But in order to remain competitive in a changing environment companies need to adapt and to continue to offer products and services that customers wish to purchase. The measures in the innovation and learning box are intended to promote a longer-term perspective to counteract the short-termism inherent in other measures. Thus new product development and the acquisition of new business and customers may be targeted. Competitive advantage can be gained by having a well-trained and motivated workforce; such measures as employees' skills and attitudes may be included here.

The balanced scorecard therefore provides a structured framework for the development of a simple but comprehensive system of performance measurement. However, it is notable that the early publications on the balanced scorecard (Kaplan and Norton, 1992 [...]) contained next to no practical guidance on how to undertake the recommended procedures. Perhaps the considerable popularity of the framework has been due to its lack of specificity, which allows it to be applied in almost any context. Other related frameworks exist, such as the results and determinants framework by Fitzgerald et al. (1991), Lynch and Cross's (1995) performance pyramid and Neely et al.'s (2002) performance prism. A common thread in all of them is that performance measures should

- Be linked to corporate strategy;
- Include external as well as internal measures;
- Include non-financial as well as financial measures;
- Make explicit the trade-offs between different dimensions of performance;

- Include all important but difficult to measure factors as well as easily measurable ones; and
- Pay attention to how the selected measures will motivate managers and employees.

It could be said that balanced scorecard essentially adopts a stakeholder perspective on the business. Shareholders and customers are clearly identified, and employees feature sometimes in the internal box and sometimes in the innovation box. Extending the idea of stakeholder analysis might suggest that the balanced scorecard could be extended to include measures that are relevant to each stakeholder group that has to be taken account of. Thus suppliers, local communities, governments and environmental lobbies might all be featured. A common addition in practice is a fifth box entitled 'corporate social responsibility', which covers some of these areas. The framework also focuses attention on internal business processes and on the longer term as well as the short term. Regardless of these extensions, the approach seems to have been found useful in a wide range of organizations – manufacturing and service, public and private – and is relatively easy to adapt to a wide range of situations.

Target setting

Having decided upon the major dimensions of performance that should be measured, the next stage is to set appropriate standards and targets, that is, the level of performance required for each of the measures identified. Clearly, higher levels of performance are more desirable than lower levels, but it may not be feasible to attain these with the current methods of working. The conflict between what is desired and what can reasonably be expected permeates the whole process of target setting. Setting targets for competing performance measures also reveals the trade-offs that may have to be made between different areas. For example, high service quality and low prices may not be compatible. Setting targets for the two areas together resolves the conflict and establishes a more explicit strategy. Thus target setting is of major importance to the process of performance management.

It is helpful to distinguish between the process of target setting and the content of the targets set. The way in which target setting is approached is of vital importance to the motivational impact of the eventual targets. A large number of studies suggest that allowing managers to participate in the process of target setting will strengthen their commitment to achieving the targets. [...] Much of the early research on budgetary control and managerial behaviour studied this in some detail (see, for example, Hofstede, 1968). It should be borne in mind, however, that managers are likely to view the issue from the standpoint of what is currently feasible and may have to be informed about the need to develop new practices. In addition the way in which the performance targets are expected to be used will influence target-setting behaviour. Managers who believe that a target will be used as a standard against which to judge their managerial performance may be inclined to set 'slack' targets that will be easier to achieve, rather than challenging targets that they may fail to meet but may still motivate them to perform well.

There are several relevant sources of information on the content of the target. What has been achieved in previous periods is always a relevant source of information as it enables judgement of what is actually feasible in given circumstances. But it is necessary to supplement this historical information with information on what is being done elsewhere. External benchmarking has become popular in recent years. This involves finding out the performance levels being achieved by competitors (either by formal collaboration or by gleaning information from a variety of sources). The requirements of customers and shareholders also provide important information on the performance levels required for future survival. These sources of external information can also provide legitimacy to the target-setting process. A difficult target may be rejected by a manager who feels that it is purely an arbitrary imposition by a demanding superior. However, if it is clearly a necessary condition for organizational survival in a competitive market place, then it may be more readily accepted as a challenge.

One of the principal ways in which targets set in different areas are pulled together into a coherent overall statement is the budgeting process. A well-set budget incorporates the standards of performance that are feasible to attain, and represents the financial consequences of the implementation of a plan of action. Ideally the budget is the expected financial outcome of an espoused strategy. Unfortunately this ideal is often not met, with the budget becoming detached from the plans on which it is based. For example, repeated budget revisions to meet financial performance targets may cause numbers to be entered into the budget with little or no idea of how these outcomes will be achieved in practice. While the budgetary process has traditionally been of major importance to the overall management of performance, in recent years budgeting has been the subject of increasing criticism (largely due to the difficulty of forecasting), and more radical approaches to perform-ance management and control have been put forward. These have been cogently summarized by Fraser and Hope (2003). The case for improving budgeting rather than abolishing has been put forward by Hansen et al. (2003).

Incentives and rewards

The next key issue to address is motivation. It is one thing to set per-formance targets, but quite another for managers and other employees to be motivated to achieve them. Generally, organizations put into place a number of incentives, both financial and non-financial, to encourage their employees to achieve the performance standards defined in the processes described above. These may include the generation of enthu-siasm to achieve a vision that has been communicated throughout the organization and to which, it is hoped, employees will commit them-selves, the use of performance appraisal and evaluation methods, and the provision of short-term financial rewards. An appropriate package of incentive and reward arrangements should be central to the design of a performance management system. However, in practice such systems are often designed in a very fragmented manner, with different departments being responsible for different aspects of the package.

In an assessment of the reward mechanisms used by organizations to encourage employees to achieve the required levels of performance, Fitzgerald and Moon (1996a) suggest that three factors are of particular importance:

1. Clarity: do they understand what the company is trying to do?
2. Motivation: what benefits, financial or otherwise, will they gain from achieving targets?
3. Controllability: are they assessed only on those factors they can control?

A feature of many successful organizations is that they have communic-ated their vision and mission to employees at all levels. Therefore the employees are clear about the organizational values they should incor-porate into their everyday activities. Although it is difficult to codify in quantitative terms, commitment and enthusiasm of this type should not be underrated. The sense of pride that comes from working for a well-known or successful organization can be a vital factor in sustaining competitive advantage. Conversely, a downward spiral of poor performance and demotivation, leading to poor employee attitudes, can prove difficult to break out of.

As well as a sense of pride in achievement, more direct incentives come into play. The long-term progression of employees in an organization is usually dependent on their being seen to perform well. The appraisal and evaluation of performance may be the subject of formal procedures and meetings or rely solely on the subjective judgement of a superior, but it is of central importance. The 'things you need to do to get on around here' is an important aspect of organizational culture of which employees rapidly become aware. Also the power politics of an organization have an impact in this area. Even more influential are systems of financial reward tied to performance. Many organizations have introduced performance-related pay, whereby employees earn extra pay for achieving preset performance targets. These have long been the norm in some types of job. For example, sales people have traditionally been paid a commission on the sales they make. These mechanisms were used less for middle managers in the UK (although not the United States) until about 1985. However, after then there was a great increase in the provision of financial rewards in both the private and the public sectors. A majority of middle managers in both sectors now receive a monetary reward for achieving performance targets.

Such mechanisms can clearly have a major effect on managerial behaviour, making it even more essential for performance measures accurately to reflect what is required of a manager. It is very easy to neglect an important aspect of performance (perhaps because it is difficult to measure) or to give it an inappropriate weighting. [. . .]

One major problem area is the use of the budget system as the benchmark for paying performance bonuses. The bonus system is often devised in isolation by a personnel or human resources department. Having decided to introduce a bonus system, they search for suitable measures of performance to base it upon. The budget is often seen as providing such a basis as it already exists in most organizations. However, what is often unanticipated is the effect this will have on the operation of the budgetary process. Whereas previously managers may have been willing to set challenging budgetary targets, or at least to submit accurate estimates of future performance, it now becomes advantageous for them to submit 'slack' estimates. [. . .]

Finally there is the issue of controllability. It may seem self-evident that managers should be held accountable only for those things that they can control, and this is a central tenet of much of the management accountability literature, where considerable effort is made to design performance measures that reflect controllable performance. But there is emerging evidence that this principle is more notable for its breach than its observance. Both Otley (1990) and Merchant (1987) have noted that managers are often held accountable for things outside their control. This may be partly due to the difficulty of splitting the controllable from the non-controllable on a black and white basis. Many things are clearly partly controllable. More fundamentally, managers may have to adapt to uncontrollable environmental changes by revising their operating strategies and plans. Hence they cannot necessarily be held accountable for implementing predetermined plans, only for achieving the desired results. This is essentially what Merchant (1987) describes as results control rather than behaviour control, and it is central to the control of non-programmed activities.

Thus incentives, rewards and the performance appraisal are central to the design of an effective performance management system. However, they are often not regarded as part of the performance measurement process and are designed in isolation from it. This is clearly inappropriate. From an economic perspective, the issue is considered at some length in the literature on agency theory, which concentrates on the design of appropriate reward mechanisms under different sets of conditions. However, this literature tends to consider the employee as an individual who is motivated solely by financial considerations. The reality is somewhat more complicated than this simple model implies, although it can be used to gain insights into real world behaviour. [...]

Information flows

The final stage in the performance management process is the provision of information on to the actual results. This is the necessary feedback process that aids adaptation and learning. In practical terms it involves what has become known as an executive information system (EIS). As Crockett (1992) has outlined, to ensure that the right strategic information flows into its EIS a company should

- Identify the critical success factors and stakeholders' expectations;
- Document the performance measures used to monitor them;
- Determine the EIS reporting formats and frequency; and
- Outline the information flows and how the information can be used.

Crockett points out that this process is complicated and time-consuming, and that it involves all levels of management. The EIS should also possess a capacity for 'drill down'; that is, the ability to provide more detailed information on areas that are being investigated in more detail.

The frequency of information provision may differ between hierarchical levels. At low levels very frequent information can be helpful. For example, hourly production and quality statistics may be appropriate for use by a production supervisor. At more senior levels, weekly or monthly reports may be more appropriate. However, it becomes more difficult to produce meaningful summary information that encompasses many different production processes and customers. Senior managers often find that such aggregate information can only be presented in financial terms. But this does not mean that the focus is only financial. In a sense the financial and accounting information provides a window into the real world of production and marketing. The 'drill down' from aggregate financial information will often need to be non-financial in nature, using such measures as quality, timeliness of delivery and customer satisfaction. This is a real challenge to the designers of EISs, and one that has yet to be fully overcome in practice.

A further issue is the use made of feedback information. At one level a measure of actual performance that shows a target has not been met is a stimulus for corrective action. It indicates that the strategy is not being properly implemented and that corrective action should be taken. However, repeated attempts to improve performance may prove fruitless. It may be that the message the data is conveying is that the strategy is now inappropriate. In this case the required action is to review the strategy and to devise other methods of achieving the organization's goals. This is the distinction that Argyris and Schön (1978) make between 'single loop' and 'double loop' learning. Although this may seem a somewhat arcane point, it is also a very important practical issue. In one case increased pressure is put on operational employees; in the other, the pressure is on senior managers and corporate strategists. It can be quite demotivating and counterproductive to pressure operating staff when they are actually achieving the organization's full potential in the current conditions. Distinguishing ineffective strategy implementation from an inappropriate strategy is a difficult but essential task.

Conclusions

Although the above scheme for the design of a performance management system may appear to be universally applicable, it is clear from practical experience that organizations should tailor each of the steps involved to their own circumstances. There is no single set of performance measures, no single basis for setting standards for those measures, and no universal reward mechanism that constitutes a perfect performance management system in all contexts. Different organizations face different operating environments and must develop strategies that accord with those environments. The so-called contingency theory of management accounting (Otley, 1980) represents one attempt to develop criteria for management accounting systems design that takes account of some of these factors. However, the research conducted by Fitzgerald and Moon (1996) in the service sector indicates that effective performance management systems have common characteristics. They conclude that the following are necessary preconditions for the attainment of best practice:

- *Know what you are trying to do.* The design of a performance measurement and management system should be rooted in a clear understanding of exactly what an organization has decided to do in order to exploit its sources of competitive advantage. This understanding should be communicated throughout the organization by means of techniques such as visioning and budgeting.
- *Adopt a range of performance measures.* Financial measures alone are insufficient to capture the complexity of modern business operations. Organizations should adopt a range of measures covering the six generic dimensions of performance: financial performance, competitiveness, quality, resource utilization, flexibility and innovation.
- *Extract comparative measures to assess performance.* Both internal and external benchmarking can be used to set standards against which performance is assessed.
- *Report results regularly.* For managers to be able to use performance information proactively it must be relevant and up to date. Appropriate frequency of reporting will differ from task to task, and by hierarchical level.
- *Drive the system from the top down.* Lower-level employees will only take the system seriously if they see it being taken seriously by senior managers.

To these we would add the following:

- *Tie performance measures explicitly to strategy.* It is all too easy to develop a plethora of performance measures; organizations should concentrate on those activities which are vital to their future success. The balanced scorecard offers one framework for doing this.

- *Remember that effectiveness is more fundamental than efficiency.* Ensure that cost reductions are not given greater importance than the achievement of output objectives.
- *Review all performance measures from the bottom up.* Check that the performance measures adopted are not easily manipulated or distorted. Put yourself in the position of employees being measures by the system, and consider how they might respond.
- *Pay attention to incentives and rewards.* It is all too easy to undo the effect of a well-designed measurement and reporting system by attaching an inappropriate reward system to it.
- *Identify the main risk factors that prevent outcome being achieved.* Consider including measures of key risk factors that need to be monitored; also consider having a measure of organizational flexibility or adaptability (that is, the capability of the organization to deal with the unexpected).

The framework outlined in this chapter may at first sight appear to be normative in nature, and indeed it is partially based on explicitly normative approaches. However, it can be used in a non-prescriptive manner to describe how a specific organization has designed and operates its performance management system [. . .]. Whilst we recognize that the framework is incomplete and concentrates on the more formal methods of managing performance in an organization, we believe that it provides a more complete basis for considering the role of accounting and other information system design than has previously existed (see Ferreira and Otley, 2004, for extensions to this framework that make it more comprehensive). Although the framework appears to be universal, more careful consideration indicates that it is in fact contingent. Each organization has its own strategy and exists in its own unique environment; I suggest that its information and performance management systems should be specifically tailored to these circumstances.

4
Currents and Controversies in Contemporary Performance Management

Carmel de Nahlik

Introduction

The area of performance management as a distinctive body of management literature is still evolving. In Chapter 3, David Otley explored some of its roots in the older operational research and accounting literatures, together with the integration of measures from those disciplines in tools such as the balanced scorecard or six-sigma, familiar to practising managers today. However, an unresolved theme underlying Otley's position statement is the tension between the quasi-scientific measurable outputs of formal processes and the less bounded 'softer' outputs of performance management processes. This chapter explores the results of that tension.

The performance management process and its consequent attempts to deal with appropriate metrics, is, itself, a worthy research area as we see in the subsequent chapters of this book. No longer is it located in the rational, bounded, hard systems, 'management as science' arena, but it is rapidly moving in to the softer systems area of 'messy problems' including stakeholder considerations, politics, power, symbolism, structure and inter-organizational relationships. So in the new world of performance management, the quasi-scientific measurement and control paradigm from economics is mapped on to the sociology and psychology literatures, with institutional effects observable as mediating factors. Whilst Chapter 3 presented a largely consensual view of performance management, we shall explore some of the currents and controversies that surround the area as seen from different perspectives. We close with a short discussion on some salient issues to managers and academic stakeholders.

Multiple levels and worldviews

The assumption that performance management is a problem-free area of management in many organizations and among policy makers was an important reason for writing this book, as performance management in practice is usually far from unproblematic and unbiased. As later chapters will show, there are no clear answers: a range of theoretical frameworks are up for debate. In this chapter, we problematize them and seek to identify explicitly some of the competing theoretical underpinnings that most chapters later take for granted.

At one of two extremes, writers have looked at performance management as a management control process linked to the audit function, thus reifying it at an organizational level. Other researchers have looked at performance management as something to be considered at the individual level and linked to a judgement of the adequacy of the individual's performance as a member of the organization. Yet another body of literature exists in which performance management is used as a method of inter-organizational comparison to benchmark the performance of the organization against a chosen peer group, with a view to its improvement.

Thus for our purposes (taking a critical overview of the field), performance management can be seen variously as: the management of stakeholders; the management of a system level under investigation by various stakeholders (who may or may not come from the same level in the system); or the management of system inter-level activities or processes as shown in Figure 4.1.

As well as operating at different levels, there are multiple ways of learning and knowing about performance management that may generate complex questions. Put another way, the understanding of performance management is subject to ontological, epistemological and value-based choices and positioning. Is performance socially constructed? Is it external? Is the perception influenced by the base disciplines of the manager and the managed, as well as any observer?

Given the context of this book, the answers to several more provocative questions may be uncomfortable to academic analysts; in particular:

- Can such different disciplines be expected to see performance management as 'the same thing', and develop a shared language for understanding it, given their wide differences in level of focus and interest?

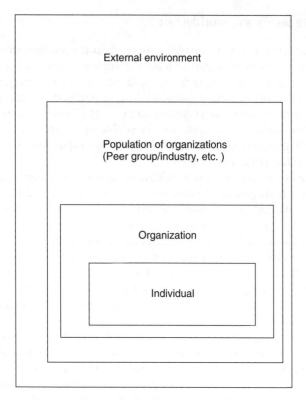

Figure 4.1   Systems view of performance management

- Can all the disciplinary perspectives contribute to a harmonious and systemic 'unified theory' of performance management or will knowledge advance more swiftly through competing explanations, stakeholder worldviews and the juxtaposition of micro and macro levels of analysis?

Performance management can be examined through multiple disciplinary lenses, at a number of levels, and from competing epistemological viewpoints. Indeed, one is obliged to question how far analysts can be confident that they are studying the same phenomenon at all! Although they are difficult to articulate in the course of everyday practice, these are some of the controversies challenging performance management's stakeholders.

Performance measurement: just a dimension of performance management?

The received wisdom is that to manage performance, you first have to measure it. So how do we measure performance? Traditionally we have looked for a change that can be quantified and thence reported, but does this necessarily lead to the desired change? If we are always looking backwards, is this useful for future performance enhancement? What of effects we cannot quantify and measure? This can become a thorny issue if we are concerned with performance relative to other organizations or individuals. Finally the measurement of performance presupposes we have an accurate working model of the relationships, but as always we must be careful of spurious correlations and hidden mediating factors.

Despite some potentially dysfunctional features, performance measurement is attractive to stakeholders in an organization because:

- For individual managers it offers a sense making device (Weick, 1969) allowing their location to be established through points of reference based on the performance measurement system. Thus terms like 'cockpit', 'dashboard', 'traffic lights' form part of the language and reinforce a perception by the manager that they can influence and control the direction of the output through either direct or perceived management of the indicators. At a psychological level this may make managers feel empowered – but is this more perception than reality? Does this matter?
- Similarly it offers a basis for selection of opportunities at each of the system levels by reference to relative positioning against the competition, based on criteria legitimized via the institutional environment as well as absolute comparators, making organizations vulnerable to 'groupthink' pressures. So we see organizations, especially firms, compared using financial ratios, which are 'norms' in the investment community. But are these the most relevant indicators for the organization's purposes? Or do the most powerful (financial) stakeholders drive and determine the measurement agenda and metrics?
- If the performance measurement and the performance management system act together as screening devices, then 'if the new opportunity fits the criteria, we should do it'. But the stakeholder benefit may be short-lived. An evolutionary view of the landscape (e.g. Levinthal, 1997) would suggest that if all species or players use the same set of rules or yardsticks then variation in performance is minimized,

and the population becomes more homogenous (Thompson, 1994). It is the heterogeneity in the population that allows for innovation (Gilbert et al., 2001) and conforming to the rules imposed by the institutional system minimizes the propensity for variation. 'Best practice' can lead to stagnation if not continually evaluated and adapted to the changing environments.

- Performance management is also affected by decision-making strategies such as the exploration /exploitation paradox (March, 1991) and game theoretic explanations (Bevan and Hood, 2006).[1] Deeper learning may be taking place about the existing 'game' within present rules, but any external change may disadvantage players who are not simultaneously conducting exploration strategies around new games with new rules. So organizations need to be scanning at the upper levels of the systems shown in Figure 4.1 constantly, in order to make sure that they have a survival plan and can demonstrate sustainable advantage relative to the competition (Grant, 1991) in order to satisfy their stakeholders.
- Performance measurement can also offer the decision maker a defence and rationalizing mechanism against challenges from colleagues above and below them in the organization: 'B followed A, therefore A caused B'. This may then be used to justify the status quo.

In spite of these potential limitations, most stakeholders tend to be in favour of metrics and measurement as a route to performance management. But what is measured, and how does this help management to move from strategic decision making to operationalization?

Consider a surplus-generating publicly owned corporation. How is its performance measured? Conventionally the performance of the investment by financial stakeholders was used as a basis for accounting-based metrics such as 'profit', 'dividends' and 'return on capital employed' and variations on these. Today these have been replaced either by more sophisticated calculations of (say) 'return on average capital employed', or measures of value enhancement such as Economic Value Added® (Stern et al., 1995) or market value added (MVA), developed by prestigious management consultancy firms with complex proprietary formulae (Lehn and Makhija, 1996). However, the core variables are still financial and therefore measurable using accounting conventions, which may be idiosyncratically interpreted within specified boundaries. (These conventions are discussed further in Chapter 12, 'An Accounting and Finance Perspective'.)

Most organizations produce accounts as activity statements for resource stewardship to stakeholders, suggesting that the pressure to count and measure things according to interpreted rules, is universal. Despite movements towards financial reporting convergence, there is still room for interpretation and organizations have a range of options open to them in terms of the numbers reported. But what of those assets which are not financial, such as intellectual property (IP) and the staff? Accounting bodies have a long-standing aspiration to offer a stewardship account of the staff or human resources, not without controversy (see, for example, Print, 2004). With the rise of Knowledge Management as a distinctive area for study, stewardship of 'knowledge assets' is also an issue for accountants, who have had the experience of brand management, brand valuation and revaluation issues to guide their thinking in this area. The lack of formal accounting for intangible assets flies in the face of theories of competitive advantage, such as the Resource Based View of the Firm (discussed below).

Both in the case of the performance metrics employed, and in the case of what is not measured, there is a risk that the performance measurement system introduced with the best of intentions (or at least legitimate ones in the context of management accountability to the organization's 'owners') can be dysfunctional. It can cause myopia, leading to deteriorating performance because in the quest for the speck of dust, the falling tree is not noticed. (In Chapter 9, Smith and Goddard introduce an extensive set of 'enemies of virtuous performance management'.) There is also the possibility that the decision makers and the firms form ossifying knowledge networks which are not benign (de Nahlik and Holloway, 2005) and stifle the creation of future knowledge which would enhance sustainable competitive advantage.

The tensions between organizational stakeholders and performance management

The stakeholder approach is now enshrined in many applied literatures from project management to public policy (see, for example, government documents like the US Executive Office of the President circular 'Planning, budgeting, acquisition, and management of capital assets', US OECM DOE, 2003), as well as featuring in the more classic organizational theory literatures (e.g. Pfeffer and Salancik, 1978). The term has also become part of the *lingua franca* of modern managers, and stakeholder maps abound in boardrooms.

Stakeholders have been defined as: '...those groups without whose support the organization would cease to exist' (Freeman, 1984, p. 31). There is a logical relationship therefore between stakeholder interests and the organization's performance.

Two issues to consider from a performance management perspective are: the process of transfer of data and information across the boundary separating internal and external stakeholders; and the use of that data and information. The rise in prominence of the 'stakeholder' construct has been paralleled by a rise in the governance literatures relating to performance management of stakeholder requirements, including those enforced by the institutional environment mentioned earlier. This in turn has led to a rise in overt performance measurement and management activity within the various system levels in Figure 4.1. However, just being a stakeholder isn't enough. Maps and 'laundry lists' of interested parties are of limited value without some form of prioritization, which is of course subjective. The activity of compiling the stakeholder map inevitably results in a movement away from the quasi-scientific approach towards the more individually centred approaches, where judgements are made about such descriptors as 'operational power', 'influence' and so on (e.g. Winstanley et al., 1995). This uneasy tension of the quasi-objective measuring and quasi-subjective prioritization activities is uncomfortable to many performance managers who are often located within what we might term the more scientifically situated functions of management accounting or internal control.

Where organizations try to satisfy the perceived interests of an undifferentiated list of stakeholders, there are likely to be problems. First, there is the direct cost of dealing reactively with the stakeholder list and responding to queries from a number of them. This cost is unlikely to be avoidable. There will be additional direct secondary costs such as time and other resource deployment which may be diverted to address the management of the stakeholder interaction process. So the opportunity cost of these two activities and associated resources needs to be actively considered by organizations on an ongoing basis, rather than reactively at times of crisis. Good strategic management involves understanding and prioritizing some stakeholder interests over others.

Second, from a pragmatic standpoint, the financial and other costs of managing relationships with stakeholders proactively are significant. In an age where (in some contexts at least) information asymmetries have fallen thanks to almost instantaneous communication, this is also a potentially volatile area of an organization's budget.

Third, the governance of stakeholders also needs to be examined as we consider the transitions taking place in organizational forms. No longer are organizations bounded, with interfaces bridged by explicit contracts (as in the view of Williamson, 1975, elaborated in other chapters). Many organizations now have a quasi-integrated supply chain, where co-operation and joint development may result in very blurred boundaries between the firm and its supplier (Wilding, 2006). As a result distinctions between internal and external stakeholders blur and transactions across the boundary may not always be clear cut. The social system nature of organizations may also mean that many of these contracts are enacted as a result of 'social capital' issues rather than the formal nature of the legal transaction (Dasgupta, 2005). This important concept merits further examination.

Social capital has been defined as the sum of the resources, actual or virtual, that accrue to an individual or a group by virtue of possessing a durable network of more or less institutionalized relationships of mutual acquaintance and recognition (Burt, 1992). In many ways this offers a more useful way of viewing stakeholder interests than through their financial stakes, focusing instead on cliques and network ties. However, identifying and measuring network ties is empirically more challenging than assessing financial flows and interests. How do we know if all ties are reported? Do network researchers have to impose their own classifications? For example, can the number of times a director and film technical expert work together, measured by each film, really be a valid proxy for other informal contacts that may reinforce the network? What of hidden networks such as professional bodies, charities and other (more or less open) membership-based organizations?

Two further examples illustrate issues around defining stakeholders within nominal boundaries (such as the firm) and the practical repercussions of managing their performance:

1. A car manufacturer 'embedding' an employee within a supplier firm. Is this person an external stakeholder or an internal one? How clear in practice is the responsibility chain? Who is responsible for managing the supplier's performance and is it represented by this individual's performance?
2. Virtual organizations (e.g. public–private or public–voluntary sector partnerships, or network organizations assembled for the life of a

project), where there may be limited involvement with the parent organizations. How are practical responsibilities allocated? Is account-ability to the parent or the partnership? Formal contractual links may be limited: how is performance managed here?

Social capital is also the sum of individual dyadic (one-to-one) ties. Mov-ing from the organizational level to the individual level in Figure 4.1, again a number of pertinent stakeholder issues arise.

At the individual level the stakeholder map will reflect the role being examined, so there may be several maps for an individual with differing perceptions of the roles, influence and power of each stakeholder. As with all perceptual maps, the result is dependent on the perception of the map owner, and may not be a shared reality, posing some issues for researchers.

Many contracts with stakeholders, either formal or informal, are of necessity incomplete (Hart and Moore, 1999) thus allowing for gam-ing behaviour to exist at the individual or organizational level (Radnor, forthcoming; Bevan and Hood, 2006). This 'gaming' approach carries over inevitably from the performance management system into the performance measurement system, when measured output from a per-formance measurement system is linked to individual rewards. Thus investments are deferred or brought forward to affect the financial reports, or personal targets are manipulated to allow for the optimal payoff to the individual manager, possibly at the expense of the cli-ent or organization if it is a zero-sum game. ('Gaming' and other dysfunctional effects of performance measurement are discussed further in several later chapters.)

Counting network ties may not be a proxy for power. Some ties are more valuable than others. Controversy can arise from the perception of the power exercised by various stakeholder groups. So for example, is it equitable for shareholder stakeholder groups to exercise the most power in the case of publicly traded firms? Does this disenfranchise the employees, without whom the firm may not generate rents? How are stakeholders in the external environment educated and informed about the range of acceptable outcomes from the performance measurement system? Too often, genuine attempts at consultation, transparency and accountability are castigated in the media for 'putting a price on life', or 'using numbers as a smokescreen' – examples abound particularly in the field of healthcare. Stakeholders may be differentially affected by per-formance measurement and management systems, sometimes in ways not necessarily linked to perceived power and influence, so issues of procedural and organizational justice need to be considered too (Greenberg, 1987; Kim and Mauborgne, 1995).

Can academics explain the nature and role of performance management?

Most of the chapters in this book present particular disciplinary or sectoral explanations for the nature and role of performance management. Some reflect a single dominant paradigm; others introduce competing forms of explanation reflecting fundamentally different ways of understanding the world, or epistemologies.

At the epistemological level, we can contrast two extreme ways of looking at PM. The first is to consider Donaldson's views of stewardship, embedded in the positivist paradigm (Davis et al., 1997). If managers are stewards of resources, then as stewards, they are accountable to their stakeholders and thence that accountability needs to be measured somehow. The second is to consider the other end of the epistemological spectrum and a postmodernist view drawing on Lyotard (1984) which suggests that the performance management and measurement system are socially constructed and politically driven. So philosophically, performance management itself is not without controversy – to manage we need to be able to measure, with all the arguments that go with the epistemology of measurement. In cultures that generally endorse the use of quantitative measurement and value rational 'objectivity', the positivist view prevails. But how does performance management work in practice – and does it really give valuable information to the stakeholders in the system? Indeed what is 'valuable' information in this context?

Returning to our earlier multilevel approach, using the institutional theory interpretations of Di Maggio and Powell (1983) and Greenwood and Hinings (1996) we can see that performance management can (and anecdotal evidence suggests, often does) become a part of the management ritual (Meyer and Rowan, 1977) legitimized by powerful external stakeholders so that it forms part of the institutional environment. Referring back to Figure 4.1, the institutional level can be identified as the location for this validation. A component of the external environment of the organization, the study of this area encompasses sociology (e.g. Greenwood and Hinings op. cit.; Selznick, 1996), and economics (e.g. Nelson, 2002) and anthropology. Performance management can also be viewed anthropologically as a ritual (Meyer and Rowan, 1977); to be a symbolic act (Greiling, 2005); and to form part of the cultural web of an organization (Johnson, 1987).

As we have already suggested, performance management can be a legitimizing device for certain behaviours and attendant outcomes, either at an individual level or at the aggregated level of a population of organizations. In the latter case, the management system for performance is legitimized by other members of a peer group and other powerful external stakeholders (Pfeffer and Salancik, 1978). Shifts and disruptions in either of these groups can cause replacement or change of 'norm' metrics, a process that can also be viewed as movements and changes in occupied spaces in the competitive landscape as a result of outcomes of a series of selection/adaptation processes (Aldrich, 1999).

Focusing on the organization's internal adaptations to its environment, the dominant strategic paradigm for some years has been the Resource Based View (RBV) of the Firm (Wernerfelt, 1984; Barney, 1991; Grant, 1991). The RBV views sustainable competitive advantage as an outcome from a melding of industry key success factors and different types of resource uniquely synthesized inside the organization to produce specialized capabilities, which are expected to be unique and valuable contributors to the firm's competitive advantage (Amit and Schoemaker, 1993). A recent variant, the Knowledge Based View alluded to earlier, suggests that sustainable competitive advantage arises from knowledge as the key resource (Conner, 1991; Kogut and Zander, 1992; Nonaka and Takeuchi, 1995; Grant, 1996; Spender, 1996).

The approach of stressing capabilities has led to the dynamic view of organizational resources (Teece et al., 1997; Wang and Ahmed, 2007). Firms constantly reconfigure their resources and capabilities as a response to change from the environment, either viewed in the macro picture (as the classic STEP analysis of Fahey and Narayanan, 1986) or as a response to different dynamics in the industries or market where the organization competes to capture 'organizational rents'. Whether this response is voluntary or not, a failure to respond, to follow a dynamic approach, is to condemn the firm to chance. Are its resources and capabilities correctly configured for continued survival and rent generation? Or is it trapped in the past and guilty of 'excess' (Pascale, 1990), or in the uncritical emulation of others, thus impeding change (Boonstra and de Vries, 2005)? Change is vital – the constant changing of the organization, its industry/markets, its environment and its stakeholders is the basis of the coevolutionary paradigm, celebrated in March (1994) and further developed by Lewin (1997; Lewin et al., 1999; Lewin and Volberda,

1999) as contribution to the organization's survival through learning and adaptation to new environments.

In all of these views managers can make a difference – they can exercise strategic choice (Child, 1972). This contrasts with the views of North (1990) and Williamson (1996) where institutional levels in the system dictate the conduct of economic and transactional activity to lower levels in the system. Indeed the 'hard' view of economists such as Williamson contrast with the 'softer' views expressed above and thus resonates with the 'hard versus soft' dimensions of Thorpe and Beasley in Chapter 2.

The strategy literature is replete with attempts to address the 'Philosopher's Stone' of actions that managers can undertake in order to improve performance, and these recipes (Spender, 1989) can also be seen in other companion applied management literatures, such as marketing. The old structure–conduct–performance paradigm is less obviously present in today's strategy literature, being supplanted by feedback systems that spiral in what is hoped will be a direction of excellence.

Fortunately, this increasing complexity in the 'real world' has been accompanied by new analytical tools, models and research techniques. These can assist researchers to examine how views of different stakeholders are affected by their location in the system or the social network; and connections between 'perceived' and 'actual' power relationships within such networks (Provan et al., 1980) and the network/knowledge relationship (Kogut, 2000).

Improved computing power and major archival databases on large firms offer ever more possibilities to researchers looking at causality, but only provided they can operationalize the research variables credibly to both academic and practitioner audiences.

However, there is a disjoint between practice and theory development that affects performance management stakeholders. Many studies are based on high-level measures derived from large public firms and using metrics that are the subject of judgement tests by auditors and managers. In today's business school we tell our students that 'turnover is vanity, profit is sanity, cashflow is reality', but it is really only in very recent studies that cashflow-based measures have appeared as performance indicators rather than income statement derived ones. This is further complicated by a predilection for cross-sectional research in which causal relationships are very difficult to hypothesize, operationalize and test. Far fewer studies are longitudinal or on smaller firms, notable exceptions being Greve (2000) and Mitchell (1991) who look at smaller firms; and Hawawini et al. (2003) who use EVA® data to look at firm survival. (Contemporary approaches to studying small firm performance management are explored further in Chapter 15.)

In terms of the operationalization of the performance management research process, again we have some deeper issues to consider. Academics raise methodological questions around data-gathering exercises and the various interested parties' perceptions of the validity and reliability of the data gathered and interpreted. These questions also affect managers in organizations carrying out performance management and indeed performance measurement activities, so they too need to be aware of potential limitations to any data gathered and then processed for use.

This is to ignore the fundamental question; however: does performance management actually have any effect on performance? Studies tend to focus on describing the selection and application of tools and techniques, sometimes reporting on changes in performance that are implicitly connected to the intervention. There remains a dearth of research designed to challenge the assumption that using one or another performance management system will affect performance outcomes more or less directly. Yet the simple process of introducing a change such as a performance management system, and paying management attention to its outputs or outcomes, may act as a 'Hawthorne effect' (Roethlisberger and Dickson, 1939). Alternatively good managers may get good results with whatever tools they adopt!

So the larger question still remains: 'how relevant is today's performance management research to practising managers?'

Towards a practice-relevant performance management research agenda

One of the taken-for-granted outcomes of performance management which makes it such an interesting and all-encompassing area for research and practice, is that of change at the levels shown in Figure 4.1. We can consider each level as a starting point for a critical performance management research agenda that counterbalances the prevailing search for the development of a 'better mousetrap' (which is apocryphally said to blame the aberrant behaviour of a single input – the mouse – for all the system's performance enhancement problems). For example:

- What effect do performance management systems have on individuals? Do they reinforce acceptable patterns and norms of behaviour ... and who judges the acceptability?

- What effect do performance management systems have on organizations? Can they cause long-term gains in the community at that system level, and how can we know? Can such systems promote dysfunctional practices as a result of pressures from the institutional environment at the next system level, when these practices become normalized and accepted?
- What effect do certain groups or coalitions in the institutional level have on the external environment as well as those levels beneath them? Do they promote change that leads to a better future for all (whatever that means)? Or might they lead organizations to indulge in uncritical emulation of each other, and act as change inhibitors?

We can also apply these questions as we consider the nature of change and innovation, and reach out from the mainstream performance management literature into areas such as organizational development and change management.

Reflecting on the dominant coalitions in the performance management practitioner and research communities, how far is practice influenced by research evidence? Do practitioners and their iconic models, which are widely and (usually) uncritically adopted, dominate? How can more rigorous academic approaches which promote good scholarship have immediate impact, when research design and peer review delay the publication of research findings? Does the legitimization process promote certain models, while excluding others that may offer better explanatory power?

Last but by no means least, we need to ask whether it is realistic to include in the research agenda the search for demonstrable evidence of causal relationships between the operation of performance management systems, and longer-term strategic performance. Given the complexities identified at each of the levels considered in this chapter, this is a challenging empirical quest, but one with significant theoretical implications.

This chapter has touched, in passing at least, on the main functions and contexts in which performance management is practised. The chapters in the next section of this book dwell on the practicalities of many of the questions raised here. We will look at performance management through a series of discipline-centred lenses to make sense of the multiple levels. Some will focus more at a macro level, others at a micro level. We can also review the questions raised in this chapter while reading about the operationalization in each discipline's viewpoint – what are the appropriate dimensions of performance in that context? Are they specific to each discipline, or more universally understood and adopted? Are there indeed different ontologies or world views of measurement in the different disciplines in which performance management is used? We revisit these questions in the final section of the book.

Note

1. In the case of the exploration/exploitation paradox, firms ration capital, both financial and other forms, to trade off breadth (or number) of learning opportunities against greater investment in fewer opportunities to increase learning – a metaphor consonant with that of scale and scope used in Hamel and Prahalad (1983). In the game theory approach, managers look at metrics and 'micro manage' to meet targets whilst potentially neglecting the higher level strategy and aims, objectives and mission of the organization (Steele and Albright, 2004).

Part II

Performance Management Research: Contributions from Disciplines and Domains

5
Performance Management: An Occupational Psychology and Organizational Behaviour Perspective

Anne Fearfull and Gail P Clarkson

> Our problem is to understand the changes that the organization (and the individual) will have to make if it is to obtain the most possible energy for productive effort.
>
> (Argyris, 1964, p. 11)

Introduction

You have no doubt heard organizations claim that their people are their most valuable and important asset. The extent to which such a view is positively reflected in the manner in which people are managed in organizations, or is a component part of organizational rhetoric is, however, a long and oft-debated topic (Legge, 1995b; Herriot, 2001; Storey, 2001; Beardwell et al., 2004). We might argue that it is not the people *per se* who are regarded as valuable, but rather their ability to work (or, as Marx might have said, their embodiment of labour power). Nonetheless, moving the emphasis from financial and technical elements to human factors can separate, qualitatively, competing organizations when it comes to performance (Pfeffer, 1998; Rucci et al., 1998).

All too often, however, work organizations have highly complex systems by which they assess the costs and benefits of everything apart from appropriate people management (Arnold et al., 2004). There is considerable ground to be covered if we are to reveal the underlying processes of, and causal links between, management of employees, employee actions and business success (Delbridge and Lowe, 1997; Sparrow and Marchington, 1998). Performance management from the more bounded perspective of the human resource management function is explored in Chapter 6. Here, taking the above extract from the work of Argyris as our starting point, in this chapter we introduce key themes and theories drawn from the interrelated disciplines of occupational psychology and organizational behaviour (OP and OB) and developed in a quest to address the complex processes and effects of performance management. As will be seen, contemporary occupational psychologists/organizational behaviourists seek not only to identify strong relationships between (aspects of) practice and (facets of) performance, but also to gain an understanding as to *why* this should be the case. To this end, a host of theories have been put forward with varying degrees of success.

Following this introduction, we set OP and OB into discipline and then historical contexts. The modern discipline of psychology takes into consideration not only behaviour but also, at least to some extent, the underlying thoughts and emotions leading to that behaviour. In this regard, we consider the key issues of employee motivation, and then turn briefly to the area of individual differences. To round off we consider the performance management challenges faced by the occupational psychologist and organizational behaviourist in the twenty-first century organization.

The disciplines of occupational psychology and organizational behaviour

Organizational behaviour (OB) is a multidisciplinary field of study, dedicated to a better understanding of the management of people at work. Theoretical concepts, research methods and general principles drawn from cultural anthropology have facilitated the OB researcher in the investigation of the explicit and implicit patterns of and for behaviour acquired and transmitted through symbols. Concepts, methods and principles based in the field of political science have assisted understanding of the role and nature of organizational power. In addition, theories, methods and principles drawn from the field of sociology have assisted OB researchers to address questions regarding the effects of organizational structure and design on behaviour at various levels of analysis and/or the societal influences upon such structures. The work of organizational behaviourists is, however, largely concerned with activity carried out at the level of the group or individual within the organization. Here, in an attempt to gain insights into the implications of issues (such as the aforementioned culture, power and structure) for the behaviour of groups and individual workers, the discipline of OB draws heavily from the general discipline of psychology and, more particularly, the field of occupational psychology (OP).

To provide a perspective on human organizational behaviour we can consider the Darwinian view on animal behaviour. From that vantage point it is proposed that it is not the 'natural' inclination of animals to live together, and that the adaptation of their behaviour towards group living has evolved only as a reaction to, and a means of guarding against, predators. This perspective has been extended and reinforced recently by anthropological research[1], which has confirmed that early humans were prey animals, which, over time, have formed co-operative 'tribes', or groups, of some kind in order to overcome predatory advances. In modern times, we have seen the development of purposively task-orientated groups, or organizations, the survival aims of which have tended towards the financial rather than the absolute. It is in this regard that we have seen psychology, and the psychologist, in the service of the human race (Karlins, 1973, pp. 1–2):

Because of his [*sic*] training the psychologist is uniquely prepared to aid man in his quest for a brighter future .... The story of psychology in the service of man is one of dedication and progress in the battle of human dignity.... It is the story of a quest for solutions and a search for problems...the story of man's struggle to achieve a rewarding quality of life.

Applied psychology has been seen as a means of enhancing the performance of people in society and thereby the performance of society itself, leading to enhancement of the quality of our lives. As a result, we might see as unproblematic the use of the discipline of psychology to remove criminal tendencies from people (McConnell, 1973); to diffuse international conflicts (Rosenberg, 1973); or to help elderly people to cope with rapid technological and social changes (Rosenfelt, 1973). We know from the work of Jahoda (1982) and others (see, for example, Hayes and Nutman, 1981; Fryer and Payne, 1986) on the socio-psychological implications of unemployment, that, by virtue of the 'latent functions' of work, the act of work and the engagement of people within a workplace is regarded as psychologically beneficial. Thus, likewise in an occupational sense, we might see the logic in using psychology as a means of improving working conditions through, in broad terms, occupational psychology: the study of employees' well-being, their attitudes and their behaviour (Warr, 2002). The term performance is (of course) just one aspect of behaviour but one key goal of this discipline is to apply psychological knowledge to maximize performance effectiveness, with much of the research in this area relating to environments where task goals are threatened by environmental conditions and workload (Hockey, 2002).

The historical context of OP and OB

The industrial revolution moved vast numbers of people from craft to factory work in eighteenth and nineteenth century Western Europe and the USA, and questions arose about how best to organize the various activities in order to attain the best possible performance outcomes. One solution was to break jobs down into their simplest components, following the 'scientific management' prescriptions of Frederick Winslow Taylor (1911) and the early proponents of 'time and motion' studies. Here all tasks were timed to find the most efficient – deemed to be the simplest – way of doing them, the task then being linked to wages through a 'piece work' system as a means by which to motivate a higher rate of production. By the mid-1900s job simplification, which necessarily fragmented or atomized the 'whole job' was applied in both manufacturing and administrative domains (Braverman, 1974).

Concerns were, however, expressed both politically (Braverman, 1974) and with regard to the negative consequences for worker mental health and the organizational implications of employee absenteeism, dissatisfaction and boredom. In this context, psychologists began the move to redesign jobs to counter both the horizontal and the vertical division of labour using theoretical models of work design and proliferating a number of job enlargement and people-centred, performance-orientated techniques under the principles of job enrichment (for example, Herzberg, 1968; Hackman and Oldham, 1975). Empowerment, high involvement and high performance work systems are all underpinned by such principles (see Parker, 2002).

The most influential theory guiding group work design was sociotechnical systems theory, particularly associated with the work of the Tavistock Institute (Trist and Bamforth, 1951). Trist and Bamforth studied the effects of the replacement of traditional 'hand getting' of coal by the 'longwall' method of mining. Following the introduction of large-scale machinery, groups of individuals had been divided into specialized groups, each person typically being responsible for a single fragmented task. This contrasted negatively with the previous method in which groups worked together to remove coal from the coalface, with high levels of autonomy over work pace and allocation of tasks. Trist and Bamforth observed that some pits had spontaneously developed a form of mining in which multi-skilled, self-selected and self-led groups were responsible for the whole collection of coal on one shift. More importantly for performance management, these groups produced higher outputs and suffered from less absenteeism. These observations laid the foundations for the concept of jointly optimizing social and technical systems when designing work. They also provided the platform for many other socially underpinned concepts, for example, the autonomous work group (Needham, 1982; Kemp et al., 1983) and team interactions, which have been shown to be strongly predictive of team performance (Guzzo and Dickson, 1996).

Concepts from OP and OB have facilitated the fine-tuning of people management or human resources practices by tapping into conceptualizations of human needs. Many contemporary practices, for example, performance appraisal and performance-related pay, are rooted in the application of psychologically defined methodologies and methods. These practices are employed as means of encouraging, or even driving, individual and sometimes group behavioural adaptation in order to manage and enhance employee performance.

Occupational psychologists use a range of research methods and designs to investigate the interaction between an individual and their work, and for the assessment of work performance. However, traditionally a large component of this has involved experimental procedures and quantitative test measures. Unsurprisingly, as the field of OB draws from a wide range of methods from other disciplines, there is no such clear tradition.

Central to the belief that such an approach or set of approaches can be successful is the notion of human motivation, in other words the particular needs, wants and beliefs that drive an individual.

Motivation

Abraham Maslow's theory of human motivation (1943), in which he proposed that humans had a hierarchy of related needs through from physiological, safety, love, esteem, to the need for self-actualization, has been highly influential in the development of work-related motivational theories. Popularly represented as a step diagram, the relationship between these needs, Maslow suggested, was that one could not step up to fulfil a higher level need until the earlier one had been satisfied. Inherent in the theory is the contention that humans strive for self-actualization and thus Maslow's theory provides the bedrock of the belief that both motivations and performance can be managed. From this standpoint, a number of approaches seeking to motivate higher and more effective levels of performance at work have been explored. By means of management education and training courses, many of these approaches, or motivational theories, have proved influential. Managers whose remit is to improve performance and productivity have been drawn towards what they perceive (or perhaps are led to believe) will assist them in achieving the 'holy grail' of enhanced performance.

We will now outline a small sample of these approaches and theories, focusing on their type and effectiveness, before going on to discuss why their effectiveness, from a management perspective, might be compromised.

1. McClelland's Achievement Theory (1961) deviates from that of Maslow in that McClelland did not believe that people had a fixed hierarchy of needs (Fulop and Linstead, 2004), but that the need to achieve (nAch), the need for power (nPow) and the need for affiliation (nAff) varied in accordance with the value placed on them by individuals. This work was developed later, prioritizing the motivational potency of power (McClelland and Burnham, 1976).
2. Herzberg's theory of motivation (1968) hinges upon enriching the job undertaken by an individual so that it is challenging enough for them to use their skills and expertise for which they were employed. Herzberg drew a clear distinction between motivational aspects of job (for example, achievement, recognition, the job content, responsibility and advancement) and those which simply stave off dissatisfaction, labelled as 'hygiene factors' (for example, adequate pay, policy and administration, supervision and conditions of work). In taking this approach, Herzberg's theory sought to counter Taylor's arguably dehumanizing approach of breaking jobs down to their simplest components and separating planning from execution. At the same time it facilitates the fulfilling 'climb' up from the basic level to achievement of the self-actualizing need.
3. Vroom's Expectancy Theory (1964) is based upon people's preferences and the value that they placed upon those preferences. In this respect, Vroom's theory shares some features with that of McClelland. However, rather than motivation being linked with specific needs (for nAch, nPow, nAff, for example), Vroom proposed that it was driven by the degree to which an individual expected to be successful in achieving that which they valued. At the core of Expectancy Theory is how the individual perceives the relationship between effort, performance and reward. As such, an individual is unlikely to put in much effort to achieve something that they do not value.

Each of these examples demonstrates the complexity of human need suggesting that, while the temptation to prioritize or privilege one motivational theory over another as a means of expediting high levels of performance may be strong, it could be considered foolhardy for a manager to do so. The 'pull' of a theory for application, it must be appreciated, could more readily or realistically be regarded as reflecting the manager's own motivational 'preferences' rather than their 'knowledge' of what motivates the employees for whom they are responsible.

Taking McClelland's theory, we can see that it is culturally neutral, or even blind, as well as being person and status dependent. On the face of things, it might appear to be a positive approach, but people with a high nAch, for example, could find managerial and supervisory functions frustrating, as their success would be dependent largely upon the achievement of others and/or their willingness to perform. This level of performance, or even willingness to perform, cannot simply be assumed. We see here a need for individualized attention as a means of motivating others. Not to countenance an individualized approach would be to court frustration or even compromise the performance of all parties. Moreover, as Herriot (2001, p. 2) states, maintaining motivation, morale and commitment cannot be resolved by 'some new motivational lever to pull, or button to press' but requires more searching consideration of the nature of the overall employment relationship (an issue we will consider below when we assess the key challenges facing OP and OB).

Yet, theories of motivation such as expectancy theory and equity theory (which examines discrepancies within a person after that person has compared their input/outcome ratio to that of a reference person – see Adams, 1963) have been seen to contribute to the enhancement of employee productivity and well-being. This is, in part, because each recognizes that behaviour is not shaped completely by environmental consequences but rather is a function of beliefs, values and other cognitive processes.

Individual motivations are, of course, but one determinant of work performance and, besides situational factors, such as physical environment, co-ordination of work activities and supervisory support, a number of individual differences have been found to have a bearing on performance outcomes.

Individual differences

Effective performance is, at least in part, seen to be a function of recruitment and selection which concern the process of choosing between people based on their potential to successfully perform a particular job in a particular organization (Robertson et al., 2002). The conventional design process begins with job analysis, '...the fundamental building block upon which all later decisions in the employment process must rest' (Cascio, 1998, p. 36), which specifies the nature of the job to be done and the characteristics by which the candidates are to be assessed.

Historically, job analytic methods have assumed that jobs were not changed by the individuals performing them. They sought simply to compare the tasks, roles and responsibilities of a job. However, more recent techniques recognize the dynamic nature of the job, individual and situational factors. Thus, they attempt to describe jobs in worker-orientated terms and are supplemented by 'competency analysis', which focuses on identifying the behaviours required to perform a job effectively. As pointed out by Robertson et al. (2002, p. 109): 'The cornerstone of personnel selection and assessment is the demonstrated existence of measurable psychological differences between people that are of importance in determining job success.'

There is a myriad of possible individual difference variables (Warr, 1987), which can be categorized as follows:

1. genetic characteristics, for example, gender, constitution and physique;
2. acquired characteristics, for example, age, education and skills; and
3. dispositional characteristics, for example, various personality types, generally defined as 'the relatively enduring individual traits and dispositions that distinguish one person from all others' (Vecchio, 1995, p. 85).

Some differences and their links with job performance are easy to identify, for example, the need for manual dexterity in an orthopaedic surgeon. In many instances there is inconclusive evidence for or against factors' influence on the quality (or quantity) of performance. For example, there is no compelling evidence to suggest that women or men are better performers *per se* and thus a need to be alert to this, as faulty generalizations can lead to making improper assumptions and potential discriminatory practices (Cascio, 1998; Cooper, 2002).

Nevertheless, psychologists have made some inroads and, in general terms, the most important individual differences for personnel selection have been shown to be cognitive ability and personality. For example, Schmidt and Hunter (1998) have established some generalizable links between general cognitive ability and conscientiousness, which have proven to be predictive of success in a wide range of jobs. Measuring these two variables it is often possible to account for 20–30 per cent of the variance in job performance, with even higher predictability in more complex jobs. Schmidt and Hunter's research suggests that general cognitive ability influences job performance largely through its role in the acquisition and use of information about how to do one's job. Individuals with higher levels of cognitive ability acquire new information more easily and more quickly, and are able to use that information more effectively.

Yet concerns have been expressed regarding the differences in scores found in different sub-groups. In this instance, the combination of cognitive tests and measures of broad personality factors which take into account differing socio-cultural experiences that might impact upon how cognitive ability is tested, can serve to increase the validity of selection decisions and reduce any group differences and potential for discrimination in selection outcomes (see Cooper, 2002). This is, however, an important concern more generally and sensitivity to a complex array of differences (in respect of, for example, ethnicity, gender, culture, disability and age) in terms of selection and management of employees more generally, pose significant challenges to the occupational psychologist and organizational behaviourist in the context of an increasingly diverse workforce.

Key challenges for the occupational psychologist and organizational behaviourist

One of the most urgent problems said to be facing contemporary managers is how to engage employees in employment relationships that will enhance individual and organizational performance (Herriot, 2001; Sparrow and Cooper, 2003). In addition to the above noted demographic and social changes, and as pointed out by Sparrow (1998, p. 124), changing organizational forms and processes themselves (for example, downsizing, delayering, outsourcing and job-based flexibility) have forced the reappraisal of many of the very basic assumptions about the design and operation of jobs and the psychological underpinning of organizational behaviour. As a result of these changes there is often a mismatch between the demands and rewards of work life. For example, the public sector is continually faced by, and needs to respond to, a changing political agenda and the motivation and engagement of employees in the organization's vision and values is proving to be of major contemporary concern (see, for example, Boyne, 2003; Ferlie et al., 2003). However, this concern exists more generally and management of the psychological contract has come to have a very prominent position in academic and practitioner literatures (for example, Rousseau, 1995, 2004; Rousseau and Wade-Benzoni, 1995; Shore and Coyle-Shapiro, 2003). Hence focus has shifted to consideration of the *implicit* as opposed to the *formal* written agreement, between the individual employee and the wider organization concerning their mutual expectations and obligations, and the consequences of such understandings for a range of organizational outcomes (Conway and Briner, 2005).

Taking a cognitive approach in the occupational environment has contributed in a number of highly significant ways to the enhancement of employee productivity and well-being. As we noted above, this applies to cognitive theories of motivation, such as equity theory (Adams, 1963) and expectancy theory (Vroom, 1964). More recently, Daniels et al. (2002) employed a cognitive approach to understanding the risks of occupational stress and found that the simplified representations of reality constructed by employees (known as 'mental models') have an influence on subsequent indices of performance. Adding a further strand, other cognitive research has demonstrated that different systems and procedures are sensitive to local context, implying that the use of standardized metrics of performance is misguided (Clarkson and Hodgkinson, 2004). Such findings have considerable implications for the understanding and management of employee performance and productivity, pointing to the need for a contingent approach to the management of behaviour, performance and reward that takes into account the particular needs and aspirations of the individual employee.

While fundamental principles of OP and OB, for example, job design involving job enrichment and autonomous work groups, have been seen to have been effective in terms of enhancing employee satisfaction and motivation, their impact on behavioural outcomes such as work performance and absence are often less clear cut. In addition, performance assessment is often based on the measurement of a limited range of actions in response to quite specific task goals. This is unfortunate as numerous scholars have concluded that it is inappropriate to attempt to assess the effect of single variables and that there is a need to take account of a wider range of work characteristics and performance outcomes/results. Moreover, there is a need to analyse the mechanisms or processes that might explain why work characteristics lead to particular outcomes (see, for example, Bramwell and Cooper, 1995; Jones and Fletcher, 1996; Parker et al., 2001; Sparks et al., 2001). In common with Houldsworth and Burkinshaw (this volume, Chapter 6), we agree that to focus on hard targets alone would be short-sighted. A concern with over-all system efficiency will allow a better understanding of performance changes in relation to broader goals and priorities of human behaviour including the implications of these for the management of both perform-ance and well-being (Hockey, 2002; Warr, 2002). Research designs with sufficient power to take account of pertinent individual differences and group processes, together with an appropriate range of outcome vari-ables, are likely to require large or relatively large sample sizes – but they will need to be sufficiently sensitive as to be meaningful to the individual. From other research (for example, Berger and Luckmann, 1967; Fearfull and Kamenou, 2006), we know that at times it is helpful to implement qualitative research methods which explore thoroughly the nature and features of individual perceptions, as people's decisions and action – and performance – are based on their own 'reality' of the situation.

Concluding reflections

Having illustrated how concepts from OP and OB have facilitated oppor-tunities to 'fine tune' people management or human resources practices by tapping into conceptualizations of human needs, we offer the *caveat* that managers have not always chosen to use this knowledge, nor to use it wisely when they have. For example, the contemporary organization is likely to be 'flatter' with wider spans of command, thus theoretically calling for greater employee autonomy, with psychological principles supporting the need for such control (Warr, 1987, 2002). Yet, in the typical, very flatly structured call centre organization, where a large and growing number of the global workforce are employed, research-ers have found it difficult to conclude other than 'that routinization, repetitiveness and a general absence of employee control are the domin-ant, although not universal, features of [...] work organization' (Taylor et al., 2002, p. 136).

Moreover, while the proliferation of techniques and methods of work-place motivation geared towards managing and enhancing performance and productivity is interesting in itself, particularly with regard to the creative elements at play to enhance worker performance, perhaps more interesting still is the apparent need for such creativity. As Fincham (1989, p. 17) has said: 'The whole notion of the "expert" design of work would hardly be necessary if jobs were skilled and responsible in the first place.' In examining the role of the social scientist in attempting to secure 'integration' or, we might say, enhanced performance, Anthony (1977, pp. 255–56) has expressed his dismay saying that such approaches:

> ... all seem concerned to achieve greater efficiency by promoting the development of organizations that are more humane, and less irksome to their inhabitants by sharing control, by allowing for greater participation, by recognizing the reality of conflict, by acknowledging the needs of employees for responsibility and growth. Both the end, of efficiency, and the means, of greater involvement, seem thoroughly benign and deserving of approval. What then explains the faint but discernable odour of stinking fish?

We can appreciate the need for a finely tuned balance of experiences provided by and through workplace engagement but, unfortunately, we have seen some managers, guided by professional and academic expertise, developing means and methods of managing through which the psychological advantages of paid employment to the individual can be capitalized upon in order to manipulate and enhance performance. With this point in mind, perhaps we should reassess Karlin's perspective on 'psychology in the service of man' outlined earlier in this chapter. We suggest this be done in the light of the arguments proposed by early contributors to the issue of performance management such as Anthony (1977) and Baritz (1960). Essentially, both of these authors questioned the degree to which organizational behaviourists/psychologists have become 'servants of power'. In closing our chapter, we would contend that further contributions to this field of work must reflect on such critical contributions as closely as they would on instrumental ones. In this way it might be possible to continue to develop the means of genuinely enhancing the nature and organization of work and the quality of performance therein.

Note

1. Dr Robert Sussman of Washington University, St Louis, Missouri at the Annual Conference of the American Association for the Advancement of Science (2006).

6

Taking a Human Resource Management Perspective on Performance Management

Liz Houldsworth and Sue Burkinshaw

Introduction

There are numerous claims, both in the rhetoric of corporate values and the practitioner press, that people are *the* most important asset of any firm. Ulrich (1998), for example, concludes that ultimately a firm's human resource (HR) community holds crucial responsibility for adding value and delivering results. Therefore, the task of successfully managing the performance of this essential organizational asset is increasingly seen as the key to the success of any organization.

Historically, the process of performance management – equated in the past with 'the dreaded appraisal', has often been parodied as time-consuming, ineffectual and de-motivating. It is against this background we seek to understand what performance management means and how its evolution in many ways tracks both the development of the concept of human resource management (HRM), as well as the changes in the macro economic, political and social environment. We acknowledge that in so doing we are adopting a rather Anglo/American standpoint, as it is from this tradition that the majority of ideas discussed here arise. Although the chapter may not consider the full range of international and cross-cultural perspectives on performance, the discussion is equally relevant for the corporate and the not-for-profit sectors; indeed one of our key observations is that in the last years of the twentieth century and early years of the twenty-first century the public sector has adopted with zeal many of the practices of the private sector (see, for example, Houldsworth and Jirasinghe, 2006).

Other chapters in this book look at managing performance from the standpoint of different academic disciplines. At the risk of appearing both biased and insular, it is our belief that the HR perspective is key and that it serves as an integrator across the disciplines of finance and accountancy, process mapping and production management, organizational psychology and knowledge management. We will leave the specifics of these disciplines to be described by those more expert in each respective field. However, we seek to remind the reader from time to time that all of these disciplines play a role in the design and implementation choices, which organizations make, as they engage in the process of managing the performance of their employees in line with organizational goals.

The next section sets the scene and provides a continuum of performance management evolution based on practitioner experience. We then examine the HR context of performance management and highlight some of the debates. In the following section we consider some of the criticisms and challenges around the implementation of performance management, and then examine reasons for its rising popularity. The final section seeks to summarize some of the earlier debates by locating performance management practice within the context of theories of HRM, and synthesizing some of the links between them.

Evolution of performance management in HRM

When thinking about performance in organizations, Corvellec (2001) has suggested that defining performance is in the eye of the beholder. It is true that the standpoint of the individual and their functional specialism seems to play a key role in how they define performance management. Certainly a whole range of disciplines including psychology, operations management, knowledge management and accountancy all claim the performance management terrain. Although mindful of the multidisciplinary nature of performance management, our emphasis in this chapter will be upon a human resources definition of performance management as it would be understood by practitioners:

> A process for establishing a shared understanding about what is to be achieved, and how it is to be achieved; an approach to managing people which increases the probability of achieving job-related success.
>
> (Hartle, 1995, p. 12)

If we begin by contextualizing performance itself, Corvellec (2001) concludes that for the large majority of management authors, an organization's performance is the result of its activity, as witnessed by the measurement of some form of output. However, to focus on hard targets alone would be short-sighted (Corvellec, 2001). The ethnologist Robert Jackall (1988) observed that for corporate managers, performance is not simply 'hitting your numbers'. It is about performing right on the organization's scene – that is, fitting the social rules that govern clothing or vocabulary, being perceived as a reliable team member or endorsing the official organizational reality as the only one.

In broad terms, therefore, performance is not only a matter of results or outputs (the 'what' of performance). It is also necessary to take into account behaviours and processes. It is useful to think of these behaviours and processes as the 'how' of performance. The 'what' and 'how' of performance together combine to make a full picture.

These ideas of the 'what and the how' of performance are just some of the themes underpinning the manifestation of performance management within organizations today. The majority of these influences upon managing individual performance, both at an individual and organizational level are far from new. The first formal monitoring systems evolved and were underpinned by the principles of Scientific Management (Taylor, 1911). These approaches were known as 'merit rating' systems, were pioneered by Scott and became established performance management systems in the 1950s. However, merit-rating systems were criticized for being subjective systems of assessment as often they were based on 'personality'. This approach was a shift away from the output-related performance measurement systems (for example, payment-by-results) associated with a 'blue collar' workforce and was adopted for the 'white collar' workforce. Commonly used factors for rating would refer to the extent to which individuals were conscientious, imaginative, self-sufficient, co operative or possessed qualities of judgement, initiative or original thinking (Armstrong and Baron, 1998).

In response to the recognition of the subjective nature of merit-rating systems, performance management processes gradually evolved into 'Management by Objectives' (MBO). MBO was a performance management process for managers, which attempted to link and integrate the organization's strategic objectives with the manager's role, to contribute to the organization and their own management development (Humble, 1972). Appraisal systems developed which included the agreement of individual objectives and an assessment of results against these objectives. Performance ratings were normally given to reflect overall individual performance or results.

During the 1990s, in the United Kingdom, it was recognized that a major shift was taking place away from performance appraisals directed and owned by the Personnel Department towards the concept of performance management. This approach emphasized the role and relationship between the line manager and the employee and the negotiation and agreement of role, responsibilities and targets. Plachy (1987) describes the approach thus:

> Performance management is communication: a manager and an employee arrive together at an understanding of what work is to be accomplished, how it will be accomplished, how work is progressing towards desired results, and finally after effort is expended to accomplish the work, whether the performance has achieved the agreed-upon plan.
>
> (p. 12)

and

> ... performance management is an umbrella term that includes performance planning, performance review and performance appraisal.
>
> (p. 27)

Figure 6.1 below provides a practitioner-based framework for understanding the evolution of performance management, which we explain in this section.

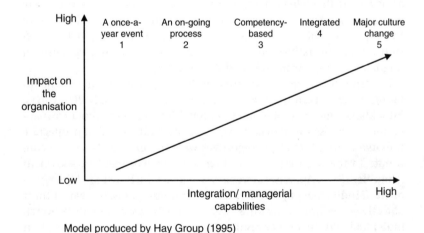

Model produced by Hay Group (1995)

Figure 6.1   Performance management continuum

Consultants within Hay Group UK, based on their experience of working with clients, produced the model in Figure 6.1; it has been found to be relevant in many sectoral contexts in the UK and Europe. It shows five different representations or levels of performance management implementation. At its most simplistic, performance management processes exist which provide a once a year 'form-filling event' and have little impact upon the organization and are not integrated with any other organizational or business processes. The next step (although it is not intended to suggest that all organizations necessarily progress via these steps) sees a move towards an 'ongoing process'. This usually involves the establishment of objectives in line with the business plan (MBO) and thus linking the actions and efforts of the individual with the requirements of the organization.

During the 1990s, performance management began to be seen as more of a core management process – capable of delivering the business vision by developing and reinforcing the key behaviours/values. Level 3 of the continuum reflects this point. At this level not just the 'what' of performance is expressed through objectives and targets, but also the 'how' of performance is invariably expressed through behavioural competencies. This is often associated with competency-based and 'soft' developmental approaches to performance management.

The background to the popularity of competencies in the UK lies in the mid-1980s when the Constable and McCormick Report (1987) set out to uncover the reasons for the UK's lack of competitiveness. They suggested the skill base within organizations could no longer keep pace with the developing business climate for reasons including the need of individuals to upgrade their skills to keep pace with continual change. In response to the needs identified in the report a structured approach to managerial training and development geared around an emerging set of 'Industry Standards' was advocated. Hence the Management Charter Initiative was born in the UK with its use of occupational competencies. This approach to management development focused upon 'outcomes' – that is the ability to perform a task satisfactorily. At about the same time, from the US an approach to competencies was gaining momentum, which had grown out of the research of David McClelland (1973). This adopted a 'process' approach with competencies defined as behavioural characteristics and attributes a person exhibits in order to be successful at work – for example, influence, team work, analytical thinking. Although National Vocational Qualifications (NVQs) continue as a qualification route in many fields within the UK (including the not-for-profit sector), their popularity within management has dwindled. Within most organizations the 'default' since the late 1990s has been to seek to define 'behavioural' competency models.

   As competency models have been adopted increasingly within organizations, their incorporation within performance management has become the vogue. They serve to link the 'how' and the 'what' of performance as well as promising a return on the investment in the competency model. Having incorporated behaviours, most organizations are positioned to try and achieve the potential benefits of integration with all other aspects of the people management cycle, as illustrated in levels 4 and 5 of the continuum. These higher levels of the continuum suggest that performance management may be perceived as a major integrative force – linking job design, organizational priorities, competencies with training and development, high potential recognition and reward. Ultimately at level 5 it is suggested that performance management can be positioned as a driver and reinforcer of organizational change.

HRM context of performance management

Key debates 1: hard or soft HRM?

> A remarkable feature of the HRM phenomenon is the brilliant ambiguity of the term itself.
>
> (Keenoy, 1990, p. 371)

This ambiguity has challenged academics and practitioners alike in seeking to define and understand HRM. The debate around the characteristics and philosophy of HRM has tended to centre on the employment relationship, the management of employee relations and the relationship of employee commitment to the employment relationship. Fundamental to the employment relationship is the effort:reward bargain (see, for example, Burawoy, 1979). This is the foundation of capitalist economies in which labour is rewarded for the effort made to produce goods and services.

   An appropriate place to start our consideration of the HRM context for performance management is the distinction between 'hard' and 'soft' HRM as described, for example, by Storey (1987). A simple way of viewing this distinction is to consider whether the emphasis is placed on the 'human' or on the 'resource'. These may be linked to developments in the 1970s when the language of 'human resources' began to creep in to the vocabulary of British academics. With this came the two notions of utilitarian-instrumentalism and developmental-humanism, now commonly referred to as 'hard' or 'soft' HRM.

It has been argued that the distinction between 'soft' and 'hard' HRM is a model, which works in theory but is not easily discernible in organizational practice. Truss et al. (1997), for example, discovered that none of the organizations they studied appeared to be adopting either a pure soft or hard approach to HRM. However, we find it a useful framework for understanding the different philosophies and approaches to performance management as we describe below.

'Soft' HRM is underpinned by the human relations movement, the utilization of individual talents and McGregor's (1960) 'Theory Y' perspective of individuals at work. Theory Y is centred on the premise that individuals are intrinsically self-motivated at work and that they seek job satisfaction, responsibility and self-development, (also known as 'developmental-humanism' – see, for example, Hendry and Pettigrew, 1990; Legge, 1995a,b). 'Soft' HR approaches centre around the skills/attitudes and behaviours of the individual. This model emphasizes treating employees as valued assets and a source of competitive advantage through their commitment, adaptability and high quality performance (Guest, 1987). Beer and colleagues (1985) are among the best-known proponents of this view on HRM and have become known as the 'Harvard school'. They place most emphasis on a 'people' focus, seeing the impact of managers on organizational climate as being at the heart of business success or otherwise, along with the relationship between management and other employees. They recognize the existence of a range of HR levers and the context of stakeholder interests as well as situational factors. The policy areas which they identify with HRM are employee influence, HR flow, reward systems and work systems.

Other authors, including Legge (1995a,b), have noted that employees working under such an HRM system are more likely to positively commit and give added value through labour, with employees feeling trusted, trained and developed, with control over their own work. We might associate this with a 'resource-based' context for HRM, with its emphasis on stressing the potential of the employee in terms of investment rather than as a cost. Such a developmental-driven approach to performance management, within a 'soft HRM model' would be manifest in the implementation of performance management processes related to approaches such as personal development plans, competency-based approaches and 360-degree appraisal.

In 'Hard' HRM, the emphasis in the approach to the management of people is on the quantitative and calculative economic costs of managing the 'headcount'. Employees are often viewed as a 'cost' in an economic and rational way rather than an investment (Storey, 1987). Within HRM literature this has been referred to as utilitarian-instrumentalism (Hendry and Pettigrew, 1990). This focuses on the importance of 'strategic fit', where HR policies and practices are closely linked to the strategic objectives of the organization with the aim of heightening competitive advantage. In terms of its view of human nature it is characterized by an underlying 'Theory X' assumption (McGregor, 1960) (that the average human being has an inherent dislike of work and will avoid it if he/she can) leading to the necessity for tight managerial control through close direction.

Within the 'hard HRM' model, performance management processes would often be reward-driven, where individual performance is measured against individual objectives/targets, linked to ratings or gradings and pay. At its most simplistic, the performance management tools which reflect the hard HRM context would therefore be 'payment by results' systems and commission-based approaches. The performance management system would be focused on differentiating between individual employees on the basis of their contribution – perhaps via performance-related pay (PRP) or other reward schemes, which take into account quantified outputs. This might be seen as an enactment of the 'partitioning' that is to differentiate between individuals as described by Townley (1993). She draws on work of Foucault (1977), who describes partitioning as one of three main methods for 'fixing' or 'locating' individuals. Partitioning therefore involves ranking – via a serial or hierarchical ordering among employees in an evaluative fashion. Contemporary manifestations of this in the workplace may be found in the increasing use of methods such as 'forced distribution'. This is the practice whereby managers are required to allocate their direct reports into 'quotas' of above average, average and below average and so on. The approach was expounded by Jack Welch and Byrne (2003) when working with General Electric. Under what he called the 'vitality curve approach' managers were required to identify the top 20 per cent of performers, the middle 70 per cent of performers and the bottom 10 per cent, who were to be managed out of the business each year. The top 20 per cent would then enjoy the majority of investment and be earmarked for their potential, with the middle 70 per cent being considered as 'solid performers' getting the majority of the work done.

Having considered how the theoretical concepts of 'hard' and 'soft' HRM might be translated into performance management practice the next section will consider other key competing perspectives.

Key debates 2: competing HRM perspectives on performance management

Beardwell et al. (2004) identify four distinct perspectives on HRM and, by implication, its contribution to performance management. These are

1. that HRM is no more than a re-titling of the personnel management function;
2. that HRM can be viewed from a strategic perspective and is a key player in driving the business forward in a highly competitive market;
3. that HRM is a new managerial discipline – a 'fusion' of the traditional pluralist perspective of personnel management/industrial relations into one approach which is managerially led and unilaterally driven; and
4. that HRM represents a resource-based model of the employment relationship which incorporates a developmental focus for the individual employee, but one in which human resources are seen as a key to competitive advantage.

We will discuss these four broad perspectives in detail below.

HRM or personnel management?

In terms of the first of these there is an on-going and long-standing debate across the academic and practitioner communities as to whether HRM is just a re-labelling of Personnel Management – 'old wine in new bottles' (Armstrong, 1987) or whether HRM provides theoretical explanations underpinning the employment relationship (Beer et al., 1985).

This debate is encapsulated in Guest's (1989) definition of HRM, whereby HRM can be defined in terms of the 'soft–hard' dimensions (discussed earlier) and the 'loose–tight' dimension.

At the 'loose' end of the dimension, HRM would be seen as nothing more than the re-titling of a Personnel Department. At the 'tight' end of the dimension, HRM is seen as being distinctly different from Personnel Management – with its own body of theory. This 'theory of HRM' relates to four main components: HRM outcomes; HRM policies; HRM as the 'cement' (for example, strategic integration, leadership, organizational culture) that binds the system together; and HRM as driver of organizational outcomes (Guest, 1989).

HRM and strategic success

A 'strategic' perspective on HRM has been around since the early Matching Model of HRM (Fombrun et al., 1984). HRM is characterized by its close alignment with business strategy (Hendry and Pettigrew, 1986), and perceived since the 1990s to fulfil a more influential role driving the strategic success of the business.

The extent to which HRM contributes to or even drives organizational strategy is debated throughout the HRM literature. Storey's (1992) model of the evolution of the HR function (Figure 6.2) captures the 'loose' and 'tight' perspectives identified by Beardwell et al. (2004), and Guest (1989).

HRM as a driver in organizational strategy is normally achieved by HRM specialists holding senior Board level positions, and through the devolution of many of the functions of HRM to line managers. In this way it has shifted into a 'strategic/interventionary' position where HRM is seen to be a strategic change-maker, helping to realign and re-shape the business in line with 'tight HRM'. The tactical, non-interventionary position on the other hand denotes the 'loose HRM' view that HRM is simply a re-titling of the personnel function.

If we strive to apply the framework of Storey to the development of performance management we might expect to see HR professionals who are still residing in the 'hand maidens' category to spend energy on reminding or checking that line managers complete the performance management process. On the other hand, if these HR professionals have clearly positioned themselves as change makers, we would not be surprised to find them working with executives to help, for example, to shape a balanced scorecard to reflect the strategic priorities which may then be communicated via the performance management process.

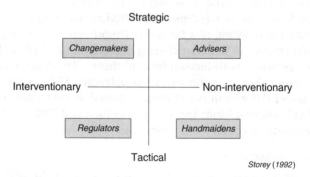

Figure 6.2   Storey's evolution of HRM

HRM: a new managerial discipline?

In terms of Beardwell et al.'s (2004) third perspective, it suggests that the values underpinning this view of HRM are predominantly individualistic and unitarist. Unitarism assumes that conflict and differing views cannot exist within an organization because both managers and employees are working toward the same goals – the organization's success.

These common interests are reflected in the 'psychological contract' (Guest, 1998). The psychological contract goes beyond the written employment contract and is subjective and promise-based. There is a mutuality of understanding between the employer and employee that is common and agreed, in relation to obligations of each respective party related to work, pay, loyalty, commitment, flexibility, security and promotion. This is reinforced by conscious pursuit of good 'person: organization fit' in recruitment and selection. Unitarism is in contrast to the dominant traditional values of personnel management and industrial relations, which emphasize collective and pluralist values (Guest, 1987).

In relation to performance management, it is straightforward to see how unitarism might be interpreted as being essentially a managerial intervention which is imposed by managers on employees, thus in keeping with the perspective that it is essentially a new managerial discipline.

Humans: just another resource to be managed?

We discussed resource-based views earlier; to recap, the performance of staff, like other assets, needs to be actively managed for optimum returns on investment. It is clear that the majority of performance management 'systems' include an element of employee development. However, the extent to which this is emphasized in practice is likely to differ. Those which emphasize it might be judged to be drawing on traditions of 'soft' HRM more than 'hard' ones. See, for example, Houldsworth and Jirasinghe (2006) who have identified 'performance development' as one of two broad 'schools' or styles of approach, the other one being more concerned with measurement and representing a 'harder' strategic control approach to HRM.

Strategy, style or outcomes?

As well as outlining the four perspectives from which to view HRM, Beardwell et al. (2004) have also suggested that it may be analysed in terms of whether it focuses upon strategy, style or outcomes. We have already discussed the strategic perspective earlier in this chapter.

The approach to HRM in terms of style, is embedded in the research of Watson (1997), Purcell (1987), Legge (1978), Tyson and Fell (1996) and

Purcell and Sisson (1983). This research centres on the role of the HR professional as an actor, within an organizational setting, who influences HRM policies and practices. The approach of HRM as 'style' is bound firmly to the principles of 'hard' and 'soft' HRM (Storey, 1989).

Research focusing on HRM as 'outcomes' centres on whether particular combinations of HRM policies and practices produce better organizational performance (Arthur, 1992, 1994; Huselid, 1995; McDuffie, 1995; Patterson et al., 1997).

The essential dilemma for academics and HRM practitioners alike is the difficulty of establishing a direct link (which is measurable and tangible) between HRM activities and processes and organizational success that is HR's contribution to the 'bottom line'. 'There is the problem of demonstrating unequivocally the contribution of personnel, as an activity, to organizational success' (Legge, 1995, p. 23).

We can see from within the chronology of Performance Management and the debates and perspectives surrounding the context of HRM, that this is a key challenge. However, the work of Thompson and Richardson (1999), Huselid (1995) and others goes some way towards establishing that a positive relationship exists between more sophisticated and innovative HR practices and increased organizational performance.

Relevant to the outcome-based approach is the extent to which employees give 'extra' in the form of discretionary effort, which would otherwise not have been forthcoming without the effect of the chosen practice(s). Authors such as McDuffie (1995) and Guest and Hoque (1996) have examined the concept of 'fit' of HRM techniques in specific circumstances and 'bundles' of practice that might affect performance. Current work explores the nature of HRM 'bundles' and the relationship between particular managerial styles, particular combinations of practice, leading to successful business outcomes (Wood and De Menezes, 1998).

We therefore suggest, that the four broad perspectives of the HRM debate and the three foci of analysis ('outcomes', 'strategy' and 'style') help us to both understand and analyse HRM and performance management practice within organizations. We shall return to this in the final section.

Challenges for performance management

We focus here on some of the main criticisms of performance management, but there is not space for detailed critiques of its underpinning HRM elements.

Given its longevity and changing guises, it is not surprising that over the years performance management has attracted a range of responses, of which Armstrong and Baron (1998) provide a useful overview. They begin by pointing out the gap in knowledge around the value of performance management, reporting that the link between effective performance management systems and improved organizational performance has been difficult to establish conclusively. They also review the available critiques and conclude that they can, broadly speaking, be divided into two camps: performance management is a good idea that doesn't work (practitioners and some academics), and performance management is a bad idea and doesn't work (academics).

In the practitioner press, for example, Fowler (1990) claimed that the performance appraisal process and MBO approach introduced within organizations soon became over-systemized and bureaucratic. He saw an increasing emphasis being placed upon the quantification of assessment criteria and objectives and results-orientation. Also the appraisal systems were typically seen as a function of the Personnel Department and not one which was owned by line managers and employees (Armstrong and Baron, 1998). Deming, the TQM 'guru', described performance, metric rating or annual review as the third 'deadly disease' of management (Deming, 1986).

Amongst more academic authors, Townley has written about the issues of power relations and control within the workplace (1993 and 1994). She emphasizes the controlling nature of performance management, particularly where individuals are ranked through paired comparisons or forced distributions. She refers to the divisions that are created internally to the work organization – for example, between headquarters and other sites, through technology but essentially via a rational classification – manual/non-manual, core/periphery workforce as discussed earlier. She views this as a form of power and control, which becomes divisive across the labour force. She describes performance appraisal as being placed at nexus of a range of disciplinary procedures: rewards, identification of skill deficiencies and potential for promotion (Townley, 1994). Barlow (1989) has similarly written about its controlling nature, in particular seeing that it relies on compliance; and Winstanley and Stuart-Smith (1996) have described the 'policing' or enforcement nature of performance management. Truss et al. (1997) found considerable gaps between the organizational rhetoric of performance appraisal and managerial practice.

Kessler and Purcell (1992) in their study of PRP concluded that performance management systems and processes become dysfunctional in three key areas: the establishment of performance criteria, the appraisal interview and the assessment of performance. Criticisms are centred on the difficulties around establishing fair and objective criteria, which are not always measurable or tangible; the lack of objectivity of the performance appraisal; and that the line-manager may not be best placed to judge the 'assessment' of performance.

The resurgence in popularity of performance management systems over the last decade has been attributed by some as part of a management re-assertion of the 'right to manage'; and that performance management processes are further attempts to elicit control over the behaviour of employees (Townley, 1993; Newton and Findlay, 1996). This is further supported in the findings of Kessler and Purcell (1992) who found that in the introduction of individual PRP systems, the managerial objectives were not necessarily about performance (or reward) but more about managerial control. The research found that the introduction and implementation of performance management and appraisal processes were being used to facilitate or support a broader process of organizational change. Other, management objectives were: to mobilize and stimulate greater employee commitment; to individualize the employment relationship; to revitalize the role and authority of the line manager; to enhance staff-management communications; and to weaken the influence of Trade Unions. It can therefore be seen that a variety of management objectives might be pursued through performance management systems. These multiple objectives and potentially conflicting objectives, account for many of the difficulties that organizations experience in the implementation of effective performance management (Beer et al., 1985). The multiple objectives and implementation difficulties of performance management may be seen as an example of Legge's perspective of HRM, in that HRM is characterized with 'potential tensions and contradictions' (Storey, 1995, p. 39). An example of this might be where performance management is presented as development-driven but is used as a tool to discipline employees and to inform the selection process for redundancy.

Despite the fact that performance management has been the subject of much criticism, take-up with organizations continues largely unchallenged. The next section considers reasons for its surprising popularity.

Why the continued growth in performance management systems?

As HR specialists have sought to acquire greater professional recognition and decision-making power, performance management has become a key element in their toolkit. HR professionals increasingly strive to couch their work in terms of its strategic nature, and heighten their influence through quantifiable outputs. However, it is unlikely that HR professionals alone would have been able to stimulate the increase in performance management activity without associated business and political pressures.

The era associated with centralization and collectivism was replaced in the 1980s with the market-based approach. There was a shift to private capital, private enterprise and a culture of individualism. The employment relationship and legislation governing that relationship changed to become increasingly individualistic and to take on a unitarist perspective.

The key impetus for the development and implementation of increasingly sophisticated performance management systems in the 1990s was the growing pressure of internationalization and organizations finding themselves operating within competitive and global markets. During this period, organizations re-structured to create flatter structures, which in turn led to increased devolvement and responsibility to line managers. Cultural shifts within organizations were also taking place, with a re-orientation to customer focus, the notions of 'productivity through people', leadership, cohesive organizational cultures and the concept of employee empowerment within the workplace. These pressures were not just confined to the private sector but also to the public sector in a drive to determine accountability and responsibility.

In the UK this was supported by the political climate of the 'New Right' throughout the Thatcher Conservative governments. The key values underpinning the New Right thinking were individualism, personal freedom and inequality. Farnham and Horton (1996), identify a range of objectives pursued by the then Conservative Government, which support the New Right philosophy. Amongst these were

- To improve efficiency and engender an 'enterprise culture'; and
- To strengthen the right to manage and a commitment to individualism.

These objectives are reflected in the philosophy underlying performance management and the performance management processes and practices developed in the 1980s and 1990s. Throughout this period there was a strong focus within organizations on creating a 'pay for performance' environment evidenced by the introduction of PRP schemes.

In this respect the economic, political, social and legal climate was 'ripe' for the growth and evolution of performance management within organizations. In support of this view, Armstrong and Baron (1998) reported that there was a substantial increase in the growth of performance management across the UK during this period. These findings are supported in the IRS (2003) Employment Review. The vast majority of respondents saw performance management as very important and one-third agreed that they had a performance culture.

Armstrong and Baron concluded from their extensive review that in the latter 1990s, performance management systems were shifting away from those which emphasized quantifiable objectives, measurable outcomes and reward (for example, individual-related pay), to those that had a stronger focus on the developmental process such as personal development plans and competency-based approaches. More recent research (Pollitt, 2006 and e-reward.co.uk, 2005) suggests that the pendulum has started to shift once more. This reinforces the view of Holloway (2002) who has described how in Western economies there has been a tendency to adopt 'new' approaches to performance measurement every few years before seeing benefits of previous implementation.

At about the same time that Armstrong and Baron were reporting their view of trends in performance management development from 1991 to 1998, a different approach was being experimented with by a number of organizations (Houldsworth and Jirasinghe, 2006). This approach takes its lead from accountancy and business process and quality movements. The main influences upon this movement can be seen to be the EFQM model and the balanced scorecard. Although they have different roots and a different set of advocates, both approaches encourage a heavier 'metric-based' view of performance than that identified by Armstrong and Baron. Indeed, Pollitt's (2005) comparative study has concluded that in northwest Europe, performance measurement has become almost universal and well established in practice, whereas he sees performance management to be still developing.

Linking performance management and theories of HRM

Just as there is no unified theory of HRM, there is no one commonly held theory or set of theories to explain performance management from an HR perspective. Instead we can see that it draws on theories/perspectives and approaches from a range of disciplines particularly those of organizational behaviour and psychology (addressed elsewhere in this book).

Table 6.1 positions performance management practice within an HRM base, drawing together some of our earlier discussion points. The table starts with 'performance management characteristics' and seeks to link

Table 6.1 Linking performance management practice to theories of HRM

Performance management characteristics	HRM theory/perspective	Manifestation in performance management practice	Other comments
Management by objectives	Strategic perspective on HRM Outcome-based HRM Hard HRM	Target setting and strategy cascade	Identifying and rewarding the 'What' of performance
Balanced scorecard approaches	Strategic perspective HRM Resource-based perspective Hard/soft approach to HRM	Highly structured approach to linking goals across the four scorecard areas	Rationality attractive, but simplest to measure hard financials and resultant scorecard is often unbalanced
Performance management as top team concern	HRM as style	HR Director positioning self and function as strategic business partner	With heightened professionalism of HRM, performance management usually seen as much more than appraisal and a key Top Team concern
Performance-related pay	Outcome-based HRM Wage-effort bargain	Ratings of performance	Holy grail for many organizations to effectively differentiate between performers in terms of pay

Table 6.1 (Continued)

Performance management characteristics	HRM theory/perspective	Manifestation in performance management practice	Other comments
Development-based approaches to PM	Soft HRM	Whole contribution of employee	Identifying and rewarding 'how' of performance as well as the 'what'
	HRM as style	Less emphasis on rating and more on development and potential based on behaviours	
	Resource-based HRM		
Employee involvement, communication and joint goal setting	Model of discretionary effort	Attempts to build motivation and buy in	Links to performance management as a change enabler
	Soft or development approach to HRM Resource-based HRM		
Measurement-based approaches to PM	Hard HRM	Emphasis on targets and standards with benchmarks for each level of performance rating	Notion of 'right to manage'
	Managerialist perspectives on HRM	Rating/ranking of performance	Often linked to pay
Forced distribution of ratings	Townley's association with partitioning	Quotas for each box-marking category	See description in Welch and Byrne (2003)

them to theories or perspectives of HRM discussed earlier in this chapter. The third column then provides a little more context by summarizing how they are manifested in practice in organizations. The fourth column provides other author comments as appropriate.

If we consider the contents of Table 6.1 we can seek some linkages between them and an earlier analysis of performance management by Holloway (2002). She focused upon contingency theory and systems theory which although relevant to performance management practice, we see as being less key within the HRM context. We do, however, see some linkages between the theories she suggests and the four perspectives and three approaches (strategy, style and outcome) outlined earlier. For example, Holloway refers to resource-based theories of the firm (Prahalad and Hamel and Grant). We see a link to resource-based perspectives on HRM in terms of the emphasis upon 'capabilities' and also to style approaches given their emphasis upon internal processes and behaviours. Similarly, agency theory and stakeholder theory have already been linked (Woodward et al., 1996) and may be seen in broad terms to link to outcome-based approaches to HRM.

The table also serves to summarize our earlier discussion by showing linkages between performance development and 'soft' HRM as manifested in coaching, development planning and attempts to build motivation. Similarly, it suggests a link between performance measurement and 'hard' HRM as manifested in the production of 'rational' targets in line with organizational strategy.

When describing the definitions of performance management, Walters (1995) argues that it is concerned with 'directing and supporting employees to work as effectively and efficiently as possible in line with the needs of the organisation'. This definition depicts a strategic HRM character, which seeks to emphasize the link of individual effort(s) to the organizational goals and objectives and fits with the view that HRM is predominantly about managing the employment relationship from a business strategy perspective.

Armstrong (2002) describes performance management as 'a means of getting better results from the organization, teams and individuals. It is about the agreement of objectives, knowledge, skill and competence requirements, and work and personal development plans. ... The focus is on improving learning, development and motivation.' (Armstrong, 2002, p. 373.) This definition underpins the notion of HRM from a resource-based model perspective.

In the mainstream HR practitioner literature, Armstrong and Baron (1998) define performance management as 'a strategic and integrated approach to delivering sustained success to organizations by improving the performance of the people who work in them and by developing the capabilities of teams and individual contributors' (Armstrong and Baron, 1998, p. 7) They continue to emphasize that performance management is a strategy which relates to every activity of the organization set in the context of its HR policies, culture, style and communication systems. This definition emphasizes the importance of shared values and cultures and reflects HRM as a new managerial discipline, underpinned by unitarist assumptions about the employment relationship.

Conclusion

Within this chapter we have sought to explain the complexity of performance management from a HRM perspective. We have seen that organizational performance management practices and processes are influenced by the theoretical perspectives of HRM (for example, soft and hard HR/loose and tight HR dimensions) and the impact of the HR approach in terms of strategy, style or outcomes.

The evolution of performance management and the development of HRM have also been seen as a response to the macro environment in terms of the political, economic, social and legal changes throughout the 1980s and 1990s. Table 6.1 illustrates the evolution of performance management alongside the underpinning debates and perspectives surrounding the HRM discipline.

We see that as with much of HRM there is no one common understanding or underlying philosophy. In fact we conclude that organizations make choices (either knowingly or at an ad hoc level) about their performance practice, much as they might do with other aspects of strategic positioning and implementation.

In the case of performance management, we can see that these decisions are based on history, the relative strength of the HR function and the current trends and fashions which abound. Given the critiques which have been levelled at performance management, we can only hope that the increasing professionalism of those working within HR will equip these individuals and their senior colleagues to make informed choices around performance management, recognizing the impact that these choices might have on both the success of the organization and also the well-being of those working within it.

7

Performance Measurement and Performance Management: The Operations Management Perspective

David Barnes and Zoe Radnor

Introduction

This chapter takes an historic perspective on performance measurement and management (PMM) within operations management (OM). After defining OM, we show that most PMM within OM today is derived from the introduction of work study/productivity measurement within manufacturing during the industrial revolution. This has led to a focus on performance measurement which has gradually evolved, reflecting changes in the concerns of operations managers and a move towards performance management. However, we conclude by suggesting that the drive for productivity and, in particular, 'bridging the gap', is still high on the agenda of many western governments, especially in the UK. As such there is a need to understand, differentiate between and manage both performance measurement and performance management within OM.

By taking an historic perspective the chapter illustrates how views of performance management both in terms of research and practice have moved in three directions within OM:

1. The broadening of the unit of analysis. Measures have moved from finite tasks and processes to take in ever larger work elements, moving towards organizational level and even to outside the organization along the supply chain from supplier to end-consumer.
2. The deepening of performance measures through tools such as the Balanced Scorecard which are linking the operational to the strategic.
3. The increasing range of performance measures as focus has shifted from economy and efficiency (input and output costs), to effectiveness (quality, flexibility, dependability, speed, outcome); and from merely measuring to managing.

These three directions reflect PMM in OM from both practice and research perspectives. Analysis of the research, theory and literature clearly indicates shifts in focus (as will be outlined in the historical analysis) as researchers and writers move the debate from unit of analysis, to models or frameworks and then, to use and context within the discipline of OM. Therefore, throughout the chapter an implicit relationship between practice, research and theory should be considered often with research leading the discussion. So that points can be illustrated, the chapter will use examples from the manufacturing, service and public sectors mainly from a UK context. However, it is possible to use these examples to reflect on lessons, issues and challenges for PMM within OM at an international level.

Background models

Operations management (OM) is concerned with the management of organizational activities which produce goods and/or deliver the services required by its customers. Slack et al. (2005) argue that one of the fundamental models within OM is the Transformation Process (Figure 7.1). This model presents the 'process' of taking a set of inputs which are to be transformed (those which are treated, transformed or converted) and the resources to do the transforming (act upon the transformed) through the process itself (which can have different focuses i.e. either information, materials or customers) to a set of outputs which can be a mixture of goods and services.

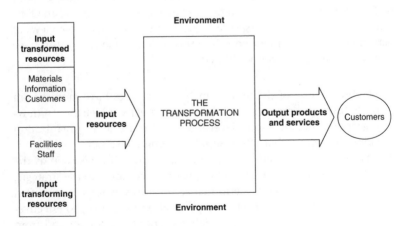

Figure 7.1   The transformation process

The transformation or operations process can occur at all levels within an organization – from a task within a department to operational level across departments and even at strategic level through the supply chain (Slack et al., 2005). At all these levels the issues for the operations manager can be considered to be similar (for example, capacity, design, managing demand, planning), as well as the need to understand or measure the efficiency, utilization or productivity of the process.

Building on this model, often considered as a 'systems view', it is possible to link to the three E's model which attempts to define economy, efficiency and effectiveness (Figure 7.2). This chapter will focus on the last two elements (efficiency and effectiveness) since 'economy' (the minimization of inputs) is rarely the main aim of performance management. The model illustrates how efficiency-focused measures linked to productivity and utilization have dominated OM. This focus developed from the industrial revolution onwards as the relationship between industrial and national financial (economic) growth was recognized. As Neely et al. observe, 'Traditionally performance measures have been seen as a means of quantifying the efficiency and effectiveness of action ... an integral element of the planning and control cycle'. However, they continue: '[This is a] somewhat mechanistic view. Performance measures also have a behavioural impact' (Neely et al., 1997, p. 1132). This has been reflected since the 1980s in a more concerted effort to measure effectiveness, and an emphasis on outcomes using softer measures such as levels of innovation, motivation and customer retention.

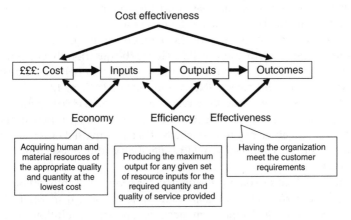

Figure 7.2   The three E's model (Radnor, 2005)

As the historical analysis will illustrate, this move has been difficult and is definitely far from complete as operations managers within the private and public sectors still have to battle with justifying their level of output and prove their levels of efficiency in order to be considered as effective. This often means that the emphasis within operations areas is still around measurement (that is, collecting measures for a 'snap-shot' picture of the situation) rather than management (using the data to make decisions and drive improvement). This can be dangerous and lead to unintentional consequences for both the process, and its outputs and outcomes. Such risks will be reflected on later in the chapter, but next we consider the history of PMM as it has accompanied the development of OM.

The history of PMM in OM

As Voss notes (1995), 'OM is very much an applied discipline ... [with] a symbiotic relationship with industry' (p. 32). It is often difficult to discern whether OM theory leads or lags industrial practice, particularly with regard to PMM. To fully appreciate the OM perspective on PMM requires an historical analysis of OM theory and practice. A review over the last 100 years leads to the identification of three distinctive time periods[1]:

- The early twentieth century – during which the foundations of OM as a discipline were laid, based on the emerging ideas of scientific management. This helped establish 'the dominant management paradigm ... [that] the role of the operations function [is] ... to manufacture as efficiently as possible. Hence the question that operations managers wanted their measurement systems to help them answer was how efficient are we' (Neely and Austin, 2000, p. 421).
- The post Second World War years up to the mid-1980s – which saw a gradual shift in OM from considering performance purely in terms of cost and efficiency to one which also encompassed other performance concerns especially quality, flexibility, timeliness, innovation and so on.
- The mid-1980s to date – during which a growing dissatisfaction with existing performance measurement systems has led to what Neely (1999) has termed a 'performance measurement revolution' (p. 207) from which OM has not been immune.

Early twentieth century

The origins of OM lie in the factories of the industrial revolution that enabled large scale manufacture for the first time. As the philosopher and economist Adam Smith (1776) had predicted, the application of the principle of the specialization of labour allied to the adoption of large scale machinery enabled goods to be produced at rates previously unimaginable using individual craft-based approaches. It is worth noting that factory owners and managers would have had to engage in performance measurement to determine just how much more efficient these practices had enabled their operations to become.

However, one of the true founding fathers of OM (and arguably its most important and influential) is Frederick Winslow Taylor. Taylor believed that it was management's responsibility to devise the best method of performing work. In the first decade of the twentieth-century he developed the concept of scientific management (Taylor, 1911). This was based on the analysis of existing work methods through observation and measurement. From this, an improved method could be developed and implemented, and its results monitored through ongoing performance measurement. Taylor's ideas were advanced by many others including Frank and Lillian Gilbreth, who developed the concept of time and motion studies, which required the measurement of every single movement undertaken by a worker in the course of performing their work. This newly developed discipline, which came to be known as 'work study', incorporated the study of work methods and the measurement of work.

The focus of scientific management was primarily on trying to increase the efficiency of individual workers. Taylor further stressed the importance of the individual worker by advocating the payment of individually based financial incentives to those workers who could increase their output as a result of the application of scientific management. This in turn required the measurement of the performance of individuals, especially their output. Thus, the emphasis of performance measurement in scientific management was at the micro-level within each operation, focusing on the work and the output of individual workers. For more macro-level measures of performance, operations managers seemed mostly to look to financial figures supplied by management accountants (although they were more likely to be termed 'cost accountants' at that time). Performance, and hence its measurement and management, was conceived primarily in terms of the volume and cost, and hence productivity. In an era of labour-intensive mass manufacture this made a lot of sense. These ideas came to dominate OM theory and practice well into the second half of the twentieth century. Their application made a significant contribution to the success of western industry in this period, and especially the United States.

Despite its widespread adoption in large tracts of industry, what became known as Taylorism was not without its critics. (For a review and vigorous rebuttal see Locke, 1982). Many of these criticisms originate from the 'human relations' movement, which had its origins in the Hawthorne experiments of Elton Mayo (Roethlisberger and Dickson, 1939), and the theories of Maslow (1954), McGregor (1960) and Herzberg (1966). This school of thought argued that worker motivation is best achieved by humanizing the workplace. From a PMM perspective these criticisms seem to centre on the impact of scientific management's concentration on the measurement of the work and the resultant performance of the individual. Its underpinning assumption seems to be that each worker's performance can be measured and assessed in isolation. However, in a factory, the performance of any one worker is usually reliant on that of others and most work is typically performed within a group. (After all, one of the points of a factory is to bring people together so they can participate in a collective enterprise.) The human relations movement argued that the social factors of work were at least as important as the technical ones emphasized in scientific management. The performance measures of scientific management usually failed to reflect this. Such criticisms led to the start of trend to broaden the unit of analysis of work measurement from the individual to the work group.

Post Second World War to mid-1980s

In many respects, the immediate post war years were a golden age for quantification in management as the newly developed techniques of management science (also known as operations or operational research, see Chapter 9 in this volume) allied to the computational powers of the first commercially available computers were added to the practices of scientific management.

However, a number of changes in the working environment led to a gradual rejection of the dominant efficiency and cost focus of PMM in OM. As discussed, there was a gradual increase in the influence of human relations movement at the expense of Taylorism. During the 1950s and the 1960s, scientific management came to be seen as a manifestation of an autocratic management style that seemed increasingly outmoded in a new democratic era. In an era of low unemployment, there was a concern to improve the quality of working life to attract and retain sufficient numbers of high calibre staff. Fuelled by the theories of the human relations school, it was perceived that performance would improve if workers were given a greater say in how they performed their work. This eventually led to experiments with self-managed teams, quality circles and other attempts at group-based participation. Workers were given more autonomy in determining how they carried out their tasks. The worst excesses of specialization were increasingly frowned upon and job enrichment and job enlargement became the order of the day.

With this rise in the acceptance of motivation theories there was a backlash against work measurement approaches, and the efficacy of performance-related pay schemes was increasingly challenged. Where financial incentives schemes were retained, these tended to become group rather than individually based. This all led to the erosion of the influence and practice of work study and measurement. OM's concern for performance measurement at the micro-level gradually disappeared. Operations managers now wanted measures that would reflect their concern for the performance of the team and larger work groupings rather than that of the individual. It is worth noting that the human relations movement was every bit as focussed on achieving productivity improvements as Taylorism. They were merely advocating other ways of achieving this. As such, the focus of concern about performance in OM remained firmly on the measurement of factors driving cost and efficiency.

As the 1960s gave way to the 1970s, questions began to be asked about the wisdom of concentrating solely on performance measurement. The previously unassailable position of US style management practice was increasingly challenged as manufacturers across the world were forced to face up to fierce competition from Japanese companies. Western companies began to lose market share to a flood of Japanese exports even in their home markets, including the US. It became apparent to consumers that Japanese manufactured goods had appreciably fewer defects than those of their western counterparts. Japanese manufacturers were also usually able to offer much greater product variety. To the thinking of western operations managers such approaches should have led to higher cost. Improved quality must have involved increased spending on quality control and assurance activities. The introduction of greater variety should have negated some of the benefits of mass manufacture. Yet, Japanese goods were usually competitively priced. Western operations managers were therefore forced to reconsider their practices, including their approaches to PMM.

Some called for better measures of efficiency so that they could assess why certain factories, notably Japanese ones, were more productive than others. Hayes and Clark (1986) concluded that what was required was 'a dependable metric for identifying and measuring such differences and a framework for thinking about how to improve performance' (p. 66). They advocated the use of Total Factor Productivity, calculated by 'dividing output by labor materials, capital and energy costs, at constant prices' (p. 72). They bemoaned operations managers' 'pre-occupation with labor costs... even though direct labor now accounts for less than 15% of total costs in most manufacturing companies' (p. 67).

However, others challenged the dominant mindset that cost should be the main concern of operations managers. Skinner's view was that 'a... major cause of companies getting into trouble with manufacturing is the tendency for many managers to accept simplistic notions in evaluating performance of their manufacturing facilities... the general tendency in many companies is to evaluate manufacturing primarily on the basis of cost and efficiency. There are many more criteria to judge performance'. (Skinner, cited in Neely et al., 1997, p. 1131.) This was inherent in the Japanese approach to OM. As Hayes and Abernathy (1980) argued, much of Japan's economic success seemed to be due to their pursuit of both efficiency and effectiveness. Western OM had almost certainly been guilty of concentrating on the former at the expense of the latter.

New measures were required to reflect the new-found concern for effectiveness. The natural starting point for this was quality – something that consumers were clearly concerned about and something that the Japanese excelled at. Initially, the focus was on eliminating defects and achieving conformance. Western operations managers turned to the application of statistics to solve their need for quality measures. Ironically, such statistical techniques were based on the work of a number of Americans – most notably Shewhart (1980), Deming (1982) and Juran (Juran and Gryna, 1980) – who had been largely ignored by their compatriots, but whose ideas had been enthusiastically taken up in post-war Japan. Such measures were initially aimed at improving effectiveness by reducing the number of product defects experienced by customers. However, their use would lead to a growing realization that improved process quality could also improve efficiency much more successfully than the traditional accountancy-based measures that operations managers often had to rely on.

The advent of total quality management (TQM) increased OM's concern to improve effectiveness and responsiveness. This, therefore, saw the introduction of customer-based measures. This linked well to the requirements of the increasingly important service operations sector for measures of customer satisfaction. In services, a level of high quality was seen as synonymous with a high level of customer satisfaction.

The lessons learnt from the Japanese experience, led to an increased understanding of the importance of the role of operations in achieving customer satisfaction and hence in the strategic success of the company. As Neely and Austin (2000) put it, in the 1980s there was 'a growing recognition that operations had a strategic role to play. Suddenly managers were interested in understanding whether the operation they managed was achieving appropriate levels of performance' (p. 422). There was a widespread view that the traditional performance measures of OM were inadequate. Neely et al. (1995) characterize these shortcomings as

- encouraging short-termism;
- lacking strategic focus;
- encouraging local optimization;
- encouraging managers to minimize variance from standard rather than seek continuous improvement; and
- failing to provide information on what customers want and what their competitors are doing.

In short, there was a recognition that OM was experiencing what Neely and Austin (2000) term 'the first measurement crisis – measurement myopia . . . [caused by] measuring the wrong things' (p. 420). The new-found concern for quality had required measures with which operations managers could track their performance. As will be discussed next, quality measures were not the only new measures that operations managers would need to concern themselves with. Many others would follow, as operations managers sought to find the 'right things' to measure. This would lead to yet more broadening of the unit of analysis of measurement and to a deepening of, and an increasing range of, performance measures in OM.

Mid-1980s to present day

The late 1980s and early 1990s saw the rise of business process re-engineering (BPR), most strongly associated with Hammer and Champy (1993). They stated that BPR was 'the fundamental rethinking and redesign of business processes to achieve dramatic improvements in critical, contemporary measures of performance, such as cost, quality, service and speed' (p. 32). The core principles of BPR are for organizations to consider themselves in terms of processes – looking horizontally across the company as opposed to functionally – and to create an environment which allows 'breakthrough'/step change improvement. Thus, the focus within BPR means that performance management becomes important to drive improvement across a number of dimensions rather than just to 'measure' the output. BPR developed a focus on the 'process' and processes that crossed departmental boundaries which allowed operations to become more clearly linked with other departments (for example, marketing). This itself allowed operations be considered more strategically and gave rise to operations being assessed or 'measured' against other objectives beyond cost and quality, including speed, flexibility and dependability (Slack et al., 2005). The majority of textbooks today on OM clearly present the 'process' view suggesting that organizations need to consider operations as processes beyond just the 'manufacturing' or 'delivery' function.

This rise of the business process view and the linking of operations across the organization with objectives beyond cost and quality has led to many of the concepts and 'measures' within OM being adopted more clearly by service companies and even the public sector. The notion of 'delivery' has been taken beyond a product to 'service delivery', with the rapid growth of the service sector and decline in manufacturing in the West. The importance of measuring the effectiveness of service delivery is illustrated by the rise of customer satisfaction measures which bombard us now in everyday life.

Both TQM and BPR allowed the focus of OM to move from merely 'producing' day-to-day towards also 'improving'. This was reflected in sets of performance measures that were becoming wider and deeper. However, as Bourne et al. (2000) note 'in the late 1980s and early 1990s, this dissatisfaction [with traditional backward looking accounting-based performance measurement systems] led to the development of "balanced" or "multi-dimensional" performance measurement frameworks. These new frameworks placed emphasis on non-financial, external and forward looking performance measures' (p. 754). These frameworks have been dominated by one particular model: the Balanced Scorecard (BSC).

Already described in Chapter 3, the BSC has grown from being a tool for organizing measures to being a device for controlling the implementation of strategy and one of the preferred strategic performance management tools of many prominent public and private sector organizations (Radnor and Lovell, 2003). If designed and implemented correctly, reported benefits are the improved articulation and communication of strategy, improved organizational control and strategic and operational process alignment (Kaplan and Norton, 2000). However, since its introduction in 1992, to improve its utility the BSC has evolved in terms of its design characteristics, design processes and usage patterns, producing what Cobbold and Lawrie (2002) refer to as three generations of scorecards:

- First Generation: Original Kaplan and Norton (1992) concept of organizing measures into clusters or perspectives (financial, customer, internal processes and innovation and learning).
- Second Generation: Making clearer links between organizational objectives and choice of measures. The objectives were related through cause and effect relationships and documented in the form of a 'Strategy Map' organized across four or more perspectives (Kaplan and Norton, 2000).
- Third Generation: Introduction of a Destination Statement (a long-term plan) which informed the choice of the short and medium-term objectives, organized into activities and outcomes with links illustrating causal relationships.

The BSC approach has been adopted by a wide range of organizations in manufacturing (BP, Motorola, Ford), commercial services (Vodaphone, Marriot Hotels, British Airways) and public services (examples in the UK include the National Health Service (NHS) and local government social services).

Clearly, frameworks such as the BSC that incorporate multiple perspectives and dimensions of performance are, in theory, well suited to application in the not-for-profit sector. The BSC, BPR and TQM all began to find 'product champions' in UK public services, especially the NHS and local government, in the 1980s and 1990s. This wave overlapped with an exponential rise in policy-driven measurement systems also strongly affecting the work of operations managers. During these decades the analysis of public sector reform in the UK focused on 'New Public Management' (NPM). There are many different (but overlapping) definitions of NPM (Pollitt, 2003). Pollitt (2001) defines NPM, amongst other things, as (see original article for further referencing)

- A shift in focus of management systems and management effort from inputs and processes to outputs and outcomes.
- A shift towards more measurement, manifesting itself in performance indicators and standards.
- A much wider use of market or market-like mechanisms for the delivery of public services.

Since New Labour came to power in the UK in May 1997, there has been a drive, and some would argue acceleration, to the restructuring of government and public services which began under the Conservative governments (Hartley, 2002). This approach taken by New Labour has been under the banner of 'modernisation and improvement' and includes many of the elements of NPM previously listed. From the Modernising Government White Paper[2] came a number of initiatives including the development of the Public Services Productivity Panel who produced a raft of White Papers tackling Health, Social Services, Welfare and Criminal Justice (PSPP, 2000). In line with NPM, New Labour has also sought to bring transparency in the performance of public services through the introduction of targets within all major government departments linked to the Spending Review (from local and central government to education, health and community care). These targets are then typically translated by individual bodies and organizations to detailed operational level measures that become a preoccupation for both operations managers and service users.

The evolution of PMM in the public policy context is discussed further in Chapters 14 and 16. In terms of direct impact on operations managers, across the public sector in response to the NPM and 'modernisation' agendas services have developed, or had imposed on them, initiatives or frameworks for performance measurement. These have included awards, tools and techniques which have been developed or initiated internally – for example, TQM programmes, Charter Mark, Investors in People (IiP) and the BSC; and initiatives and programmes that have been imposed, driven or initiated from central government. In the UK, these initiatives have included: for local government – Best Value and Comprehensive Performance Assessment (CPA); in the Health Service – waiting list targets and star ratings; and in education – primary school tests and secondary school exam result league tables. All of these approaches have led to published results indicating either performance against a threshold position (for example, star ratings for NHS trusts) or a position in a league table (for example, list of good or poor performers). Pidd (2005) offers the following classification of the early twenty-first century performance regime:

1. National Standards set out in Public Service Agreements (PSAs);
2. Devolved funding and flexibility with reporting structures specified;
3. Benchmarking against similar units (for example, 'family groupings' and Benchmarking clubs in the Health Service);

4. Transfer of Best Practice being encouraged through awards which are won in competition (for example, the Beacon Council Award in the UK);
5. Audit and inspection in order to be held to account for the PSA targets; and
6. Service, units and managers meeting targets and getting rewarded for doing so for example, greater autonomy in spending powers.

Pidd and others (including Smith and Goddard, in this volume; Goldstein and Spiegelhalter, 1996; Royal Statistical Society, 2003) also provide critical assessments of the impact of this regime which space precludes us from outlining here. Fundamentally, performance measurement in the public sector has continued to centre around control, accountability and reporting, based on efficiency (in order to justify to the public 'value for money'). Performance management related to improvement in operations processes and outcomes has been far less prominent – even neglected – in some areas of the public sector. As well as the intrinsic technical complexity of understanding the causal relationships involved in long-term outcomes of public service provision, this 'neglect' reflects the political complexity of public agencies working together over long periods to drive real improvement.

Looking back and looking forward

So what does history tell us?

The sections above have plotted the history of PMM in OM taking us from Smith and Taylor to Kaplan and Norton through the manufacturing, commercial service and public service sectors. We have seen how the focus on performance within OM has moved from measurement based on efficiency and productivity in relation to cost, to management on a broader more strategic level considering operations from a number of perspectives.

Johnston and Clark (2005) describe PMM within OM as about 'Communication, Motivation, Control and Improvement' with many organizations developing and using a range of measures across the whole organization in assessing its performance. We can adapt the transformational model (Figure 7.1) to exert feedback control (Figure 7.3). Outputs are measured, compared with a given target value and the difference between the two is fed back into the input side where a 'controller' takes corrective action by adjusting either the transforming or transformed inputs.

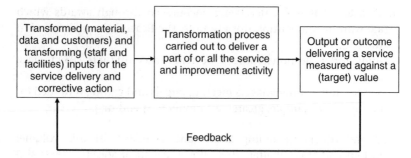

Figure 7.3   Systems view of performance measurement and management (Radnor, forthcoming)

This feedback control systems views suggests a performance management system is one which provides information on the matters of importance (communication), promotes appropriate behaviour (motivation), provides a mechanism for accountability and control (control) and creates a mechanism for intervention and learning (improvement) (Fischer, 1995; Haas and Kleingeld, 1998; Neely, 1998). However, what this view does not do is differentiate between performance measurement, performance reporting and performance management. The historical analysis has shown that the moving boundaries of PMM in OM has meant that for many researchers and others engaged in the field, the terms 'performance measurement' and 'performance management' have become interchangeable. However, we argue that it is important to consider them as different concepts.

Lebas (1995) describes performance measurement as including measures based on key success factors, measures for detection of deviations, measures to track past achievements, measures to describe the status potential, measures of output and measures of input. On the other hand, performance management involves training, team work, dialogue, management style, attitudes, shared vision, employee involvement, multi-competence, incentives and rewards (Lebas, 1995, p. 12). He argues that '[although the] processes involved in performance measurement and in performance management are not the same...they feed and comfort one another' (Lebas, 1995, p. 12). In other words, PMM are not separable although distinction should be drawn between them. Performance measurement is the act of measuring the inputs, process and outputs; while performance management comprises the response to the 'output' measures, adjusting inputs via the feedback loop or taking other appropriate correction action (illustrated in Figure 7.3). It is also worth noting that the escalation of performance measurement, control and accountability has been associated with an explosion of performance reporting. Operations managers, particularly in the public sector, complain that 'literally hundreds of measures are reported internally and externally a month'. This has led to the development of departments whose role it is to 'feed the performance measurement and reporting beast' with little comprehension of the purpose or result in the activity. Interestingly, this vast amount of data and information is often not used by central government or politicians in any meaningful or systematic way (Pollitt, 2004).

Therefore, seeking to differentiate the terms performance measurement, performance reporting and performance management from an OM perspective, the following definitions are suggested:

- Performance measurement is about assessing, either quantitatively or qualitatively, the output of an activity or process.
- Performance reporting is about giving an indication of the level of output or outcome of the activity or process (usually against some form of target).
- The purpose of performance management is to motivate behaviour leading to improvement and innovation.

Thus while performance measurement and reporting reflect the reductionist concerns with efficiency, productivity and utilization that dominated the majority of the twentieth-century, performance management (albeit building on performance measurement) is concerned with effectiveness and a broader, more holistic, even qualitative view of operations and the organization which characterizes PMM from the 1980s until today.

Future challenges of PMM in OM

Considering the historical analysis given above, what then can be concluded about the future and, importantly, the challenges of PMM in OM both for researchers and managers?

The first point to make is that the drive for productivity has not really disappeared. In a world of increasing global competition, the low wage economies of the developing world and the need for transparency and accountability pose a significant challenge to operations managers in the manufacturing, commercial service and even public service sectors. As Taylor demonstrated so long ago, measurement is the starting point for improving operational performance. The challenge is in measuring the right things and using those measures as the basis for managing perform-ance improvement. Adding more and more performance measurement and performance reporting, without performance management, can be counter-productive.

The second challenge follows from this. How should performance measurement and performance management within OM be developed in the future? In particular, can OM provide a link across all func-tions/departments of an organization? The BSC (and similar perform-ance management frameworks) emphasize the importance of taking a multi-functional perspective on performance management linked to organizational strategy. But the process perspective provided by the BPR movement highlights the need to link operational activities across the firm and along its supply chain. The challenge then is how to develop a manageable and coherent set of performance measures for an organ-ization's business processes, rather than a proliferation of unconnected measures for individual operational tasks and activities.

Third, how can the lessons, issues and successes within the private sector help the development of PMM in the public sector particu-larly in terms of OM? Whilst managing operations in the public sector undoubtedly throws up a new and different set of challenges, there is much to be learnt about PMM from the private sector. Many of the PMM issues that arise in the public sector have been faced before within the private sector. The challenge is to learn how to adapt, not merely adopt, and apply private sector experiences to best effect.

Fourth, there is a need to develop more predictive tools in performance management. Historically, the underlying premise of performance man-agement is based on 'feed back' rather than 'feed forward'. This implies getting things wrong before you can get them right. There is much that could be done to incorporate the lessons of organizational behaviour into performance management. A greater consideration of the 'software' rather than just the 'hardware' of performance management, using it to change behaviours of operations managers not just the systems they manage, would surely yield massive benefits. Exactly how to do this remains one of the great challenges for performance measurement and performance management in OM.

These four observations illustrate that in terms of OM, PMM will continue to broaden (across departments and supply chains), deepen (through the use in the public sector) and extend in range (development of predictive tools). On one level this development of performance meas-urement and performance management in OM is good and important but on another it could be bad and dangerous. Operations managers across all the sectors need to remember that PMM are tools and means, and not an end in itself. Although understanding economy, effectiveness and efficiency are important, the extent to which they are measured, analysed and reported should be balanced with need to manage and deliver improved goods and services. The focus needs to be beyond internal targets, reporting and outputs to using PMM to understand and drive performance in terms of customer satisfactions and outcomes. As the saying goes, 'you can't make a pig fat by weighing it!' but only by weighing it do you know if it is losing or gaining weight – so you can make a decision about what to do.

Referring back to Johnston and Clark's (2005) description of performance measurement we can extend this to consider reporting and management for OM. Control can refer to performance measurement, communication to performance reporting and motivations and improvement to management. Lebas (1995) clearly states that 'All those who have focussed exclusively on measurement, without understanding that measures are only telling what the consequences are of the decisions that created the context for performance, missed the opportunity to gain control over – to gain mastery of – the process of creating performance and success for the firm or for the organizational unit under scrutiny' (p. 13). Building on this, therefore, it is important to have elements of the three (measurement, reporting and management) in an effective performance management system which, as this chapter has demonstrated, is not always the case.

In terms of the research agenda for PMM within the OM discipline, there needs to be further work on the definitions and concepts surrounding performance measurement, reporting and management. To date, the debate has been around measurement and management but as this chapter has illustrated real understanding should be created in terms of reporting, related to the extent and effect of it. Related to this, and considering the points made above, researchers can support practitioners in identifying appropriate measures, across business processes and across sectors, that allow effective (predictive) decision making.

The majority of research within OM to date has been fairly descriptive (case studies and surveys). More reflective or paradigmatic research is needed where questions, concepts and even theories are built around understanding the relationship between the system and the behaviours of the system and organization. From its theoretical background, OM is in a good position to do this and should attempt to widen the philosophical questions that are now emerging within performance measurement and performance management.

Notes

1. These dates are indicative rather than definitive. There are no clear defining moments and the transitions from one era to the next should be seen as evolutionary and gradual rather than revolutionary and abrupt.
2. In Britain, government White Papers set out policy that is due to come before Parliament; in this case see Modernising Government, Cmnd. 4310, Cabinet Office, 1999. London: The Stationery Office.

8
Managing and Measuring Project Performance

David Bryde, Fiona Lettice and Martin Wickes

Introduction

Over the past 25 years the discipline of project management has evolved from being a specialist sub-domain of operations management, grounded in the disciplines of management sciences and operational research (OR). Today it is a multidisciplinary subject, drawing from and incorporating theories and concepts of other business and management-related topics, such as strategic management, quality management, performance measurement, information technology (IT) and finance. This new project management paradigm, which is broader in its conceptual base and areas of application than the traditional project management paradigm, is exemplified by the development of the subject of performance management in the context of managing business projects. This chapter provides a brief review of the influence of practice on project management and the increasing interest in the performance management of projects. The key trends in project management research are presented, from an initial focus on Project Critical Success Factors and a restricted set of performance criteria (the Iron Triangle) to an increasing recognition of multidimensional performance criteria. These start to encompass value-based performance measurement, psycho-social measures and links to strategy and programme management. An integrative framework is then presented which unites these various evolutionary strands. Finally, some challenges remain for both researchers and practitioners in the field and these are discussed at the end of this chapter.

Influence of practice on project management

What has driven the evolution of a new project management paradigm? An academic perspective suggests that the developments in the wider field of project management have been led by innovations and changes in practice rather than by theoretical advancements (Maylor, 2001). It is certainly true that the contexts in which project management is practised, like most operational environments, have seen much change in the past two decades. In the case of project management, it is no longer merely a set of practices employed either by project-focused businesses, such as aerospace or construction, or by all types of organization on an *ad hoc* basis for 'special' initiatives. Rather, it is often the defining structural attribute for many organizations.

The need to develop new project management capabilities and structures has presented practical challenges. Project team members are often required to work in knowledge areas they are unfamiliar with, operating as trans-disciplinarians and they need to be able to understand quickly new technologies, markets, people and organizations. Further, project workers face the trials of having to satisfy a myriad of stakeholders, each with a different perspective of what constitutes a successful project or programme; and this complexity is often compounded for those working in matrix organizational structures, which have dual lines of reporting to functional superiors as well as project superiors.

These practical challenges mean that the management of projects is often problematic. Projects and their interrelationships with stakeholders have become increasingly complex, and so they have become increasingly difficult to co-ordinate and control. Practitioners are therefore trying to develop solutions to address these specific problems. For example, a degree of regulation is sought through the implementation of formal project management methodologies, such as PRINCE2 (OGC, 2002) (process control) and optimizing outputs and outcomes for project stakeholders is the aim of the implementation of new performance measurement systems (performance control).

Growth in interest in performance management

An interest in the subject of project performance has been fuelled by a number of high profile reports, including public policy documents, into levels of success in project environments. A consistent finding from these reports is that poor performance (defined in a variety of ways) is a cause for concern and new ways of working need to be developed to address the concerns. In the United States, a series of reports by the Standish Group has focused on the poor performance of IT and software projects (see for example, Standish Group International, 1994). In the United Kingdom, the issue of poor performance and the need to improve programme and project performance has been identified in both the public and the private sectors. In the public sector, the Office of Government and Commerce identified continuing weakness in project delivery in the 'Improving Programme and Project Delivery' (IPPD) report (OPSR, 2003). Case studies of large-scale projects, published by the National Audit Office, emphasize new ways of working to maximize performance. For example, on the Heathrow Terminal 5 project the Major Projects Agreement (MPAF, 2005), which is a new performance and employment framework for large-scale building services engineering projects, is being utilized to provide a framework for the management of performance between the client and contractors. In the private sector, the landmark reports by Latham (1994) and Egan (1998) highlighted poor performance in the UK construction sector and led to the establishment of the Key Performance Indicator (KPI) Working Group, and then in 2002, of the Construction Best Practice Programme by the then Department of Trade and Industry and Rethinking Construction. The KPI Working Group (DETR, 2000) developed a model of project performance for construction companies to benchmark their performance, comprising seven key performance indicators: the typical time (for completion), cost (of completion and in-use) and quality (defects and issues) indicators; and then the more construction-specific indicators of client satisfaction (with the product and service), change orders (originated by the client or the project manager), health and safety (accidents and fatalities) and business performance (encompassing financial indicators such as profitability, Return on Investment, Return on Capital Employed and so on).

Whilst it is possible to attribute developments in project management to practitioner-oriented advances, as discussed earlier, momentum for change has been maintained through the publication of these reports, which has put project performance high on the agenda of government, regulatory bodies, unions, trade associations, in addition to the organizations involved in either commissioning project work or providing for project delivery.

Trends in project management research

Research into project critical success factors

Prior to the 1980s, the focus of research and theory development in terms of project performance management was on the identification of project critical success factors (CSFs). Implicit was acceptance of the concept of success factors, developed by Daniel in the 1960s, that 'in most industries there are usually three to six factors that determine success; these key jobs must be done exceedingly well for a company to be successful' (Daniel, 1961, p. 116). From this concept, Rockart (1979) developed a CSF method for meeting the information needs of top executives. This method focused on understanding the objectives and goals of the company and the factors (CSFs) critical to their achievement. The CSF concept or method has been applied to project environments, with project CSFs being 'those inputs to the management system that lead directly or indirectly to the success of the project' (Cooke-Davies, 2002, p. 185). A comprehensive body of literature exists, both survey-based and case studies, which contributes to an increasingly long list and wide range of project CSFs; though certain CSFs are consistently identified as needing particular attention. These include establishing common agreed project objectives, gaining top management support and appointing an appropriate project manager and team. Westerveld (2003) and Iyer and Jha (2005) provide relatively recent reviews of the project CSF literature. In most of the early work there was an acceptance or assumption as to what good or poor performance meant in project environments. It was measured in purely functional terms, that is, did the product work or not; and in terms of the tasks carried out, that is, was the project completed on time, within budget and to a given specification (Kerzner, 1998). The focus of effort was on establishing the influences on project performance not on how performance is defined.

The traditional paradigm – the Iron Triangle

Measuring performance in terms of whether the project completed on time, within budget and to a given specification has been described as the Iron Triangle, Golden Triangle, Solid Triangle or Triple Constraint (Atkinson, 1999; Gardiner and Stewart, 2000) of project management (for ease of reference referred to as the Iron Triangle from hereon). Early theoretical and practical developments in the field of project management were aimed at maximizing performance in terms of the Iron Triangle, through adherence to budgets (meeting cost objectives), schedules (time) and the provision of deliverables linked to specifications (product quality). Methods that focused on managing performance against cost and time-criteria were developed post-World War Two, namely: cost and schedule control systems criteria; and critical path analysis (CPA, also known as critical path method, or PERT – programme evaluation and review technique). For more information on these methods, see, for example, Gordon and Lockyer (2005).

The Iron Triangle is still emphasized in contemporary practice (White and Fortune, 2002). Achieving time, cost and quality objectives is important to both the project team and the client organization because the measures provide an objective view of how well the project is managed. That said, it is also the case that the continued pre-eminence of the Iron Triangle is in part due to the fact that time, cost and product quality metrics are relatively easy to develop and implement; and also cost, time and quality objectives are within the control of the project organization (Pinto and Slevin, 1988).

New approaches to research on project success

From the 1980s onwards, criticisms were being reported in the wider performance measurement literature reflecting dissatisfaction with narrow financially oriented perspectives of traditional performance measurement frameworks (see, for example, Ghalayini and Noble, 1996; Bourne et al., 2000). Such criticisms, which had led to the development of frameworks which took a broader stakeholder perspective like the Balanced Scorecard (BSC) (Kaplan and Norton, 1992), applied also to the exclusive focus of project performance management on the Iron Triangle. Specific criticisms were: the measures may result in an objective appraisal of a project but, being so narrowly focused, did not provide a balanced view of the performance of the project from a reasonable cross-section of stakeholders; and the measures considered projects from a tactical perspective, detached from the high-level, longer-term strategic imperatives that exist in organizations. But perhaps of most concern was the recognition of an erroneous assumption at the heart of the framework: that if the Iron Triangle was met, then the customer *must* be satisfied. Anecdotal evidence from high profile project failures showed this was clearly not true in the case of all projects. For example, a company may launch a new product on time, within budget and to the defined specification. But if the product did not sell, then could the project which developed the new product be considered a success?

The recognition that good and poor performance could be distinguished by criteria other than the Iron Triangle was the driver of a new wave of development in project performance management, which we call the 'project success criteria research genre'. (The term 'key performance indicator' is often used instead of 'success criteria'). Each piece of research has added to the body of knowledge concerning the topic of project success criteria. For example, specific findings of studies include

- Technical-related criteria are given greater emphasis than cost and time-related criteria (Might and Fischer, 1985).
- The emphasis given by an organization to time-related criteria has diminished (Kerzner, 1989).
- The importance of project success criteria changes over the life of a project (Pinto and Slevin, 1987).
- The emphasis given to project success criteria influences the importance attached to planning or tactical factors (Pinto and Prescott, 1990).
- The emphasis placed on criteria relating to the future are more important to people whose project has finished than to people whose project is unfinished (Shenhar et al., 1997).
- The emphasis given to the internal-related success criteria of time and cost is a response to senior management pressure rather than customer expectations (Wateridge, 1998).
- Criteria for measuring customer satisfaction take precedence over the internal-related success criteria of time and cost (Tukel and Rom, 2001).
- The emphasis given to time, cost and external customer-related criteria varies depending upon the level of technological uncertainty at the start of the project (Shenhar et al., 2001).
- There are universally important criteria, but some criteria are more important to specific industry contexts, for example, ROI is emphasized by investment organizations (Maltz et al., 2003).

An outcome of this research genre was the agreement that performance in project environments is multidimensional (Shenhar et al., 1997) and that different people would focus on different dimensions at different times as part of their assessment of the success or otherwise of a project. For example, an architect may consider success in terms of aesthetic appearance, an engineer in terms of technical competence, an accountant in terms of spend under budget, a human resources manager in terms of employee satisfaction and a chief executive in terms of stock market value. However, a pessimistic view of the outcome of the studies of project success criteria is that the variables – internal versus external perspectives, different stakeholders, stage in the project life cycle, business sector, and project characteristics – interact in a variety of complex and dynamic ways that makes it difficult to derive any simple solutions that can be usefully applied to project management practice. Another criticism is that many of the studies of project success criteria have tended to be hypothetical and focused on developing normative models; asking how performance of projects ought to be measured rather than how it is measured in practice.

Although research into project success criteria seemed to develop in a rather *ad hoc* and piecemeal fashion, with little evidence of a unifying holistic framework emerging, one point of convergence was the gradual emergence and acceptance of a distinction between 'project management' performance and 'project' performance (De Wit, 1988). Evaluating project management performance involves assessing performance not only in relation to the Iron Triangle but also in terms of how the project is managed through its life cycle, that is, the quality of the process; whilst evaluating project performance is broader in its perspective and includes an assessment of the longer-term effect of the final product or service on the customer and other key stakeholders (Baccarini, 1999). For example, the Thames Barrier Project took twice as long to build as planned and was four times the proposed budget, but was considered a success as it provided a profit for the key stakeholders (Morris and Hough, 1987).

In identifying elements of performance beyond the Iron Triangle, there is evidence of the influence of theories and concepts of quality management and total quality management (TQM), with the recognition that 'quality' was not only an output from the project, as defined in the Iron Triangle, but also linked to the 'quality of the management process', that is, the project management performance (BSI, 1995, 2000). So measures relating to the management of risk (the number of unforeseen risks impacting the project), the re-use of organization knowledge and the manager's ability to sell follow-on work would be additional ways in which the project management performance could be monitored.

In the field of quality management, one important debate was linked to understanding the relationships between quality and satisfaction. One view sees high levels of performance in terms of quality as an antecedent to high levels of satisfaction, whilst another view shows that quality levels can be low but satisfaction still high. A desire to understand the link between elements of project and project management performance and satisfaction levels is an important driver behind the project success criteria research genre, with the aim being to establish what elements of performance influences levels of satisfaction with projects.

Different authors highlighted the importance of different attributes, with little evidence of any strong unifying concepts binding the various studies together. For example, one author would define 'satisfaction' in

terms of an overall perception from an individual, and for the organization by an increase in market share and by technological breakthrough;
whereas another author would highlight attributes relating to the implementation process, the perceptions of the project's value and the concern
for and attendance to, the client's needs. Therefore, it would be difficult
to argue against the 'charge' levelled (Winch et al., 1998) that the subject
of defining successful project and project management performance was
developing in a fragmented fashion.

Despite this fragmentation, the influence of quality management,
albeit often implicit rather than explicit, is clearly present. The internal
focus on the quality of the project management process could be categorized as being typical of a quality assurance approach, which is an
early stage of evolution in quality management (Dale et al., 1994). Here
the emphasis is on demonstrating to the customer, through the project
management performance, that the project team are 'doing things right'.
The external focus on the attributes of satisfaction could be categorized as
typifying a TQM approach, a higher level of quality management evolution, in which performance combines elements of 'doing the right thing'
as well as 'doing things right'. This distinction between doing the right
thing and doing things right can be seen to have informed the move
to distinguish between project and project management performance
and to provide the underlying theory for emphasizing process-related
measures of performance when assessing the effectiveness of project
management.

Value-based performance measurement

Another response to the perceived limitations of traditional performance measurement methods, which focused on a narrow range of mainly
financial-based measures, has been to focus on methods that provide
a single, value-based measure of performance (O'Hanlon and Peasnell,
1998). This approach has been evident in the literature on corporate financial management, with the establishment and trademarking of the
concept of 'Economic Value Added' (EVA®), by Stern Stewart & Co.
Although having evolved from the Cost/Schedule Control Systems Criteria (C/SCSC) developed by the United States Department of Defense in
the 1950s, the project management Earned Value Method (EVM) is conceptually rooted in this desire to provide single value-based performance
measures. In the case of EVM, this is achieved through the integration of
methods for measuring performance against the time and cost objectives
into a single measure of value (Fleming and Koppelman, 2000).

Psycho-social measures

Whilst the debate about project versus project management performance could be described as extending approaches to measuring performance outwards in terms of the time horizon, and downwards in terms of a customer focus in the supply chain, another strand of development focused further up the chain. It can be argued that satisfaction could be defined not only by the customer or client but also by groups internal to the project, such as the project manager and project team members (Cleland, 1986; Nicholas, 1989; Tuman, 1993); and that their desired outcomes, whether they be task-oriented or psychosocial-oriented (Pinto and Pinto, 1991), are important measures. The psycho-social orientation has been extended further up the supply chain, potentially incorporating a wide range of stakeholders such as: sponsors, users, customer, team, project organization and suppliers. Psycho-social measures relate to the motivation, training and development, and the rewards and recognition system employed for the extended project team. This focus on stakeholder well-being is highlighted in the British Standard Institutes' definition of project management, which states that it is the 'planning, monitoring and control of all aspects of a project and the *motivation of all those involved* in it ...' (BSI, 2000, p. 10, emphasis added). This provides the rationale for theoretical developments in the literature, such as Theory W Project Management (Boehm and Ross, 1989), which aims to create win-win scenarios for project team members. Implicit in the statements of proponents of the psycho-social perspective is that the increased cost associated with generating, collating and analysing psycho-social data is far less than the disruption that would be caused by ill-motivated staff or the recruitment and induction costs of replacing staff who resign.

The link to strategy

The final development relates to the performance of the programme and the role of projects within such programmes. Programmes contain multiple and related projects (Pellegrinelli, 1997) that often have a shared strategic intent (OGC, 2007; Lycett et al., 2004) and therefore programme management performance relates to the efficiency and effectiveness of programme-level operations. Theorists and researchers have begun to consider how to measure programme performance and, in this respect, knowledge developed in the domain of strategic management has been applied. For example, the strategic management view (Johnson and Scholes, 2002) that progression towards strategic objectives of the organization (such as increased market share) is a salient measure, has been recognized in the programme management literature. Certain measures have also been drawn from research that has investigated the management of strategic projects, for example, the development of the technological base of the firm and creating new marketing opportunities (Shenhar et al., 1997). Other measures are aggregated from the project-level measures. For example, if the number of unforeseen risks impacting projects across the programme is deemed to be excessive, this may initiate a programme-level response to improve capabilities in this area.

An integrative framework of performance for managing projects

Figure 8.1 (Wickes, 2005, p. 105) shows a framework of performance which brings together the various evolutionary strands of project and project management performance measurement described above. It takes an integrative and holistic view of the various research genres that have been present over the past 20 years. It brings together the strategic Programme-Level perspective; a Project Management viewpoint incorporating the Solid (or Iron) Triangle, an internal perspective and an external perspective; a view on Project Performance; and one from the standpoint of the Extended Project Team.

Where programmes comprise multiple projects, clear integration and aggregation of measures are needed at both levels of the performance framework. In addition to the standard Iron Triangle (cost, quality, time) measures, the Internal Perspective focuses on the project team and the project management process and considers measures that span from pre-project through the timescale of the project and also post-project. The External Perspective again spans from pre- to post-project, but considers measures from the customer and key stakeholder perspectives. Feedback and communications are particularly important in this perspective. The Project Performance Perspective is task focused and is where many of the traditional financial measures and value metrics are found. Project outputs are also included. The Extended Team Perspective covers many of the psycho-social measures, such as motivation, training and development and reward and recognition.

Challenges for research and practice

Since the 1980s, there has been a shift in emphasis in relation to measuring and managing performance in project environments, which has involved a move away from an exclusive focus on the Iron Triangle to

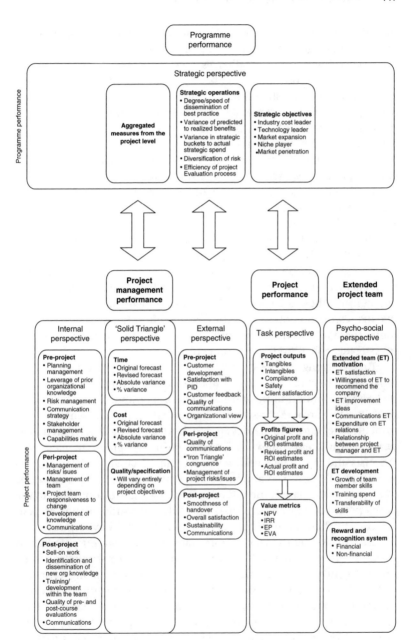

Figure 8.1 A framework of programme and project performance
Source: (Wickes, 2005, p. 105)

multidimensional or value-based measures. It has also seen a delineation of project management and project performance.

However, there are still challenges. One challenge relates to terminology. Although efforts are being made within the project management community to establish commonly agreed terms, that is, through the development of a project management Body of Knowledge (APM, 2000), there is still often confusion as to the meaning of the terms 'project critical success factors', 'project success criteria' and 'project key performance indicators'. The terms are sometimes used inter-changeably and different organizations subscribe to different meanings. This lack of clarity is reflective of the lack of integration and absence of unifying frameworks that has typified the development of theory and practice in the field.

A second challenge relates to the theoretical and practical development of methods based on a single value-based measure of performance, such as EVM. There is little agreement as to the usefulness of such an approach and although theoretical benefits of using EVM have been claimed, such as cost savings, improved analysis, communication and control, these are countered by the argument that the benefits of making it work do not warrant the cost and effort (Raby, 2000). Furthermore, there has been little empirical study of a systematic nature that investigates how EVM impacts on performance.

A final challenge relates to the body of research on project success criteria, which having stressed the importance of an array of measures, can make a contribution to the development of metrics that will be used in practice. The outcome of research suggests that the requirement is for performance measures and metrics approaches that are flexible enough to be adapted to different contexts. Whereas 20 years ago, project management theorists and researchers used terms like Iron Triangle and Triple Constraint, which conveyed a message of solidity and certainty to describe models of performance, the future challenge will be to contribute to the development of multidimensional and multi-observational models characterized by their ability to deal with change, dynamic environments and uncertainty. Rather than solid, iron triangles, the emerging paradigm is perhaps better equated with fluid polygons: changing shape depending upon the influence of a variety of complex and interacting variables, such as the type of project stakeholder and stage of the project life cycle.

However, other disciplines that have gone down a similar path have encountered difficulties. In the literature on corporate financial management, for example, there has been criticism of approaches that use such multiple indicators of performance, with the argument put forward that whilst such models provide new metrics, they are often isolated and not linked, either with other metrics or with the main financial metric of the company (O'Hanlon and Peasnell, 1998; Strack and Villis, 2002). Indeed, in operations management, reference has been made to the 'metrics maze' (Melnyk et al., 2004), which in the context of projects seems particularly pertinent as the route to a commonly agreed set of defined project and project management performance measures, with corresponding metrics, has proved to be long and tortuous so far.

Conclusion

Projects have become more prevalent in organizations in the last 20 years, driving a need for better project management capabilities and structures. Related to this, project performance has become a significant issue, especially as poor performance in high profile projects has received more attention from the public and government bodies.

An early focus within project management research was on project critical success factors and the Iron Triangle of cost, quality and time. More recently, it has been important to start to consider customer expectations more centrally, influenced to a large degree by the field of quality management. Value-based performance measurement and psycho-social measures have also become more important in the recognition that multiple perspectives of performance are increasingly required. Where organizations are trying to deliver their strategy through programmes of multiple projects, a programme-level view is also required, which may be an aggregation of project measures but is likely to require new measures to monitor progress towards an organization's strategic objectives. The authors have developed an integrative framework of performance for managing projects to bring together these numerous and evolving strands. Despite the recent developments and increasing research and practitioner interest within the project performance field, several challenges remain – to establish unified terminology; to develop value-based performance measurement methods and evaluate their benefits; and to understand more fully the fluid polygon (as opposed to the iron triangle) paradigm that is emerging and requires a constantly changing shape to respond to complex and interacting variables such as type of stakeholder and stage of the project lifecycle.

9

Performance Management and Operational Research: A Marriage Made in Heaven?

Peter C Smith and Maria Goddard

Introduction

The practice, teaching and research of management is peculiarly vulnerable to fads. A cynic might suggest that this is the result of a lively market in management gurus, in which the latest management concept is promoted as an indispensable tool for the modern manager. However, it might also be the case that some apparent fads do indicate a real change in the preoccupations and needs of managers. The explosion in interest in performance management (PM) since the mid-1990s may indeed be one such case.

For many years the concept of PM was synonymous with the micro-management of employee behaviour. It certainly has roots in Taylor's concept of 'scientific management', and Currie (1959) claims that elements of PM can be traced back to the thirteenth century. The predominant early interest was therefore from the perspective of HRM, although some industrial companies had quite advanced management control systems in place by the 1970s. However, the concept of PM has progressively broadened in recent years, to the extent that by the 1990s it had become closer to implying a concern with the strategic management of an entire organization, or even economy. Unusually for a management trend, PM appears to have reached the public sector at around the same time as it started to penetrate the commercial sector (Holloway, 1999), providing opportunities for cross-fertilization of ideas and practices.

In spite of the enormous growth of interest in PM, a precise definition of the concept is elusive. For example, an Organisation for Economic Co-operation and Development (OECD) report on PM in the public sector notes that the growth in interest in PM has been stimulated by the increased devolution of responsibilities in many public sectors, and the associated need to develop explicit models of accountability and performance measurement, but fails to arrive at a specific definition (OECD, 1996). This difficulty reflects the different connotations of PM that exist, an issue we explore further in the next section by examining the organizational context within which PM must operate. We then describe what we perceive to be the four fundamental building blocks of PM: formulation of strategy; development of performance measurement instruments; application of analytic techniques that seek to interpret such measures; and development of instruments designed to encourage appropriate organizational responses to performance information. The paper concludes with some reflections on possible future developments.

The context of PM

Whereas the most common criteria for performance *measurement* are probably still financial, the traditional definition of PM places the individual employee as the focus of attention. In this context, the definition of performance is assumed to be relatively uncontentious, deriving from an organizational strategy that is taken as given, and the principal interest is in the instruments available to optimize performance. It therefore emphasizes organizational control within an established set of objectives. In this vein, PM can be characterized as '... an integrated set of planning and review procedures which cascade down through the organization to provide a link between each individual and the overall strategy of the organization.' (Rogers, 1990.)

More recently commentators have recognized the limitation of such 'top-down' philosophies, and have sought to broaden the scope of PM to include conscious reflection on strategy, objectives and organizational culture. For example, Rashid (1999) advocates a philosophy of 'cascading up' of ideas to complement the traditional top-down approach. Pollitt (1999) is typical in characterizing PM as a set of five processes that extend beyond the organization's boundaries: setting objectives; assigning responsibility; measuring performance; feedback of information to decision making; and external accountability.

The diversity of views on what constitutes PM is reflected in the diverse disciplines that have sought to make a contribution to the topic. Examples beyond HRM include operations management, marketing, finance, accounting, organizational behaviour, economics, psychology, political science and, of course, operational research (OR). Each discipline contributes its own language, traditions, preoccupations and prejudices to the topic. Neely estimates that a news report or article on PM has appeared every 5 hours since 1994, and that in the United States alone a new book on performance measurement appears every week.

The range of perspectives on PM can be loosely captured in diagrammatic form (Figure 9.1). The narrow view of the PM role is represented by the inner loop. Strategy, objectives, organizational structure and culture are taken as given, and the purpose of PM is to ensure that the organization is 'steered' in some sense optimally within that context. The broader view of PM is more dynamic and is indicated by the outer loop. It recognizes that the organization must continually review the context within which PM is conducted, and be prepared to amend strategy if circumstances (such as customer feedback, technological developments or a change in priorities) suggest it is needed. It must be emphasized that this simple double loop representation is very simplified (for example, it ignores important complications such as partnerships between autonomous organizations). However, it captures the essence of the increasingly important strategic element of PM.

A persistent theme in the modern PM literature is the increased devolution found in the modern organization, and the associated increased need for conscious surveillance of relatively autonomous elements of the organization. Delegated decision making is unproblematic only if

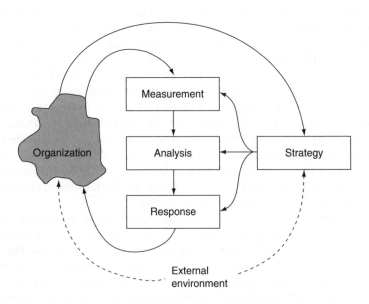

Figure 9.1   Schematic representation of the performance management process

the centre has full information on the actions and outcomes of the devolved unit and a way of controlling these actions, or if the objectives of the centre and the devolved unit coincide. In practice, neither of these requirements is likely to be fulfilled, and so a 'principal : agent' problem arises (Milgrom and Roberts, 1992). It is the relationship between the centre (the principal) and the devolved unit (the agent) that forms the central concern of PM.

In the extreme, the devolved unit might become an entirely autonomous player in an external market, competing without particular favour for the business of the parent organization. In these circumstances, the market becomes the principal instrument of PM. The purchasing organization specifies its requirements, and the intention is that – if the market is assumed to be competitive – optimal performance in terms of the required product's price and quality will ensue. Poor performance will simply lead to financial failure of the devolved unit. At the other extreme, the organization might retain the devolved units strictly within its direct control, and instead seek to optimize performance by means of a portfolio of managerial devices, such as performance measurement, incentives and appraisal.

The choice of organizational form (crudely characterized as market or hierarchy) has been the subject of a flourishing strand of economic enquiry, stimulated by the work of Williamson (1975). There are of course numerous potential intermediate forms, such as the 'internal' markets (or quasi-markets) introduced in organizations such as the BBC and much of the UK public sector in the 1990s (Bartlett et al., 1998), under which the devolved units remain within the organizational hierarchy, but are to a greater or lesser extent exposed to internal or external competitive forces.

Some economists argue that those designing organizational form should seek to minimize the costs associated with devolution (Milgrom and Roberts, 1992). These comprise two broad categories: transaction costs and agency costs. Transaction costs comprise the direct costs associated with specifying the centre's requirements (perhaps in the form of formal contracts), monitoring performance (information systems) and rewarding the agent (perhaps in the form of incentive payments). Agency costs comprise the indirect costs that arise because of devolution, in the form of a divergence between what the principal ideally wants from the agent, and what is actually provided.

Ouchi (1979) extends Williamson's model by arguing that the choice of optimal organizational form in a specific situation depends on two broad contextual considerations: the nature of the production process and the ability to measure outputs. Markets are optimal when knowledge of the production process is poor but outputs can be accurately measured – that is, when contracts can be readily written and performance monitored by observing outputs. Conversely, hierarchies might be preferred when knowledge of the production process is good but outputs are difficult to measure – that is, when behaviour can be readily controlled through rules of process. When information on both production process and output measurement is poor, the organization may have to resort to what Ouchi calls 'clan control', under which performance is determined by social and cultural norms rather than markets or bureaucracies.

Numerous other considerations might influence the choice of organizational form. For example, the nature of the uncertainty confronting an organization (both in demand for products and supply of inputs) might be an important determinant. The optimal choice is moreover likely to vary considerably between industries, and to change over time, as technologies, information systems and markets develop. Organizational form nevertheless defines a crucial context within which PM must take place. The PM literature is mainly concerned with a hierarchical organization in which some element of devolution has taken place. The rest of this paper therefore examines PM in this context. However, it is worth emphasizing that the strategic element of the PM process should in principle keep under review whether organizational form and processes remain appropriate.

Four components of PM

In this paper, we adopt the more recent strategic approach to PM. Our interest is therefore in *organizational* performance, and the extent to which purposive managerial action can contribute to such performance. Important early work in this area was undertaken within the OR tradition by Stafford Beer (1966), who emphasized the cybernetic nature of the management process. However, the most sustained academic thought on these issues has been undertaken by management accountants interested in organizational control (Otley, 1999). Their accounting perspective has led to an emphasis on financial aspects of performance, a shortcoming that is readily acknowledged in the literature. However, many of the models they have developed are relevant to all aspects of performance. We exclude from consideration here action that might influence the external environment, most notably in the form of marketing, and instead focus on actions that influence activity within the organization. There are then four broad categories of actions that constitute PM:

1. *formulation of strategy* to determine what constitutes performance;
2. development of *performance measurement instruments*;
3. application of *analytic techniques* to interpret such measures; and
4. development of instruments designed to *encourage appropriate organizational responses* to performance information.

The success of a PM system will depend on how well these four indispensable elements of the PM process are welded into a coherent whole. We now consider them in turn, in each case touching briefly on the existing OR contribution.

Formulation of strategy

As noted above, most PM endeavour takes organizational strategy and objectives as given, and seeks to develop managerial instruments within that framework. It pursues the 'inner control loop' of Figure 9.1. Yet in a rapidly changing and consumer-led environment, most organizations need continuously to reappraise and reformulate their strategy if they are not to fail. Particular challenges face the relatively new breed of organizations such as the 'dot com' companies where the environment can be particularly unstable and unpredictable, and where success is possible only if constant adjustments are made to strategy. In the public sector, organizations are required to reconsider their strategy following major policy shifts or changes in the political environment. A concern for strategy might also embrace organizational structure, incentive mechanisms and organizational culture, each of which might have important bearing on long-run performance. For example, a healthy organization in the private or public sector is likely to nurture an element of entrepreneurial ambition amongst its employees if it is to respond successfully to a changing environment (Osborne and Gaebler, 1992).

As Dyson (2000) shows, in principle OR has much to offer in the development of organizational strategy. However, numerous authors have bemoaned the traditional reluctance of OR to address strategic issues (Ormerod, 1997). Why should this be? A common theme amongst commentators critical of OR's absence from concerns of strategy is that – in contrast to the inner loop – the 'outer control loop' is by definition messy, unstructured and not amenable to quantification. The search for strategic threats and opportunities cannot be reduced to a mathematical programme, or be readily described in analytic terms, or even be easily distilled into coherent educational texts. This lack of structure is anti-pathetic to the mainstream OR tradition. Indeed, where attempts *have* been made to consider strategy, they have tended to be subsumed into easily measured aspects such as extent of diversification activity, rather than non-traditional metrics that focus on the strategies themselves (Murray and Richardson, 2000).

For this reason, the most promising tradition within OR likely to offer a strategic component to PM is probably represented by the flourishing variants of the 'soft' methodological approach (Rosenhead, 1989). The open-minded and eclectic philosophy underlying soft OR approaches is well suited to problems of strategy, for which the 'harder' OR tradition is rarely likely to be relevant. In particular, soft systems methodology has been specifically developed for use in ill-structured and messy problem contexts where there is no consensus about how to define the problem nor how to tackle it (Checkland, 1985). It is appropriate where complex organizational structures and processes are the norm, which will cer-tainly be true in the public sector, and also in many other institutional contexts. The embracing of 'soft OR' in the UK in the 1980s by the Oper-ational Research Society greatly enhanced the potential contribution of OR to the strategic aspect of PM.

Performance measurement instruments

The revolution in information technology has led to the potential for enormous improvements in the quantity, quality, timeliness and cost-effectiveness of data relating to performance. Yet in many organizations, although the potential for such data capture is recognized, the real-ity has often been that the systems structure and systems information made available to managers is partial, of poor quality and late. [. . .] The principle underlying such methods [as the Balanced Scorecard (Kaplan and Norton, 1992)] is that past success may not be a reliable indic-ator of future success. Instead, the methods seek out measurable aspects of current *process* that are likely to be strong indicators of currently unmeasurable future *outcome*.

In many respects, the practice of performance measurement has been led by the public sector, where the absence of financial measures of success naturally led to the development of multidimensional measure-ment instruments (Likierman, 1993). To date, there has often been an absence of theory to inform the development of public sector schemes, but the general principles adopted have been analogous to their commer-cial counterparts: namely, indicators of current process should capture aspects of unmeasurable future outcome. The added complexity is that there is often less consensus amongst public sector stakeholders as to what constitutes relevant outcome (Smith, 1996).

Prominent examples of public sector performance measurement schemes in the UK include the local government performance indicator system (DETR, 1999) and the NHS Performance Assessment Framework (NHS Executive, 1998). Characteristics of such schemes tend to be that they are incomplete (rarely capturing all acknowledged aspects of performance), prolix (comprising numerous indicators of performance) and opportunistic (measuring what is measurable rather than developing new systems for PM purposes). Possibly as a result of these weaknesses, it has hitherto been rare to find a performance measurement system completely integrated into the managerial processes of a public sector organization. The NHS Plan published in July 2000 seeks to remedy this by placing the NHS Performance Assessment Framework at the centre of NHS managerial attention (Department of Health, 2000). In a similar vein, the 'Best Value' system seeks to integrate a national performance measurement system into the strategic planning process in English local government (Audit Commission, 1999). Making these laudable objectives operational is likely to be a formidable challenge.

OR practitioners have often been central to the development of organizational information systems which are a key element in any PM system. Indeed it is instructive to note that the US Institute for Operations Research and the Management Sciences (INFORMS) defines OR and Management Sciences as 'the professional disciplines that deal with the application of information technology for informed decision-making'. The distinctive role of OR is often to examine the 'whole system' within which the information system must operate (Checkland and Holwell, 1998). The OR Society's development of the *European Journal of Information Systems* is testimony to the profession's central interest in this issue.

Analytic techniques

Performance data are frequently worthless until they are translated into meaningful signals of performance. For example, the accounting tradition is to convert activity data into measures of profitability. Hospitals might report activity in terms of average lengths of patient stay. However, such naïve approaches are in general woefully inadequate – and indeed irrelevant – for most purposes. The complexity of the modern organization has therefore led to the development of more sophisticated analytic techniques, designed to secure more sensitive measures of performance.

Broadly speaking, analytic techniques seek to understand the reasons *why* a particular indication of performance is observed. For example, in order to undertake a comparison of variations in the performance of hospital surgical departments, as measured by clinical outcome, it might be necessary to seek to gain an understanding of the extent to which variations in outcome are due to:

1. variations in *case mix*, or the characteristics of the patients being served;
2. variations in the *nature of resources being used* – poorer results may be the result of (say) an inappropriate mix of resources (such as an outdated configuration of capital stock);
3. variations in *priorities* regarding outcome – some providers may choose to place a greater emphasis on (say) quality of survival at the expense of (say) higher mortality;
4. variations in the *external environments* – for example, the contributions of other agencies, such as local personal social services, to outcome;
5. variations in *accounting treatments* – there may be some flexibility in the way that data are collected or recorded;
6. *data errors* – the quality of data might vary substantially between providers;
7. *random fluctuation* – many performance measures are highly vulnerable to such fluctuation, considered to be entirely outside the control of the provider;
8. variations in *quality of services* – usually the key performance measure to most stakeholders.

Two broad approaches to disentangling these sources of variation exist: cross-sectional and longitudinal. The cross-sectional approach seeks to understand a unit's performance data by examining equivalent data from comparable organizations, and is intrinsic to the benchmarking movement. The intention is to quantify the unit's performance (say, quality of service) relative to other organizations – after adjusting for all the other sources of variation not related to performance noted above. In contrast, the longitudinal approach looks at year-on-year performance changes in a single organization, and must inevitably be used when there exist no comparable units, or where comparison is highly problematic.

Intellectual effort has concentrated on the cross-sectional approach, although the extent to which senior management is interested in disentangling cross-sectional sources of variation may vary considerably,

depending on context. In principle, an interest in managerial performance suggests that the analysis should seek to adjust for all sources
of variation not attributable to managerial action. This is not always
achieved. For example, the early league tables of academic success in
English schools were published without correction for any of the above
types of variation, in spite of impassioned appeals from academics to
do so, and the existence of techniques to address the complex analytic
problem (Goldstein and Spiegelhalter, 1996; Mancebon and Molinero,
2000). On the other hand there may be good reasons for not adjusting
examination results – for example, there are legitimate concerns about
how any 'risk adjustment' should be undertaken. However, it is worth
noting that failure to treat devolved units (schools) fairly within a PM
system might lead to serious inefficiencies in system behaviour, such
as not being able to attract teachers to 'problem' schools (Milgrom and
Roberts, 1990a). In other words, an inadequate technical basis for PM
leads to an unsatisfactory *strategic* environment.

The intellectual challenge offered by the need to interpret crude performance measures has proved attractive to academics, particularly in
the realm of productivity analysis. Indeed the performance *measurement* function has become synonymous with performance *management*
in much of the literature, and an impressive battery of analytic techniques has been assembled. The *Journal of Productivity Analysis* is a good
source for recent developments. Within the statistics tradition, multilevel (or hierarchical) modelling has been dominant (Goldstein, 1995).
These techniques assume that outcome can be ascribed to a hierarchy
of causes (for example, the local authority, school, class and individual
in educational outcome), and seeks to ascribe measured outcome to
each of these 'levels'. Clearly these methods are most appropriate when
hierarchical institutional structures are in place.

The econometrics tradition has focused on the development of cost
functions and production functions, most specifically through the use
of stochastic frontier analysis (Morrison, 1999). These techniques seek to
model the determinants of 'performance' in line with economic models
of production. Specifically, they assume explicitly an element of inefficiency, which is modelled as a negative influence on performance. The
strength of such models is that their specification can be tested for consistency with theory, and they can be used to test hypotheses. Their
weaknesses are that they require extensive data, that they require possibly restrictive assumptions about model specification and that their
use becomes impractical with production processes of any complexity. In particular, one of the key constraints in PM is a lack of detailed

knowledge of the relationships and transformations between inputs and outputs.

Perhaps because of its linear programming formulation, OR researchers have concentrated their analytic efforts on the application of data envelopment analysis (DEA) (Charnes et al., 1995). DEA seeks to quantify the degree of technical inefficiency of a unit relative to comparable organizations in a multi-input, multi-output context. It has spawned a small research industry, and numerous applications have been reported (Hollingsworth et al., 1999). In many respects DEA represents the apotheosis of the performance indicator movement (Smith, 1990). However, reports of DEA being used in earnest in the PM process are rare. This may be because of its many practical weaknesses: model specification depends on user judgements, and cannot readily be tested; alternative plausible specifications might offer quite different results; DEA models are highly vulnerable to data errors; if the production process is at all complex, the ability of the technique to detect inefficiency is quite limited (many units are designated 100 per cent efficient).

Numerous other analytic techniques designed to help make sense of performance data exist. Cluster analysis is often used to identify 'families' of comparable organizations. Factor analysis might be used to reduce the number of dimensions of performance. In healthcare, various risk adjustment methodologies have been used to assess clinical performance, and analogous techniques have been developed in other industries.

Most of the approaches mentioned here are 'feedback' techniques: historic performance is analysed and the inferences fed back to managers for appropriate action to be taken. However, there is also an important role for what management accountants refer to as 'feed-forward' techniques that seek to alert managers to future outcomes. Various forecasting techniques offer important OR contributions in this respect. In particular, critical path analysis represents perhaps the apotheosis of the 'inner loop' control philosophy. If the objectives and structure of a project management problem are clear, then critical path methods offer important insights into optimal managerial responses to changed circumstances.

In spite of this impressive intellectual endeavour (or possibly because of it), competing analytic techniques frequently yield quite different estimates of relative performance (Iezzoni, 1997; Jacobs, 2001). This uncertainty can lead strategists to question their usefulness or veracity. Moreover, the techniques often appear to be impenetrable to the non-expert. For these and other reasons, their impact on policy appears to have been modest. One can point to some concrete influence – for example, a suite of analytic techniques is used by the UK water regulator to set performance targets for water companies and rewards are based on results (OFWAT, 1999); similarly, it has been suggested that future efficiency targets for the police forces may be devised in this way (Spottiswood, 2000). However, the concrete influence on organizational policy has not yet matched the impressive methodological advances made over the last 25 years.

Encouraging appropriate organizational responses

The most finely honed performance measurement system can prove worthless, even dysfunctional (for some stakeholders at least), if it is not embedded within an organizational environment that encourages appropriate behavioural responses on the part of managers (Milgrom and Roberts, 1992). [...] The intention should be to encourage appropriate system responses through the use of incentives and other managerial devices. Incentives can be designed or accidental.

Designed incentives seek to link a target to some aspect of measured performance, and attach a reward (or penalty) to performance achieved in relation to the target. Rewards can be at the individual or organizational level, and may be financial or otherwise. The important characteristic of 'designed' incentives is that the rules of the game are set in advance and are observable by all parties.

In addition to these purposive systems, there exist in most organizations 'undesigned' (or accidental) incentives. Many undesigned incentives arise from poor design of explicit incentive schemes, and can be seriously dysfunctional. They have been documented in a wide variety of research traditions. In synthesizing this experience it is possible to identify at least nine enemies of virtuous PM (Smith, 1995), listed here with some concrete examples from healthcare.

Tunnel vision

'Concentration on areas that are included in the performance indicator scheme, to the exclusion of other important unmeasured areas.'

Example: numbers of people on hospital waiting lists have hitherto preoccupied UK health-care managers as the primary process performance measure, possibly to the detriment of important but unmeasured dimensions of performance (for example, clinical outcomes).

Measure fixation

'Pursuit of success as measured rather than as intended.'

Example: a 5-minute waiting time performance criterion in Accident and Emergency departments led to the widespread employment of a 'hallo' nurse in UK hospitals, which is costly and may have no impact on any aspect of patient satisfaction or outcome, serving merely to meet the formal requirement for patients to be seen by a nurse within 5 minutes.

Sub-optimization

'The pursuit of narrow local objectives by managers, at the expense of the objectives of the organization as a whole.'

Example: use of the proportion of operations carried out as day cases as an indicator of surgical efficiency does not acknowledge the increased burden the use of day case surgery may place on agencies outside the hospital sector, such as social service departments or primary care.

Myopia

'Concentration on short term issues, to the exclusion of long term considerations that may only show up in performance measures in many years time.'

Example: curative services (as measured by short-term process) may be given higher priority than preventive services (as measured by long-term outcome).

Complacency

'Lack of ambition for improvement brought about by an adequate comparative performance.'

Example: an apparently middling performance when judged against others on surgical survival rates may appear satisfactory and inhibit the search for further improvement.

Misrepresentation

'The deliberate manipulation of data by provider staff, including "creative" accounting and fraud, so that reported behaviour differs from actual behaviour.'

Example: adverse patient satisfaction reports might be unaccountably 'lost'.

Misinterpretation

'Incorrect inferences about performance brought about by the difficulty of accounting for the full range of potential influences on a performance measurement.'

Example: is a high rate of 'did not attend' at an outpatient clinic due solely to the actions of the clinic, or do other, uncontrollable influences (such as patient characteristics) have an important influence?

Gaming

'Altering behaviour so as to obtain strategic advantage, particularly prevalent when targets are based on year-on-year improvements.'

Example: an NHS hospital might have 'gone easy' on performance against its NHS efficiency index (which was based on an annual percentage improvement) so that it did not receive unduly demanding financial targets in the future.

Ossification

'Organizational paralysis brought about by an excessively rigid system of measurement.'

Example: a low rate of inpatient readmissions has hitherto been considered an indicator of good practice – however, its use might inhibit the take-up of an efficient new technology that requires frequent readmission.

A common theme from these observations is that understanding the *full* impact of PM on the behaviour of individuals within the organization is a crucial element in the assessment of PM systems. The incentive stage is often seen as merely a matter of setting appropriate targets for managers. The adverse consequences arise because individuals and systems respond to undesigned as well as designed incentives. Formal targets are therefore likely to be seriously misleading unless viewed within the context of the entire set of incentives, both designed and accidental, that is built into the system. However, although the subject of a respectable accountancy tradition, most notably through the journal *Accounting, Organizations and Society*, the behavioural response stage in the PM process has been under-researched. Even where research *has* addressed the impact of performance measurement, attention has tended to focus narrowly on success as measured by the chosen performance measures themselves, rather than on any broader system-wide evaluation (Holloway, 2000). [...]

It is possible to hypothesize numerous other organizational responses that can be put in place to mitigate some of the adverse responses suggested above. To take just one example, 'complacency' can be challenged by basing targets to some extent on year-on-year improvement as well as cross-sectional performance – but this development may in turn increase the potential for 'gaming'. The appropriate response is therefore likely to be highly dependent on the organization and industry under scrutiny.

Thus the 'response' stage of the PM process is very under-developed, and has hitherto been the domain of organizational behaviour specialists, management accountants, psychologists and economists, most especially in the context of agency theory (Milgrom and Roberts, 1992). Nevertheless, as commentators such as Russell Ackoff (1978) have long argued, it is fertile territory for future OR activity, possibly in collaboration with other disciplines such as psychology, sociology and economics. This is a complex area that deserves further attention, especially as the nature of incentive structures will vary greatly depending on the environment in which the PM system operates. Most notably, appropriate responses may vary substantially between the private and public sectors, where the nature of the funding and resource mechanisms, motivations of employees, labour markets and the overall aims of the PM process can differ enormously.

Discussion

The literature on PM is eclectic, diffuse and confused. The definitive 'general theory' of PM remains elusive, and is unlikely ever to emerge. Important contributions can be found in fields as diverse as strategy, organizational behaviour, operations management, industrial economics and accountancy. A cursory search of any publication database reveals that most academic publications still use the expression 'performance management' in the context of HRM. This connotation of PM is of course often a vitally important determinant of organizational performance. However, it is only one of the potential contributory factors embraced by the broader definition of PM we adopt here.

Within the inner loop of PM described earlier, most activity to date has been concerned with performance measurement. In the corporate sector, numerous instruments along these lines can be found, amongst which the 'balanced scorecard' has been dominant. In the public sector, the instruments of performance *measurement* have developed rapidly, in the form of large information systems and sophisticated analytic techniques. However, in both sectors the more elusive behavioural aspects of PM have received comparatively little attention. We would argue that the entire PM movement might be compromised if this weak link in the feedback cycle is not afforded increased attention.

There have been some attempts to integrate performance measurement instruments into a more general framework of PM. For example,

Kaplan and Norton (1996a) show how the balanced scorecard approach might be viewed within the context of corporate organization, culture and environment and the recent developments in British healthcare and local government will merit careful scrutiny. The Business Excellence Model has also been widely used by the government in the context of the public sector (EFQM, 2000). However, such work is at best exploratory, and we have a long way to go before a satisfactory theory of PM can be put forward.

The outer feedback loop to strategy has received least academic attention (Milgrom and Roberts, 1990b). This is hardly surprising, given that the nature of such second order feedback is – almost by definition – likely to be unpredictable and difficult to formalize. Nonetheless, this should nevertheless not detract from its central importance, and there have been some notable, if isolated, cases of successful soft systems interventions. We can merely add our voices to the ritual to call for more research in this area (Langfield-Smith, 1997).

The discussion has suggested that contingent factors are likely to play a crucial role in determining optimal approaches to PM. This message has been a constant theme in the important management control literature (Otley, 1980), and suggests that specific characteristics might include

- the technology employed (for example, whether manufacturing or service sector; an established technology or one subject to rapid change);
- industrial structure (for example, monopoly or competitive market, public sector, regulated sector or competitive sector);
- organizational structure (whether imposed or chosen; the extent and nature of internal devolution);
- external environment (for example, demand uncertainty, supplier characteristics);
- strategy; and
- nature and relative power of stakeholders (shareholders, customers, citizens, patients, politicians).

In conclusion, we have shown that there is a distinctive OR tradition in each of the four categories of action that constitute PM. However, the contribution of OR has been partial and is less well-developed in some areas than in others. We have explored the reasons for this. In terms of *formulation of strategy*, the main obstacle relates to the 'messiness' of the process, which prohibits quantification and the neat formulaic approaches represented by traditional OR. The soft systems approach is far better equipped to deal with complex and unstructured situations than more traditional OR approaches, and we would expect to see further applications of this approach to PM issues emerge over time. OR has contributed substantially to the development of performance *measurement instruments*, especially in terms of organizational information systems and one must hope that operational researchers – with their broad systems perspective – will redouble their efforts in this area. Contributions to the development of *analytic techniques* in PM have come from a variety of disciplines, but the main emphasis in OR has been on the application of data envelopment analysis. Whilst the methodological approaches have become increasingly advanced, we have argued that, for a number of reasons (such as presentational complexity and a tendency to get different results from different techniques), the impact on policy has been rather modest. OR analysts are not alone in needing to devise better ways of communicating complex results to non-experts which could strengthen the link between research and strategic policy, and there may be a role for some generic social research to establish more effective links between the production of evidence and its influence on organizational policy and practice (Davies et al., 2000). The issue of *behavioural responses* to PM and the role of incentives has been relatively neglected by OR analysts to date. Their main focus has been on the use of target-setting to achieve specified goals and the narrow evaluation of the success of the PM system judged only in terms of the chosen performance measures themselves. Again, OR analysts are not alone in their relative neglect of this vital element in the PM system. There appears to be great potential for collaboration with other disciplines to make progress on this in future.

The need for PM arises most urgently in hierarchical organizational structures where no natural market exists, precisely the circumstances in which OR can make its most compelling contribution. There is therefore every reason to believe that OR has a great contribution to make to the PM movement, and one must hope that the discipline will seize the opportunities presented by the recent explosion of interest. It will be interesting to return in 10 years time to see whether that hope has been realized.[1]

Note

1. Acknowledgements – The authors would like to acknowledge helpful comments from Jacky Holloway at the Open University and two anonymous referees. They are in part funded by the UK Department of Health.

10
Marketing and the Bottom Line: Assessing Marketing Performance[1]

Tim Ambler

Introduction

Top management is naturally preoccupied with its firm's wealth. You might expect it to be equally preoccupied with generating it, but the astonishing fact is that, on average, meetings of top UK management devote nine times more attention to spending and counting cash flow than to wondering where it comes from and how it could be increased.[2] The monthly accounts commonly have just one line for the sales revenue from immediate customers. The rest concerns spending and storing it. The source of the cash flow – the end users – does not even get a mention.[3] The same pattern characterizes many other firms in the US and around the world.

Accountants seem to imagine that a pile of money will grow if only you count it often enough. Large companies are understandably concerned with certainty, but re-counting the same money does not make it any more certain. The same profit and loss account numbers are planned, budgeted, forecasted, then reforecasted, without getting the company any closer to the marketplace. The point is simple: if you want to know what your future cash flow will look like, investigate where it comes from – the market. A farmer whose livelihood depends on a river flowing through his land will be concerned with the upstream situation, especially if the river could be diverted to a neighbour's property. Companies should be just as concerned with their upstream wealth, and whether their competitors are diverting it. Our research shows that companies that look to the sources of cash flow – those that think about the market – are more profitable.[4]

Understanding where corporate wealth comes from involves questions like 'Why do consumers buy now?' 'Why might they buy more (often)?' 'Which other kinds of people might buy these products for other reasons?' In industrial or business-to-business sectors, who are the 'consumers' or 'end users'? The train driver has quite different interests from those who buy the trains.

Over the last 30 years, large firms have kept ahead through acquisitions (spending cash again) but not through organic growth.[5] In other words, these leaders, such as Unilever, have been paying too little attention to their consumers. They have been looking at the bottom line – net profits or shareholder value – rather than at what generates it. Analysts today are looking a little closer: survival depends on basic wealth creation. And wealth creation is exactly what marketing does.

The first edition of [the book from which this chapter is drawn] summarized a 30-month research project into 'Marketing Metrics', and this second edition update[d] that with research in the US. Similar work has also taken place in Australia, China, Scandinavia and Spain. [The purpose of the project was] to report best practice in marketing performance measurement, to show how it could be better and to share these concepts and language. The project sponsors recognized that, unlike accountants, marketers are divided by their understanding of even common words such as 'marketing' or 'brand'. And as well as clarifying the financial aspects of marketing, the project sought to pinpoint the non-financial factors that lead to business success. [. . .]

Is your metrics system good enough?

Too many companies dismiss the importance of marketing merely because they do not understand what it is. Take the Confederation of British Industry, for example. In their 1999 Fit for the Future campaign,[6] innovation and competitiveness are rightly extolled, but marketing and customers of any kind barely get a mention. Alec Daly, the campaign chairman, says, 'We want companies who find it difficult to innovate talking to those where innovation is inbred; companies who find it difficult to control cash, talking to those who find it second nature; and companies who need and want a step change in their competitive performance, exposed to those who have already done it.' This is all admirable, but it is also production oriented, and ignores the outside world – the market.

To evaluate marketing performance, we first have to clarify what marketing is

When people say 'marketing', they may mean any one of at least three things: 'pan-company', 'functional' or 'budgetary' marketing. The first, perhaps ugly, expression describes a holistic view of marketing: it is what the whole firm does, not just the 'marketers', to secure customer preference and thereby achieve higher returns for the shareholder. According to the UK publishing company EMAP, 'Marketing is central to our business here. This is a total marketing company and everyone is interested in marketing.'[7] Consciously or not, every business in the world engages in marketing in this primary sense and would be bankrupt otherwise.

Pan-company marketing is not an option but a necessity: firms engage in it whether they recognize marketing or not. The difference lies between those who consciously espouse this customer-oriented philosophy and those who market by happenstance.

'Functional' marketing is what marketing professionals do and this varies from business to business. It limits marketing to the activities of one department. Few small companies have marketing departments and even large firms, like the Unilever beauty products subsidiary Elida Gibbs, are dispersing their marketers throughout the organization. In terms of responsibility, some marketers are not accountable for profits whereas others see this as their main charge. Some have charge of product specification, pricing, sales and trade marketing functions, whereas others are seen as staffers, outside the main direction of the business.

The third definition sees marketing as expenditure which means largely advertising and promotion. When people talk of the 'return' on marketing, this is the marketing they generally mean. But the incremental gains from advertising and promotional expenditures should be evaluated in the context of the wider meaning of marketing.

The first definition of marketing is the most important. Only a minority of companies have separate marketing departments, or separate marketing budgets, but they all have end users to satisfy. We shall address the secondary meanings, but we are going to focus on maximizing marketing health throughout the whole company's business in order to maximize corporate wealth. 'Marketing' needs to include employees (the internal market) and innovation that impacts customers because these, possibly more than advertising and promotion, create new cash flow.

Even not-for-profit organizations, such as charities and national governments, have to be concerned with marketing in this sense. Without inward cash flow they would not be able to achieve their objectives. Marketing, in short, is the creation and harvesting of inward cash flow. [. . .]

Brand equity is an elephant

Brand equity, for many companies, is far their biggest and most valuable asset. It lacks the attention it deserves because it is not on the balance sheet and it is hard to measure. Furthermore, it is a relatively new, perhaps only 20-years old, part of the business scene.

The first step is to describe the beast from a number of points of view. Some commentators recognize the value of customers while others see brands and others again see competitive advantage. This gives the impression that we are looking at different things whereas in reality we are only looking at different aspects of the same thing.

Any complex asset, such as an industrial building, can be measured in all manner of ways. To make sense, we have to know the purpose of measurement. A glazier will want to measure windows when a tiler will want to measure the roof. Brand equity (the asset) is frequently confused with its value. Certainly the financial valuation is an important measure of a brand but it is only one measure and the number will differ according to the purpose of the valuation. A brand may not be worth the same to a seller as to a buyer.

The question arising, therefore, is how a firm should select the brand equity metrics in its particular situation. How it names this beast, for example, 'reputation' in a professional services business is secondary to understanding it and measurement is part of that. Managing brand equity is a crucial role of marketing and thereby of transferring value from the market to the shareholder. It is the upstream reservoir of cash flow, earned but not yet released to revenue.

Financial fallacies

Chief Executives, being busy people, are quite often appalled by all this marketing mumbo jumbo and demand a single number for performance or a single number for brand equity. The modern fashion is to bring everything down to shareholder value. That is what business is for and managing for value provides a universal framework.

That is a tempting road to take but [...] it is a dead end. Brand valuation is barely more helpful to brand management than putting a price on Mount Everest helps mountain climbing. Even those business issues that can be quantified cannot necessarily, still less usefully, be translated into financial numbers. The assumptions needed for the conversion go far beyond what the data can sustain. For example, we know that a psychological contract exists between a company and its employees. Maybe we can measure how strong that contract is, on a five-point scale from very committed to very uncommitted, but few companies would care to assign a financial value to that commitment.

Modern management uses measurement to plan improvement and to learn from what is actually achieved. With learning, change can be predicted and then tracked from period to period in a controlled way. More importantly, sharing the business model can give direction to the whole firm. Financial proxies lose the reality of that process.

The second major difficulty is that we cannot measure the future. Management needs to predict the outcomes of their actions, or their options, but they cannot be sure of them. A number of modern techniques such as customer lifetime value (CLV) and brand valuation are based on taking the present value of future cash flows. These techniques are useful for choosing between various investment choices, but not for reporting on the progress made by marketing to date. In a sense they take the credit for future marketing activities and thereby deflect attention from the situation today.

A final [...] danger of these techniques is tunnel vision. By projecting future income streams from current awareness, we do not allow for the wider world [...]. The narrower our understanding of our brand and its customers and competitors, the narrower and more risky is the tunnel of vision. Innovation by our firm and others will reveal opportunities beyond anything now in the plan. Marketing eyes need to open wider to these peripheral developments, some of which may prove important new sources of cash flow. CLV, for example, is distorted by working from the current customer database rather than what it might be. Shareholder value is a useful technique for determining how best to spend cash flow but it makes little contribution to understanding where it comes from.

Important as financial metrics are, they distort reality and provide the illusion of control. Cannabis does much the same.

Metrics evolution: How did we get where we are?

Reporting on marketing to top management is, or should be, an intimate part of the way a firm does business. A new metrics system should not be bolted onto processes which otherwise continue unchanged. Since the metrics need to reflect business strategy, implicit or not, it follows that they should evolve along with the strategy. What is discarded is almost as important, and often more controversial, than what is added.

It is probably not very sensible to step straight to an ideal metrics solution. Culture and metrics need to evolve together over time but that can be accelerated. [... As] the experience of leading companies shows, [the ...] process is influenced by the size and type of business and its competitive sector. Know the metrics your competitors see but do not limit yourself to those numbers. Otherwise, the knock-on effect of metrics on strategy is likely to result in copycat marketing.

The general pattern of development begins with top management having little appreciation of the significance of marketing metrics. As the recognition of the need for control measures grows, they turn to the accountants for basic financial indicators such as sales, costs and profits. It then becomes clear that these are retrospective. Indicators need to be closer to customer and competitor and therefore have to be non-financial such as behavioural (for example, loyalty, penetration) or what people have in their heads ('intermediate', for example, awareness and attitudes). Very soon, top management is swamped by numbers. Marketers are asked to select a dozen or so key indicators. The final stage, to which many aspire but few achieve, uses the full database of metrics and performance to select those indicators which predict future performance.

A practical methodology for selecting the right external metrics

[We now move] from how metrics evolved to how management can develop them. Changing even the external market metrics turns out to be a major problem.

Some of the troublesome areas include assembling a comprehensive database, gaining agreement that these are company-wide measures, not just private communication between the CEO and the marketing department, and the interaction between metrics and strategy. As noted above, to what extent should firms select the same measures as their competitors and where should they differ? Their source may dictate the choice: some research can only be gathered on a shared basis and other metrics are available only from the standard packages that market research agencies make available.

A single brand company operating in just one market has a much simpler problem than the multi-branded multinational. To what extent should metrics be standardized across all brands and territories? Different markets will want to use their own indicators, strategies will differ and consistent information may simply not be available from data suppliers.

Very large companies may, like Unilever, have scope for a department that specializes in marketing information, independent from their marketers. But for most companies, the only function in a position to integrate financial and non-financial marketing metrics is the finance department. In other words, turning over market research responsibility to the Chief Financial Officer (CFO) has much to commend it:

- Marketers are widely seen as selective and/or manipulative in the way they present information. Independence would add credibility.
- Metrics are not a high priority for marketers despite the increasing pressure for accountability. Most managers are tired of surveys and questions from business schools. Even so, we [the project researchers] were surprised by the low interest shown by marketers. With honourable exceptions (notably those who contributed to [the book *Marketing and the Bottom Line*]), marketers are more interested in making runs than scoring. Perhaps this is as it should be.
- Marketing information is widely dispersed in large organizations. Only part of it exists in the marketing department, even if there is one. The finance function routinely penetrates all sections of the firm.
- Alignment, or consistency, is needed across functional and geographic boundaries as well as across hierarchical management levels. Ways to evaluate the marketing mix (advertising, promotions and pricing) need to be consistent with evaluating marketing as a whole. Again, the finance function is skilled in assembling consistent information.
- The costs of marketing information should be treated in the same way as other management information costs, such as the management accounts, and not deducted from the marketing effort.
- The finance function should be within the marketing tent in order to understand where the cash comes from. Thankfully, we found the old adversarial relationship between marketing and finance to be largely a thing of the past, but direct responsibility for the numbers will help cement the partnership.

In short, this is a minefield but at least knowing where some of the mines are and their nature improves the odds of getting through. Standing still is not an option for long.

Using metrics to improve innovation performance

[We will now move] from the external marketplace to the two main internal indicators of marketing performance: innovation and employees. The mantra 'innovate or die' is broadly accepted but implementation is tough and finding the right performance indicators is even more difficult. Top managements want to monitor 'innovativeness' and yet few believe that key performance indicators (KPIs) provide the solution. Boots the Chemist, the UK's major health and beauty care retailer, appointed a director of innovation, but carries out little measurement beyond the number of product launches and the proportion of sales from recent launches.

The quality, not the quantity, of innovation is the crux. Indeed, many large firms today suffer from an excess of innovation, or initiative overload. The three phases of innovation (creativity, development and implementation) require different skills. Culture (the way things are done) and process (what is done) are merely enablers, not drivers.

3M very successfully uses just a few simple metrics, such as the proportion of sales due to recent innovations. Many other firms have copied these metrics, but few have succeeded because their leadership styles and cultures are different. The moral is that firms should get away from the detail and first measure these bigger picture variables.

Thus it is mostly a question of leadership and then culture rather than process. In large companies, much of the process gets in the way and should be dismantled. These metrics prove to be very similar to those used for assessing employer brand equity, that is, what the employees carry around in their heads about the firm they work for.

Employee-based brand equity

Some companies, and especially consumer service companies, see employees as their first customers. If management correctly markets to employees, then the front-line employees will take care of the external customers. In this perception, internal marketing becomes, for the top management, even more important than external marketing and therefore its own set of metrics is the more crucial. Whether 'marketing' includes employees is academic: synergizing human resource and marketing skills can bring rich rewards. The 'employer brand' concept helps these two functions to learn from each other. Tobacco company Gallaher, for example, sees marketing in pan-company terms and has marketing, sales and financial people working together in teams.

Which segment of 'customer' is the most important depends on when you ask the question. Employee issues will need to be addressed first and the end user will be satisfied last. Marketers will plan things the other way about, that is, start with the consumer, but the motivation of all the segments needs to be measured whichever way the company goes.

Many firms now measure employee indicators but few cross-fertilize employee and customer survey techniques and measures. They should. The relationship between employee and customer satisfaction is commonplace. BP found, unsurprisingly, a good correlation between the two. To some extent, employees can provide, far more cheaply and easily, proxies for external research though this needs careful quality control. In a service company especially, customers form their impressions, that is, brand equity, from their interactions with the employees.

Brand transparency

Beyond customers, competitors and employees, the contribution of other stakeholders to cash flow is indirect but it can be influential. [We examined] the interaction between the company and its shareholders, sometimes proxied by analysts. We researched the disclosure of market metrics to shareholders in annual reports.[8] Broadly, 85 per cent of company respondents agreed that shareholders are entitled to information about brand equity, often their most valuable asset. At the same time, few companies supply many metrics at all [. . . although to strengthen the acquisition and retention of investors] it is in the interests of companies that they should.

Assessing the performance of the marketing mix

Returning to the nitty gritty of marketing expenditure, most CFOs want to know the particular contributions from advertising, promotions and other parts of the marketing mix. This is not the return on marketing as a whole, which is meaningless, but whether increasing or decreasing the elements of expenditure increased profits and/or brand equity. Better still, they would like to know this ahead of time when budgets are set.

Few companies have fully grasped just how fundamental marketing and brand equity are and the consequential unwisdom of focusing on efficiency ratios such as ROI but they are moving in this direction. We found increasing emphasis on effectiveness (achieving what matters) rather than doing the wrong things more cheaply. Of course, companies want both effectiveness and efficiency and to measure the contribution of each element of the mix to those ends. [. . .]

While too many unknowns prevent this [evaluation] being a science, a few techniques [. . . are available to] help and, importantly, at least achieve internal consensus on the optimal expenditures. Furthermore, the different elements of the mix, for example, electronic media, have their specialist metrics which warrant separate consideration.

Getting the right metrics to the top table

Gaining this consensus requires both the top management and the specialist marketers to be looking at the same performance indicators. Shell calls it the 'line of sight'. Aligning metrics with strategy and aligning key measures both across functional silos and up and down the hierarchy sounds easy but it is not.

[However,] practical steps to bringing it about [can be taken]. Managers are wedded to the metrics they have and this type of change takes more time than they can divert from daily priorities, or think they can divert. Ship-to-ship transfer in the open ocean only looks attractive when you know your ship is sinking. Wait that long to modernize your marketing metrics and it is too late.

The fuzzy future

[We end on a cautionary note....] A business cannot be run just by numbers. Standardize everything and it will die. Shifting management bonuses to marketing metrics, as users of the Balanced Scorecard have discovered, may be unwise. Ignoring the indicators of cash flow and the reservoir called brand equity is terminal but so is ignoring everything else.

Top management should be wary of calls for oversimplification. We are not dealing with a hygiene matter where boxes can quickly be ticked before moving on. Indeed, using marketing metrics in a mechanistic way denies their very purpose. Even if the metrics are the same, the sources of cash flow – the reasons why consumers buy and might buy more – are the discussions which the metrics should trigger. The book [*Marketing and the Bottom Line*, from which this chapter is an extract] offers a design process to decide the right marketing metrics for your company, taking both the tailored and general points of view into account.

A certain fuzziness helps the firm achieve a great future.

Further reading

Aaker, D. A. (1991) *Managing brand equity*, New York: Free Press. See also (1996) *Building strong brands*, New York: Free Press.
Ambler, T. and Barrow, S. (1996) 'The employer brand', *Journal of Brand Management*, Vol. 4 (3 December), 185–206.

Ambler, T., Barwise, P. and Higson, C. (2001) *Market metrics: What should we tell the shareholders?* Centre for Business Performance, Institute of Chartered Accountants in England and Wales.

Anderson, E. W., Mazvancheryl, S. and Fornell, C. G. (2002) 'Customer Satisfaction and Shareholder Value', MSI Conference on Measuring Marketing Productivity, Dallas, October 3.

Arganbright, L. and Thomson, K. (1998) 'The buy-in benchmark', the Marketing and Communication Agency Ltd. and Market and Opinion Research International: London.

Barwise, P., Higson, C., Likierman, A. and Marsh, P. (1989) *Accounting for Brands*, London: London Business School and Institute of Chartered Accountants in England and Wales.

de Geus, A. P. (1997) *The living company. Growth, learning and longevity in business.* London: Nicholas Brealey.

Gale, B. T. (1994) *Managing customer value*, New York: Free Press.

Heskett, J. L., Sasser W. E., Jr. and Schlesinger, L. A. (1997) *The service profit chain: how leading companies link profit and growth to loyalty, satisfaction, and value*, New York: Free Press.

Keller, K. L. (1998) *Strategic brand management*, Upper Saddle River, NJ: Prentice Hall.

Marketing Leadership Council (2001) *Measuring marketing performance*, Corporate Executive Board: Washington DC (August).

Marketing Leadership Council (2001) *Stewarding the brand for profitable growth*, Corporate Executive Board: Washington DC (December).

Meyer, M. W. (1998) 'Measuring and managing performance: the new discipline in management', in Neely, A. D. and Waggoner, D. B., eds, *Performance measurement: theory and practice*, vol. 1, Cambridge: Judge Institute, xiv–xxi.

Mintzberg, H. (1994) *The rise and fall of strategic planning*, Englewood Cliffs, NJ: Prentice Hall.

Narver, J. C. and Slater, S. F. (1990) 'The effect of a market orientation on business profitability', *Journal of Marketing*, 20–35.

Perrier, R. (ed.) (1997) *Brand Valuation*, 3rd edition, London: Premier Books.

Rust, R. T., Zeithaml, V. A. and Lemon, K. N. (2000) *Driving customer equity: how customer lifetime value is reshaping corporate strategy*, New York: The Free Press.

Sahay, A., Kohli, A. K. and Jaworski, B. J. (2000) 'Market driven vs. driving the market: conceptual foundations', *Journal of Academy of Marketing Science*, 28(1), 45–54

Slater, S. F. and Narver, J. C. (1994) 'Market orientation, customer value, and superior performance', *Business Horizons* (March–April), 22–8.

Srivastava, R. K. and Shocker, A. D. (1991) 'Brand equity: a perspective on its meaning and measurement', Cambridge, Mass.: Marketing Science Institute, working paper no. 91–124.

The Conference Board (1999), 'Aligning strategic performance measures and results', Report no. 1261-99-RR.

Thomson, K. (1998) *Emotional Capital*, Oxford: Capstone.

Notes

1. Chapter 10 is based on the Executive Summary of the second edition of *Marketing and the Bottom Line*, by Tim Ambler, a book which provides a critical guide for marketers to make marketing fully accountable. The chapter captures the essence of the key messages in Ambler's book, which incorporates a framework for evaluation, numerous examples and recommendations for management action. To convey the flavour of the original material, we have retained the author's structure and headings; and key references from the original publication are appended as Further Reading.
2. Marketing Metrics project research with UK PLCs, December 1999.
3. Operational matters, supplies and suppliers, corporate governance, employee issues, interest, taxes, dividends and capital expenditure take far more time than the motivations of the ultimate customer. But these are all ways to spend, or at least count, the cash, not increase its flow.
4. We found a 0.25 correlation between customer orientation and performance. The precise figures vary but this result is similar to comparable studies.
5. David Cowans' Marketing Forum Presentation, Oriana, September 1999.
6. Website: www.fitforthefuture.org.uk
7. Quoted in 'The Role of Marketing', research report by KPMG, 1999, 7.
8. Tim Ambler, Patrick Barwise and Chris Higson (2001) 'Market Metrics: What should we tell the shareholders?', London: The Centre for Business Performance.

11

Open Performance Management: The Internet and Electronic Observability

Steve Little

Introduction

Information systems play a key role in the process generally described as 'globalization' and, as a consequence, new perspectives on performance measurement are emerging as new information and communication technologies (ICTs) are deployed to maintain cost-effective transactions across an emergent global production system. The relationship between new information technologies, globalization and social and economic exclusion has become a focus for discussion amongst a range of social theorists (Castells, 1996, 1997, 2000; Giddens, 1999; Ohmae, 1995). This chapter focuses on the implications of this new connectivity and observability for performance management.

The diffusion of ICTs from the advanced economies in which they were developed to a wider range of locations has allowed global production networks to emerge. Whether dealing with manufacturing or services or any combination of these activities, performance now reflects a more openly negotiated set of measures in an increasingly networked environment. The production chains linking peripheral sources of materials with a technologically advanced core can be managed and for the first time monitored closely and continuously. This integration of ICTs into business processes presents the opportunity to capture data on performance at a relatively low cost.

Tapping the data streams of the value chain from suppliers through to customers offers new insights into performance and also presents an opportunity to leverage the internal resources available for performance management with those of a wide range of stakeholders. Increasingly value is added through the organization of the data and information generated by the control and coordination of these processes, whether the volume and value of the transactions are high or low. For example, the e-business model of Amazon not only tracks each customer's on-line behaviour but also then prompts them with suggestions that may elicit further information. This both adds value to the transaction for the customer, and shapes further that customer's profile. This approach is equally valuable in business-to-business relationships within the production chain, and at high value. Aero engine manufacturers now sell the power from their engines as a guaranteed output for the customer, while the real-time monitoring of these engines in use through satellite technology delivers the level of performance measurement necessary to deal with the most demanding client. However, the monitoring by a firm also facilitates monitoring of the firm by customers, and while this tension has become acute in certain sectors, ultimately it offers a redefinition of performance measures in concert with a wider range of stakeholders.

Governments, or at least those with a commitment to democratic accountability, have found that their performance at local and national level is subject to new forms of electronic public scrutiny, most strikingly (at the time of writing) in the case of the logging of 'rendition' flights on the Internet and the subsequent calling to account. Top-down models of e-government based on traditional relationships are challenged by such public engagement. This new transparency offers advantages and disadvantages to both sides. In Britain, self-assessment of personal liability for income tax is an initiative which places a burden on taxpayers who in return expect a level of support based on their experience of 24/7 responsiveness in the commercial sector, not on their traditional transactions with government.

The remainder of this chapter sets out the wider context in which performance is now judged, and provides examples of both reactive and proactive responses to a new networked transparency.[1]

The context of new performance dimensions

Dicken (1998) describes a generic production chain drawn from Porter (1990) to analyse the dynamics of the global economy. In common with Porter's representation of the value chain the model allows the identification of the critical support activities which support each stage of value creation. Dicken separates these into flows of materials, personnel and information on the one hand and technology and research and development functions on the other. Innovative components of this system often emerge from smaller and medium sized specialist companies which in turn must take into account requirements determined by a global system. However, participants and contributors at all levels of specialization must respond to both severe cost competition and shorter product life cycles in which to recover investment. Product differentiation and customer support can maintain demand for goods and services and maintain premium prices for them.

Many established companies have responded to the competitive pressures on their cost-base by shifting towards the higher value end of the production chain. Such a shift makes the distinction between products and services less obvious. It also leads to an intensification of knowledge requirements since a focus at this end of the chain requires closer adjustment to cultural variation among users and customers. This pursuit of higher value activities can be seen in both new and established forms of production, as with the examples of new e-business models and established aerospace companies.

Once an organization begins to operate in an external information space, its own performance becomes exposed to external scrutiny and benchmarking becomes an activity undertaken by consumers and consumer groups, as described by Naomi Klein (2000). Klein argues that there is a shift in focus by what were formerly manufacturing organizations, hollowing out material production through outsourcing and replacing it with a form of cultural production intended to maximize intangible values. She argues that the apparent global expansion of high profile brands is in fact accompanied by the progressive subcontracting of all functions except the management and development of the brand itself. This represents the logical end point of outsourcing strategies facilitated by both a reduction of transaction costs and the alteration of the relative advantages and economies of size. These changes place intellectual capital leveraged by technology at the core of business. Brands are becoming the carrier of the core values and emotional capital of what were once physically extensive organizations that have been reduced to sets of networked relationships.

The Internet now represents a key communication base for social and political movements and freedom of access to it is increasingly regarded as part of broader freedom of expression (Reporters Without Borders, 2006). As the skills and awareness of the new monitoring capability have diffused a reverse panopticon has been created, in which formerly peripheral locations can shadow the developments at the 'centre' and can develop a capability set of their own that can be electronically inserted into the broader pattern (Little and Grieco, 2008, Forthcoming).

The global deployment of brands therefore creates global exposure, increasingly exploited by the campaigns targeting high profile brands. As noted above, entry into a global electronic space brings the prospect of profiling and monitoring of and by external stakeholders. Campaigns which challenge brand identity have emerged from within organizations, as with the 'Walmartyrs', employees of retailers Wal-Mart reporting their work experiences,[2] as well as from the traditional labour movement and broader social campaigns. The emergence of a countervailing meta-brand in the form of the logo of the fair trade movement represents the cooption of the approach by its critics.

Even where value chains and networks operate across a range of jurisdictions actions can be monitored relatively easily in the electronic form. The complex coordination afforded by the global ICT structure has been mirrored by a counter-coordination initially within labour movements traditionally concerned with communication. The traditional long distance coordination among dockside workers was supported by a website which proved critical to these efforts during the Liverpool Dock dispute of 1995–1998 (Bailey, 2006). South African activists have leveraged their skills in international mobilization developed during the apartheid era to develop Internet campaigns in collaboration with social movements around HIV and health issues. More traditional workplace concerns are also being pursued through this technology uniting workers for Volkswagen from Germany, Brazil and South Africa in campaigns over pay and conditions, with grass-roots activists circumventing the position of the union hierarchy. Equally significant is the organization of the consumers of the goods and services produced by transnational systems. The growth of the Fair Trade movement is one consequence of such monitoring, where traditional consumer perceptions have been leveraged by the electronic environment in which organizations now operate. All of these movements present challenges to the definitions of performance and related goals espoused by commercial organizations.

Open performance monitoring: cases and examples

The interaction between company strategy and stakeholder campaigns shows evidence of both conflict and synergy between the internal perception of priorities and objectives for performance, and the dimensions of performance seen as critical by external constituencies. This interaction increasingly takes place in cyberspace, and the following examples represent both the process that supported the discourse and an archive of action. The examples here involve two high value global industries – pharmaceutical and aerospace.

Example I: The pharmaceutical industry: Defence and counter offensive

The life-saving technology provided by the pharmaceutical sector has attracted particularly close attention from consumers. Pressures on 'big pharma' from wide-based social movements of the vulnerable are having their effect. The concessions made by pharmaceutical companies over the pricing of AIDS drugs in Africa represent a triumph of political pressure over legally defined intellectual property rights which undermine the logic of existing company strategies.

Not surprisingly, the pharmaceutical industry provides examples of how definitions of performance and value have been contested for some time.[3] For every 5000 to 10,000 compounds screened by the testing process, only some 250 will become lead candidates for clinical trials (Bernard, 2002). Of these as few as five drugs will enter clinical testing, with only one likely to achieve approval for use at the end of the three phases of clinical trial. Much of the protected licensed period will have elapsed before this drug is sold into a market in which governmental and private medical insurers are becoming increasingly concerned about cost inflation. Once the protection expires, other cheaper manufacturing locations are able to produce generic substitutes for the original proprietary product.

The high attrition rates at every stage and the need for the recovery of vast costs means that companies are searching for increasingly elusive 'blockbuster' products. There are failures in use and controversies over value, efficacy and cost. The world wide vice-president of GlaxoSmith Kline (GSK) was reported as claiming that most drugs work on less than 50 per cent of patients for a variety of reasons (Connor, 2003). In this context, strategies for reducing the costs of such uncertainties are sought. The strategies sought include the involvement of low cost manufacturers and the accommodation of the generic market in profit models and the use of brands to maintain the value of a drug in the face of generic substitutes.

Global electronically facilitated pharmaceutical production networks are emerging to challenge older integrated single company chains. However, this same global electronic technology has allowed the emergence of more transparent meta-governance forms (Grieco et al., 2003) with the stakeholders now including governments and regulators plus the ultimate end users of the products. With the advent of globalized information technology, the drug development process is increasingly forced to accommodate the concerns of the ultimate stakeholders – the users of the drugs and those with the conditions and diseases targeted by global drug manufacture.

In the developed economies, the use of certain drugs is also being monitored beyond the formal regulatory processes. For example, on 13 October 2002 a television broadcast on the anti-depressant Seroxat used the BBC website to elicit responses to the programme from users of the drug. These are now incorporated into an article in the *International Journal of Risk and Safety in Medicine* available online (Medawar and Herxheimer, 2003/4). In response the *British Medical Journal* website provided a review article defending the class of drugs, selective serotonin re-uptake inhibitors or SSRIs, to which Seroxat belongs. It argues that the benefits of these drugs outweigh any problems (Cowen, 2002). A Seroxat Users Group website was available to promote the follow-up Panorama programme 'Seroxat: e-mails from the edge', which was broadcast on 11 May 2003 and this site continues to carry campaign information.[4]

The model of intellectual property being promulgated as a global standard through the World Trade Organisation (WTO) Agreement on Trade Related Aspects of Intellectual Property and Public Health (TRIPS) agreements and the WTO is the one favoured by the major international pharmaceutical companies. However, the advent of the AIDS crisis in both developing and developed countries during the 1980s led to campaigns and actions which, in key cases, have achieved the political neutralization of intellectual property rights. The TRIPS agreement makes provision for the 'compulsory licensing' of protected drugs under emergency conditions. Such production is intended for use only in the country of production; however, many countries affected by AIDS do not have the necessary production facilities and inevitably drugs are acquired as unauthorized 'grey' imports. In April 2001, in the face of concerted campaigns in both real and cyber space, 39 pharmaceutical companies withdrew from a legal action in the South African courts. This intended to use TRIPS rules to stop South Africa from importing or producing these cheap versions of patented AIDS drugs. Their withdrawal in effect, surrendered intellectual property to which they were legally entitled in the face of globalized political opposition. After failing to negotiate drug discounts from multinational patent holders, Brazil, Thailand and Cuba also opted to manufacture generics representing a clear challenge to the basis of the larger patent system. The 20-year market monopoly under TRIPS has been neutralized.

This monitoring of the global pharmaceutical industry demonstrates how distributed technology can provide a monitoring and mobilization device which widens stakeholder participation. It also forces companies to re-evaluate their understanding of performance in both financial and social terms by adding a meta-regulation by the wider stakeholder community to the governmental regulation of this industry's activities.

Example II: SARS collaboration and synergy

The campaigns around the AIDS crisis have led to an opening up of governance and meta-governance of the life science universe and this has had positive results in other areas. The rapid formulation and coordination of a global response to disease was demonstrated by the highly distributed discourse around severe acute respiratory syndrome, or SARS. From early 2003 the Centers for Disease Control (CDC) Atlanta and the World Health Organization provided online information on the progress of SARS.[5]

Both the US Department of Defense Global Emerging Infections Surveillance and Response System (DGEISR) and Asia Pacific Economic Cooperation (APEC) websites continued to provide monitoring and a world SARS map remained available from the Indian company maptell.com for several years after the outbreak abated. During the crisis it was possible to compare the reactions of various national governments by visiting the heath ministry websites of, among others, Singapore, Taiwan and Australia (Little and Grieco, 2008, Forthcoming).

It is clear that the big pharmaceutical companies and big governments such as the United States have become aware of the vitality of the negative image they have invited by permitting the development of institutional structures which preclude the world's poor having access to essential treatment. There is a growing awareness in business generally that the end user has the ability to organize globally in respect of product markets and in government that policies can be monitored and challenged.

The collaborative and synergistic response to the SARS outbreak and the continuing collaboration over a potential avian influenza pandemic demonstrates that a positive response to initially threatening interventions can be advantageous, and that ICTs have revolutionized the speed and extent of such collaboration.

Example III: Aerospace – inclusion and incorporation

Aerospace is a sector in which the external perceptions of stakeholders have been incorporated into the product development cycle to improve performance and sustain relationships. This phenomenon is more often associated with customer engagement in fashion-oriented consumer goods and has grown from a model of 'viral marketing' in which information is distributed surreptitiously through the social networks of potential customers (Kharif, 2000).

Boeing has a history of successful incremental development within successive technologies (Gardiner, 1986; Little, 2004). The impact of computer-aided design on the cost of development is evident in comparison between its products from the 1970s such as the Boeing 757 airliner, with the 1960s 727 model. By the 1990s, the design programme for the Boeing 777 model was highly dependent on integrated computer-aided design systems which allowed significant savings in development time, and reduced the need for physical models and prototypes to a minimum (Sabbagh, 1995).

The relationships between aerospace manufacturers and aircraft operators have been close for decades, the development of aviation milestones such as the Lockheed Constellation and the Boeing 747 Jumbo Jet were instigated by key customers. The Boeing Company has distributed elements of both manufacturing and component production to target markets, with, for example, Japanese and Australian contributions providing risk-sharing and promoting buy-in. Airbus, as the principal rival to Boeing, is now moving to establish an assembly line in China, currently the major growth market for mid-sized commercial aircraft (Matlack et al., 2006).

However, as with the emerging networked pharmaceutical production system, there has also been a shift in the understanding of the relationship between prime and sub-contractors and customers. A combination of an increasing variety of leasing arrangements and the deployment of satellite technologies now allows the real-time remote monitoring of aircraft in flight. As noted earlier, this has led to new forms of customer support, and a refocusing from sales of aircraft, aero engines and spares to the support of 'power by the hour' in order to capture a more stable income stream.

The Boeing 'world design team' is a concept that extends the relationship with traditional stakeholders to the end users of the company's products, including frequent flyers, accessing an additional perspective on performance.[6]

In addition to assembling some 35 per cent of the new 787 from its plants around the US, Boeing also draws upon key foreign companies, both in their home locations and, in the case of Toray (a former textile company now expert in new generation composite materials), in their US-based operations. The software necessary to the coordination of these complex contributions is also a joint development with Dassault Systemes of France.[7]

The aerospace value chain has developed to capture suppliers and customers and to enrol both into the performance management system. At the same time, the extension of the electronic coordination developed for manufacture to the broader user base allows the incorporation of customer feedback into the design system itself.

Conclusion: performance as the managing of presence and expectations

When Manuel Castells described 'informational politics in action' (Castells, 1997, p. 333) he was concerned with one aspect of globalization: the reliance on simplified mass communication. He argued that this inevitably reduces the complexity of political discourse. However, elsewhere in the same volume he describes very different and complex forms of electronically mediated communication by dissident minorities: Zapatista rebels in Mexico and Militia groups in the USA. The former have become the commonly accepted symbol of the use of the Internet as a base for political opposition from the marginalized. In response, the Mexican Federal Government has established its own presence in cyberspace itself, providing links to independent and critical coverage of events via its own website (Little et al., 2000).

Other governments have sought to operate in this new space, and the concept of 'e-government' is attractive in terms of economy, efficiency or both. SMS text has been trialled in conjunction with traditional postal voting in an attempt to increase voter turnout for UK local government elections. A more adventurous initiative is the on-line electronic petition system developed for the Scottish parliament. Griffin (2003) argues that this innovation allows central monitoring of devolved government functions.

However, other events have shifted the expectations of stakeholders further. The Hutton Inquiry (Hutton, 2004) posted UK Cabinet papers normally kept secret for 30 years on the Internet, along with the full transcripts of the evidence presented to the enquiry. This opening up of the political process via Internet presentation permitted the global external audience to make their own assessments of the relationship of the official judgement to the detailed evidence. The narrow legal interpretation of Lord Hutton was subject to a broader political judgement, just as the narrow interpretation of intellectual property by 'big pharma' was compromised by wider political mobilization around the affordability of HIV treatments.

Elsewhere, however, pharmaceutical companies have engaged with campaigns and pressure groups where these coincide with their interests. For example, the adoption of Roche's Herceptin for the treatment of advanced breast cancer followed campaigns in several jurisdictions. The manufacturer became involved directly in one campaign through the canvassing of patients to elicit their support for the use of the drug for early stage cancers, expanding the potential market, but also exposing a wider range of patients to the significant side effects (Boseley, 2006).

The aerospace sector offers a paradigm for more open and positive engagement with feedback, solicited and unsolicited, through acknowledgement of its potential value. This co-option of potential criticism and its incorporation in performance monitoring represents a more robust response which fits with Bray's formulation of a 'New public relations' (Bray, 2005). This allows communication to the stakeholders from the workers directly involved in an issue, relying upon their understanding of the company's goals and values to shape their presentation. Control is replaced by monitoring and mentoring in order to achieve a more direct and honest engagement with stakeholders.

An organization adopting Bray's approach faces two challenges. The first is to identify and interpret the external responses and reactions that reflect an adverse external perception of the organization. The second is to identify and lead appropriate changes in corporate objectives and emphasis that will meet such a potential shortfall in performance and legitimacy. The research challenge of these changes in practice is to develop means to capture effectively diverse grass-roots initiatives, and to track changes in corporate systems, which would allow meaningful access to stakeholders within the dual constraints of commercial confidentiality and data protection legislation.

Notwithstanding these constraints, this chapter has illustrated some of the potential offered by the integration of ICTs into business processes, for innovative and affordable global performance management research.

Notes

1. The web addresses in this chapter were correct at the time of access in July 2007.
2. See http://walmartwatch.com (accessed 27 July 2007).
3. See, for example, http://www.global-campaign.org/bigpharma.htm (accessed 27 July 2007).
4. See http://www.seroxatusergroup.org.uk/ (accessed 27 July 2007).

5. See CDC at http://www.cdc.gov/ncidod/sars/ and the WHO at http://www.who.int/csr/sars/en/ (both accessed 27 July 2007).
6. See http://www.newairplane.com/ (accessed 27 July 2007).
7. See http://www.newairplane.com/ (accessed 27 July 2007) and follow the 'Launch 787 DreamLiner Site' link for details of systems and structure suppliers.

12

An Accounting and Finance Perspective on Performance Measurement and Management

Stan Brignall

Introduction

Managers measure organizational performance in order to improve it; thus performance measurement is part of the process by which management teams manage the improvement of performance over time. Management is a team activity involving people with different functional responsibilities and disciplinary backgrounds, yet traditionally most measures of organizational performance have been financial in nature. More recently it has been widely recognized that what constitutes organizational success is multifaceted and means different things to different people. Accordingly, models of multidimensional performance measurement and management have been developed which have fostered an interest in the interrelationships among different performance dimensions, including those between financial and non-financial performance measures.

In what follows we shall first consider in more detail the conventional view of accounting and finance performance measures. Three main functions of such performance measures are then identified and considered in turn: financial performance as a business objective; financial performance measurement as a tool of financial management; and finally as a means of motivation and control. In the next section we examine the criticisms of mainstream financial performance measurement and consider how new financial performance metrics aim to overcome them. Yet these new metrics are only a partial answer to these criticisms so in the penultimate section of the chapter we consider some of the models of multidimensional performance measurement that have led to new directions in strategic performance management, such as Kaplan and Norton's 'strategy mapping' concept. In the final section of the chapter we consider the current problems and challenges for research in these areas.

The conventional view of the accounting and finance role

Traditionally, organizational performance management has focused on the use of quantitative financial measures of primary interest to shareholders. In most writings on accounting and finance it is usually assumed that managers of for-profit organizations should be trying to maximize their shareholders' wealth. The extent to which this actually happens and the conditions for ensuring it does so are the subject of Agency Theory (Jensen and Meckling, 1976). Jensen and Meckling argue that asymmetries of information among owners and managers cause control problems which can be tackled by the use of incentives such as share options to encourage managers to align their goals with those of shareholders. In this context, accounting information such as that in the annual report and accounts enables shareholders to monitor the performance of managers to see if they are acting in shareholders' interests. In a similar fashion, managers use management accounting systems to control the actions of subordinates in the process of management control.

One of the strengths of financial performance measures is that accounting uses a common measure of wealth: money. But the use of a common measure still leads to two different yet complementary approaches to measuring stocks and flows of money: cash versus accruals accounting. Under cash accounting, money received and paid by a business entity in a period is recorded; if cash received exceeds cash paid out, the cash balance will increase. Under the accruals approach income earned from sales made in a period (but not necessarily received in the period) is matched against expenses incurred (but not necessarily paid) in the same period: if income exceeds expenses a profit is recorded for the period. In practice an organization's books and accounts record its transactions in a double entry book-keeping system culminating in the usual periodic financial statements: the profit and loss account, the cash flow statement and the balance sheet. Of the three, the balance sheet is prime as the cash balance at the end of the accounting period and the profit earned in the period are inserted into the balance sheet to enable it to 'balance' the entity's liabilities against its assets.

The use of ratio analysis of an organization's financial statements to interpret its performance was arguably pioneered by the Du Pont Company. In for-profit organizations, the ultimate focus is on an organization's return on investment (ROI), which can be expressed as a percentage and compared to the organization's cost of capital to see if the return is adequate. In not-for-profit organizations, such as charities, the ultimate purpose is not to earn a profit but to provide a service while breaking-even (or remaining within agreed budgetary limits). In the public sector there is a greater range of objectives: some organizations may be expected to earn a real rate of return on their assets while for others it may suffice to break-even. ROI is a ratio, where the numerator is profit before interest and taxes (per the profit and loss account) and the denominator is total assets (taken from the balance sheet). This ratio can be decomposed into two other ratios (return on sales and asset turnover) that in turn can be further decomposed in a 'pyramid of ratios' covering various aspects of cash flow/liquidity, operating profit and asset utilization.

Under Generally Accepted Accounting Practice (GAAP), an organization's assets are usually recorded in its balance sheet at their historical cost less depreciation to date, although long-lived assets may sometimes be revalued to correct distortions caused by inflation. GAAP is an amalgam of various accounting disclosure requirements, which in the UK include Companies Act legislation; the London Stock Exchange listing requirements; International Financial Reporting Standards (IFRS); the recent Operating and Financial Review, requiring forward-looking information; and so on. In addition, there are guidelines on Corporate Governance regarding such matters as the separation of the roles of chairman and chief executive, the role of non-executive directors and so on. Finally, to ensure that agency relations between owners and directors are not breached, there is the role of the external auditor who is paid to give an opinion as to whether the accounts give a 'true and fair view' of the financial performance of the firm during the relevant accounting period (typically a year). One might hope that with such a multiplicity of rules and regulations the information contained in a company's accounts might be relied upon. But various scandals in recent years, such as Enron and Worldcom in the US, have led to further tightening of the regulatory regime such as the American Sarbanes–Oxley Act 2002, which required considerable investment in assuring the independence of the audit function, evaluation and disclosure of internal controls concerning financial reporting, and enhanced protection, compensation and sentencing provisions.

In the foregoing, it has been assumed that the level of analysis for financial performance measurement and subsequent management is the whole firm (or a group of companies). This need not be the case. For example, one might wish to measure the performance of an individual employee, of a product, a department, a factory or a division. Equally, one might be trying to measure performance from outside the organization (as an investment analyst, perhaps) or within the firm, perhaps as a senior manager wishing to evaluate the performance of a division of the firm. Obviously, differing levels of analysis and viewpoint will lead to differing requirements for financial information. Many commentators have identified three main functions of financial performance measurement and management:

1. As a (some would say *the*) primary objective of a business organization.
2. As a tool of financial management.
3. As a means of motivation and control.

We will consider each of these in turn in the next three sections.

Financial performance as a business objective

The financial objectives of a for-profit business primarily concern the needs of the external suppliers of debt and equity capital. External financial reporting in adherence to GAAP is intended to meet these needs. In particular, the business's residual owners (shareholders) seek to hold their agents (managers) accountable for the performance of the assets entrusted to them. The economic returns to shareholders comprise dividends and capital gains on the market value of their shares. Such total returns for a period may be divided by the share value at the start of a period to calculate the rate of return. This may be compared with that available elsewhere from investments with a similar degree of risk, as rational investors expect to be compensated for bearing higher risk by receiving higher returns. As earnings determine what can be paid out as dividends in the long run, shareholders and their agents (such as investment analysts) are primarily concerned with financial measures like earnings, earnings per share (EPS), dividend yield, dividend cover and ROI.

Financial performance measurement as a tool of financial management

Various commentators have argued that an organization's accounting and finance function performs three main activities (Johnston et al., 2002; Mouritsen, 1996; Sheridan, 1994):

1. transaction processing: the sales, purchase and general ledger main-
   tenance and periodic external reporting, principally to shareholders.
   This is the traditional domain of financial accountants.
2. financial management: management of the cash flow and Treasury functions such as hedging foreign currency risk, making capital
   structure decisions (the appropriate mix of debt and equity finance),
   calculating tax liabilities and formulating dividend policy. In many
   large organizations today most aspects of financial management will
   be carried out by finance professionals, not accountants.
3. management accounting: the provision of regular and ad-hoc financial information to senior and operational managers such as
   information for planning, control and performance measurement,
   including capital investment decisions, budgeting and ratio analysis.
   In twenty-first century organizations this is the area most involved in
   performance measurement and management.

This third broad area of activity is therefore of most importance to the
subject of this chapter: the contribution of accounting and finance to
organizational performance management.

Financial performance measurement as a means of motivation and control

Divisional performance measurement

The origins of accounting go back into history, examples including lists
of inventories compiled for the Egyptian pharaohs. In the middle ages
'stewardship accounting' involved stewards – managers of large estates
owned by the nobility – giving an annual account of their stewardship
of the estate while the owner was absent, attending the King's court.
The development of double-entry bookkeeping by the fifteenth-century
Italian monk Luca Paccioli not only improved the accuracy of the recording of accounting transactions but also facilitated the preparation of the
primary financial statements.

More recently, Johnson (1991, 1992) identifies three stages of American industry's development over the past century and a half, each
successive stage being associated with greater complexity and consequent control problems. In the first stage, manufacturing organizations
took the form of individual factories producing relatively homogeneous products with performance measurement systems (PMSs) focused
on the collection of financial and non-financial data about the efficiency of input/output activities in conversion (production) processes.

In the second stage, where companies grew by vertical integration, PMSs focused on measures of margins, net income and ROI, a notable example being the Du Pont Corporation and its pyramid of ratios introduced in 1912.

In the third stage, product diversity increased and the range of markets expanded, causing control problems such as increased organizational size and complexity and highlighting the limits to a manager's span of control. In response, many organizations created *multidivisional* (M-Form) structures, as seen at General Motors (Chandler, 1962; Sloan, 1964; Williamson, 1975). Under the well-recognized heading in management accounting textbooks, 'divisional performance measurement' (DPM), between the 1930s and 1990s conventional divisionalized PMSs in the US and UK used accounting budgets, standards and targets ('budgetary control': cf. Solomons, 1963) to control operating processes in the pursuit of strategies leading to the achievement of organizational goals (Nanni et al., 1990). Divisionalization was intended to optimize local decision making (by decentralization), enable closer monitoring of operations and act as a training ground for future top managers. Necessary conditions for divisionalization to succeed were a reasonable degree of divisional autonomy and independence and performance measures that accurately and unbiasedly reflected the true performance of the division and its manager.

So, mirroring practices at the overall organizational level, in DPM senior managers use budgetary control to hold divisional managers accountable for those costs, revenues and assets for which they are responsible and which are controllable by them ('managing by the numbers' – cf. Ezzamel et al., 1990). However, the evaluation of divisional financial performance has been affected by the distorting effects and the erosion of divisional autonomy caused by transfer pricing (Hirshleifer, 1956) where divisions trade with each other. Another problem is arbitrary overhead allocations (Thomas, 1975) in which costs are moved away from the point where they can be controlled. Accordingly, it is true to say that the use of budgetary control has been controversial, with worries about local optimization but corporate sub-optimization; high monitoring costs because of the problem of information asymmetry between corporate and divisional managers and the duplication of activities in separate divisions.

Many writers, such as Hopwood (1972), have also emphasized the importance of appropriate management control style in preventing behavioural problems in budgetary control. Broadly, the findings in this area state that subordinate participation in budget setting is desirable up to a point, beyond which they may take the opportunity to build in 'budgetary slack' to make budgets easily attainable. More controversially, in response to the perceived problems of budgetary control, the 'beyond budgeting' movement (Hope and Fraser, 1999) has recently advocated the abolition of budgeting. This does not imply an abandonment of formal planning but rather a preference for a more decentralized, participative approach to managing the business, with greater emphasis on rolling forecasts, key financial and non-financial performance indicators and 'stretch' targets often based on 'world-class' benchmarking.

In the history of DPM there have been continuing technical debates over the rival merits of ROI and residual income (Amey, 1975; Tomkins, 1975) as financial performance measures. Most commentators are now agreed that residual income, under which a cost of capital charge is deducted from operating profit, is conceptually superior to ROI as it explicitly allows for risk. A positive residual income is the accounting equivalent of a positive net present value, implying a return in excess of the risk-adjusted cost of capital that adds to shareholder wealth (known as the 'Fisher–Hirshleifer model'). In contrast, it has been noted that ROI in any 1 year rarely corresponds with a company's (or division's) economic rate of return (Edwards et al., 1987; Kay, 1976; Peasnell, 1982). In recent years the residual income concept has been further refined by consultants Stern Stewart into measures of Economic Value Added (EVA®). Other forms of modern shareholder value-based management include Shareholder Value Analysis (SVA: cf. Rappaport, 1987), which identifies seven 'drivers' of shareholder value and advocates selection among strategies using net present value analysis. However, whilst such developments in unidimensional financial performance measurement are to be welcomed, they are still open to criticism.

Beyond financial measures for management control

The use of financial measures as the predominant mode of controlling operations has been widely discredited in recent years by management accountants (for example, Johnson, 1992) and operations management experts such as Thomas Vollmann (Dixon et al., 1990). Whilst financial measures are obviously relevant to shareholders, they are less so to other stakeholders such as customers, employees and suppliers, so devising PMSs appropriate to these other stakeholders with differing information needs is now a major problem for PMS designers. The problems with traditional performance models are not confined to their financial orientation, as they also fail to recognize the move in advanced economies from manufacturing to services as the dominant employer and source of GDP (Fitzgerald et al., 1991). In addition, not all organizations are conducted for profit, and there is a large public sector in most advanced economies that is increasingly adopting or adapting private sector approaches to performance measurement and management. An example here is the use of the Balanced Scorecard (Kaplan and Norton, 1992) as a basis for the UK National Health Services' Performance Assessment Framework (Department of Health, 2001).

To this broadening in the types of organization must be added new forms of organizational structure (Bartlett and Ghoshal, 1993). Typically these involve a move away from the traditional M-Form to flatter, more responsive and flexible organizational structures in response to increased competition and the greater pace of change (Lee, 1992; Otley, 1994; Srikanth, 1992; Whittington et al., 1999). For example, many large organizations such as the UK National Health Service have many of the characteristics of network organizations (Thompson, 2003), while others engage in joint ventures and strategic partnerships to help them beat the competition. Business process re-engineering has been an important facilitator of many such structural changes (Hammer, 1990) with which management accountants have not always engaged (Johnston et al., 2002). One other recent feature of organizational change is the rise of shared service centres (SSCs), a variation on outsourcing. These have recently included financial shared service centres (Herman and Brignall, 2005), usually focusing on the centralization of the transaction processing aspects of the accounting and finance function (see above).

Eccles and Pyburn (1992) argue that one of the major limitations of using financial performance measures such as EPS and ROI as measures of organizational performance, is that they represent lagged indicators which are 'the result of management action and organizational performance, and not the cause of it' (p. 41). Organizational success, according to Emmanuel and Otley (1985), depends not only on the achievement of financial measures, but on how well the organization adapts to the environment within which it exists. Success, they argue, is a multidimensional concept, and the aspects that relate to that success change over time and between one individual or group in the organization and another. 'To attain satisfactory levels of performance in each of these dimensions requires the control and co-ordination of a variety of activities carried out by different people' (Emmanuel and Otley, 1985, p. ix). Writing in 1989, Turney and Anderson argued that the accounting function had largely failed to adapt to the new competitive environment which organizations increasingly found themselves in, where continuous improvement in the design, manufacturing and marketing of a product (or service) were key requirements of success. In particular, where strategies depend on non-financial dimensions of performance, their success may be endangered by what they described as 'obsolete' and 'restrictive' accounting control systems. The development of strategic management accounting (SMA) goes some way to recognizing the deficiencies of traditional PMSs by adding information on competitors' costs and market shares (Simmonds, 1983). However, SMA fails to recognize the importance of non-financial determinants of competitive success such as quality and flexibility, and the views of customers and other stakeholders such as employees and suppliers. On the basis of the foregoing arguments, traditional financially based systems of PM seem in need of change, even where they incorporate new financial metrics such as EVA®.

New directions in strategic performance management

Some 20 years ago the publication of 'Relevance Lost' (Johnson and Kaplan, 1987) irrevocably changed the management accounting and performance measurement (PM) agendas. Among their many criticisms of management accounting at the time, Johnson and Kaplan argued that its research and practices were dominated by the needs of external financial reporting to shareholders. This, they said, had led to inaccurate product costing systems in which overheads were attached to product units based on simplistic volume bases such as direct labour hours. Whilst these costs were accurate in aggregate, and so adequate for external reporting, they were highly inaccurate for individual products where they made differing demands on manufacturing resources other than direct labour, which was in any case a fast-diminishing proportion of total costs. In response, Cooper (1987) and Cooper and Kaplan (1988) proposed the development of activity-based costing systems in which overheads with similar causes were grouped into activity cost pools, each with its own individual 'cost driver'.

Johnson and Kaplan also recognized that traditional financial performance measures are not only too late and too aggregated but also poor proxies for aspects that matter to customers like quality and delivery speed. Subsequently, various multidimensional PM models have been developed, such as the Balanced Scorecard mentioned earlier, the 'Performance Pyramid' (Lynch and Cross, 1991) and the 'Results and Determinants Framework' (Fitzgerald et al., 1991), and rapidly adopted by companies wishing to stay ahead of the competition. Since then research has focused on how such models can best be implemented (Brignall, 1993; Fitzgerald and Moon, 1996b; Kaplan, 1994; Kaplan and Norton, 1993) and developed into tools for strategic performance *management* (Brignall and Ballantine, 1996b; Kaplan and Norton, 1996a). The goal of strategic performance management in the early twenty-first century is to improve organizational performance by recognizing the chains of cause and effect among different dimensions of performance in an organization's Strategy Map (Brignall, 2002; Kaplan and Norton, 2000, 2001). Identifying such chains of cause and effect is difficult (Brignall, 2002; Nørreklit, 2000) but might help meet the differing needs of multiple stakeholders (Doyle, 1994), such as shareholders, customers, employees and environmental activists (Brignall, 2002). In addition, as many of these models concentrate on performance management at the strategic business unit (SBU) level, it has been recognized that measurement of performance at the corporate level will affect what is measured elsewhere (Goold and Campbell, 1987). Accordingly, it has been proposed that the models' scope needs to be broadened (Brignall and Ballantine, 1996a) to reflect this within a contingent approach to information systems design (Brignall, 1997).

Such holistic approaches to strategic performance management and improvement are now being aided by developments in information systems and technologies. Integrated organization-wide information systems such as Enterprise Resource Planning (ERP) systems have greatly expanded a manager's span of control, enabling the removal of hierarchical layers of management also associated with the implementation of Business Process Redesign (Hammer, 1990). The vendors of ERP systems claim they provide 'an integrated solution for planning, executing, and controlling business processes *horizon-tally* across the value chain. [...] SAP R/3 (the market leader) integrates processes such as sales and materials planning, production planning, warehouse management, financial and management accounting, and HR management' (Norton and SEM, 1999, p. 38). ERP brings together performance information from all of a business's main functions, including accounting and finance, and so facilitates the adoption of multidimensional approaches to performance measurement and management. This may be further enhanced by Strategic Enterprise Management Systems (SEMSs) such as that developed by SAP, which has the Balanced Scorecard at its heart (Brignall and Ballantine, 2004).

Conclusions: changes and challenges for research and practice

While many companies still use traditional financial performance measurement systems, the current state of the art has moved on. New financial performance metrics such as EVA® have made an impact but do not remedy all the old problems. In particular, they have little to say about non-financial aspects of performance. The advent of better-integrated information systems such as ERP is enabling organizational change and reconfiguration (Scapens and Jazayeri, 2003) in which multidimensional performance models such as the Balanced Scorecard and their associated strategy maps bring together financial and non-financial performance information with the aim of meeting the needs of a wide range of organizational stakeholders. In this scenario, financial performance measures are still necessary but are only part of the measurement and management of organizational performance.

The changes in performance management detailed in this chapter have caused changes in the roles of management accountants and finance professionals. Better computerized accounting information systems such as ERP and shared financial service centres (Kris and Fahy, 2003), for example, have freed accountants to add value and play a greater role in the decisions of the senior management team (Brignall et al., 1999; Johnston et al., 2002), including the strategic measurement and management of organizational performance in a context of constant change. Organizational change is omnipresent and management accountants are playing their part in it, supporting performance improvement initiatives like activity-based costing, process change (Brignall et al., 1999) and benchmarking (Holloway et al., 1999).

These developments are being studied by accounting academics using a wide variety of research methods, such as action research, surveys and case studies, whether of a cross-sectional or longitudinal nature. This research spans the various research paradigms identified by Burrell and Morgan (1979) and embraces many different theories, such as actor network theory (Briers and Chua, 2001), agency theory, complementarities theory (Brignall and Ballantine, 2004; Milgrom and Roberts, 1995), contingency theory (Brignall, 1997), institutional theory (Burns and Baldvinsdottir, 2005) and structuration theory (Giddens, 1984; Scapens and Macintosh, 1990). And, increasingly, accounting researchers are working in interdisciplinary teams, reflecting their recognition that organizational performance is a multidimensional construct that is managed by teams of managers from different functions and disciplines.

This wide variety of approaches to management accounting research, including research on performance measurement and management, has not been without its critics. A recent example of 'paradigm wars' was encapsulated in a 'debate forum' edited by Kari Lukka in the *European Accounting Review* (Vol. 11, no. 4, 2002). In this debate, various accounting academics (Hopwood; Ittner and Larcker; Luft and Shields; Lukka and Mouritsen) take issue with Zimmerman's (2001) criticism of the state of empirical research in management accounting and his assertion that only economics-based (and, hence, positivist) management accounting research has any status or potential. At the risk of oversimplification, for the purpose of this chapter it is probably sufficient to note that the writers cited above all call for a variety of approaches to management accounting research, rejecting Zimmerman's call to privilege economics-based research.

Indeed, accounting is an unusual discipline in that it draws its theoretical background largely from aspects of behavioural science, sociology and organization theory, but its models are drawn from neo-classical economics and mathematical theory. This diversity arises because although accounting models are constituted through numbers, these numbers reflect human agency, which is driven at least in part by organizational rules, norms and incentives deriving from the three dimensions of social structure proposed by Giddens (1984): signification, legitimation and domination. Accounting reduces the complexity of organizational transactions and in attempting to quantify them, represents these transactions in codified forms. The choices made in the construction of these codes reflect the social and political relationships of the model builders and the distribution of power throughout the system.

Because of these unique characteristics, accounting studies are ideal candidates for the use of multi-methodology and multi-theory research. Empirical research methodologies are needed to establish the mathematical relationships between the distributions of accounting estimates but to understand and explain the behaviour and complex organizational characteristics that have produced those estimates, an interpretative analysis is more compelling. The problem the accounting researcher faces then becomes one of reconciling the philosophical and, in any actual research study, the political differences underlying two different research methodologies. Yet despite the problems, we would expect a continuation of management accounting research from a wide variety of paradigms, methodologies and theories, including more multi-methodology and interdisciplinary work.

13
Measuring and Managing Intangible Assets

Bernard Marr[1]

Introduction

Intangible assets such as knowledge, brands, relationships, organizational culture and intellectual property are primary drivers of competitiveness and organizational performance in today's global economy. Indeed, it is estimated that the level of US corporate investment in intangible assets, around $1 trillion annually, is at about the same level as investment in tangible assets (Lev, 2002). A survey commissioned by the consulting firm Accenture confirmed that most executives around the world believe that intangibles are critical for the future success of their businesses (Molnar, 2004). However, at the same time, most of them also agreed that their approaches to measuring and managing intangibles were either poor or non-existent.

Not only commercial enterprises are stressing the importance of intangible assets; not-for-profit organizations as well as governments are also recognizing the importance of their intangibles. In order to position itself at the forefront of the knowledge economy, the European Union, for example, aims for its membership countries to invest a minimum of 3 per cent of their GDP into research and development (R&D) initiatives. In the United Kingdom, the then Prime Minister Tony Blair wrote in the 2003 Trade and Industry White Paper that intangible resources such as creativity and inventiveness are the greatest source of economic success but that too many firms have failed to put enough emphasis on R&D and developing skills (DTI, 2003). The UK's Secretary of State for Trade and Industry added that increasingly it is the intangible factors that underpin innovation and the best-performing businesses (DTI, 2004).

In the view of the Brookings Task Force on Intangibles, the large and growing discrepancy between the importance of intangible assets to economic growth and the ability to identify clearly, measure and account for those assets is a serious problem for business managers, investors and governments (Blair and Wallman, 2001). However, in this chapter I will argue that 'objective' measurement of intangible assets poses huge challenges and for that reason makes objective reporting and accounting for intangibles difficult, if not impossible. I therefore argue that today's focus should be on assessment of intangible assets for organizational decision making and learning. I will outline some of the key reasons for measuring intangible assets and then discuss the limitations of traditional measurement as well as their resulting implications for measuring intangibles. First, however, it is important to define such assets.

Defining and classifying intangible assets

The growing importance of intangible assets is underpinned in theoretical terms by the resource-based view of strategy (discussed further in Chapters 4 and 14). The most valuable resources are those that provide a unique competitive advantage, supporting the organization's core competencies. For the purposes of this chapter, it is safe to equate 'intangible assets' with 'intellectual capital', 'knowledge assets' or 'intangible resources'. But if something is intangible, how do we know it is important?

Intangible assets are non-tangible resources that are attributed to an organization, support its competencies and thus contribute to delivery of value to its stakeholders. They are not confined to factors that differentiate 'leading edge' companies or characterize specialized 'knowledge firms', but core generic elements that should not be taken for granted. The following typology of human, structural and relational resources, makes this clear:

Human resources: the workforce's skill-sets, depth of expertise and breadth of experience; their aptitudes, attitudes, flexibility, loyalty and motivation. These resources leave when staff go home at night, go on holiday, resign or retire.

Relational resources: the relationships between the organization and outside organizations, groups and key individuals – customers, alliance partners, pressure groups, investors and so on. Both formal (or contractual) and informal relationships are crucial to the effective operation of modern, frequently global, supply chains. Brand image, corporate reputation and service or product reputation reflect the quality of such relationships; and today's public services and governments are just as aware of their reputation as commercial firms.

Structural resources: key factors studied by researchers from many disciplines, including the ways organizations are structured, their core processes and policies, information systems and databases, leadership and management style, culture and values, routine practices and intellectual property (often protected by law).

Clearly 'intangible assets' will encompass the critical success factors in many organizations, whether commercial or not-for-profit, and form the basis for capabilities and core competencies. However, it is important to remember that their significance as value drivers is context-dependent and will change over time, and in conjunction with the tangible resources with which they interact.

Reasons for measuring intangible assets

Measurement has a central role in our society. However, when it comes to intangible assets, the reasons why we endeavour to measure and what we consider as measurements have some distinctive features.

One key reason for measuring intangibles comes from the widening gap between what companies disclose in their traditional annual reports and what really matters to their stakeholders and wider society. Driven by the ever-increasing gap between book and market value, many people have called for improved transparency in organizational reporting. This movement has led to initiatives especially in Europe, where a series of projects funded by different European Governments and the European Commission helped to produce guidelines on how companies can produce improved reports disclosing the value of their organizations in general, and their intangible assets in particular. Legislation has been passed to improve transparency in organizational reporting. In Austria, for example, the government has introduced a law that makes it compulsory for all universities to report on their intellectual capital. At the same time new accounting guidelines are being developed and standards are being questioned and reviewed. With the introduction of the International Accounting Standards and stricter compliance regulations, more emphasis will be placed on accounting for and reporting of intangible aspects of organizational performance.

Measuring intangible assets can also influence people's behaviour. Measures focus attention and direct our behaviour, especially if they are linked to compensation systems. Many companies realized that by basing their compensation systems only on financial performance they encourage short-term thinking. In order to counterbalance the short-term focus, attempts are being made to balance financial measures with measures for intangibles, which are often seen as leading indicators and drivers of longer-term performance.

A third reason for measuring intangible assets is for strategic learning purposes. In order to make decisions about the future strategic direction of an organization, it is critical to understand the drivers of performance and competitive advantage. And more often than not it is the intangible assets that are the key drivers of future performance and sustainable competitive advantage. For that reason organizations require mechanisms that allow them to assess their intangible value drivers.

These reasons for measuring intangibles represent three more general purposes of performance management:

1. *Reporting and compliance* – measures are used to communicate with the organization's stakeholders, be it either voluntarily or compulsorily for compliance reasons.
2. *Controlling people's behaviour* – measures are used to motivate people and change their behaviour. Measures are used to quantify the value of compensation for compliance with objectively verifiable standards of work (Austin, 1996, p. 193).
3. *Strategic decision making and organizational learning* – measures are used to inform management decisions, to challenge strategic assumptions and to continuously learn and improve.

Each of these categories has its limitations, as discussed below.

The limits of measurement

Measurement has been defined as the assignment of numerals to represent properties (Campbell, 1928). It is seen as the assignment of particular mathematical characteristics to conceptual entities in such a way as to permit an unambiguous mathematical description of every situation involving the entity and the arrangements of all occurrences of it in a quasi-serial order (Caws, 1959). Whereas these technical definitions have been especially useful in disciplines such as physics, in management we talk about organizational performance measures. These have been defined as parameters used to quantify the efficiency and/or effectiveness of past action (Neely et al., 2002).

An *effectiveness* measure of performance reveals how many units of the purpose were accomplished. It is a response to the question, 'Are we doing the right things?' On the other hand, an *efficiency* measure of performance reveals how many units of the purpose were accomplished per unit of resources consumed. It is a response to the question, 'Are we doing the things in the right way?'

(Mason and Swanson, 1981, p. 15)

Often the emphasis in measurement is on quantifications and numbers, with the intention to provide us with an *objective, uniform and rigorous* picture of reality.

However, this seems to work better in some areas than in others. We find it easy to quantify things like profits, return on assets or cycle times and we can count incoming orders, service visits or rejected deliveries. Some important characteristics though are not easily counted or quantified. Aspects like organizational culture, our know-how, the strengths of customer relationships or the reputation of our brand are all inherently difficult, if not impossible, to measure. In turn, they may be particularly challenging to manage and change.

Albert Einstein, one of the great thinkers of the 20th century, emphasized that 'Not everything that can be counted counts, and not everything that counts can be counted.' The problem arises when we use numbers to measure things that can never be measured in a traditional 'measurement' sense. Boyle (2001) writes:

We admit that numbers can't reveal everything, but we try to force them to anyway. We tend to solve the problem by measuring ever more ephemeral aspects of life, constantly bumping up against the central paradox of the whole problem, which is that the most important things are just not measurable. The difficulty comes because they can *almost* be counted. And often we believe we have to try just so that we can get a handle on the problem. And so it is that politicians can't measure poverty, so they measure the number of people on welfare. Or they can't measure intelligence, so they measure exam results or IQ. Doctors measure blood cells rather than health, and people all over the world measure money rather than success. They might sometimes imply almost the same thing, but often they have little more than a habitual connection with one another. They tend to go together, that's all.

(p. 30)

When it comes to the more intangible aspects of our organizations we must rely on proxies or indirect measures (Blair and Wallman, 2001). And these often only capture a fraction of what we want to measure. Organizations are often prepared to sacrifice rich realities in order to achieve alleged rigour and clarity through measures. The American social theorist Daniel Yankelovich said that 'The first step is to measure whatever can be easily measured. This is OK as far as it goes. The second step is to disregard that which can't be measured or give it an arbitrary quantitative value. This is artificial and misleading. The third step is to presume that what can't be measured easily isn't very important. This is blindness. The fourth step is to say that what can't easily be measured doesn't really exist. This is suicide.' [2] The implications of these measurement limits are discussed below.

Implications for the use of measures

The mechanical objectivity that we often aim for in organizational measurement serves as an alternative to personal trust (Porter, 1995). Measures provide a moral distance and make knowledge impersonal in a quest for objectivity. Objectivity is required for the first two measurement purposes outlined above:

1. Reporting and compliance requires objectivity and in many cases even external auditing. Organizations use external auditors to provide an objective verification of the numbers they put in their annual reports. And some companies such as Shell, for example, go even further and also use external auditors to audit their numbers on environmental and social performance.
2. Using measures as a means of controlling people's behaviour necessitates objectivity, especially if measures are linked to reward and compensation.
3. In both scenarios personal trust is replaced with what are believed to be objective numbers. There is, in fact, a complex relationship between trust and quantification. For example, when farmers and merchants didn't trust each other to provide the right amount of wheat, they could use the standard barrel stuck to the wall of the town hall, which would measure the agreed local bushel (Boyle, 2001). It has been demonstrated that throughout history we were often able to win greater trust for claims by giving them quantitative expressions (see, for example, Gooday, 2004; Porter, 1995). Nevertheless, it is dangerous to replace trust with measures, since the big assumption

is that we can measure everything that matters. The fact is that what matters the most in modern-day organizations is difficult to measure and often impossible to express in meaningful numbers.

Examples abound of the dysfunctional consequences of measurements replacing trust. One comes from food standards. Similar to the farmer and merchants using the standard barrel, today, we rely on standards to facilitate international trade. The US food standards, which are administered by the Department of Agriculture, specify that, for example, a 'US Fancy broccoli stalk' has a diameter of not less than two and a half inches, or that the colour of a Grade A canned tomato is at least 90 per cent red.[3] The same applies to the European Union, which specifies the standard bend of a banana or the size and shape of apples. We presumably all agree that what really matters are the intangible factors such as the taste and nutritional quality of this produce, but these are again difficult to measure. The standards are almost entirely based on the easy-to-measure physical appearances of the produce. And, in fact, studies have found that this has encouraged farmers to use dangerous pesticides, not to increase yields, but for the only purpose of maintaining cosmetic appearance to meet such standards (Sugarman, 1990).

The case against the mechanistic use of accounting performance measures was powerfully made by Thomas Johnson and Robert Kaplan (1987) in *Relevance Lost*. While accountants are working hard to regain relevance, many organizations are exploring alternative routes for providing more relevant information in the form of voluntary reports. There is a clear requirement for such numbers-focused performance measurement to enable organizations to report to external stakeholders or comply with regulations and laws. The problem arises when such measures are used to entirely different purposes.

Measures can be used to influence what people do. As Agency Theory suggests, employees (agents) rarely have the same objectives as the owner or instigator of a business (the principal) (Holström, 1977; Ross, 1973, and see Chapters 9, 12 and 14). Thus the principal puts measures in place that will guide the behaviour of the agent, and therefore align their objectives. However, this model can only work if the principal can measure all critical dimensions of performance. More often than not, a gap exists between what we *want* to measure and what we *can* measure.

Meyer argues that 'people will exploit the gap between what we want to measure and what we can measure by delivering exactly what is measured rather than the performance that is sought but cannot be measured' (Meyer, 2002, p. xxi). This causes dysfunctional behaviour and sub-optimal performance. Take the example of a sales manager, whose main objective it is to visit customers in order to introduce a set of new products, which these customers will hopefully want to buy. The optimal performance comprises some easily measurable dimensions, for example, number of sales visits and amount of time spent with customers; as well as some difficult-to-measure dimensions of performance, for example, quality of the sales visits and preparation for the visit. However, too often organizational measurement systems only concentrate on the aspects that are easy to measure, which regularly causes sub-optimal performance. In the above example, it is easy to see how sales managers would make many unproductive or unnecessary customer visits at the end of the month just to make up the numbers. (The classic example is referral interviews in a government agency, where number of interviews is measured whereas the quality of referrals is not; see Blau, 1963.)

The creation of an environment in which trust is replaced with numbers to increase control is socially divisive. Imposing control measures on people activates the self-centred drives of organization members and as a result, rank, territoriality, possessiveness, fear and anger will dominate social relationships:

> Compensating people for performance on multiple measures is extremely difficult. Paying people on a single measure creates enough dysfunctions. Paying them on many measures creates even more. The problem is combining dissimilar measures into an overall evaluation of performance and hence compensation. If measures are combined formulaically, people will game the formula. If measures are combined subjectively, people will not understand the connection between measured performance and their compensation.
>
> (Meyer, 2002, p. 8)

The view that no measurement system can be designed to preclude dysfunctional behaviours is far from new (Ridgway, 1956). Austin (1996) makes a very strong case that measurement for controlling people's behaviour does not work in today's organizations. Instead, we should focus our efforts on what he calls 'informational measurement' used for learning and strategic decision making.

Measuring intangibles for strategic decision making and learning

So far, we have noted some general challenges of designing performance measurement systems that achieve the objectives set for them. Most systems still focus on tangibles. What happens when intangibles are the key to success? I argue that the main reason for measuring intangibles is for decision making and learning. For this, we also need to extend the meaning of measurement to not only focus on the narrow sense of measurement used in physics or mathematics. I propose that the term *performance assessment* is used, rather then 'measurement'. It is, therefore, not only about quantification and the assignment of numerals. To quote Dee Hook, founder of the Visa credit card network, 'in years ahead, we must get beyond numbers and the language of mathematics to understand, evaluate and account for such intangibles as learning, intellectual capital, community, beliefs and principles, or the stories we tell of our tribe's values and prosperity will be increasingly false.'[4] Performance assessment is about the systematic collection of information to enable comparison of a given situation or status relative to known objectives or goals; it enables organizations to evaluate performance. Inherent in it is the notion of value. Performance assessment can, therefore, not only take the form of numerals but also the form of, for example, written descriptions, symbols or colour codes; indeed, all that is required is for those involved to share the code.

As we all know, the perceived value of something is ultimately in the eye of the beholder. For some of us, a Rolex or Patek Philippe wristwatch is valuable and we are willing to pay several thousand dollars or euros to own one. We might see the value in its mechanical perfections, in the craftsmanship, in the design or we might value it as a prestige symbol. If we only want a device to tell us the time, a simple Timex or Swatch would do the job perfectly. This means, in order to assess the value of anything, we need to understand the value system and, in this case, how the watch fits into this value system. The same is true for organizational resources and especially for its intangibles for which there is rarely a secondary market to determine a financial value. For example, the know-how of building engines is essential for Honda but of little value to a financial services firm.

This is why we have to start with the value creation logic or business model of any organization. This puts the intangible resources into the context of the strategy and allows organizations to create a cause-and-effect model of how these intangibles contribute to firm performance.

It provides us with the necessary strategic information of how value is created and what resources and competencies matter; it therefore supplies the starting point for an evaluation. It also allows us to take into account the context-specific value and interdependencies between resources. For example, it is impossible to value a brand name without taking into account all the other important factors, such as reputation, people, processes and so on. Cases such as Enron have shown how a brand name can disappear overnight if the supporting resources such as reputation and customer relationships fall away.

Clearly any social context it is hard, if not impossible, to capture the whole truth in one measure. I prefer therefore to use the word *indicator*, rather than 'measure'. An indicator 'indicates' a level of performance, but it does not claim to 'measure' it. If, for example, we introduce a new indicator to assess customer satisfaction levels, this indicator will give us an indication of how customers feel; however, it will never 'measure' customer satisfaction in its totality.

Assessing performance and selecting indicators

Many books on performance measurement written for practising managers assume that all relevant performance data is either already available or can be easily collected. Unfortunately, for intangibles this is mostly not the case. Even though organizations might have a lot of performance data, they often lack relevant and meaningful information about their intangible assets. Instead of relying on data that is available in existing IT systems, organizations should first identify what they would really like to assess, and then compare it with what they have already in place. This allows them to see how close they can get with their existing indicators to what it is that they want to assess.

In many cases, relevant, reliable and cost-effective data are simply not available. Given the opportunity to collect data specifically for the purpose in hand (rather than as a by-product of the requirements of regulators, auditors or top management), innovative approaches to designing the performance indicator set and performance management system are also desirable. One way to get a good idea about how to assess performance in a particular area is to ask the people that are most closely involved in this area. Assessing performance for strategic learning means that people have to believe in the indicators and use them to inform their decision making. Therefore, involving people (both internal and external) at all stages is critically important, in order to establish their perceptions both about relevant indicators of performance, and relative performance using those indicators (Boyd et al., 1993; Ketokivi and Schroeder, 2004; Venkatraman and Ramanujam, 1987).

The importance of perceptual data indicates that qualitative methods have much to offer, both to the manager designing systems for evaluating the performance of intangible assets (human, relational and structural resources) and to academic researchers. Large-scale surveys and questionnaires still have a place in this field, and Internet technology can reduce the cost and enhance their attractiveness considerably (see, for example, Dillman, 1999). Numerical and non-numerical data can be obtained in order to, for example, rank competitors, evaluate the service delivery or organizational culture, or assess the level of relationships with different suppliers. But understanding perceptions about intangible variables requires rich, often unstructured and highly nuanced data.

Space limits preclude detailed discussion here of methods but the following have already been tested and found useful in this field (Marr, 2006; and see also Denzin and Lincoln, 2005):

- Participant and non-participant observation, including the use of video and audio recording, narrative and pre-formatted reports (Russ-Eft and Preskill, 2001).
- In-depth interviews – guided conversations with varying degrees of pre-established topics (Yin, 2003), generating both verbal and non-verbal data (for example, body language).
- Focus groups – facilitated group discussions usually on pre-determined topics, often involving the same people on several occasions so trust is established and self-censorship of views is reduced.
- Mystery shopping, giving the researcher the same experience as 'real' customers – ideal for eliciting staff attitudes, availability and clarity of information and so on.
- Peer-to-peer assessment – where employees assess each others' performance (anonymously or openly), providing direct feedback to improve their practice. (This approach is intrinsic to internal benchmarking, and '360 degree feedback' appraisals.)

Conclusions

In this chapter, I have argued that the measurement of intangible assets – human, relational and structural – poses significant challenges if it is approached from an accounting or objective reporting perspective. Because of the difficulty of deriving meaningful objective measures for intangible assets, I argue that organizations should concentrate on the assessment of their intangible assets for improved decision making and learning. Here the constraints of traditional measurement theory need to be broken to yield meaningful and relevant information.

Instead of trying to quantify the unquantifiable, indicators can be used to assess performance of intangible elements in order to guide management decision making and strategic learning. Deriving meaningful and reliable indicators requires innovation in research design, whether by academic investigators or practitioners and their consultants. Putting the evaluation of intangible assets into practical use is best approached participatively, and is not without some risks and costs. But for many organizations, including those in the not-for-profit sector, it is no longer possible to manage performance meaningfully without including intangible assets.

Notes

1. This chapter is based on parts of Marr, B. *Strategic Performance Management: Leveraging and measuring your intangible value drivers* (Oxford: Butterworth-Heinemann, 2006).
2. From an interview with Daniel Yankelovich, quoted in Adam Smith [pseudonym of George J. W. Goodman], *Supermoney* (London: Michael Joseph, 1973) p. 286.
3. See: Austin, R. D. *Measuring and managing performance in organizations* (New York: Dorset House Publishing, 1996) p. 13.
4. Quoted in Boyle, D. *The sum of our discontent: why numbers make us irrational* (New York: Texere, 2001) p. 29.

14
Political Economy Perspectives on Performance Measurement

Tony Bovaird[1]

Introduction

This chapter explores the conceptual basis for performance measurement within political economy. It shows that competing perspectives in economic theory suggest different approaches to measuring performance – and that some perspectives even suggest such measurement is irrelevant or potentially counter-productive. It explores how key concepts in performance measurement are handled differently in each school of political economy, highlights the self-reinforcing nature of many of the questions asked within political economy, and offers some lessons from conflicting paradigms of performance measurement.

Because economic analysis mainly focuses on service-wide performance measurement, the chapter does not deal in detail with performance management at the organizational level, although some management issues in performance measurement are highlighted.

The context – the key concepts in performance measurement

In this section we look at how some of the key building blocks in performance measurement are interpreted within different schools of political economy.

Differing interpretations of 'performance'

The concept of 'performance' is interpreted variously in the social sciences and in management studies. The interpretation used here will be a deliberately pluralist formulation – that 'performance' is the level of satisfaction of stakeholders' expectations. In each model of political economy, there has been a tradition of defining 'performance' from the perspective of one stakeholder in particular. For example, welfare economics judges the performance of an economic system in terms of its ability to optimize a social welfare function, defined on the utilities of all residents of a polity. Public choice theory normally assumes that consumers' welfare should be optimized in public and private resource allocations. In Marxist models, it is the interest of the working class which forms the basis of prescription.

In addition, there are three dimensions of 'performance' which need to be considered in any strategic analysis – performance in the domain of the organization, in the domain of the service system and in the domain of the communities to which these services are intended to be delivered (Bovaird, 1994). Consequently, a particular set of strategic initiatives may be judged as successful in one domain but as failures in another domain.

Thus 'performance' is not a unitary concept, with an unambiguous meaning. Rather, it must be viewed as a set of information about achievements of varying significance to different stakeholders.

The objectives of public agencies and private firms

Performance assessment is commonly assumed to be intimately bound up with objective setting. In practice, this is not always so, and even when it is the case, the relevant objectives are often difficult to establish and contested by different stakeholders (Bovaird, 2004). However, most schools of political economy have largely ignored the intra-organizational dynamics which influence the objective-setting process and have focused on those objectives dictated by the organization's external environment. In the case of private firms, this has usually been assumed to be profit-oriented, for example, rate of return on investment or shareholder value added, although alternative objective functions such as sales maximization (Baumol, 1959) or growth maximization (Marris, 1964) have been postulated.

In the public sector, different schools of political economy generally distinguish between the generic aims of public action and the specific objectives of a single agency. For example, welfare economics assumes that the public sector pursues the generic aims of economic efficiency and equity. Individual agencies are expected to have more specific objectives in terms of tackling or compensating for specific market failures or redistributing welfare towards particular social groups. However, the objectives of public agencies are highly disputed. Contrasted with the 'public interest' approach embedded in welfare economics is the assumption in Marxist analysis that the state's objective is to serve the interests of the dominant fraction of capital.

Performance information: internal reporting vs. external reporting

In general, we can postulate five different roles for performance assessment systems: signalling strategic direction, informing resource allocation, enabling control, informing learning or providing propaganda. Each of these roles can be played out internally within an organization or in managing the relationship with external stakeholders (either on behalf of an organization or its network). Each of these roles involves a measurement process and a reporting process. To be useful, performance reporting must not only provide information on the past, which is relatively straightforward, but also highlight measures from which the long-term functioning of the organization can be inferred (Meyer, 2002). Such inferences are, of course, surrounded by high levels of uncertainty.

In practice, most schools of political economy are almost exclusively concerned with the use of performance measurement in the realm of external reporting, for example, in determining grant payments between levels of government or in monitoring achievement against contract specifications (although principal–agent theory also models relationships between different internal actors). This means that they normally give relatively little weight to ensuring that the performance indicators (PIs) used for external performance are paralleled by similar PIs used inside the organization.

Appropriate performance measurement systems

Political economy tends to be relatively ecumenical in relation to the appropriate measurement systems for establishing performance levels, accepting PIs from several disciplinary approaches:

- the engineering approach, which relates the expected output to the specified input at each stage in the value chain and thus measures the input/output ratio (the productivity rate);
- the statistical approach, which extends the engineering approach by providing empirically tested information on the strength of relationships in the input/output process, standardized in the light of data about factors over which there is no managerial control (for example, through regression analysis or data envelopment analysis);
- the systems approach which sets objectives for each work unit or individual and measures the achievement of these objectives ('Management by Objectives', or its modern variant in quality management approaches – 'fitness for purpose');
- the management accounting approach, which measures the achievement of a set of financial results by each cost/performance centre

(keeping to financial control targets, unit costs, 'contribution' per unit of output and so on), which was amalgamated with the systems approach in the PPBS and Zero-Based-Budgeting systems of the 1960s and 1970s;

- the 'conformance to specifications' variant of quality management approaches, which advocates the use of a checklist of attributes of a product (and its production process) or service together with its service delivery system (along the lines of Lancaster's 'characteristics' approach (Lancaster, 1966)); and
- the consumer marketing approach, which measures consumer satisfaction (sometimes in terms of willingness-to-pay, sometimes in terms of 'gaps' between consumer expectations and perceived characteristics of the product or service).

The engineering and statistical approaches, particularly in relation to the modelling of input:output relationships, are integral to all political economy models of performance assessment. How well an organization meets the 'demand' for its services (whether this is based on user demand or social need) can be modelled by the systems, management accounting or 'conformance to specification' approaches, all of which are consistent with the objective-maximizing calculus in most schools of political economy. However, the most common approach is that from consumer marketing, which derives from the subjectivist economics of the neo-classical school and was elaborated in welfare economics.

Measuring 'performance' in different schools of political economy

There is no one way in which the concept of performance is integrated into the analytical frameworks of political economy. The schools of political economy to be considered here are:

- welfare economics;
- public choice theory;
- principal–agent theory;
- Austrian economics;
- new institutional economics; and
- classical and neo-Marxism.

Welfare economics

In the welfare economics framework of analysis, the first best conditions for a welfare optimum (as postulated by the general equilibrium theory variant of neo-classical economics) are unlikely ever to be met in practice, whether in a free market economy, a social market economy or in a centrally planned economy. This justifies government intervention to correct 'market failures', which are typically categorized as:

- chronic tendencies to disequilibrium;
- imperfect competition;
- externalities;
- lack of information in production or in consumption;
- ignorance by some actors of their own best interest;
- existence of non-excludable goods or services;
- existence of goods or services with zero marginal costs;
- discrimination by an economic agent against producers, consumers or providers of inputs on grounds unconnected with the cost involved in employing them or meeting their needs;
- uncertainty; and
- 'merit goods' which we desire others to consume for reasons unconnected with our own welfare.

This framework then leads to measuring public sector performance in terms of how much market failure has been corrected by the intervention of a public agency. This approach has the virtue of neatness and intellectual clarity. It became embodied in the technique of 'cost-benefit analysis' (CBA) in the 1950s and 1960s, which had widespread conceptual acceptance in the USA and the UK and which still lurks behind much of the policy evaluation techniques of the World Bank and many United Nations organizations (Boardman et al., 2006). The key measurement issues revolve around how to measure the extent of welfare losses arising from market failures such as externalities and the economic value of their removal through government intervention. In theory, this can be done either by measuring the aggregate changes to the *sum of consumer and producer surplus* or by valuing the *total willingness to pay* in society for all changes introduced by government intervention and then subtracting the *opportunity costs* of the resources used up. However, CBA as a decision algorithm suffers from a number of conceptual and operational difficulties, which have meant that it continues to be largely confined to appraisal of major infrastructure projects in the transport and water sectors. The 'willingness to pay' approach, as one element of CBA, has found wider acceptance in informing health and environmental policy.

The greatest conceptual problem for welfare economics is the theory of the second-best. This states that, if the conditions for the 'first-best' solution are infringed, then the conditions for the 'second-best' solution may be so altered that they have nothing in common with the conditions for the first best. Since 'first-best' conditions can be assumed never to obtain in the real world, they are of no significant interest, because they may bear no correspondence to 'second-best' conditions. Hence, there can be no presumption of superiority for such rules as 'marginal cost pricing' or 'free trade' or 'public securing of the provision of goods and services for which willingness to pay is greater than long-run marginal costs'. While cost benefit analysis can be rescued if we can measure all deviations from the conditions for 'first-best' solutions, in practice this is very difficult.

This is not to say that welfare economics has been a blind alley for those wishing to measure performance. While the fancy superstructure erected by cost-benefit analysis on the foundations of welfare economics must be abandoned, some very practical and useful insights have emerged, which could valuably be incorporated into governmental approaches to performance measurement. In particular, the approach has highlighted the central importance of understanding of the underlying rationale of non-market provision, without which performance measurement is doomed to be superficial – for example, a service may be labelled as 'high-performing' although it could easily be provided as well by other agencies.

Secondly, the welfare economics approach has highlighted the particular power which attaches to measures of marginal cost of provision (as opposed to unit costs) and to consumer willingness to pay (or, more generally, 'willingness to make sacrifices') to get a service (as opposed to actual revenues collected). In the public sector, it has emphasized the importance of discounting future flows of costs and benefits by a social discount rate (rather than market interest rates). Moreover, the analysis of economic rents which emerges from welfare economics (refining the earlier analysis of Ricardo) has recently formed the basis of the resource-based view of the firm (for a critique, see Lippman and Rumelt, 2003) and Economic Value Added® as a central performance measure for the firm (Kay, 2000).

Public choice theory and public sector performance

Public choice theory has been defined as 'the economic study of non-market decision making, or simply the application of economics to political science' (Mueller, 2003, p. 1). It is an approach which emphasizes that not only markets but also governments can fail. It is natural that, because of its desire to expose the many ways in which governments fail, public choice theory has shown rather little interest in recommending how governments could perform more successfully.

However, there are a number of strands of public choice theory which are relevant to performance measurement. In particular, this section will consider performance measurement through:

- measuring the elimination of government failures;
- measuring cost differences between publicly and privately provided services; and
- measuring the constitutional and pressure group constraints on budget-maximizing bureaucrats.

The set of 'government failures' which are suggested by public choice theory include instability (the political business cycle), inefficiency, manipulated agendas, bureau budget maximization and the rent-seeking and wealth-transferring efforts of interest groups. Clearly, these could be further classified into political failures and bureaucratic failures. The extent to which these behaviours are implicit in actual government interventions can be explored in practical cases. In addition, in so far as some government actions are devoted to eliminating these behaviours, a conceptual framework can be constructed to estimate, at least partially, the extent of their success. Of course, there is an implicit contradiction in such approaches to measure the success of any government intervention, in that public choice theory emphasizes that all public interventions will, at least to some extent, fail.

Performance assessment through measuring cost differences between publicly and privately provided services has been a longstanding issue in public choice economics. In general, there is no firm evidence that state enterprises are invariably less efficient than their private sector counterparts (De Alessi, 1980; Parker, 1985). This conclusion has been confirmed in relation to cost savings brought about by move to marketizing public services in the UK (Walsh and Davis, 1993). More importantly, the limitations of this kind of performance assessment have been long known – in particular, they typically pay little attention to quality differences between services compared (Coulson, 2006).

The third major area of performance assessment arising from the public choice framework is the measurement of inefficiencies created by budget-maximizing bureaucrats and the effectiveness of the constitutional and pressure group constraints placed upon such bureaucrats. Niskanen (1971) has argued that bureaucrats have an incentive to deploy resources in order to produce goods or product characteristics that will not be readily monitored, and that elected politicians avoid supporting policies with hidden benefits for the unorganized majority in order to deliver political goods to special interest groups. Dunleavy (1991) has contested Niskanen's model as simplistic and unrealistic and distinguishes several different types of budget of interest to the 'budget-maximizing bureaucrat'. He argues that the benefits to a bureaucrat of a budget increase are mainly associated with increases in budgets for directly controlled expenditure (mainly in-house staff), while the management costs arising from a budget increase are largely associated with an increase in the budgets associated with external providers or partners. Bureaucrats are therefore likely to desire to maximize the former rather than the latter. Performance indicators for how successful a bureaucrat has been in this attempt might therefore consist of the ratios of these types of budget. Naturally, different stakeholders will interpret each of these ratios differently. Senior officials in the agency might be expected to interpret as favourable a high level of in-house to overall budget, while external partners might prefer a lower ratio.

Principal–agent theory

Principal–agent (or agency) theory is concerned with the design of incentives for efficiency under conditions of asymmetric information. The principal is assumed to be less informed than the agent about the conditions facing the organization, and may be unable to monitor the agent's behaviour with precision. Asymmetry of information gives rise to imperfect incentives and inefficiency is the result (Vickers and Yarrow, 1988, p. 92).

The principal seeks to induce the agent to make its pricing, output and investment decisions in accordance with the interest of the principal, given the cost conditions which exist. The agent, however, is typically better informed than the principal about cost conditions, and is interested in maximizing his/her own outcomes (Vickers and Yarrow, 1988). In these conditions of information asymmetry, allocative inefficiency is the result and agents make positive 'supernormal profits' owing to their 'monopoly of information' (Vickers and Yarrow, 1988, p. 100).

Principals will seek to structure situations so as to allocate information to those who will use it most effectively to increase the size of the organizational surplus. However, this co-operative motive is entangled with incentives for conflict, since agents with access to certain information may use it to enhance their claim on the surplus at the expense of the principals. The stronger the conflict motive, the less useful will be the information allocated to agents. Agreements that may be desirable to all participants may therefore not be concluded because of asymmetric information. Consequently, one or both sides can gain if monitoring takes place, whether agreed voluntarily by the agent or imposed by the principal. Agents and principals may therefore share some information while at the same time guarding and manipulating other information (Ben-Ner, 1993, pp. 209–10).

The principal can limit divergences of interest by imposing monitoring upon the agent, thereby incurring monitoring costs. For example, in local government, elected officials are the agents of local voters and the monitoring is done by other politicians (especially the 'Opposition'), by voters (either at the ballot box or by 'voting with their feet'), by bureaucrats, by funders (for example, taxpayers or other levels of government) and by the media (press and broadcasters) (Zimmerman, 1978). However, in the public sector there are often multiple principals, who may emphasize different aspects of the agent's performance, making monitoring much more complex.

An accounting system which allows the agent discretion in reporting selective subsets of information, thereby presenting different financial conditions to different groups, will be preferred by the agent to an accounting system which reports a single unified set of information and reduces the agent's discretionary powers in reporting (Zimmerman, 1978, p. 125). Zimmerman has placed a major dampener on the hopes of public choice theorists in respect of the likely efficacy of their reforms. He argues

> critics and would-be reformers [in his field of reform] fail to recognize that the public's demand price for financial information is quite low (perhaps negative if assimilation costs are significant). [. . .] Accordingly, public officials have little incentive to adopt many suggested reforms. [. . .] Given that the typical (rational) voter will not incur the monitoring costs to affect municipal decisions, municipal accounting reforms, which lower the user's processing costs [. . .] are likely to

produce very small benefits [since they impose costs on the agencies and therefore on the voters. . . .] The media will increase their level of monitoring only if there exists a demand for such 'news' or if it is more likely that the media will uncover scandals. [. . .] What [many would-be reformers of municipal politics] fail to recognize is that the 'defects' in the reporting system they are trying to change are merely symptoms of a more fundamental problem.

(Zimmerman, 1978, pp. 134–5)

This analysis suggests that the hoped-for benefits of performance measurement in the public choice framework may be significantly overestimated.

Austrian economics

Austrian economists turn welfare economics on its head. In the Austrian view, entrepreneurs constantly strive for market advantage, creating monopolies and disequilibria for their own exploitation. Far from disapproving of this and attempting to root it out, as recommended by classical and neo-classical economists, Austrian economists welcome it as the very dynamic which gives competitive market systems their beneficial welfare characteristics.

Given the dynamism, and therefore the inherent instability of the market system, Austrian economists oppose attempts at planning, whether by the state or by 'strategic planners' inside firms. Planners lack the necessary information on costs and consumer wants – and, even if the planner attempts, at great cost, to obtain the necessary information on prices and outputs, such information will be out of date and of little use; only the competitive market provides organizations with relevant and contemporaneous information.

With these assumptions, clearly there can be no rationale for the public provision of goods and services through planned economies and no need for public sector performance assessment, since public policy failure can be assumed from the start. In this perspective, the ideally appropriate performance measure for most public policies, whether macro-economic, micro-economic or social, would be the absence of such policies. Furthermore, the same analysis applies, at least to some extent, within private firms – success comes from staying 'close to the market', not from strategic planning based on performance information.

New institutional economics

Unlike welfare economics, public choice theory or the Austrian school, the various schools of institutional economics generally have no systematic statement of the end state towards which regulation should direct economic actors. Rather they generally have some operating rules for regulatory activity and are relatively unconcerned about the infringement of 'second best' conditions, since they assume that there is no set of rules by means of which more than temporary equilibria and local optima can be achieved.

In these circumstances, one might expect a readiness to recommend reliance upon a pragmatic set of PIs in order to judge the performance of a service system or of specific organizations within it. In fact, there is relatively little interest in issues of performance measurement in the main variant of this approach which has been popular since the 1970s – the 'markets, hierarchies and networks' (MHN) approach, which builds upon the transaction cost economics analysis of Williamson (1975; 1985) and has been set out cogently in Thompson (2003).

The measurement branch of transaction cost economics is concerned with 'ways by which better to assure a closer correspondence between deeds and awards (or value and price)' (Williamson, 1985, p. 81). Conceptually, in the MHN approach, one would expect PIs to be identified in terms of reductions in transaction costs. Those organizations which could achieve such reductions would be expected to be more successful; and the governance structure which minimized transaction costs for any given service system should be that which public policy seeks to bring about. However, Williamson is cagey about the prospects for practical work in this area: 'The three main dimensions in describing transactions are frequency, uncertainty and the condition of asset specificity. None of them is easy to measure, although empirical researchers have found proxies for each' (Williamson, 1985, p. 391). Indeed, he suggests that 'although the measurement branch of transaction costs economics has made considerable headway during the past decade [...], the relevant dimensions for ascertaining where the measurement difficulties reside remain somewhat obscure' (Williamson, 1985, p. 81). In spite of much theoretical interest in this approach over the last three decades, there has been little empirical advance on this position. An assessment by David and Han (2003) found empirical support for some elements of the theory (for example, asset specificity) but considerable disagreement on how to operationalize some of its central constructs and little empirical support for some of its core propositions.

Classical and neo-Marxism

Classical Marxism attempts to provide a rigorous framework for demonstrating the degree of exploitation of workers within any given configuration of the forces of capitalist production and distribution, regulated by dominant fractions of capital; but it refuses to 'play the game' of policy evaluation and design of regulatory systems – the only improvement which it seeks to the capitalist system is its overthrow. While classical Marxist analysis does seek to show how capitalist firms maximize surplus value, the calculus by means of which this is done is at the level of the competitive market system, rather than at the level of the organization.

In the Marxist paradigm, public policy reflects the long-term demands of private capital and the balance of class forces within society (Gough, 1979). It is therefore entirely to be expected that PIs for public agencies should heavily emphasize the leverage of private monies into public projects and services and the achievement of commercial or quasi-commercial rates of return on investment. However, Dunleavy and O'Leary (1987) distinguish three different approaches to the state in the writings of Marx and Engels: the instrumental, arbiter and functionalist models, with different implications for the management function in the state and, potentially, for the procedures used to assess the performance of state institutions. In the *instrumental* model, the state is regarded only as an instrument for the reproduction of capital and is held to possess only that degree of autonomy which it needs to perform this function (Katznelson, 1992). Social reforms forced out of the state in the form of concessions to organized dissent may be welcomed as both demonstrating and nurturing the potential for organized resistance; or rejected as dangerous, leading to short-termism and 'economism' (Lenin, 1902); but performance measurement has no useful role. In the *arbiter* model, the state is seen to play a role in mediating the destructive conflict between different fractions of capital. This necessitates closer mechanisms of inter-agency control, one of which might conceivably be performance measurement. Finally, in the *functionalist model* of state organization, changes in the economic base determine changes in the political and legal superstructure. Policy-making styles are assumed to vary in accordance with what is optimal for the functions concerned. Performance measurement might help to indicate which organizational forms are most in line with structural conditions.

Thus policy analysis in the Marxist paradigm serves a different role from that in other paradigms: it is meant not only to explain the organizing actions of agents (capitalists, officials of the state and workers) but also to explore how most efficiently capitalism can be brought to that point in its development at which it can be most easily precipitated into the socialist mode of production. Analysis of performance measurement in this paradigm attempts to explain *why* it has come to be used rather than *how* it might be used more appropriately by the different class interests which attempt to influence state decision making.

The various schools of neo-Marxist analysis tend to be more optimistic about the possibilities of successful political action against dominant class interests, so that regulation is not viewed simply as a fight amongst fractions of capital, and suggestions can legitimately be made on strategies to make industrial restructuring less disadvantageous to the workers and the localities involved.

The most influential school of neo-Marxism in recent years has been that of French regulation theory, principally identified with the works of Aglietta (1979) and Lipietz (1992). They suggest that the tensions of capitalism are regulated by specific institutional forms, societal norms and networks of strategic conduct. Each epoch of capitalism has its unique accumulation regime and its corresponding mode of regulation. Late twentieth-century capitalism is 'post-Fordist', in which the mode of regulation is based on a fragmented social structure, dual labour markets, individualized rather than collective enterprise (and bargaining) and a targeted welfare state.

In this reworking of traditional Marxist concepts, there is no attempt at a 'totalizing theory' – rather regulationist theory suggests that the state's regulatory activity must be tailored in ways which are sensitive to the overall business system and to operating conditions in the branch of industry in which it intends to intervene. There is active disagreement on the implications of such interventions for the overall performance of the business system. Although the concept of 'socially necessary labour time' offers potential for a critique of waste in capitalist production, based on benchmarking between organizations and sectors, this is rarely attempted in a systematic way. Similarly, although the concept of 'surplus value' in classical Marxism has direct parallels with 'economic rent' in classical and welfare economics, neo-Marxists have not attempted to use this part of the classical Marxist toolbox to analyse the performance of private or public sector organizations.

This approach to the role of the state therefore accepts that many mistakes will be made and that the state has to engage in a learning curve in developing and refining the mode of regulation appropriate, in its circumstances, to the regime of accumulation. One strand of regulation theory, urban regime theory (particularly identified in the UK with the early writings of a non-Marxist, Gerry Stoker) suggests that the development of the 'enabling authority', carrying out contract management based on an explicit system of PIs, represents the creation (by the Thatcher government) of a particular form of local government suited to post-Fordist economic and social conditions (Stoker, 1989).

Performance measurement as a set of reinforcing rituals?

The model of political economy which is used to understand organizational actions will inevitably influence not only the definition of organizational performance which is used, but also the conclusions about the level of performance exhibited by any given set of organizations. For example, adopting the public choice approach to explaining public-sector behaviour can lead to performance assessment being interpreted essentially as comparison of public providers with 'best practice' private-sector providers. In this case, performance assessment would, almost inevitably, show that market provision was superior, since the dice are loaded in this direction from the start.

If, on the other hand, the welfare economics paradigm is used, so that the PIs used highlight the extent of market failure and its correction by government intervention, then this draws attention to the undesirable features of market outcomes and serves to suggest that market forces need to be regulated. This message will be all the more strong if no attempt is made to measure the extent of 'government failure' arising from the interventions.

Thus there is a self-reinforcing mechanism, by which the choice of an analytical paradigm tends to constrain the data collected in such a way that the assumptions of that paradigm are not tested – indeed, they are usually not even exposed. This is particularly dangerous in the case of performance assessment, since its very rationale and legitimacy is based upon its claim to provide a searching and rigorous critique of the performance of the agency or service system concerned.

Moreover, 'lock-in' to dysfunctional performance management systems may arise from the 'perverse control syndrome' (Bovaird, 2004).

Here, very clear PIs are set for line staff (often to achieve more managerial control) but then staff use them to exercise control upon their own top managers, by distorting measurement and reporting systems to ensure that they report a message in line with what their managers want to hear, whatever the underlying reality. This can make performance measurement a threat to the survival of any agency which has adopted it.

Learning lessons from conflicting paradigms of performance measurement

Given the wide range of world views commonly clustered under the umbrella term 'political economy', it is no surprise to find that political economy provides no agreed framework for how performance measurement should be carried out. However, the implications of this conclusion are important. Each perspective has its own model of performance measurement, containing potentially useful lessons for policy makers and practitioners. They therefore each have a claim to influence the everyday practices of organizational life. However, the insights from each perspective can only appropriately be applied to the questions which that perspective seeks to address. It is therefore important that stakeholders are aware of the political economy model behind any given set of PIs. This alerts them not only to in-built assumptions but also to possible biases in data used. Stringing together a performance measurement system from an odd assortment of conceptual tools which address fundamentally different questions is likely to lead to policy failure (in public sector organizations) or strategy failure (in private firms).

Many governments are espousing models of political economy, such as public choice theory, while simultaneously adopting mechanistic measurement systems for performance which are totally at odds with the assumptions of that model. This is not a sustainable position and is likely to lead eventually to a crisis of confidence in current ways of developing, using and reporting performance measures.

Of course, it is possible that performance measurement fulfils an essentially symbolic purpose and that its results are not actually of much interest to any of the stakeholders concerned. We know that politicking is often based on vivid, directly relevant anecdotes rather than performance information and on appeals to misplaced views of 'common sense' rather than theory. Since each of the schools of political economy considered here does provide some fruitful material for populist 'sloganeering', and none is particularly useful in distinguishing rhetoric from reason, it seems likely that political economy will remain for the foreseeable future more a way of justifying existing prejudices about performance rather than a way of driving improvement in performance measurement.

Note

1. An earlier version of this chapter was published as Bovaird (1996). The author is grateful for the comments of Jacky Holloway and for ongoing discussions with Arie Halachmi, which have helped shape the arguments in this chapter.

15
Performance in Small Firms

Richard Thorpe and Jean Clarke

Introduction

Since the 1970s it has become increasingly common for academics and policy makers alike to claim that the impetus for economic growth and innovation depends on both improved performance of existing small firms and increasing the number of start-up companies. Herbig et al. (1994, p. 37), for example, report: 'small, new businesses have been the main driving force for the economic growth of the 1980s, contributing virtually all the new jobs during that decade'. This belief that small firms are the driving force of Western economies is a relatively recent occurrence. Up until the 1970s interest from policy makers and academics was limited and it was assumed that economic development was based on mass production by large companies (Carr and Beaver, 2002). Following the first oil price shock in 1973, many large companies were hit by severe economic problems, and increasingly began to be seen as inflexible and slow to adjust to new market conditions. Against this background, in Britain, the government initiated a comprehensive inquiry into the role of small businesses in the economy. The final report (the Bolton Report) was presented in 1971 and suggested that small firms were integral to a successful economy, thus sparking much interest in the performance of small firms.

The major rise of discussion and interest surrounding small firms occurred in the 1980s with studies such as Birch's (1987) analysis of the place of small firms in the US economy suggesting that small firms created most new jobs. Sentiments such as these were also seen in governmental policies in several countries which sought actively to promote small business activity through policies that aimed to improve small firm performance and make self-employment more attractive to aspiring entrepreneurs (Huse and Landstrom, 1997).

This governmental interest in start-ups and small firm performance has continued to grow, according to Huse and Landstrom (1997), concurrent with deepening economic problems and increased unemployment in many Western countries. In parallel, academic studies in the field of small firm performance have proliferated with researchers concentrating on both internal factors such as owner-manager personal attributes and external factors such as market structure and interest rates (e.g. Baum and Locke, 2004; Birley and Westhead, 1990a, b; Brockhaus, 1982).

Yet despite the large number of studies it is difficult to distil a coherent picture of the phenomenon of small firm performance (Davidsson et al., 2004). The vast majority of studies of small firm performance remain based on de-contextualized, objectivist approaches often treating the owner-manager and their context as mutually exclusive properties. The problem with de-contextualized approaches is that small business growth and development is very much related to the values and 'life views' of the owner-manager and their perception of what satisfactory performance is. Therefore, in this chapter we adopt a more contextualized stance which proposes that it is more beneficial to view performance as an idiosyncratic construct. By this we mean performance is uniquely defined by those involved in performing, rather than some external evaluation of successful performance. We therefore propose that the key to supporting small firms is not to espouse a generic strategy but to allow the owner-manager and others in the business to engage with their own particular strategy for the firm through facilitating a process of reflection and dialogue.

We subsequently put forward three performance measurement systems, which we argue may be used as 'boundary objects' or tools to mediate communication in organizations, emphasizing the process of communication SMEs engage in rather than the content of the tool. This is a finding that emerged strongly from an ESRC-supported 'Evolution of business knowledge' project, that investigated knowledge acquisition in small and medium sized firms and highlighted the usefulness of such systems around which managers could discuss and debate (Thorpe et al., 2008).

This chapter is in some ways a microcosm of the rest of the chapters in this book, as it represents a smaller, illustrative discussion set in a particular context, of the larger issue of performance. Yet in doing this it also attempts to carve out a unique input to the book by putting forward a contextualized, subjectivist approach to performance differing greatly from prescriptive mainstream approaches.

SME performance: government interventions and academic research

As described above, in recent decades small firms have been seen as a major building block of the economy and governmental policies across the USA, Britain and the rest of Europe have been oriented around improving their performance. Many of these policies concentrate on removing negative influences in the external environment which are seen as hindering the performance of small firms. Armstrong (2001) highlights such negative influences as excessive taxation, bureaucracy and red-tape and risk aversion towards new ventures from banks and other sources of capital. The policies which are put forward to counter these negative influences and consequently improve the performance of small firms include 'tax concessions for small businesses, de-regulation in the name of reduced "compliance costs" and a wide range of subsidies, mostly offered through the mechanism of competition so as not to offend the sensibilities of the individualistic self-starter' (Armstrong, 2001, p. 536). These policies appear to be grounded in the belief that once negative external influences have been removed growth and improved performance will be a natural consequence as the small firm is allowed to blossom in an enterprise-driven culture. As Armstrong (2001, p. 534) argues, these policies assume the absence of high performance in the small firm sector 'is due to its suppression, either by hostile systems of ideas, by regulative restriction or by a denial of the material upon which it can operate'.

Other governmental policies have concentrated on developing the individual owner-manager in the hope that such development will lead to the growth and development of the business. Yet while funding has been consistently available to help SMEs take advantage of such initiatives (Stewart and Beaver, 2004), SME response to these schemes has remained mixed. Matlay (2004), for example, found a relatively high awareness of initiatives but low usage rates among a sample of 600 SMEs. As the Council for Excellence in Management and Leadership (CEML, 2002) report, although there is a plethora of publicly funded schemes available many of them are perceived to be overly bureaucratic and disconnected from SME needs, driven by Government agendas and funding rather than attention to demand for such opportunities from SME managers. This supply-side mentality has resulted in schemes which fail to connect with the existing small business environment, which is characterized by heterogeneity and a pursuit of a multiplicity of objectives. It seems that developing any SME is contextually specific and dependent on a large number of factors (Goss and Jones, 1997), making it difficult to decipher what skills and attitudes should be emphasized in SME training (Gibb, 2002). Indeed, the UK government's Performance and Innovation Unit (PIU, 2001) argues that both the need for and type of training required by the typical SME will be dependent on the type of business and its lifecycle, the size of the organization and the need required to address immediate business problems, suggesting that any developmental activity needs to be contextually situated within that particular SME's environment.

On the academic front this juxtaposition is also evident between studies which aim to understand external influences and those which concentrate on understanding the individual owner-manager's effect on the performance of the firm. Concentrating on the external dimension, Birley and Westhead (1990a, b, p. 236) highlight a complex world in which 'suppliers; buyers; the strength of competition; ... interest rates; company taxation; degree of dependency on a small number of customers; ... extent of complexity and uncertainty in the market served; ... and social, legal and political conditions' are among the many factors that may affect small firm performance. Porter's (1980, 1985) ideas in particular have been very influential in this area. He argued that the fundamental basis of above-average performance in the long-run is sustainable competitive advantage, identifying five groups whose actions may limit a firm's profitability namely: competitors, customers, suppliers, new entrants and suppliers of substitute products. Of particular importance to small firm growth, he suggests, are competitors' strength and customer concentration. However, there is a question over how useful the concept of competitive advantage is, as Klein, J (2001) claims despite the ubiquity of the model, the central concept of competitive advantage is notoriously difficult to define. Furthermore, while the recipes for achieving competitive advantage are highly prescriptive, they have been widely discredited by numerous researchers. Indeed Klein, J (2001, p. 1) suggests that Porter's model is at worst 'nothing more than a tautology: successful firms are successful because they have competitive advantage, which in turn cannot be defined in any other way than as a quality that brings about success'. A number of other researchers have suggested that the dynamism of the industry, or the unpredictable nature of environmental change inherent to the industry within which a firm operates (Duncan, 1972), are important factors, as high performing firms are more often found in industries and regions that are more dynamic (Carroll and Hannan, 2000; Davidsson and Delmar, 1997). Yet once again such research appears to be reporting on growth that has already occurred rather than offering any insight into how small firm performance may be improved.

On the internal side, academics have also concentrated on how the owner-manager's personal attributes may affect the firm's performance, with many of these studies examining such attributes in an objectified and prescriptive manner. For example, early research in this area concentrated on the context-independent personality characteristics of the owner-manager as the source of improved performance in small firms. The aim behind such approaches was to identify what characteristics a small business owner-manager should have to ensure they would grow a business successfully (e.g. Brockhaus, 1982; McClelland, 1961). Other more recent studies aim to highlight a more behaviourally oriented view of performance. In particular, these studies highlight characteristics such as effective scanning, interpretation and communication of information in the environment around as related to development and growth (e.g. Baum and Locke, 2004; Baum et al., 1998; Forbes, 1999). A major problem with these approaches is that they overemphasize the importance of individual or personality factors in the operation of entrepreneurship, and minimize the role played by the complex interaction between the individual and wider social or societal pressures. Indeed, these interactions have been shown to impact the decision of whether an individual becomes self-employed and their opinion of what satisfactory growth is (Dickie-Clark, 1966; Scase and Goffee, 1980; Stanworth and Curran, 1973). Yet, the vast majority of government initiatives aiming to increase performance in small firms have not accounted for such complex interactions and emphasize either the external influences which affect small firm performance or generic owner-manager characteristics as separate from their unique context. Recently, academics have suggested that performance needs be addressed in a more subjective, idiosyncratic and situated manner, concentrating on the owner-manager within their own unique environment (Thorpe et al., 2005b; Cope, 2005; Cope and Watts, 2000). In the next section, we put forward an argument which suggests we should approach performance in a way that is socially, relationally and contextually based, focusing on the owner-manager as situated within a particular environment which places limits on their choices of action.

SME performance: a contextualized approach

The majority of the academic understandings and governmental approaches to small firm performance described above are based on de-contextualized, objectivist approaches towards small firm development and treat the owner-manager and their context as mutually exclusive properties. They therefore treat owner-managers as disconnected and isolated beings, who may be studied through their responses to various external stimuli using positivistic methods, which control extraneous (social) variables. As Stainton-Rogers et al. (1995) argue, the underlying problem with these de-contextualized approaches to research is that an individual is never in a situation not subject to social influence and therefore it is not possible to separate them clearly. Rather, the owner-manager is part of and involved in the creation of the conditions, which make up their world through engagement, interaction with the circumstances around them. The individual owner-manager as distinct from their environment is not a viable unit of analysis as they are part of and create the complex systems within which they are situated (Chell, 2000). Therefore, the owner-manager and the performance of their small firm may not be examined as simply present at hand but rather they must be placed within a social context that places restrictions on their action possibilities. While governments and academics have stressed the importance of improved performance in terms of capital growth and employment creation, in the context of the smaller firm, viewing performance in this way can be both misleading and unhelpful. When incorporated into SME development services, this focus has resulted in emphasis being placed on financial returns and profitability rather than aiming to engage with individual SME owner-managers and their aims and ambitions for growth.

However, as Beaver et al. (1998) found, small business growth and development is very much related to the values and 'life views' of the owner-manager and their perception of what satisfactory performance is, highlighting that small firms 'are fashioned by the actions and abilities of the principal role players and owe much to their personal perceptions of satisfactory performance and business direction' (Beaver et al., 1998, p. 160). While many businesses undoubtedly could grow, a significant number choose not to, preferring instead to remain of a size where family influence and control can be maintained. Indeed, as Davidsson et al. (2004) note, 'most firms start small, live small and die small...they never embark on a significant growth trajectory'. While small firms are often viewed as 'tiny acorns' from which large oak trees can grow, the reality often is that many wish to remain 'small bonsais'. Indeed, Gray (1992) notes that the predominant motive for self-employment is the desire for independence and the freedom to pursue non-business goals. Therefore, small business performance may be viewed as positively motivated business intentions and actions on the part of the owner manager (Gray, 2000). In this view, performance needs to be understood as an idiosyncratic construct, which as explained in the opening section suggests that successful performance may only be defined by those who are doing the performing – what is successful for one owner-manager may not be defined as successful by another. Therefore, performance cannot be properly grasped without a thorough understanding of the desires, aspirations and ambitions of the owner-manager and also what is possible within their own unique environment.

In our empirical research (Clarke et al., 2006), we have found that taking such a contextualized approach to SME growth and development may be particularly useful. This research focused on a longitudinal evaluation of a government-sponsored action learning initiative in the Northwest of England involving the use of action learning in 19 SME learning sets established involving 100 SMEs. Action learning is based on the premise that learning comes about through reflection followed by action to solve 'real world' issues contextually embedded in the owner-manager's environment (McGill and Beaty, 1995). Reflection and discussion take place in small groups facilitated by a set adviser. The owner-managers involved in this study reported that giving them the opportunity to take time out to discuss real issues relevant to them, allowed them to 'disengage' with the everyday running of the business and reconnect with their long-term goals for the business. It seems this was particularly valued because a 'space' was created by someone else where the owner-managers could think past the operational and onto strategy. Indeed, the pressures on small business people are often so intense that without such space, attention is only paid to the short-term, the weekly cash flow or the next week's order, not the development of the business which requires a long-term focus. Therefore, it appears that by removing owner-managers from their operational environment, and putting them in a situation where they discuss their own unique business aims, a sharper strategic focus may emerge for those who want their business to move in this direction. We are not prescribing that all owner-managers should move to a longer-term, strategic focus; but rather suggesting that opening up such 'space' gives owner-managers the chance to re-engage with their aims and ambitions regarding the business, whether this be to grow and develop or to remain at a small size where their control can be maintained.

The key, it seems, to supporting SMEs is to facilitate them in some way which provides them the opportunity to engage with their own ambitions regarding their business. However, while the opportunity to engage in action learning proved useful for the SMEs involved in our study (Clarke et al., 2006), it is often not practical or even possible for SME owner-managers to remove themselves from the business for any length of time. Interestingly in other research focusing on the creation of knowledge in SMEs, Thorpe et al. (2005b) found the use of 'boundary objects' or tools which mediate communication within an organization may also facilitate owner-managers in engaging with their aims and ambitions for the business. While it is possible that such 'boundary objects' may take the form of diverse number of artefacts, Thorpe et al. (2005b) suggest that performance measurement systems may allow certain dilemmas, contradictions and ambiguities within context to be discussed and reconciled, leading to coherent strategy and goals for an SME.

Performance measurement systems are defined by Garengo et al. (2005, p. 25, citing Neely et al., 2002) as 'balanced and dynamic systems that are able to support the decision-making process by gathering, elaborating, and analysing information'. However, it is essential to emphasize here that while such tools are often applied in a prescriptive manner (recommending certain courses of action and particular strategies), the important factor is not the content of the tool itself but rather the communication which the tools may mediate. Therefore, rather than recommending some particular form of strategy or process, what is important is the opportunity for reflection and dialogue that these tools may create, allowing the owner-manager to re-engage with what is important to them in their own particular strategy for their business. In the next section, we put forward three performance management systems, which may be used as 'boundary objects' and applied in a contextualized manner, facilitating communications in small organizations.

Mediating communication: the use of performance measurement tools

This section outlines three examples of performance management which we propose, through drawing on the findings of Thorpe et al. (2005b), may work as boundary objects in small companies helping to mediate communication and bringing about more cogent strategies.

First we examine the Balanced Scorecard (Kaplan and Norton, 1992) which is currently in widespread use, and a growing body of evaluative research into its effectiveness (examples of which have been mentioned in earlier chapters). Secondly, the Business Excellence Model (BEM) is examined (the framework for assessing applications for the UK Business Excellence Award). We have chosen these performance measurement tools in particular as both are increasingly being applied in the small firm sector (Anderson et al., 2001; Taylor and MacAdam, 2003). The final measurement tool is Gross Value Added (GVA), a method of measurement used by support agencies such as Business Link throughout the UK. In this example, we refer to recent research we have conducted which provides a worked example of applying this tool in a contextualized manner (Thorpe et al., 2005a).

The Balanced Scorecard

The Balanced Scorecard is a high-profile model which has attracted much attention from both practitioners and academics (Nørreklit, 2000). It is based on the premise that whereas the conventional focus on organizational performance tends to be backwards looking and financially based, what managers actually need is a balanced set of performance measures which focus on a broad range of aspects of the organization relating to its priorities for success. As a consequence, the performance indicators need to be balanced between the financial and non-financial and need to come with both 'lead' and 'lag' indicators, as well as intervention and monitoring measures. The Balanced Scorecard identifies and integrates four different ways of looking at performance: financial, internal business processes, customers and organizational learning. Figure 15.1 below illustrates the basic Balanced Scorecard model with the 'original' four generic perspectives or dimensions present.

These balanced sets of indicators are said to be linked in a cause-and-effect relationship and together provide the manager with a comprehensive understanding of the key operational factors, which will drive the organization's future performance (Kaplan and Norton, 1996a). There have, however, been a number of criticism of the Balanced Scorecard. In a critical examination of the model, Nørreklit (2000) argues that the assumption that there is a cause-and-effect relationship between the indicators is flawed. For example, she highlights that customer satisfaction does not necessarily yield good financial results; but rather chains of action which yield high level of customer value at low costs lead to good financial results. Therefore, the relationship is logical rather than causal, since it is inherent in the concepts. Nørreklit (2003) further argues that

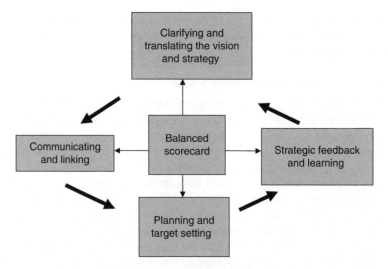

Figure 15.1 Kaplan and Norton's description of the balanced-scorecard process. Adapted and reprinted by permission of Harvard Business Review. Exhibit from 'Using the Balanced Scorecard as a Strategic Management System' by Robert S. Kaplan and P. Norton, January–February 1996a, p. 77. Copyright © 1996 by the President and Fellows of Harvard College; all rights reserved

the concepts and claims of the Balanced Scorecard are based on confused and unsound argumentation, and that rather than being a new and convincing theory, the Balanced Scorecard and its subsequent popularity is merely the result of a form of persuasive rhetoric.

Notwithstanding these criticisms, the Balanced Scorecard may also be used to clarify and gain consensus about strategy, align departmental and personal goals to strategy and obtain feedback to learn and improve strategy, rather than being applied simply as a performance measurement tool (Kaplan and Norton, 1996a). Indeed, Anderson et al. argue that the greatest benefit of the Balanced Scorecard for SMEs is often based on clarification of the strategic vision and the associated priorities and objectives in such a way as to build a consensus. For our purposes, the use of the Balanced Scorecard in this way is more appropriate as it may act as a tool to mediate communication within the organization and gain a coherent and meaningful strategy for all members of an organization. However, it must be ensured that there is collective effort between all parties in the organization, during the building of the scorecard and during the subsequent implementation (Anderson et al., 2001). As Nørreklit (2000) highlights, in addition to being rooted in employee commitment and something realizable, the scorecard needs to be rooted in the language of the employees.

The EFQM's Business Excellence Model

The European Foundation for Quality Management (EFQM) Business Excellence Model (BEM) is a framework designed to act as a general management system and to help improve the basic managerial processes of the organization (EFQM, 2001). It is promoted as 'a practical tool to help organizations do this by measuring where they are on the path to excellence; helping them understand the gaps; and then stimulating solutions' (British Quality Foundation, 2007). While is it widely applied in the literature as a performance measurement tool, it initially emerged as a framework from the European Quality Awards, which were launched in the early 1990s with the support of the European Organization for Quality and the European Commission (EFQM, 2001). The model's philosophy is that regardless of the sector, size, structure or maturity of a business, all organizations need to establish appropriate management systems. It is essentially a non-prescriptive framework based on nine criteria, five of which are 'enablers' (i.e. what the organization does) and four are 'results' (i.e. what the organization achieves). It is often presented diagrammatically in the form shown in Figure 15.2 below.

While theoretically the model may be used by any organization regardless of sector, size, structure or maturity, the award was originally designed for large private-sector organizations. Therefore, in 1996

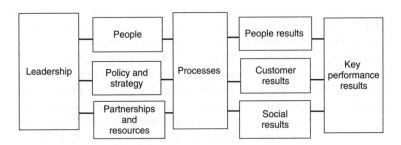

Figure 15.2 The measurement model of the EFQM.
Source: Adapted and reprinted with permission from EFQM Self-assessment Guidelines, European Foundation for Quality Management (2001)

specific guidelines for applying the BEM in SMEs were launched following a pilot study in 1995–1996. The BEM is applied in organizations
through a process of self-assessment often with a number of individuals
within the company acting as a self-assessment team who assess their
organization against each criterion. This process aims to help the organization identify strengths and areas for improvement, with the ultimate
aim being to allocate a score for each of the criteria. However, this process of scoring against set criteria can often be problematic for SMEs. As
Taylor and McAdam (2003) report, the 'one right way' approach of the
BEM could be misleading for small companies which have very different issues and drivers from the large private founding companies of the
BEM. However, rather than emphasizing the scoring and comparison on
the criteria, we argue that this process of engaging in dialogue about the
strengths and problems in an organization can highlight the goals and
ambitions of the owner-manager and other actors in the organization
allowing them to be discussed and potentially integrated. It therefore
works as a process of mediating communication in an organization and
potentially designing a cohesive strategy that has been agreed on and
understood.

Gross Value Added

In recent years, the UK Government has used Gross Value Added (GVA)
as a measurement of productivity improvement. An increasingly wide
range of geographical and sectoral figures for GVA are available including
calculations of GVA by cluster, region or sub-region. One consequence of
such developments is that SME support agencies such as Business Links
are now required to collect GVA data from their clients in an attempt
to provide evidence of improvements in performance, and a measure of
the success of any interventions. GVA recognizes that the use of profit
as a measure of the performance of a company is fraught with difficulty
as companies often 'distort' the profit figure over any given period for
a number of reasons, for example, through what they allow for depreciation. GVA uses the same accounting information which firms have
to collect to make quarterly and annual returns, but the line drawn in
the profit and loss account is placed slightly higher so as to include not
only profit, but wages and salaries and depreciation. As a result, it gives a
clearer (and some would say more useful) picture of the performance of
the firm. However, within these approaches to GVA, the focus is on GVA
as an output measure of the creation of wealth but not on the creation
process itself.

Therefore, while GVA is an output measure of the creation of wealth by organizational activity, it may also allow the owner-manager and others in their business to reflect on how the business may be structured in a variety of ways which can add value. Once again we are emphasizing the process of discussion and dialogue that will take place as an opportunity to communicate about long-term goals. Thorpe et al. (2005a) aimed to show how such a process could work through giving emphasis to GVA as a communication tool in a small owner-managed business. Our approach was broadly consistent with collaborative action research which stresses the importance of establishing a partnership between the researcher and the researched; a strategy it is argued which leads to the development of shared understandings (Reason and Bradley, 2000; Reason and Rowan, 1981). Five employees from the SME along with the MD and the Finance Manager were selected to form a GVA project team which discussed and developed a GVA strategy over a period of months (see Figure 15.3). At each stage of the process participants were asked to provide feedback relating to their understanding of GVA and its relevance to company interests. The results suggested that participants found

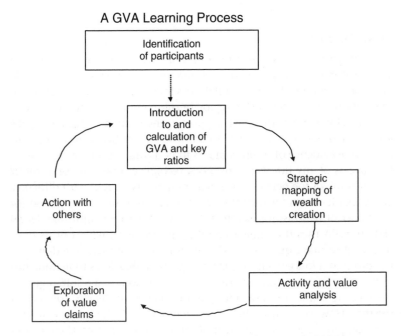

Figure 15.3 A GVA Learning Process, taken from Thorpe et al. (2005a)

this process developed their understanding of processes within the business and helped them develop 'open' new questions about where they wanted to be in the future. Therefore, through a contextualized approach GVA could be a very useful tool to aid discussion and reflection on performance.

Conclusions

This chapter has examined a number of concepts in relation to performance management in the small firm sector. The first part of the chapter has considered a number of theoretical explanations and emphasized the importance of a contextualized approach for the improved performance and development of SMEs, rather than the objectivist and de-contextualized approaches which dominate the area.

In the final part of the chapter, attention is turned to three different frameworks which we have proposed may be used as 'boundary objects' or tools to mediate communication in organizations, through an emphasis on this dialogic process rather than the strategy espoused by the particular tool. While there are particular problems with each framework which we have highlighted, our emphasis is not on the strategic orientation of the tool itself and whether the tool is 'right' or 'wrong'. Rather we concentrate on the process dialogue which it encourages which may bring coherent strategies to small firms, regardless of what this strategy may be. We offer this approach as an alternative to mainstream strategies offered by governmental agencies which often focus on objectified measures such as capital growth and employment creation. Such generalized offerings from support agencies result in generic strategies and simplistic assumptions about the desire for SMEs to grow and develop. As Shotter (1993) highlights, such attempts by outsiders to provide alternative ideas for business development can be viewed by owner-managers as dangerous or deviant and rejected as unworkable or wrong for 'their' business. By trying to enforce contrived structures on SMEs not in touch with their contextual environment, policy makers are likely to continue to face failure. Rather in approaching small firm performance we must 'join them in their world' (CEML, 2002) and embrace and understand the small firm sector as one characterized by heterogeneity and the pursuit of a variety of different objectives.

16

Performance in the Public Services

Richard Kerley

Introduction

> To measure and control performance is seen as a crucial element of securing efficiency and effectiveness in government, at a time when both its cost and performance is under scrutiny.
>
> (Alford, 1992, p. 1)

> It is often hard to measure performance in the public service, especially in terms of quality and effectiveness. However, it is wrong to overstate the difficulties. The important thing is to be clear about what each service is intended to achieve, and what distinguishes a good service from a poor one. Quality and effectiveness can be monitored in various ways, including feedback from users, and more (and better) inspection.
>
> (Audit Commission, 1986, p. 4)

> ...there are...a host of political, bureaucratic, conceptual and technical problems in implementing such a regime of extensive PIs for different public services.
>
> (Wholey, Director of US General Accounting Office, cited in Aristigueta, 1999, p. 5)

Alford was writing in the context of Australian government, Wholey speaking of the United States and although the opening quotation from the Audit Commission refers to arrangements in England and Wales, similar views hold good for the entire UK.

Although concerns about 'efficiency' and 'performance' in public services have been part of the discourse of some governments for years – even centuries – this concern has been increasingly emphasized in the past two decades, regardless of party of government or the country governed.

In their 1989 publication *First steps in Measuring Performance for the Public Sector*, Jackson and Palmer cite publications which are all post-1980, and in the period since that publication, the volume of work produced on performance and the public services has increased dramatically. To some extent, discussion about performance in the public services is coloured by a wistful assumption that it is all much easier in the trading sector. Jackson and Palmer express this view at the start of their paper: 'In much of the public sector the bottom line of profit does not exist. Financial performance and the impact of services are difficult to assess' (Jackson and Palmer, 1989, p. 1). The presumption that 'hard to evaluate' public services may be contrasted in some way with the much more robust signals of achievement and performance available through a trading company with 'a bottom line' and 'profit' is a fond delusion though one that is widely held.

However, it is a tempting fallacy to assume that the publication of corporate turnover, profit figures and earnings per share is a simple and failsafe indication of how well an organization is doing – the famous 'bottom line'. Measuring effective performance in large and complex organizations is very difficult. This is not a novel observation; the late Peter Drucker first pointed out 50 years ago that '[...] no one single yardstick is "the" measure of performance, prospects and results of a business; [...] success, like failure, in business enterprise is multidimensional' (Drucker, 1968, p. 85). Contemporary examples such as Enron make this point graphically for any observer who doubts the substance of his comment.

This chapter explores the purpose, and the implications of introducing and developing performance management in public organizations. Although much of the illustrative material is drawn from Great Britain, similar developments can be charted in other countries and therefore some examples are drawn from overseas.

The historical, political and economic context

A concern for the effective management of performance in the public services simply reflects and echoes some of the themes that have underpinned management theorizing for much of the past two centuries. This is the proposition that the management process is about setting objectives and then seeking to achieve those objectives. Fayol (1949) and Taylor (1911) would both readily have recognized the concept of performance as we discuss it today, though they approached it from different perspectives, with Fayol focusing on the organization and Taylor principally on teams and individuals as part of the system of production.

The approach to managing performance in the public services in the industrial and post-industrial period owes a lot to the development of such highly rationalistic 'scientific' approaches to management and fits closely with the Weberian tradition of a rational bureaucracy. In some ways, the introduction of performance measurement into the public services is not a neo-liberal imposition associated with privatization policies, but very much part of the bureaucratic tradition discussed in the context of the contrasting efficiencies inherent in 'markets' and 'hierarchies' (Niskanen, 1971).

One other linked aspect is deep rooted in the commonly found governmental concern for balancing the needs of government for expenditure on public services with keeping tax levels down and spending public money wisely and frugally. In 1780, Lord North set up the Commission for Examining the Public Accounts, with the purpose of examining not simply government expenditure but also the organization and efficiency of governmental activities. In 1866, with the Exchequer and Audit Act, Gladstone created the forerunner of the current British Auditor General, an office which now provides much of the detailed analysis of government performance in the UK and is paralleled in the United States by the General Accounting Office (Day and Klein, 1987). Governments everywhere have over time established systems, procedures and forms of organization to monitor and improve the performance of public services.

Governments everywhere have also been periodically gripped by an enthusiasm for achieving greater efficiencies and more effective performance from governmental and public service organizations. The papers of US President Lyndon Johnson show that after his initial burst of correspondence and speeches about the assassination of his predecessor John Kennedy, his first major letter to members of his government was a circular urging economy and efficiency in each of their departments – 'more bang for our buck' (Johnson, 1968). Governments in earlier eras (Geddes in the 1930s UK; Hoover in the 1920s USA) have often sought such economies, both by reducing the range and scope of public services and also by seeking to improve the performance of them. The political drive which in America led to the Government Performance and Results Act (1993) was motivated by concerns about efficiency and economy in government as well as by the political motivation of President Clinton and Vice President Al Gore.

Such sporadic initiatives by governments have increasingly come to be replaced by policies, legislation and executive actions intended both to achieve economies and enhance the performance of public services on a continuing basis. Such efficiency drives intended to enhance government performance have paralleled the growth of public spending from the second half of the twentieth century onward. It has also been associated with the emergence and transfer of ideas drawn from the various different approaches and forms of analysis applied to strategic business planning and transferred into the public services. The post-Second World War wave of such ideas was led by 'management by objectives' (MBO), a process first clearly discussed by Drucker (1968) in *The Practice of Management*. The ideas expressed there came to have a significant influence on the way in which managers in private and public organizations came to see management within those organizations.

The themes of MBO originated in America, and were translated across the Atlantic into both British industry and British public services. During the 1960s and the 1970s, such ideas surfaced with different titles but often with very similar forms in the public services as PPBS (Planning, Programming and Budgeting Systems) in the USA and PAR (Programme Analysis and Review) in the UK. Such approaches to large-scale planning and their attempted utilization in the public services, fitted in well with the enthusiasm of the 1960s and early 1970s for more 'rational' and 'scientific' approaches to decision making. In various public services, this represented in a specific form a very clear example of the 'rational planning' approach to management. Additionally, the way in which some of the leading proponents of effective performance management – for example, the Audit Commission – present their ideas is very clearly based on a simple control loop system of management:

1. Make policies;
2. Set objectives;
3. Allocate resources and take action;
4. Monitor performance; and
5. Review (and amend) policies.

By the early 1980s, the very pronounced and complex linkage between attempts to improve performance, the aspiration in some areas of public service to establish a rational planning process, and the assumption that 'business methods' would be more effective than traditional public administration approaches were fully articulated. Clear examples can be seen in many of the early documents produced by the Audit Commission for England and Wales after its creation in 1983. The establishment of the Audit Commission followed legislation introduced by Michael Heseltine, the government minister most enthusiastic about promoting the efficient performance of public services (Heseltine, 1987, pp. 15–28). The first director of the Audit Commission, Sir John Banham, had gained earlier experience with the McKinsey consultancy and adapted the McKinsey '7S' (Pascale, 1990) model of good organizational practice into the thinking of the Audit Commission. One early publication (Audit Commission, 1986, p. 83) states

> Economy, efficiency and effectiveness do not just happen. In almost every situation changes – often uncomfortable changes, involving people doing things differently – will be involved. Those organizations in the public and private sectors which have been successful in securing beneficial changes have created an environment that thrives on challenge and change, by managing the following elements (vision, strategy, structure, systems, staffing and skills, style) in such a way as to reinforce each other.

The combination of ideas about developing more effective performance, the supposed virtues of business approaches, and the rational approach to planning influenced the climate of ideas from the 1960s onwards, with accelerating pace into the 1990s and the new century – regardless of governing party. This has had a direct impact on the organization of public services that has been seen particularly in central government in Britain with the development of approaches such as more intensive financial management, the creation of government agencies and the metamorphosis of the Private Finance Initiative (Conservative) into the Public Private Partnership (Labour) (Pollitt and Bouckaert, 2000). Such trends also influenced local governments (Boyne, 2001, 2002) and the health services (Klein, 2000).

In the United States, the Clinton federal government formalized this synthesis of approaches into a declaratory programme – led by the Vice President – the National Performance Review, which expressed the ambition to create a government that: 'works better, and costs less.' (Gore, 1993, p. 3.) This US review led directly to legislation (Government Performance and Results Act, 1993) which required federal, state and local government to implement measures intended to track performance government and act upon recorded failings.

The focus on performance in the public sector was, through the period following on from the oil shocks of the 1970s, at first more apparent in local and central government than it was in the health services. It also was driven by a growing recognition that in many cases performance management was weak throughout the public services. Although based in Australia, Hughes (2003) makes an observation that he argues has universal relevance: 'By any standard, performance management in the traditional model of public administration was inadequate, and this applied to either performance of individuals or the organization' (p. 205).

In some public organizations, changes intended to address perceived weaknesses of performance were accelerated through the mediation process of the major management consultancies which carried forms of analyses and sometimes prescriptions across borders (Saint Martin, 2000). This again demonstrates a linkage between the business-derived strategic planning processes promoted and circulated by the big consultancies such as PA and McKinsey, and the impetus for change in public bodies.

In different public organizations there were attempts to create review mechanisms as 'watchdog bodies', where some comparison can be made with the Public Accounts Committee in the House of Commons and the Ways and Means Committee in the US House of Representatives. The initial experience of many such bodies and departments appears to have often been limited to relatively small-scale and circumscribed tasks which attracted attention because they enabled short-term system rationalization to be effected and cost-savings to be achieved. Thus during the earlier phases of the development of performance management in the public services, it was the minutiae of management practice (procurement, minor functional duplication) rather than major programmes and strategic issues (effectiveness of health interventions, the outcomes of secondary schooling) that were explored.

It is clear that in various countries and jurisdictions, even in the most decentralized such as Switzerland where change grew from cantonal level, the impact of measures intended to enhance performance impacted on the various levels of government and their agencies whether they were deliberately intended to do so or not (Schedler, 2000, p. 80). The widespread finding of research appears to be that levels of government and quasi-governmental bodies have permeable boundaries that enable management ideas and reform initiatives to interpenetrate across the organizational divide. What is less clear, however, is whether the diffusion of such ideas owes much to formal theories of how we might understand performance and attempts to improve and enhance it, or is merely herd-like emulation of ostensibly good practice.

Theories of performance

Such developments in performance management and the manner in which they have emerged and been explicitly supported and explained by government have rarely been accompanied by any explicit theoretical justification. Even those ministers most interested in the development of effective management in the public services (for instance, Michael Heseltine) rarely express their ideas in such terms, relying on either intuitive sentiment or claimed practical experience. One major international exception is Roger Douglas (1993), former Finance Minister of New Zealand, a country which wholeheartedly embraced radical political and administrative reform in the 1980s onwards (Boston et al., 1991). Douglas clearly outlines in his valedictory account the conceptual bases for his major institutional and legislative changes. When we set such a thoughtful personal account alongside more consciously theoretical academic work (Boyne, 1998; Eliassen and Kooiman, 1993) and empirical international studies (OECD, 1991) we can draw out some of the theoretical premises that underlie the development of performance management in the public services. These themes tend to be inter-related in a complex manner but we can nevertheless distinguish some key elements.

Economic theories

Those which have greatest influence on the development of performance in the public services are theoretical work related to principal/agent relations (agency theory) and the incentivization of economically rational individuals or entities. The collective staff of public organizations are assumed to be agents working for a principal (government), though of course this is made more complex because of debates about who really is the 'principal' in any representative government (Dunleavy, 1991). The designation of defined and often discrete units whose performance is measured and recorded is clearly intended to make the principal/agent relationship more specific and more amenable to control. So governments in various jurisdictions have created 'agencies' with targets and performance measures they are required to achieve. Achieving such performance targets can be seen as a substitute for profit in the classical economic model. In some cases (although the trends are mixed both between and within jurisdictions), senior managers are financially rewarded for achieving such targets, in an attempt to create concrete financial incentives.

The more abrasive claims of the public choice theorists (Mueller, 1989; Niskanen, 1971) may at first seem to take us beyond measuring public service performance to a more normative view that it is axiomatic that public services are better controlled by, in effect, extending forms of choice for service users and competition between providers. Niskanen, in particular, observes that without control and measurement, bureaucrats will seek to maximize their own interests in 'the ease of managing the output of the bureau' (ibid, p. 38). This author is perhaps the firmest and most long standing of the proponents of a view that control and measurement of performance are, in the absence of competition, an absolute necessity to restrain self-serving bureau building.

This said, there are clear linkages between such theories and the form and extent of performance measurement in the public services. Thames Water and all the other English water companies ceased to publish performance indicators of service-level achievement in the year that they were privatized as PLCs (following the passage of the Water Act 1989). They did this on the grounds that the spur to better performance was now profit and such data was no longer relevant to the public, and was in any event not required to be published by trading companies. Interestingly this is a discussion that re-emerged vividly almost two decades later, with the debate over the potential requirement on companies in the United Kingdom to publish an Operating and Financial Review (HM Government, 2006).

Management theories

We must be careful, in the contentious climate of discussing highly debatable public sector change, to distinguish between practices imported from the private to the public sector and the theoretical premises which underlie different forms of managerial organization and action. So in the former category, for example, are the various attempts to introduce individual and collective financial reward as a means of enhancing public sector performance – 'performance-related pay'. In various jurisdictions, such attempts have been made in civil service functions; in healthcare and in education. But such financial incentivization is not universal in the private sector, where it is often recognized that it may be inappropriate and indeed, rests on weak theoretical propositions which new disciplines – such as behavioural economics – are challenging.

In considering the relevance of theory, we can identify two significant strands of management theory that have major implications for examining performance management in the public services. The first (also referred to above and derived from economic thought) is the enhanced emphasis on the objectives of the organization and the implications this has for performance. Public services have, in the past, been criticized for over-concentrating on the *processes* of decision making and service delivery rather than the volume or quality of *outputs* and eventual *outcomes*. The increased concentration on outputs that the measurement of performance signals is a significant change based on ideas developed over many years of management theory and still subject to contestation and testing.

As already observed, active (and even retired) politicians do not often lay claim to major theoretical underpinnings for their actions and choices. In the actions of the three Blair governments in Britain, and the predecessor Conservative governments of the 1980s and 1990s, we can observe policy developments based on unstated or sometimes confused theoretical foundations.

The major changes of organization form and architecture, and the adoption of different organizational forms in different public services, owes something both to contingency theory and to the concept of 'organic' versus 'mechanistic' forms of organizational structure as being contingent on the environment in which the organization operates (Burns and Stalker, 1966). The 'public services', though often referred to as though they were an homogeneous entity, are quite heterogeneous in purpose and form. The armed forces serve a different function from health-care organizations and both operate in a different 'market' environment from, say, publicly supported theatre and music, where willing audiences engage in discretionary social expenditure.

Although much derided at the time when first expressed, Tony Blair's often repeated phrase 'what matters is what works' is actually a statement that owes something to a synthesis of management theories tested in some very different settings (Burns and Stalker, ibid). It is clearly intended as a means, even a prescription, for enhancing performance by using different organizational forms contingent on circumstance. But even here the government then demonstrated some of the confusion referred to above, appearing to contradict its own espoused policies by seeking to impose a common model of purpose and organization on different types of public bodies regardless of evidence about the contingent nature of 'best practice'.[1]

However, both in the action of central government and even when there are degrees of discretionary choice available to public service decision makers we can see elements of that 'herd-like' phenomenon (or 'isomorphism') referred to above. The analysis of this process in the works of critics such as Di Maggio and Powell (1983, 1991) is relevant to the widespread adoption of mechanisms for performance measurement and management.

The modernization of public service performance management

Despite the rhetoric of party debate and dispute, which ostensibly emphasizes differences between the political parties, it is apparent that the actions of governments from the mid-1970s onwards have followed a consistent and common trend in trying to enhance performance in the public services. If anything, it was the Conservative government of 1979–1992 that shifted the debate on public services beyond the narrow focus on cost-cutting of the mid-1970s and the period of International Monetary Fund (IMF) crisis to a broader concern with performance.

In 1982, the UK government launched the Financial Management Initiative (FMI) in central government at the same time as the Audit Commission was being established to review local government. 'Efficiency and Effectiveness in the Civil Service' which described the FMI, referred to what are still very familiar and key principles of performance management in government:

> ...to promote in each department an organization and a system in which managers at all levels have:
>
> 1. a clear view of their objectives, and means to assess and, where ever possible, measure outputs and performance in relation to those objectives;
> 2. well defined responsibility for making the best use of their resources, including a critical scrutiny of output and value for money;
> 3. the information (particularly about costs), the training and the access to expert advice that they need to exercise their responsibilities effectively.
>
> (HM Government, 1982, p. 2)

A later Conservative government introduced the 'Citizens' Charter', initially derided as a trivial initiative, but one that was launched with an explicit focus on improving performance in the public services, and which subsequently led to the requirement for local authorities across the UK to collect and publicize performance indicators related to various services (Audit Commission, 1992). As the responsible minister argued in a contemporary radio interview:

... Well, of course [public services] need investment and they get investment but it would be a very strange thing if the government and the public services were the only great corporation or supplier of goods to people in the world that didn't have a quality control department; that didn't have a constant campaign to try to raise quality.

(William Waldegrave, interviewed on the BBC Radio 4 'Today' programme, 14 April 1993)

In that short extract, Waldegrave manages to emphasize the drive on quality and investment as significant words and phrases which characterize the drive to enhance performance in public services, both in that decade with a Conservative government and into the twenty-first century with Labour governments. Interestingly, and although much criticized at the time of launch, it is still possible and considered desirable for public agencies to be awarded 'Chartermarks' for high-quality service delivery.

The period under review in this chapter has seen a shift in political thinking which has led to representatives of all the major political parties placing great emphasis on the effective delivery of public services. Such ambitions motivated many of the changes introduced by the Conservative governments of the 1980s and 1990s and the word 'delivery' has become a *leitmotif* of the 'New Labour' governments, with ever increasing emphasis placed on the performance of different public services. At the time of writing, the delivery ambitions for these services are itemized through annual Public Service Agreements, and those for each major department of state are publicized through the 'Spending Review' section of the Treasury website under 'Public Service Performance' (HM Treasury, 2007).

This increased emphasis over the recent period on achieving enhanced performance has led to the emergence of a discourse on public services that places great emphasis on achieving 'targets'. The HM Treasury website contains direct guidance documents on the objectives and targets agreed for each government department. These in turn allow exploration of the subsequent expanded targets set for various non-departmental public bodies, agencies and independent bodies such as local authorities. In the case of the Home Office, for example, a limited range of higher order targets numbering approximately six expand, at the level of a typical police force, to between 50 and 60 performance targets (West Yorkshire Police Authority, 2007).

This plethora of targets has itself been the subject of sustained – if sometimes overstated – claims from various sources. The then Leader of the

Opposition, Michael Howard MP, claimed in one campaign statement that if elected, his government would: '... sweep away bureaucracy and political correctness. ... He will promise to scrap performance indicators and targets' (Howard, 2004).

The criticism of the use of targets for various public services as a means of enhancing their performance can also be found in more measured terms in documents such as 'On Target? Government by measurement' (House of Commons, 2003).[2] In preparing their report, the Public Administration Select Committee, drawing upon academic advice and evidence, stipulate the assumptions underlying their enquiry: 'That the public wants and expects sustained improvements in the delivery of public services, which is also a Government priority; that service providers in receipt of public funds ought to be publicly accountable for their performance; and that setting targets can be one means of stimulating better performance by those who deliver services' (ibid, p. 5).

In stating these assumptions, the committee helpfully summarized some of the broad themes that characterize current debates about performance in the public services. They also, implicitly in the extract cited, and explicitly elsewhere in the report (ibid, pp. 31–34) assert the value of measuring performance. Even more strongly, the report argues that performance measurement: '... cannot and should not be abolished. The accountability and transparency it [the measurement culture] brings are now an inherent part of our public administration' (ibid, p. 32).

In this observation, the parliamentary committee focus on tools of data collection and recording that are central to understanding the management of performance in the public services: performance indicators, which we will consider in more detail next.

Performance indicators and the research agenda

Performance indicators (PIs) are central to any understanding of how performance is managed in the public services. It has been argued by Day and Klein (1987, p. 243) that the information inherent in such PIs represents: '... the lifeblood of accountability ...'.

A number of alternative definitions have been employed by various writers about PIs; there is, however, a common form of words found in many British government publications, and it seems most appropriate to focus upon that. The following typical definition is taken from an early report by Her Majesty's Inspectors examining Further Education in Scotland but could readily apply to other similar public service organizations (and still has a very contemporary ring): 'a performance indicator is a statement, often quantitative, about resources deployed and/or services provided in areas relevant to the particular objectives [of the college]' (HM Government, 1990, p. 3).

The same authors also quote approvingly from an unattributed comment which urges that the emphasis should be on 'indicators as guides or signals rather than as absolute measures'. This passage continues in a similar vein to explain that: ' . . . because no single indicator is a perfect instrument and because each one is limited in its scope it is essential that a *range* of performance indicators be employed' (emphasis in original, p. 3).

So here is a classic dilemma of measuring performance in the public services, and a dilemma that faces all those who manage public services. The dilemma takes a similar form to the observation that Drucker made about profit and business performance in *The Practice of Management*. Good performance appears and is assumed to reflect effective management, and it is indisputably common sense and correct to attempt to measure this, but there is no absolute and unequivocally definitive way of doing so. A powerful analogy used by Carter et al. (1992) is to suggest that PIs can be viewed as either the 'dial type' or 'tin-opener type'.

Unfortunately, research into performance measurement in a number of public service settings suggests that it takes a considerable amount of time to move beyond the easy accumulation of relatively simple data sets which we could describe as the dial type. Over 20 years ago, Pollitt (1986) examined one local authority – Bexley – which was relatively advanced in employing performance measurement. His analysis of the several hundred PIs reported, showed that 75 per cent of the PIs referred to 'efficiency and economy' indicators. Only a very small percentage (1 per cent) related to effectiveness, and according to his observation none of them referred to quality of service. More recently, although the volume of PIs that government has required to be published has increased[3], Boyne (2002) has also shown that any increasing proportion of such information now focuses on the efficacy and quality of services. His conclusion is encouraging for those who are proponents of performance measurement and those who argue that such measures improve in their efficacy with experience and adaptation (for example, Hughes, 2003): 'Performance Indicators have improved and cautious congratulations are in order' (Boyne, 2002, p. 24).

Others researching within approximately the same time frame (for example, Sanderson, 2001) have demonstrated that the largest proportion of data collected and analysed still tends to favour more readily measured aspects of economy and efficiency over effectiveness and quality of service. There remains, however, a case for arguing that even the collection of apparently simple data on performance – if analysed and utilized – could have a significant impact on the performance of public services. This could be particularly powerful at the extremes of professional behaviour. It is apparent from official reports into both infant deaths at the Bristol United Hospitals Trust and the Harold Shipman murders that even a casual scan of performance information would have been very indicative of atypical (and in the Shipman case criminal) behaviour by highly qualified public service professionals working in settings where a high trust relationship had always been assumed to assure high performance (Shipman Enquiry, 2007).

The original Audit Commission view (1992) on what form PIs should take emphasized the importance of getting the balance right when defining the terms of measurement, collecting and then publicising such data. '... indicators must be understandable to the public, and sufficiently objective to provide valid comparisons, but without at the same time excessively simplifying the aim of the service or creating incentives to distort provision in order to perform well on a particular indicator' (p. 2).

Much contemporary research focuses on the effectiveness and validity of collecting such data and assessing whether it contributes to more effective organizational performance in public organizations. In healthcare, it has been argued that the publication of such data can encourage risk-averse performance amongst professionals engaged in problematic and risk-susceptible activities such as surgery (Bridgewater, 2003). In other fields such as local government the work of Boyne (1996, 1997, 2002) has concentrated on precisely this topic. Similarly in the United States, Moynihan and Ingraham (2001) have investigated the extent to which it is necessary to do more than simply publish performance data in order for it to be used either by the public or by engaged professionals and managers. Of course, it is sometimes the case that extensive use of performance information to create league tables may encourage dysfunctional practices and lead to occasional lapses into malfeasance by individual public managers (Anonymous, 2002; Royal Statistical Society, 2003).

Within the context of the United Kingdom, one of the most interesting developments in recent years has been the extent to which the impact of devolution in Scotland and Wales has led to both policy divergence between the countries and different approaches to measuring and recording government performance. The extent to which this is of potential concern to different layers of government and the broader society has been commented on by the Office for National Statistics and the Statistics Commission (Hodgson, 2005).

Conclusion

The measurement of performance in the public services remains a complex issue, though not as uniquely complex as is sometimes assumed. The emergence and consolidation of the routinely collected performance data is now commonplace for all public services. This will continue to develop and become more readily accessible, particularly with strengthened public access to official information. This enhanced data in itself is of enormous value in enabling researchers to develop a better understanding of how to measure performance more effectively. Developing a better understanding of how better measurement relates to better management, however, is an even more complex challenge for the researcher.

Notes

1. Space limits preclude wider discussion of the emergence of the evidence-based policy movement in the 1990s, exhorting public policy makers and practitioners to implement 'what works' on the basis of research evidence. However, the importance of understanding contextual factors is acknowledged by, for example, Nutley et al. (2007).
2. At the time of writing this chapter and at the time of this report being prepared, the Committee was chaired by a former academic with an intellectual background in politics and public administration.
3. Local authorities in England with responsibility for the full range of local government services were required in 2005 to collect and publicize some 520 PIs – a greater volume of PIs per authority than in either Wales or Scotland.

17

Performance Management in the Voluntary Sector

S Andrew Morton

Introduction

Although performance management is a fairly crowded research discipline (Thorpe and Beasley, reproduced as Chapter 2 in this book), it has received relatively little academic attention as it is applied in the so-called 'voluntary sector'. Yet the practice of performance management has been growing there for some years, albeit lagging behind activity in the public service sector.

This chapter aims to add to our understanding of what performance management is by examining developments in the voluntary sector. Through the perspectives of literature and research on the sector, this chapter will explore whether it has a distinctive organizational performance management agenda. We will then identify the key philosophies and models that appear to inform it. Finally, we will attempt to identify the tensions involved in developing a contextualized approach to performance management. The focus throughout will be on learning from the recent history and dynamics of the UK environment, with a particular interest in the service-provision side of the sector.

Definitions and research streams

The voluntary sector has attracted relatively little research interest, possibly because a precise conceptual definition of the voluntary sector is still lacking and possibly because it may not exist as a distinctive sector at all (Salamon and Anheier, 1994). Researching the sector 'is as improbable as any similar claim to be researching the public sector or the corporate sector [...] as a whole' (Halfpenny and Reid, 2002, p. 536). It is certainly a diverse sector: 'Indeed, researchers who have attempted a definition or classification often remark that the array of organizational forms, activities, motivations and ideologies that exists between the state and the market is so confusing as to render the task inherently impossible.' (Kendall and Knapp, 1996, p. 16.) Its scope is correspondingly broad, incorporating service provision, self-help or mutual aid, advocacy and campaigning, and groups providing services to voluntary organizations (Nathan, 1990).

To make sense of the sector, one immediately struggles with finding a name for it – 'voluntary action', 'voluntary sector', 'third sector', 'non-profit' or 'not-for-profit', 'non-governmental organizations' and 'charity' (among other designations). Charities are the easiest to distinguish with their purpose as having a 'public benefit' established in law, unlike the rest of the voluntary sector (Kendall and Knapp, 1996; Lock, 1998), and they are regulated in the UK by the Charity Commission. The Commission, set up in 1853, originally investigated breaches of trust in the use of publicly-collected funds; from the 1990s onwards successive legislation has extended control over registered charities.

The term 'non-profit organization' emerged from economists in the United States in the 1980s and emphasizes the constraint on profit distribution of certain organizations. Etzioni (1973) rejected a narrow view of the economy in preferring 'Third Sector' to describe hybrid organizations that avoided profit as their goal while adopting the private sector's responsiveness to the market and the public sector's values.

The concept of 'voluntary' organizations refers to the absence of compulsion (Kendall and Knapp, 1996) and focuses on the use of voluntary effort (Halfpenny and Reid, 2002). Defining this has attracted considerable academic attention. One stream emphasizes its economic accountabilities – 'roughly that sector which is neither the private sector nor the public sector' (Wise, 1995, p. 1); 'organizations which occupy an intermediate position between the state and the market' (Kendall and Knapp, 1996, p. xi). The Nathan Report defined voluntary action as 'not directed or controlled by the state and [...] in the main is financed by private, in contradistinction to public funds' (Nathan, 1952, p. 1) and this reinforced the post-war Beveridge position that voluntary organizations were marginal to public services. Whether this in-between sector now exists is debateable. From 1979, Conservative governments' preference to purchase services from the market created a more central role for voluntary organizations in welfare delivery (Halfpenny and Reid, 2002). New Labour has further mainstreamed the voluntary sector as a policy actor (Cabinet Office, 2002; Kendall, 2003; Blackmore, 2005) and the 2002 HM Treasury Cross-Cutting

Review promises it an even more integral role in service provision (McLaughlin, 2004).

This accountability view recognizes that while, in classical economics, the market generally ensures that goods and resources are distributed, the provision of public goods by governments may fail to meet demand (Kendall and Knapp, 1996). Voluntary organizations exploit gaps and performance failures in government public service provision (Hansmann, 1980; Weisbrod, 1988).

A second research stream defines the sector structurally and operationally. Arguably the most influential is Salamon and Anheier's (1994) proposition that the voluntary sector organizations are:

- formal structures with constitutions;
- independent of government and self-governing;
- not-for-profit; and
- voluntary – philanthropic in their motivation and involving volunteers.

Such organizations have distinctive patterns of financial management (Osborne, 2006a). For instance, they differ from public bodies by receiving voluntary income that is not the product of taxation. Unlike private companies they do not distribute surpluses to shareholders.

The drawback of such a broad definition is its over-inclusiveness; it includes organizations involved in health, education and research, development, housing and others. Kendall (2003) excludes organizations not 'traditionally thought' of as voluntary in describing the 'narrow voluntary sector' (NVS), as distinguished from Salamon and Anheier's 'broad voluntary sector' (BVS). Still, neither position in this framework is entirely satisfactory and does little more than to draw lines around certain organizations. It gives little sense of the identity of the sector as a whole and what distinctive pressures, processes and outputs it might have.

A third stream of analysis takes a more pragmatic view – as it has evolved, terminology has become elastic (Kendall and Knapp, 2000) and there is little to be gained from trying to stake down phenomena which are changing anyway (Halfpenny and Reid, 2002). As Theuvsen (2004) notes, the sector's position vis-à-vis the for-profit sector has been changing for the last decade and practices regarded as distinctively 'for-profit' are being adopted by the voluntary sector. In this view, seeking pure definitions or labels seems a fruitless task, especially if terms are used interchangeably within the sector anyway.

The real issue is whether voluntary organizations experience distinctive pressures and challenges. If so, academic study of the sector should usefully add to our understanding of the scope and purpose of performance management.

Distinctive? A literature overview

At its crudest the distinction is that commercial business is interested in profitability and the voluntary sector is not, which partially explains why the latter has paid little attention to performance measurement (Wise, 1995; Palmer, 1996). Management practices were a low priority in the 1980s in a sector built on goodwill and informality, which perceived itself as different from private enterprise (Omisakin, 1997; Cunningham, 1999). However, pressures in favour of them increased through the 1990s with increased competition for funding, dependence on statutory funding and the demands of a 'contract culture' that accompanied it. Still, as Alatrista and Arrowsmith (2004) note, distinctive organizational goals, performance measurement and accountability structures even now constrain take-up of management practices from outside the sector. In parts of the sector, performance management is also resisted as marginal to core operations and regarded cynically as a public relations (PR) exercise (NCVO, 2005d). Alarmingly, consultations by NCVO with voluntary organizations found few staff or trustees who understood the term 'performance improvement', and even if they recognized the term many took it to refer to individual rather than organizational performance (Quality Standards Task Group (QSTG), 2004).

In turn, the sector has received scant attention from management theorists who saw it as marginal to the economy (Batsleer, 1995) and this helps explain the asymmetry now in research coverage of performance management. For instance, as recently as 1998, of the 1721 published documents in the Chartered Management Institute's information database, only ten referred to the voluntary sector. Well-defined service commitments within the sector tend to block out HRM-inspired visions of integrated management (Kellock Hay et al., 2001). Little research on the sector has explored the use of performance management as an integrated system, combining the management of organizational, team and individual objectives (Armstrong and Baron, 1998). Such ideas have generally been perceived as more appropriate to other sectors (Cunningham, 1999).

Attracting more research interest are performance 'measurement', 'assessment' and 'improvement'. Macro-level concerns – regulation, public service contracting, beneficiary satisfaction, changes in public and social policy, development of a coherent voluntary 'sector' – drive investment in performance measurement rather than performance management processes. The impetus, for instance, for voluntary organizations to use quality management tools, according to the Centre for Voluntary Action, is from funders, often promoting specific standards, and from a perceived need to gain legitimacy in their eyes (NCVO, 2005b). The pressures are immense – from public sector Best Value thinking, governmental insistence on evidence-based policy making and from major institutional funders like the Community Fund in the UK who take a powerful lead on outcomes-based project funding. There is a lively debate about impact measurement and whether this is viewed from the macroperspective of civil society and the role of voluntary organizations or that of the organizations themselves (Reed et al., 2005).

Macro-level research has arguably been to the detriment of research at the micro-level of individual organizations (Vigoda, 2001; McLaughlin, 2004). While research over the last 20 years has 'gathered increasingly reliable information about [voluntary organizations'] resources', Halfpenny and Reid in their 2002 overview of sectoral research, mourn the neglect of small-scale, localized agencies. Further, while sectorally sensitive performance measurement models have emerged, detailed guidance for organizations on how to use them is yet to surface; as yet, the main benefit of research is to 'raise the debate on the wider role and impact of the voluntary and community sector' (NCVO, 2005c, p. 2).

Research, then, splits roughly two ways: one, at a policy level, often interpreting the sector's options for performance management in the context of the government's plans for public and voluntary sectors (for example, Kendall and Knapp, 2000); the other, at a case-study level, examining individual organizations' choices and performance management practices (for example, Dunn and Matthews, 2001) as a means of evaluating sectorally appropriate approaches. Between these lie a number of reviews, the most important being the Johns Hopkins Comparative Nonprofit Sector project, led by Salamon and Anheier, which produced a series of national analyses in the mid-1990s. The space in-between is also inhabited by more normative literature, in the sense of prescribing good practice (for example, Hudson, 2004), deriving from the research, advice and advocacy activities of organizations (in the UK) such as the Directory for Social Change and NCVO.

If we place all this within Thorpe and Beasley's (2004) typology of performance management research, it is 'hard' and 'applied' (in the sense that the sector is driven by accountability and compliance issues) with 'convergent' views on the nature of performance management with a mixed 'urban'/'rural' focus: there is relatively little research crowding in the sector but it has been confined to a small range of issues within the sector. This is likely to change as the performance measurement agenda broadens beyond external compliance and as a range of performance criteria relevant to the sector is established.

A distinctive sector?

What, then, makes the voluntary sector 'distinctive', if it is at all? Prompted by the consultations around the 1989 White Paper 'Charities – a framework for the future', the National Council for Voluntary Organizations (NCVO) sought to set out a number of distinctive characteristics:

Voluntary organizations

- are free from the immediate demands and constraints of the market, as they do not have to generate profits;
- do not need statutory backing for what they do, unlike local authorities;
- remain subject to the law, but their independence allows them to be self-regulating and to have a flexibility and responsiveness that organizations in other sectors may lack;
- set their own priorities and have freedom to change them to meet new needs or to fill gaps left by State provision;
- offer a variety of channels for people to become involved with others in an immediate and personal way;
- provide opportunities to exercise individual initiative, to offer creative solutions to what otherwise might seem to be insurmountable problems or to be innovative;
- have room for the enthusiast and, on occasion, for the eccentric; and
- contribute to the healthy functioning of a plural and democratic society (Nathan, 1990, p. 18).

Additionally, the external environment was changing: privatization and contracting out of services meant that voluntary organizations became part of mainstream service provision (Osborne, 2006c; McLaughlin, 2004). The effect of such changes after 1979 was that the traditional independence of voluntary organizations was under threat by greater accountability to government through contracting.

Given these sectoral features, Wise (1995), Hind (1995) and Kendall and Knapp (2000) all reject the relevance of performance measurement seen wholly in accounting terms: voluntary organizations are not tied to a corporate finance cycle. Performance cannot be measured reliably by a single indicator. This is echoed by the NCVO's analysis that 'compared to the private sector, voluntary and community sector (VCS) performance measurement is generally far more complex' because outcomes are less tangible and tend to be more people-centred (NCVO, 2005c, p. 1). From a non-governmental organization (NGO) perspective, Fowler (1998) agrees that financial returns cannot be measures of performance for organizations that offer services to those who cannot meet their full costs. Moreover, assessing performance poses peculiar problems for voluntary organizations:

- project delivery depends on the involvement of multiple actors;
- their behaviours are influenced by forces often out of their control;
- achievements often depend on control over resources which may not be possible;
- time-scales leading to completion of projects can be very long; and
- the goal of human development depends on integrated action and cannot be atomized into separately evaluated projects.

Three main conclusions emerge from these discussions about the sector's distinctiveness. First is that the lack of accountability to shareholders imposes a heightened obligation on the sector to be socially and publicly accountable (Drucker, 1990). 'Performance management is particularly important in Third Sector organizations because, unlike businesses, few have the benefit of strong market forces to provide an external check on performance' (Hudson, 2004, p. 171). In reality, performance management and accountability are not alien to sectoral values, but endemic to them: 'Few voluntary organizations are strangers to outcome or performance assessment of one kind or another: their very existence often requires them to argue their effectiveness in tackling social problems, supporting vulnerable individuals or promoting particular causes' (Kendall and Knapp, 2000, p. 106). Further, there are very clear accountabilities even if they do not include shareholders. Organizations are under pressure for improved reporting when public service contracts are accepted (Blackmore, 2005) even though voluntary organizations are not democratically accountable in the way that public sector providers are (Kendall and Knapp, 2000). Voluntary organizations have multiple external and internal stakeholders and often struggle with juggling reporting obligations (QSTG, 2004; Reed et al., 2005). So, the big issue is not whether voluntary organizations are accountable but how they deal with multiple accountabilities (Wise, 1995; Fowler, 1998; Kendall and Knapp, 2000; NCVO, 2005c) within their performance management systems.

The second conclusion is that performance management approaches have to be appropriate to deal with the distinctive features and dynamic operating environment of the voluntary sector (Drucker, 1990; QSTG, 2004). Management models have been borrowed from other sectors (Courtney, 1996) to fill the gaps in more home-grown research; and Theuvsen (2004) notes with concern how 'mimicry' as well as economic and governmental pressures have led to the common use of some management techniques like strategic planning. Pressure from formal regulation introduces performance reporting mechanisms into the sector which, in some quarters, raises questions about their adequacy to capture the nuances and scope of voluntary activity (NCVO, 2005e). This reaction, on the one hand, has inspired critical thinking about the architecture of performance measurement: what measures are appropriate or inappropriate and whether creating standardized measures of performance should be an aspiration for a diverse sector (NCVO, 2005d). On the other hand, the reaction has encouraged sectoral research to develop methodologies and performance indicators beyond those borrowed from both public and private sectors (Dunn and Mathews, 2001; Kendall and Knapp, 2000; NCVO, 2005c).

Emerging models

Although performance management models in the sector are more emergent than established, there is a general consensus about the purpose of performance management. It is 'essentially an internal organizational tool concerned with the utilization of organizational resources, against a number of priorities and organizational objectives' (Osborne, 2006b, p. 217). It provides a 'feedback loop' between the major actors – trustees, managers and staff – and corporate goals (Hind, 1995; Hudson, 2004). The literature highlights two main accountability dimensions: to the public at large, users and members, funders, government and other external stakeholders (Wise, 1995; Kearns, 1996; NCVO, 2005b); and to internal regulators – trustees, managers – to monitor achievements and conduct and ensure the organization's mission is delivered (Hudson, 2004; QSTG, 2004; Blackmore, 2005).

Of these, external accountability is becoming the increasingly dominant driver for performance management in the sector (Lock, 1998). In comparison to literature on accountability in the public sector, research here is still insubstantial (Kearns, 1996) although the emphasis has already been skewed towards assessing financial performance (Connolly and Hyndman, 2000; NCVO, 2005e). Leat (1993) advocates a much broader performance assessment agenda acknowledging process and programme accountabilities as well as financial ones. That said, several studies show that voluntary organizations fail to do this well (Connolly and Hyndman, 2001; Palmer et al., 2001; Cabinet Office, 2002; Charity Commission, 2004), calling into question their capacity to partner government in service provision (McLaughlin, 2004). Both the skewedness and effectiveness of current performance management practice, alongside the debate on appropriateness, have stimulated investigation into new models.

Strategic planning

Mainstreaming of voluntary organizations by Conservative Government policy in the early 1980s required more robust management systems to replace 'muddling through' (Landry et al., 1985). Thus, one of the earliest modern models was provided by strategic management and planning. The essential theory is that management processes, such as performance management, are aligned with strategy. The process is a systematic one and involves establishing a vision which informs the organizational mission and this in turn determines the strategies, then their objectives and supporting processes.

The model, promoted by the Directory of Social Change through Hudson's work on managing voluntary organizations (Hudson, 2004), emphasizes the importance of systematic management to 'holding people accountable at different levels'. Wise (1995, p. 41) argues that the strategic management cycle of needs-vision-mission-aims-actions can helpfully feed into the operational performance management cycle of aims-inputs-transfer/delivery-outputs to create an integrated model for the sector (Figure 17.1).

As an essentially 'borrowed' model the caveats, as Hudson admits, surround its 'fit' to the sector. Voluntary organizations frequently lack integrated systems to capture data on performance and only recently have systematically introduced performance indicators as a management tool (Hudson, 2004). Further, Bart and Tabone's large-sample primary research into the hospital sector (1998) found that while mission statements had some value as 'performance-enhancing drivers',

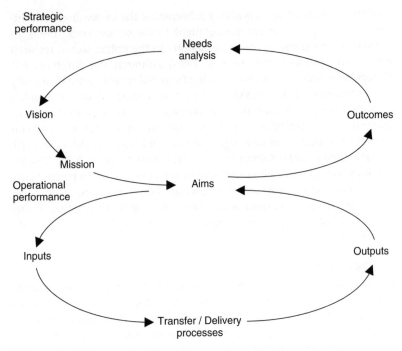

Figure 17.1 Figure-of-eight model for value for money.
Source: Wise, 1995, p. 41

few organizations' systems were fully aligned. Most failed to link their management processes to their mission. Least aligned of all were HRM processes designed to link people performance to organizational goals. Nonetheless, voluntary organizations appear to have taken up the principles of strategic planning in recent years and tend to sharply focus on their mission (QSTG, 2004).

Quality systems

Osborne (2006b, p. 217) notes that 'the experience of services by their beneficiaries and their impact on them' overlaps with the task of performance management. The quality management approach represents a second model or group of models used within the voluntary sector. Case-studies, such as Dunn and Mathews' (2001) account of the Cedar Foundation in Northern Ireland, chart the use of several models. They note the use of 'soft' outcomes related to user satisfaction rather than 'hard' outcomes in an approach that is highly participative – incidentally one of Drucker's recommended hallmarks of a sectorally appropriate performance management approach (1990). The Cedar Foundation adopted a strategic planning model on to which it grafted several models and standards – Investors in People, the EFQM 'Excellence model', ISO 9002 and the Balanced Scorecard – with the advantage of gaining a holistic performance assessment approach with templates of performance indicators drawn from the respective models. Their relevance, argue Dunn and Mathews, is that they meet accountability requirements by external funders and purchasers as well as focus on beneficiaries.

There are caveats too for borrowing quality standards. Voluntary organizations, according to NCVO and the Futureskills 2003 survey, are generally aware of available models – 94.4 per cent aware of Investors in People and 53.4 per cent aware of EFQM for instance – but they are rarely adopted. 39.3 per cent registered for Investors in People and only 8 per cent for EFQM. One factor accounting for such rejection is the 'not-invented-here' syndrome: PQASSO, a quality standard developed by the Charities Evaluation Service in 1997 for voluntary organizations is the most used of all standards, accounting for 46 per cent of the Futureskills survey respondents. Other factors are a lack of capacity, and resistance to standards which are seen as a distraction to core operational obligations (Centre for Voluntary Action Research (CVAR), 2004).

Perhaps most serious are the potentially distorting effects of multiple quality standards that are being driven by funders (NCVO, 2004). On the one hand, there is a danger of 'decoupling' where imposed performance measures are inappropriate to actual performance and are regarded with resentment. On the other hand, there is a danger of 'colonization' in which organizations are distracted from their core mission in order to comply with external measurement standards (NCVO, 2005c). Researchers at London South Bank University in 2004 evaluated the Community Fund's use of 'preferred' outcomes indicators to assess funding applications and revealed a variety of bidding behaviours to make projects 'fit' in with them (Macnamara et al., 2004).

'POW' – the public sector and beyond

Arguably, the most dominant investigatory model in use among service-oriented voluntary organizations is influenced by the 'production of welfare' (POW) framework. Though influenced by other disciplines, POW is based on economics theory and breaks down production activity into inputs (resources), outputs (services and products) and outcomes (ultimate impacts on users and beneficiaries). The framework has given new public management its essential performance criteria – efficiency, effectiveness, equity and economy (Bovaird et al., 1988) – and in the voluntary sector has been described as the 'Value-for-Money Triangle' (Wise, 1995).

With the introduction of formal, statutory regulation of charities at the beginning of the 1990s, the Nathan Report (Nathan, 1990, p. 13) identified 'a growing need for efficiency and effectiveness' related to demands inside and outside the sector. The Report promoted performance measurement based on outputs and performance against agreed objectives ('effectiveness') and the ratio between inputs and outputs ('efficiency'), adding that cost efficiency measurement was inadequate on its own. Noting concerns about over-use of quantitative evaluation, the Report commended establishing performance indicators to evaluate management, resources, structures, methods of working and procedures as well as economy measures and control over inputs.

Osborne (2006b, p. 218) raises doubts about the 'rationalist tradition of decision-making' which underpins this approach, since it relies on accessibility and availability of performance data when the 'bounded' reality of the sector is that limited information is held by different parties. Osborne strains at the leash of the POW framework and argues for a more contextually sensitive model for the voluntary sector. First, there are other competing models around the sector including the 'political' approach, in which assessment is used as a means to an end to promote or prune activity, and the 'pluralist' model which acknowledges multiple stakeholder requirements for performance review. Second, indicators need to be developed respective to different levels of performance – organizational, team, individual. Third, specific sectoral needs for performance measurement have yet to be established. These he goes on to define:

- context monitoring, including assessment of the corporate environment, collaborations with other agencies and partnerships;
- strategy monitoring, checking alignment of processes and aims;
- progress monitoring, assessing targets-on-time;
- detailed activity monitoring;
- impact monitoring, measuring achievement of high level objectives; and
- catalysis monitoring, assessing impacts on other agencies.

Extending POW

Kendall and Knapp (2000) argue that a multiplicity of stakeholders and their preferred measurement standards, specific accountabilities (for example, to the public, funders or government) and internal, operational needs for performance data, demands 'indicators that range beyond those conventionally employed in for-profit firms and public organizations' (p. 129). Just as Osborne extended the POW framework by examining the foci of performance measurement, Kendall and Knapp propose extending performance criteria beyond efficiency, effectiveness, equity and economy (NCVO, 2005c). This new managerialist approach is deficient because it fails to measure:

- the effect of trust and voluntarism;
- the capital that lies within networks of people and collaborating agencies who together may produce a qualitatively different quality and type of impact; and
- innovating behaviour in the sector geared to improving or developing different kinds of service provision.

To Bovaird's public sector-derived criteria, Kendall and Knapp now add choice and diversity, social justice or equity, participation, advocacy and innovation. The production of welfare process is not a closed system and organizations are influenced by both the meso-context of their networks and the macro-level context of society, politics and policy. The latter context, encompassing government, professional rule-makers and powerful social values, may be perceived to be remote by stakeholders in the production system; but it has powerful indirect influences such as the expectations placed upon professional workers, as well as operating more directly through, for example, government funding decisions. The 'meso-level' social context often acts on welfare production systems in a more benign way, as relationships built on trust cross organizational boundaries through communities of interest and practice, geographically proximate groupings and virtual networks (Kendall and Knapp, 2000, pp. 115–17).

Thus the POW framework is extended even further to encompass the influential contexts of performance. But – given the power of the macro-context in particular – has the 'context' not taken over some of the 'text'? Performance management, at least in some areas of service provision, is in danger of being dictated by external stakeholders rather than having an internal rationale such as being intrinsically good practice. The attendant difficulty is that organizations pay lip service to external requirements and develop *ad hoc* management processes that are seen to distract them from the real business of service (Macnamara et al., 2004).

Modernization

The fifth model raises immediate concerns about the impact of government on the sector:

> The recent governmental 'cross-cutting review' of the role of the voluntary and community sector (VCS) in the provision of public services in the UK... establishes a distinctive voluntary sector modernization agenda that involves the VCS in embracing the core tenets of the New Public Management, including a commitment to professional management, an adherence to standards of audit and performance management and an embracing of contractual approaches to inter-organizational governance.
>
> (McLaughlin et al., 2002, p. 556)

McLaughlin et al. thus chart the resurgence of an old managerialist model in a New Labour skin. The Cross-Cutting Review promises to integrate the voluntary sector into public service provision as never before but it highlights two difficulties with performance measurement practice. One is that the lack of consistent and accurate performance data in the voluntary sector makes it impossible for organizations to demonstrate how they might contribute added value to service provision. The second is that if organizations cannot provide performance data evidence, the government cannot include them as partners in public service provision.

The modernization 'model' proffered by government would require improving information from this sector, developing a standardized information return that helps compare providers and their performance, agreement on reporting standards and a timetable for introducing new management information systems. This model McLaughlin believes 'will require further extension of managerialist approaches into the VCS' (McLaughlin et al., 2002, p. 560) and will split the sector into two – the modernized and the non-modernized who will be effectively marginalized as contributors to civil society. This is an explicitly imposed model which suffers from difficulties well-defined in the literature of being top-down and assuming a too standardized approach to performance management.

Tensions

Throughout this analysis, clear gaps in research have been described that are related to the relatively unsophisticated development of performance management in the voluntary sector. Just as clear are important unresolved tensions which will colour and define future initiatives. To conclude, I want to identify the tensions that are likely to influence the continuing research agenda in the sector.

Distinctiveness vs. standardization

A large proportion of literature on the sector has tried to establish the sector's distinctiveness. An immediate difficulty here is in defining its identity as distinct from other sectors since the voluntary sector is increasingly drawn into a public service agenda and is evidently influenced by other-sectoral management models and techniques (Theuvsen, 2004). The pressures against organizations' autonomy are immense. Lock (1998, p. 410) believes that 'the contract culture is changing the very nature of charities and their regulation'. Stoker notes the pressure in favour of charities having legal duties to publish their performance criteria (Charity Commission, 2004). McLaughlin (2004) is highly critical of neo-corporatist prescriptions from government and urges the sector to stand against 'one best way' modernization ideas.

Some kind of standardization of performance measurement and reporting, of course, is important to retain public confidence (Charity Commission, 2004), but despite the publication of a Statement of Recommended Practice for charities (SORP) in 1988 and its revision (SORP 2) in 1995, voluntary organizations still struggle with complying (Palmer et al., 2001). The problem is general and deep: 'Existing performance reporting at the level of individual voluntary and community organizations (VCOs), sub-sectors and the VCS as a whole is limited. This implies that there is inadequate performance information to support VCOs and VCS efforts to improve performance' (NCVO, 2005e, p. 6).

Moreover, no agreement has yet emerged in the literature on what sets of performance criteria are important and appropriate to a diverse sector. (There is much greater clarity about what criteria are *not* (Kendall and Knapp, 2000)). Outcomes measurement has gained some currency in the sector as a distinctive approach but it nonetheless causes confusion and some resentment as being too funder-driven (Macnamara et al., 2004; NCVO, 2005d). Difficulties remain with measuring soft outcomes, with long time-scales, with different types of impact and types of activity where outcomes are hard to establish. As the NCVO admits, 'tools for impact assessment are still in their infancy' (NCVO, 2005d). New performance criteria to evaluate processes that have been proposed in recent years are, Kendall and Knapp (2000, p. 129) admit, 'inherently difficult to pin down'.

For the sector to win the debate about being distinctive it has to define its particular economic role and identity. As Blackmore (2005, p. 2) remarks, those organizations which accept public service contracts will need to establish 'the distinctive value they bring to public services'. The pressure on developing meaningful performance criteria and measurement models will remain intense so long as public accountabilities exist.

Internal vs. external rationales

The importance of accountability as a primary driver of performance management introduces a second tension. While external rationales are well defined and covered by research (for example, Connolly and Hyndman, 2000), the debate continues on what this will mean for conceptualizing performance management in the sector and, indeed, for the sector as a whole. On the other hand, internal rationales for performance management are less defined and relatively neglected in the literature. Nonetheless, voluntary organizations are called to account both externally and internally (QSTG, 2004).

With pressures from regulation and stakeholders, assessing organizational performance is an unavoidable issue, even if the sometimes-competing claims of multiple stakeholders make it difficult (Kendall and Knapp, 2000). Voluntary organizations are 'increasingly subject to influencing agents' (Kellock Hay et al., 2001, p. 240). If McLaughlin's (2004) prognosis is borne out they are likely to lose a leading role as agents of modernization by being suborned as the subjects of it.

How far voluntary organizations integrate external performance standards into their own vision, mission and culture is questioned by several commentators. Some of these standards are rejected outright as too costly, bureaucratic, irrelevant and measuring the wrong things (NCVO, 2004; QSTG, 2004). Funders, purchasers and inspection agency requirements that preferred quality standards are used are ostensibly in a bid to raise quality; there is evidence though that organizations adopt them simply to enhance their ability to compete for contracts (Kellock Hay et al., 2001) and enhance their legitimacy (Theuvsen, 2004).

The other side of the debate is how far voluntary organizations have robust internal regulation mechanisms, and arguably the power of external audit bodies have inhibited their development (Palmer, 1995). A lack of resources available for administration is 'exacerbated by the pattern of funding, which favoured short-term project working over sustained development funding for infrastructure' (Kellock Hay et al., 2001, p. 253). The 'every penny counts' mindset bred from organizations' keen sense of public accountability takes investment away from internal management including HRM, training and performance appraisal of staff (Cunningham, 1999; Alatrista and Arrowsmith, 2004; QSTG, 2004). Thus both research and the practice of performance management in the sector appear to be unequally strung between reporting for external accounting purposes and collecting performance data internally for organizations' own learning and development (NCVO, 2005c).

Macro vs. micro

The third tension concerns the symmetry of the levels at which performance management research is, or will be, conducted in the voluntary sector. Halfpenny and Reid (2002) are concerned that:

> ... the stress placed by both policy analysts and researchers on partnerships, inputs and output measures gives prominence to those voluntary organizations that are structured, formalized and professionalized, and therefore capable of cooperating or competing with public and private sector organizations. This 'professional turn' diminishes the attention given to the messy and muddled yet vibrant sorts of voluntarism that often spring up as collective expressions of opposition to state and private sector policies and practices.
>
> (p. 543)

This echoes McLaughlin's (2004) view that modernization leads to only a 'selective engagement' between government and certain kinds of voluntary organizations.

Clearly, the movement towards 'professionalism' is unstoppable in the current regulatory climate and should therefore retain a major place on the voluntary sector research agenda. Considering too the macro-perspective of the sector's contribution to achieving the goals of civil society, those organizations sophisticated enough to manage the accountability demands of properly evidenced performance assessment should continue to receive attention. However, there is a real danger of losing sight of the role of 'patchwork quilt of social services' (Fowler, 1998, p. 150) who may plug the gaps left by well-resourced larger voluntary organizations who, in turn, plug bigger gaps in public services.

Vigoda (2001) identifies an inverted pyramid of research coverage of organizational performance: at the top, broadest attention has been given to private and public sectors with more restricted treatment of the voluntary sector. Further down, these studies have focused on macro-issues such as efficiency and effectiveness, with the least attention given to examining the workings of individual organizations trying to cope with changing contexts. Vigoda thus poses a challenge to researchers to redress the balance and regard the voluntary sector as a rich focus for research.

Conclusions and reflections

This overview has revealed a dynamic and changing performance management agenda in the UK voluntary sector. It will likely continue to evolve as organizations refine their identities vis-à-vis their public sector partners and the market. As such the relatively narrow focus of research is likely to widen as the voluntary sector comes to grips with regulatory and public accountability issues and with broader performance criteria beyond the strictly financial. Emergent models are throwing up exciting questions about outcomes assessment, different levels and contexts of performance, and appropriate forms of performance data that will satisfy the needs of both external stakeholders and regulators and internal management.

Many of these issues are not limited to the UK context, though we have mainly concentrated on it here. Kearns (1996), commenting from a US perspective, identifies accountability as one of the key debates in non-profit organizations; he argues how organizations should answer public expectations across a wide spectrum of indicators, from organizational performance to ethicality of behaviour. The relative neglect of the sector in research circles, which we have noted in the UK, is also repeated elsewhere. Cooper, as long ago as 1990, called for greater attention to the non-profit sector in the American literature on accountability, which he described as 'neither substantial nor sophisticated' (1990, p. 18).

We have seen throughout this analysis how the sector is struggling to develop its own measurement and assessment approaches, extending beyond tools and philosophies belonging to other sectors, while sometimes being held uncomfortably to account by the systems of service-partner and donor stakeholders. This kind of struggle we saw at work in the use of quality assessment frameworks in the sector. Looking forwards, this chapter has outlined a number of unresolved issues which will influence the development of performance management approaches – moves to standardizing performance reporting, questions about the continuing impact of regulation on the sector, and, indeed, what the sector will even look like in the future.

Part III

Towards a Multidisciplinary Perspective on Performance Management

18
Viewing Performance

Richard Thorpe and Jacky Holloway

Introduction

When this book was first conceived, we envisaged that this chapter would be able to bring together all the disciplines and fields of study with which we were working and present them in a single schema. Our inspiration for this was a paper by Easterby-Smith (1997) in which he examined the concept of organizational learning from a multidisciplinary perspective. What he was able to create was a template that allowed the reader to understand the concept from a range of different disciplinary perspectives. By doing so he was able to offer a more holistic understanding. As our aim was similar – namely to seek a better understanding of the often very distinct contributions relating to performance that are embedded in the diverse set of academic disciplines and traditions that focus on aspects of performance and how it can be measured and improved – we initially began by adopting the same framework used by Easterby-Smith (1997) and attempted to use his categories. Through such an approach, we aimed to gain a better understanding of what constitutes performance management, especially in multidisciplinary contexts, and by so doing to contribute to improved practice and theory.

We first identified the base discipline from which the conceptualization of performance arose (such as psychology, economics or engineering), and the ontology or system of belief that underpinned the way in which each discipline set about researching the topic within their particular field. We then moved to understand better the research methods that were being used and the 'problematic' which forms the basis of any particular study or enquiry. Our initial expectation was that from this analysis we might observe a set of prevailing drivers within each discipline; for example, a view that performance was predominantly about human behaviour or the quality of the information that could be brought to bear in any particular set of circumstances. From the perspective of understanding the nature of the discipline, and an understanding of what counts as knowledge or truth, we would then, we believed, be in a position to identify the contribution each discipline brought to the field. Furthermore, we deduced that only by understanding the contribution each discipline makes and how it has emerged would we be able to suggest how it might be possible to construct effective multidisciplinary teams of researchers or practitioners to take our understanding of performance to a new level.

In reality, what we have arrived at is a rather incomplete framework or schema. This is because on analysis of the disciplines they appear to be at varying stages of development with respect to models, methods and theoretical contributions. They are also diverse in terms of the extent to which we could discern explicit or even implicit theoretical roots and ontologies. Notwithstanding, we have drawn out a number of themes which our disciplines and sectors exhibit and these are presented in this chapter, together with some emerging lessons for performance management practitioners. Many of these themes are not fundamentally new and have been identified before (for example, see Bowey et al., 1986) but warrant restating, given the evidence provided by the contributions made to this book.

Common themes

Although most of the chapters in Part II were written to a common brief, the early stage of development of performance management research in many fields meant that the data was not robust enough to reveal detailed patterns within each discipline. What was possible though, on analysis of the content of all the chapters, was to identify some general emerging themes and patterns that were common across all the disciplines and sectors.

Simple unitary measures

One strong trend that many of our writers mention is the way practitioners quickly move away from relying on one measure (or a very small number of measures) to suites of performance measures and indicators that better reflect the performance management and control objectives which they address.

Single measures, they indicate, may have been useful at a time when activities were more predictable (or thought to be more predictable), but soon both practitioners and analysts recognized these failed to take account of such things as operational scale and the interdependence that exists between factors. Also the traditional unitary measures depended upon the nature of the industry and discipline that was undertaking the measurement; hence HR specialists measured the performance of people, and operations managers measured the performance of machines. Seeing the deficiencies in unitary measures, particularly how they failed to pick up the importance of inter-dependencies and were prone to 'gaming', subversion or manipulation led to a move to identify multiple measures that reflected the different dimensions that made up the performance of an enterprise.

Efficiency and effectiveness

In our review of the history of performance measurement and management, we could see some disciplines collecting an ever-increasing array of data to reflect the performance of a firm in their search to account for the variability of input and several kinds of output, or combinations of outputs. Their aim was to produce a classical 'production function' which might often, depending on the disciplinary perspective, be represented mathematically.

Crudely stated, this theoretically orientated approach to productivity that seeks to capture and measure as many variables as humanly possible, bears little relationship to what academics observe on the ground as managers strive to improve the performance of their organizations. Despite this, financial analysts have achieved fame by using such 'whole system measures' as they sought to judge the viability of particular enterprises. For example, in the 1970s Clarkson and Elliot of the Manchester Business School were able to predict the collapse of Rolls Royce several months before it happened, and Ingham and Harrington (1980) proposed a system (or pyramid) of financial ratios to compare the performance of companies in similar industries in order that relative performance could be assessed. What is striking here is that the multiple measures used by those managers who tried to measure the whole system were still rather static. They still only measured the easily measurable (e.g. output volumes, person-hours deployed or financial costs incurred) and they still retained their focus on efficiency, only showing how to do the known tricks faster. There were few signs of a shift to effectiveness measures incorporating notions of relevance, and even fewer incorporating a strategic dimension related to the requirement to retain or develop future competences or capabilities.

In some respects, public services have led to the development of more sophisticated measures (for example, of longer-term impact, cost-effectiveness, user satisfaction and value added). The public sector has also exhibited a tendency to develop excessively complex performance indicator systems however, with dozens of potentially conflicting politically driven targets. Public service modernization in many countries since the 1980s (characterized by various forms of quasi-market and partnership arrangement and wider citizen involvement) has engendered more externally focused performance management systems than those found in many companies still today.

Embracing soft and more strategic aspects of performance

What we see from the contributions in Part II is a gradual move away from a simple focus on the 'harder' (easy to measure and usually quantitative) variables in organizations and a move over to embrace a range of 'softer' measures that signal a recognition of what the organization might need to do in order to be successful into the future. In many of the chapters, we see a widening of the concern for performance from inside to outside the firm or organization through a concern to understand stakeholders of all kinds, from customers to pressure groups. A few disciplines are actively engaged with concerns in relation to environmental matters that also serve to signal their understanding of not simply the immediate impact of what the organization does, but also of the implications for wider society.

Mintzberg (1982) recognized many years ago that effectiveness implied the combination of productivity with relevance, and required not simply an optimum combination and efficient use of inputs (whatever they were to be) but additional factors such as judgement, initiative and adaptation. It was the growing importance of qualitative components that were missing from many judgements being made about performance. From a similar period, we find detailed national and international debates in healthcare and education about the nature (and affordability) of 'high quality' services (see, for example, Maxwell, 1984); and early attempts to employ performance management frameworks such as quality assurance, devised for manufacturing, in the service sector.

It is clear that over the years each of the disciplines we have examined has widened their understanding of the kinds of performance measures in use. This reflects a shift towards measurement and management systems that address the real priorities of, and issues faced in, the organization and away from measures especially in the public sector that tackle a short term (often politically embarrassing) problem.

To affect overall organizational performance, contingency theorists have provided insights into ways of devising performance measurement systems that link business strategy with organizational culture. Viewed in this way, as systems components, performance systems can be seen not only as a means of measuring things, but also as part of a policy instrument that works to influence change by carrying appropriate messages that reflect and influence behaviour in particular ways. If one takes a contingency perspective, then the quest is not for one type of measure for all situations and businesses, but for more appropriate sets of measures of inputs, processes, outputs and outcomes that 'fit' particular circumstances. (See Holloway, 2002 for some contributions from contingency and systems perspectives to performance management systems design.)

The importance of process and change

As Lawler and Bullock (1978) observed when commenting on changes to payment systems, most approaches to the design of measurement systems are top-down; they assume that those at the top of an organization are capable of making all the necessary decisions. What we again see from the chapters in Part II is that if a wider process of consultation takes place in the design of performance measures, three things happen. The first is that both management and employees learn more about the priorities being measured and what changes might be needed to be made to support them. Second, if this happens then there is a better chance of a broader set of measures emerging, as happens with the balanced scorecard approach, that will, for example, measure important processes and not simply support functions. (By the latter we mean those 'support' activities that do not exist as entities in their own right, but instead exist only to better deliver the product or service; for example, the HRM or accountancy functions within a firm.) Use will also be made of external as well as internal measures. And third, and perhaps most importantly of all, there would be a critical mass of individuals committed to change and the success of whatever is decided.

What we can detect from the trends in Chapters 5–17 is the adoption of action research approaches to data collection and change with respect to performance management. These link strategy with learning and design, as opposed to linear traditional rational planning and implementation. Measurement then has become part of an interactive process that places emphasis neither on the system itself nor solely on the simple matching of the performance measurement system to the organizational circumstances, but instead recognizes that a good management team can

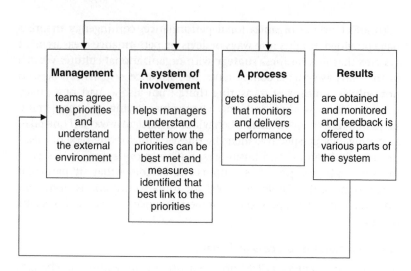

Figure 18.1 An inclusive performance measurement design approach

achieve success through a robust process of engagement and iteration. The participatory process serves then to drive the organization forward in the direction in which its performance can be maximized (Figure 18.1).

What then are the approaches we might recommend?

First, broadening and deepening our understanding of performance management processes as illustrated by the above themes can help us to draw some conclusions about the scope for more effective performance management systems. Without wishing to be prescriptive, evidence from our discipline and sector reviews suggest the following promising approaches.

Drawing on as wide a range of information sources as possible

The action research approach to performance management identified in some disciplines recognizes that learning and changing amongst organizational members are social processes, in which the experiences of the organizational world are developed and shaped through contacts with others. As a consequence, if behavioural change is to be one of the outcomes, solutions need to be found by listening to the views of others. In the context of performance management, an important task for managers will be to create clarity of purpose in such situations and, through the resulting debates and a process of fact finding, establish a clearer view of 'who wants what' within the organization. This clearer view or account of what would otherwise be contested issues in the organization offers employees a better climate within which performance can be managed and understood. Evidence of how this process might work already exists in studies conducted within particular fields of management (for example, in the approach adopted by *Investors in People* and in approaches to payment system design and implementation, Thorpe, 2000) but has never really been brought together as lessons for the field as a whole.

What managers might begin to consider is how they can develop a process that uncovers the understandings, expectations and motivations of organizational members and matches these to a thorough environmental assessment of the priorities the organization will need to focus on if it is to succeed. In some chapters, we have seen these explorations encompass a wide understanding of stakeholder views in a global as well as a societal context.

This process might well need to be undertaken at two levels. At the senior management level, to clarify the organization's priorities might include a clear understanding of the organization's value and supply chains in order to uncover the organization's core capacities which incorporate present skills as well as accumulated knowledge and organizational processes. At a more operational level, the challenge is to communicate these to the workplace and to learn from employees how these core capacities might be best measured (qualitatively as well as quantitatively) and how change might be best achieved.

Such a process appears to us to be extremely important in helping managers really understand their organizations, even if the problems of collecting information, consulting and revising ideas prior to implementing change are likely to demand considerable time and effort; there are few short cuts.

Engaging the commitment of senior managers

The change literature is full of examples where David has managed to beat Goliath and new systems have been gradually modified or subverted on implementation. What the research literature indicates (Kotter, 1995; Pettigrew and Whipp, 1993) is that senior managers need to be involved at the beginning of every change and have the commitment and competence to carry though the programme if it is not to be modified or subverted by others in the organization pursuing different goals and objectives. Senior level involvement will also ensure that a close link is established and maintained between the strategic and the operational, and that coherence in the performance measurement systems are maintained. Middle managers should also not be overlooked and a clear role in designing and implementing any process should be identified if they are not to feel threatened or disenfranchised. It is also important that employees at this level have prior training and clear briefings if they are to feel confident in their roles. The commitment of employees at junior levels can be greatly influenced by how they perceive and experience the commitment of those at more senior levels. Powerful messages can come from relatively small but symbolic cuts associated with performance management systems, serving to undermine change.

Ensure that key staff at all levels make a contribution

As with any significant organizational change, to improve performance systematically it is important to encourage participation by establishing a large enough coalition of staff to drive through the changes.

The experience of organizations making change has shown that providing both formal and informal opportunities for participation dramatically improves performance. The key here is good human resource management practice in particular (Pettigrew and Whipp, 1993) especially the involvement of organizational members (at any level) who can see a wider context than simply their current role. The processes of leadership, team development and information seeking that are intrinsic parts of powerful approaches such as benchmarking and the balanced scorecard need managing in their own right (Francis and Holloway, 2007). Such approaches generally require inputs from different functions, and involve examining key internal processes in depth as well as looking outside the organization for comparators, all of which can be uncomfortable especially for newly established multidisciplinary teams.

Be process led and let the identification of the measures emerge – in contrast to having a preconceived view of what the measures should be

As we have indicated, the importance of process has been vastly underrated and 'tools' such as the balanced scorecard and benchmarking serve not merely as tools in their own right, but also as vehicles around which debate and discussion can take place leading to new understandings and action.

The strategic nature of designing a performance management or measurement system can not be overstated. As performance integrates with culture, a process of change that involves many will permeate a large area of the organization and require the re-organization and revision of procedures. It provides the opportunity for improving performance in a variety of ways – what Pettigrew and Whipp (1993) refer to as 'coherence'. These improvements might be in the area of communication, central procedures, technology or training – essential processes supporting the desired outputs and outcomes.

The complexity and unpredictability of such systemic interconnections is often underestimated in performance management system design. There are very few simple 'cause–effect' routes to better performance. For example, research studies have shown that when payment systems are used as interventions and catalysts for broader organizational changes they have led to improvements in motivation. But simply linking 'pay' to 'performance' rarely has the desired effect.

Performance measurement systems affect almost all other sub-systems of an organization, both directly (e.g. training, development and appraisal procedures) and more pervasively via information systems, job design, management style and organizational culture. Investment in gaining an in-depth understanding of input–process–output–outcome relationships almost always pays off.

Emerging messages for performance management

We have already acknowledged that the discipline and sector studies assembled in this book reflect 'work in progress', as most authors have been venturing into largely uncharted territory. They and their peers may undertake, or advise on, performance management using their specialist knowledge; but like most specialists they had not previously taken stock of their contribution to wider knowledge about performance management in the way that we asked them to do for this book. Nonetheless, their combined wisdom leads us to highlight the following, generic and cross-discipline messages. Some consultants who engage in process consultancy (for example, Employment Relations Ltd.) are already clear on the approaches that need to be employed but the key points we feel need to be taken into account by anyone designing, implementing or managing a performance measurement or management system include:

1. Being clear about what needs to be prioritized – no organization can measure everything so choices have to be made.
2. During the prioritization process, there needs to be clarity on what the different functions are in the organization and how they relate one to another. As a consequence organizations need to consider how they

can measure processes and identify intra-organizational priorities. It is accepted that these may well be different between different products and services or between different processes within an organization.

3. In connection with the above, organizations need to be careful not to overemphasize the performance of sub-systems or support functions at the expense of those activities that really add value to the enterprise. Within an organization, attention should be paid to cross-cutting processes that make sense to customers, both internal and external.

4. To ensure coherence, tensions that might exist between different functional areas need to be made more explicit and resolved. If not they may rapidly damage the performance management system.

5. Measures should include qualitative aspects of performance, the 'how' as well as the 'what'. A proper understanding of customer satisfaction or staff motivation, or a particular capability embodied within the staff might be extremely challenging and require imaginative use of measures.

6. Linked to the qualitative nature of performance measures, inputs into a system, such as the competence of staff for a particular role, might be far more important than the recording of outputs. They therefore need to be carefully understood so that knowledge of how organizational change can be facilitated and properly understood can be used to protect the future of the organization.

The focus here has been on implications of contemporary performance management research findings for managers and organizations. In the concluding chapter, we take stock of the 'state of the art' in our selected disciplines, and assess the implications for the future performance management research agenda. We also reflect on the wider messages for business schools as key players in the development of performance management practitioners.

19
Conclusions and Reflections

Jacky Holloway and Richard Thorpe

Introduction

In this closing chapter we take stock of the trends revealed in the discipline and sector-based analyses, and revisit the case for more explicitly interdisciplinary or transdisciplinary performance management research and practice.

Much of the dissemination of our emerging knowledge about the process and impact of performance measurement and management takes place via business school-based management education, training and development (from vocational training through to MBA and doctoral programmes), as well as research outputs. These activities bring most management academics into regular contact with practitioners – but how far does what we teach reflect the real world challenges of managing performance, and contribute to the sharing of effective practices? And what is the perceived relevance of academic research to the wider community?

In concluding this volume we reflect on the implications of the knowledge of performance management assembled here, for business school teaching. We also consider whether academics could do more to exploit the opportunities available to them to undertake research, both on what practitioners do in the name of performance management and on its effects.

Is the whole more than the sum of the parts?

In Chapter 18 we discussed some general themes and messages for managers, arising from an overview of the accounts of performance management included in Part II. Each discipline contributes some distinctive elements to a broadening and deepening appreciation of the nature and

259

challenges of performance management. But given the degrees of commonality in the language, research methods, dimensions of interest and even performance management techniques applied by practitioners, we wonder whether what we observe is the emergence of a generic approach to performance management research and practice.

Clearly we have presented a highly complex field operating across many levels and contexts and, as a consequence, it appears unlikely that we are on the verge of being able to offer the reader a single framework for investigating or explaining performance management practices and their impacts. (Whether this is desirable, is a philosophical and ontological question not really appropriate for this book!) But perhaps now, it is possible to simplify the picture somewhat and make it slightly easier for researchers and practitioners to make sense of what is required of organizations in terms of their performance management capabilities as they seek to find ways to meet those needs.

Table 19.1 summarizes some of the key characteristics of all the disciplines and sectors featured in this book, as an aid to comparing and taking stock in terms of research approaches and practical issues addressed, and identifying gaps or neglected areas in practice or research.

By scanning Table 19.1, some general impressions can be drawn which have wider implications for researchers in particular.

Let a thousand flowers bloom . . .

First, a broad sweep across the wide selection of disciplines and sectors yields a complex and diverse picture both of research and management activity. Where there are signs of convergence they mainly relate to:

- the adoption of a handful of contemporary PM tools such as the Balanced Scorecard (unsurprisingly, given its multidimensional approach) by practitioners who are studied and/or advised by researchers;
- the sustained popularity of efficiency measurement (again unsurprising, since very few organizations or sectors today can afford waste!); and
- the use of a relatively narrow set of research methods.

To expand on the last point, although a growing number of disciplines are introducing qualitative, ethnographic or systemic research methods, the majority have roots in more positivistic approaches and few disciplines show any signs of abandoning their quantitative tools (surveys, statistical analysis, mathematical models and the like). Indeed

Table 19.1 Key features of performance management practice and research

Discipline/focal sector	Main levels of focus for PM activity	Dominant dimensions of performance addressed	Research 'paradigm' or preferred approaches	Emerging trends in practice	Emerging trends in research
Strategic management [see in particular Chapter 4]	Markets, industry sectors; firms	Efficiency, effectiveness (goal attainment, e.g. market share)	Quantitative (economics-based); complex modelling, e.g. networks; intra-org. processes and capabilities	Identifying core value drivers and how to protect and enhance them; moving away from 'what is our market share?' to 'how can we change?' 'what are causal relationships & environmental influences?'; stakeholder perspectives explored	Resource-based, knowledge-based views still growing; how to identify and measure key dynamic firm capabilities; elements of structural contingency theory Dynamics of manufacturing processes Interplay between strategy and culture (corporate, national)
Occupational psychology and organizational behaviour	Individuals, groups, within organizations	Efficiency Effectiveness (Mainly operational)	Primarily quantitative, sometimes experimental	Job (re)design, simplification of operations; occupational stress (costs/effects of) Wider systems perspectives becoming more common	Occupational stress (causes of); qualitative approaches becoming more common, as perceived to add explanatory value

Table 19.1 (Continued)

Discipline/focal sector	Main levels of focus for PM activity	Dominant dimensions of performance addressed	Research 'paradigm' or preferred approaches	Emerging trends in practice	Emerging trends in research
Human resource management	Ranges from strategic level (including resource-based view) to operational – linking effort to reward	Efficiency and effectiveness of people, predominantly at an operational level in the context of individual's roles	A move to qualitative indices (still at an early stage) that makes the link to the need for cultural fit and a process approach	To link individual goals with organizational priorities and the development of a competency 'process' approach that connects the *what* with the *how*; PM as integrating mechanism linking, e.g. job design, training and development and organizational priorities; also a managerialist strand, e.g. move to metrics, EFQM, balanced scorecard	Views about *hard* and *soft* HR and investigations into an RBV on performance; strategic integration of leadership and change in line with the debates about what HRM is or ought to become; emerging critical dimension, e.g. MBO is really about re-establishing authority and pay is about re-establishing control, not managing performance
Operations management	Small group/ operational,	Efficiency, effectiveness	From quantitative and reductionist	Increased complexity away from single	Cross-disciplinary studies, e.g. with

moving up supply chain	(immediate); awareness of strategic impact growing; quality (multidimensional)	to more qualitative; company case studies (mixed data)	operations and efficiency to systemic connections along supply chain; from internal focus (e.g. BPR) to externally driven change (TQM, benchmarking, balanced scorecard) Recognition of effect of operations on strategic performance	marketing, information management/systems Qualitative studies, e.g. of innovation and change Transfer of methods across sectors, e.g. supply chain partnerships, 'lean', from manufacturing to NHS
Project performance Usually group within organization; or time-limited multi-organization network	Efficiency (e.g. EVA); effectiveness Past: time/budget/specification; becoming more systemic	Mainly rational, quantitative; becoming more holistic	Project failures exposed limits of 'time/budget/specification' approach. Becoming more inclusive – whole life cycle focus; whole systems; BSC; multiple stakeholder perspectives considered	Developing multidimensional measurement tools (but ideally the ones leading to single figure); widening out, e.g. measuring strategic impact; examining stakeholder views of 'success'

Table 19.1 (Continued)

Discipline/focal sector	Main levels of focus for PM activity	Dominant dimensions of performance addressed	Research 'paradigm' or preferred approaches	Emerging trends in practice	Emerging trends in research
Operational research	Organizational goals, individual or group impacts	Efficiency, effectiveness; predictability and control	Positivistic origins; becoming more diverse but still mainly quantitative	Intrinsically quantitative professional work (in-company and consultancy); behavioural elements seen as external and independent contingency variables	'Soft OR' introduced qualitative, participative approaches, but rarely applied to PM; application areas slowly widening from manufacturing and logistics; computer modelling increasingly powerful
Marketing	Organizational goal setting (e.g. shareholder value, brand equity)	Efficiency, effectiveness; looking for strategic insight; gradual acceptance of need for innovative/ idiosyncratic measures to handle complexity of products and markets	Shifting from rational/quantitative, to creative/future oriented/qualitative; a *good* measure, rather than *the* measure	The need to understand the idiosyncratic nature of how value is added and a need to know where value comes from, requiring and understanding of context, not simply shareholder value;	Understanding role of information in corporate success in different contexts; detailed operational use of measures; critical appraisal of measurement of shareholder value, brand equity

Information and information management	Whole networks of firms and markets; sub-systems and elements	Ethics Equity Efficiency Effectiveness	Mixed – modelling, quantitative and qualitative; micro and macro	an examination of the role played by finance in the decision-making process Innovation – new services, markets, modes of operation – design, control Fighting for survival; process improvement (e.g. benchmarking); understanding stakeholders and supply chains	Observing and reflecting on emergent trends, e.g. use of information to control workers; impact of information asymmetries on power relationships; speed of growth and change, impact of e-business; boundaries and global reach
Accounting and finance	Firm, internal management control; international regulatory environment	From economy and efficiency towards effectiveness and multiple measures	Moving from almost all historical and quantitative to more behavioural and future-oriented	How to measure value, not just budgetary control, especially in public sector	Challenging rational assumptions; studying behavioural responses to PM, especially dysfunctional effects; regulation; complexity;

Table 19.1 (Continued)

Discipline/focal sector	Main levels of focus for PM activity	Dominant dimensions of performance addressed	Research 'paradigm' or preferred approaches	Emerging trends in practice	Emerging trends in research
				Compound measures and models (e.g. EVA, BSC, activity-based costing) Working with other disciplines, e.g. for benchmarking	support for managers implementing, e.g. ABC, BPR
Intangible assets	Firm, mainly	Market-based measures, e.g. (variants on) return on assets Process measures Effectiveness	Mainly quantitative; developing qualitative approaches to perceptions, behaviour	How to value intellectual assets, e.g. brands, for balance sheet and valuation of company/assessment of performance. What processes create value?	Contextual issues, understanding cultural values and significance Globalization Technical issues around definitions; legal issues
Political economy	Three main levels: organizational, systems, and from	Extending from traditional efficiency focus, to	A range of (mainly quantitative) perspectives:	No agreed framework; gradual	The need to take a broad intra-organizational

the perspective of consumers; internal and external	account for past, present and future performance; strategic direction – resources and control; links to learning and change	engineering, systems, management accounting, consumer marketing, conformance to specifications	emergence of attempts to reconcile the information and agendas from very different perspectives (practical application, mainly indirect, e.g. via accounting, marketing, consumer behaviour)	view of the dynamics of the organization; growth of critical strands (e.g. the symbolic role and purpose served by performance measurement); competing theoretical influences; contributions to interdisciplinary studies
Small firms Individuals; whole organizations	Quantifiable outputs – e.g. asset growth, jobs created; Value to owners (qualitative)	Past – mainly quantitative; Now, more qualitative, interpretive, participative	Mostly short term, seeking stability/ status quo rather than growth; Some (with support from outside) taking longer-term view and assessing capabilities, needs of supply chain and new markets	Qualitative – understanding value of organization to owner-manager is essential to assessing performance; encouraging strategic thinking via tools (e.g. EFQM, GVA); assessing resources, e.g. human capital; individual behavioural studies

Table 19.1 (Continued)

Discipline/focal sector	Main levels of focus for PM activity	Dominant dimensions of performance addressed	Research 'paradigm' or preferred approaches	Emerging trends in practice	Emerging trends in research
Public services	All levels, but especially whole 'units' within systems; local economies	Efficiency	From mainly quantitative, to mixed (e.g. eliciting multiple stakeholder perceptions)	A lot of externally imposed models and measures being applied	Supporting practice, e.g. culture change, efficiency modelling
	Centre: periphery relations	Effectiveness (long and short-term impacts)		Managerial agendas driving (policy-led) internal control	Analysing complexity; evaluating impact of PM per se especially dysfunctions
		Equity		Professional and inter-organizational relationships affecting outcomes	Provision of 'evidence' for evidence-based policy and practice
		Accountability		Using evidence in practice	

| Voluntary sector | Traditionally macro, concerned with regulation and policy context; gradual shift to micro level – focus on targets/measures preferred by funders seeking to influence processes and outcomes | Efficiency, effectiveness, related to contracts and compliance; growing interest in responsiveness and accountability in face of increasing regulation, although voluntary sector still has considerable freedom to set its own priorities | Rejection of quantitative accounting measures in favour of embracing as far as possible measures that take account of multiple stakeholders | In many ways the approach has been towards pressure to use tools *imposed* from funders; creeping pressure to embrace the modernization agenda that has taken over from the managerialist agenda from the 1990s; growth of partnership working, networks; where does responsibility for performance lie? | To develop measures beyond those borrowed from the public and private sectors – soft measures such as user satisfaction; to research integration of systems to address complexities of, for example, diverse sectoral needs, different levels and multiple stakeholders |

developments in software packages for both research and practitioner use are extending access to powerful quantitative performance information and analysis tools.

What the table and data on which it is based do not show are some of the newer approaches to management research that are appearing in some business schools, but are not yet seen as mainstream. For example, storytelling, drama and narrative approaches to data collection, offer different kinds of insights that could offer important understandings. New analysis tools and video and Internet-based qualitative data sources, online surveys and focus groups, collaborative action research and community participation methodologies are all finding a place in management research, especially associated with business histories, management of change, policy making or inter-organizational relations. Also under-represented (or perhaps just under-reported) are theory-driven studies, although we know that theory building and testing is often not an explicit outcome of many studies. Some particularly under-theorized areas are discussed later in this chapter.

Researcher or researched?

What is perhaps surprising is the degree of overlap between the areas of performance management that are engaging management practitioners, and those that researchers are involved with. One could assume that this reflects high levels of collaborative, user-focused research (encapsulated by the concept of 'Mode 2' research discussed below) – and that is probably quite a fair assumption. At the time of writing, 'third mission' research is growing fast in the UK, reflecting in part the growing emphasis on regional development and local economic and social partnerships. Many business schools also have their origins in engineering departments, vocationally oriented former polytechnics or professional training institutions, where research was intrinsically linked to the needs of industry or practitioner groups. Some disciplines in some universities and independent research units depend on consultancy or commissioned research for much of their income, which helps to sustain more theoretical or 'blue skies' research where government funding is scarce. Other research units are jointly owned (for example, university spin-off companies), or funded to offer training to practitioners (for example, in charity management, innovative manufacturing processes or service evaluations), or have a tradition of working in partnership with post-experience Masters students on substantial work-based projects. The possibilities for collaborative research that spans immediate applicability in industry, links to teaching and theory or methodology development are increasing rapidly.

A question to ask here therefore is 'What added value is obtained through research: industry partnerships, that could be put to wider use in theory development or safely generalized to performance management practice more widely?' A likely answer, we suspect, would be 'Relatively little, because findings are commercially sensitive, or insufficient data were collected, or the context was so unusual that generalization would be dangerous'. Each of these barriers to obtaining better value from research is avoidable if addressed at the design stage, but only if the stakeholders regard it as sufficiently important.

Back to our roots?

A final general observation is that in spite of the diversity and synergies noted above, much performance management research still takes place within single discipline departments and teams. People adopt the level of focus, epistemological frameworks and comfortable dimensions of performance that are 'normal' in their discipline. Indeed the silos are potentially even deeper, given the handful of underpinning academic fields that seem to have done most to characterize the 11 disciplines touched on in Table 19.1 – principally economics, psychology and statistics/mathematics. (Sociology, geography, anthropology, social policy and the newer field of complexity science are among others that could have been mentioned too, but frankly compared to economics and psychology in particular their influence is extremely muted in the performance management area.)

In the three sectors (or 'application areas') described here we also find discipline-based contributions – not least because even small firms, when they start to develop differentiated structures, tend towards functional or discipline-based arrangements. And in turn, larger academic departments often use industry sectors as part of their sub-structures (service operations management, social marketing, public sector finance, charity leadership and so on). However, in the UK at least, with the increasing use of networked partnerships of providers in the public and voluntary sectors and growth of project-based commercial work (as routine manufacturing and service operations are outsourced off-shore), it is timely to develop more sophisticated ways of researching the synergistic impact on performance of requiring multiple disciplines and organizations to work together in new ways. As the chapters on accounting and finance, project management and the voluntary sector in particular indicated, effective multidisciplinary team working needs careful management in order to perform well; but potentially the 'whole' can be greater than the 'sum of the parts'.

Indeed perhaps it is most unusual to have produced a book like this one, with a set of authors many of whom have worked together in small groups and certainly find much in common socially, and yet who have also happily produced accounts of the kinds of performance management that they teach about and research into which are predominantly grounded in single disciplines! Admittedly, the authors were asked to provide accounts that would enable 'outsiders' to understand their worlds in some depth, but it is apparent that unless there are specific reasons for crossing discipline boundaries many people can get by 'on their own'. Each discipline has students who expect discipline-based courses, research clients with specialist projects and enough of a formal identity to drive theory development within discipline boundaries. So perhaps a more pertinent, if somewhat uncomfortable, question is: 'Why collaborate across disciplines?'

We return to these three impressionistic themes in the 'Research agenda' discussed below. But first, having raised the thorny topic of academia: industry relations, we look a bit more closely at the context in which performance management research and teaching take place.

Messages for management academics

The start of the twenty-first century has been characterized by the growing visibility of global businesses, exponential growth of Internet-based services and often-contested fragmentation of formerly state-owned sectors. Business and management have become mainstream mass media topics and, the authors would argue, a transformational force in society, being central to the operation of public, private and voluntary bodies. Management is no longer confined to the business pages of broadsheet newspapers, and with its 'popularization' has come the unfortunate side-effect of being open to all kinds of criticism.

Management academics seem particularly vulnerable to criticism on the grounds of supposed irrelevance, superficiality or assumed distance from the 'real world' of business practice. How often have we heard potentially fruitful innovations dismissed as 'another management fad', unpopular evidence of poor performance summed up as 'just management-speak', and media-savvy business school professors dismissed as 'so-called gurus'? Academics in turn are often scathing in their reviews of 'airport bookstand' books and magazines that prescribe the latest quick fix for the busy manager, in spite of the obvious existence of demand for such publications. Yet many of those same academics are employed as part-time consultants by business owners and public policy makers; they create stimulating learning environments for students at all levels including practising senior managers; and develop deep insights into corporate life through long-term action research programmes and commissioned evaluation studies. What does this messy scenario tell us about the prospects for serious growth in the quantity and quality of empirical evidence, leading to sound theorizing, about performance management in all its guises?

Since the 1990s in many countries undergraduate business and management studies have shown sustained growth in student numbers, and postgraduate programmes (MBAs, discipline-based specialist degrees and Doctor of Business Administration or DBAs) remain popular even if the growth curve has levelled off. International students flock to universities in Europe, North America, Australia and New Zealand, while indigenous offerings in emerging economies are rapidly gaining ground, often based on Western models in terms of content and structure. Yet American MBAs in particular have been criticized for their lack of relevance to the needs of businesses, in terms of both their academic content and their modes of delivery. Indeed some of the harshest critics of business school programmes, especially MBAs, come from within academia. Bennis and O'Toole (2005) entered the debate by illustrating the extent to which MBAs and the professors who teach them are removed from business practices. Their claims echo those of Pfeffer and Fong (2002) and earlier concerns voiced by Mintzberg (1976, 2004). Business schools, they all argue, have been for too long focused on 'scientific' research and analysis and less concerned with developing those qualities and abilities that can accommodate the complexities of organizational life. Starkey and Tiratsoo (2007) develop this theme when they argue that business schools need to be judged less on an increasingly out-of-date curriculum and much more in terms of the extent to which they develop the human capital to tackle a complex modern world.

On the other hand, business school clients who claim that business schools are not producing the kind of graduates that both business and society need, also have a role to play: in the redesign of teaching programmes; support for students (internships, sponsorship etc.); and by being open to new modes of teaching and learning. In the UK, in particular, professional associations and business leaders have been partners in the development of undergraduate and Masters 'subject benchmarks' that have shaped twenty-first century curricula, especially in terms of key skills for future employees. Many academic programmes are directly linked to professional accreditation, and when professional requirements change, so do the courses. The world of business education that the authors of this book inhabit features practice-based and work-based learning, vocationally oriented 'foundation degrees' supported by employers and an ever-growing range of modes of delivery from in-company teaching, through 'blended learning' combining classroom and distance teaching, to entirely online programmes. The traditional full-time MBA course for aspiring (but inexperienced) managers, and its 'executive' variant for those seeking to underpin their experience with a qualification, are now relatively small segments in an increasingly fragmented market.

Of course, there are debates to be had about retaining an appropriate degree of separation between 'education' and 'training', and policy issues relating to who should pay for higher education if it is increasingly driven by the needs of employers, but at least in some countries it is possible that both educational attainment and organizational performance will improve as a result of the 'teaching relevance debate'. However, the route from high-quality management research into better teaching can be a long one. It takes time to assimilate new knowledge into teaching programmes, and management practice and business environments change far more rapidly than researchers can hope to keep up with. Thus in management and business education perhaps more than most fields the relationship between teaching and research should be direct and continually evolving.

The 'research relevance debate' may take longer to produce fruitful results, however. Academic researchers are normally required to explain the relevance of their proposed work to 'users' when applying for funds; and research associated with the improvement of national economic performance is often favoured. Managers are increasingly expected to justify their decisions on the basis of 'the best available research evidence', as if there were a body of knowledge comparable to that in medicine and other older professions. Yet one safe assumption is that much management practice is undertaken *without* explicit reference to the best available research evidence. Several writers on the emerging topic of evidence-based management (Pfeffer and Sutton, 2006a, b; Rousseau, 2006; Rousseau and McCarthy, 2007) discuss at length how this may reflect shortcomings in American management education, but also point to organizational and individual antipathies towards research in the context of management work. Certainly there are individual psychological traits that affect how likely a person is to seek out and use research-based information in their work, but a lot of other (professional and organizational) cultural, social and economic factors play a part.

Rousseau and McCarthy also point out that 'management' is not a profession in the traditional sense of having control over (legal) requirements for entry and training, and expectations of continuing professional development (CPD) are extremely varied. Furthermore, the lack of a shared management language particularly between functions or disciplines can limit the kinds of peer discussions about evidence and practice that are found in medical staff rooms. So engaging users' interest in research is not always easy; and persuading practitioners to contribute to the research process can be surprisingly challenging especially in organizations where performance is problematic. Many managers undertake research-like activities as part of their normal work (focus groups for new product development or user satisfaction feedback, organizational development programmes and the like), but do not feel confident enough in their research skills to participate more explicitly in research. Particularly, if their only training was in quantitative approaches and survey design, they need opportunities to learn relevant qualitative methods (Skinner et al., 2000). But CPD and DBA programmes, practitioner journals, more accessible textbooks and 'self-help' groups are all helping manager-researchers to gain confidence and skills, and significant numbers of practitioners now participate in management conferences and seminars in the UK at least.

As well as the requirement to demonstrate relevance to users and wider society, management research now has to meet ever-stricter criteria of rigour (Pettigrew, 1997). It is treated as a mainstream social science in terms of performance criteria such as double blind peer reviewed journal papers and methodological rigour in funding proposals. Newer and innovative qualitative methods often struggle to be understood by reviewers more familiar with quantitative or positivistic approaches, and sub-disciplines with roots in economics or psychology still tend to dominate in terms of funding allocations. As earlier chapters have shown performance management is under-theorized in many disciplines (as indeed are many other areas of management and organizational behaviour!), so there is a parallel pressure to develop theory far more actively than in the past.

Accepting Lewin's dictum that 'there is nothing so practical as a good theory' (Lewin, 1951, p. 169), as an applied field (like medicine, education and engineering) the need for growth in empirical research at all levels is a clear requirement, over long and shorter periods of time. Management research questions are rarely best addressed under laboratory conditions, so multiple methods and partnerships with the providers of data are also essential. Most management knowledge is 'co-produced', even if none of the protagonists set out with this as a specific objective. One of the more fruitful debates within management research that is particularly apposite for performance management researchers has been around the adoption of 'Mode 2', 'practice relevant' research as the norm (Gibbons et al., 1994; Starkey and Madan, 2001; Tranfield and Starkey, 1998).

To expand briefly, as mentioned in Chapter 2, Gibbons et al. (1994) distinguish between two modes of knowledge production. 'Mode 1' they characterize as the 'traditional' approach to knowledge generation occurring within the context of existing institutions and academic disciplines. This would include multidisciplinary working of the kind that we have seen described in a number of chapters above. But ' . . . multidisciplinarity is characterized by the autonomy of the various disciplines and does not lead to changes in the existing disciplinary and theoretical structures. Cooperation consists in working on the common theme but under different disciplinary perspectives' (Gibbons et al., 1994, p. 28). The agenda is seen to be an academic one that makes a distinction between fundamental and applied knowledge. If one subscribes to this view then the dissemination of knowledge will occur downstream of production and there will be less concern for practical relevance.

'Mode 2' in contrast is characterized as transdisciplinary (for current purposes, synonymous with interdisciplinary), where knowledge is created in a particular context, a context that values those involved in practice and aims to co-produce knowledge.

> Interdisciplinarity is characterized by the explicit formulation of a uniform, discipline-transcending terminology or a common methodology. The form scientific cooperation takes consists in working on different themes, but within a common framework that is shared by the disciplines involved. Transdisciplinarity arises only if research is based upon a common theoretical understanding and must be accompanied by a mutual interpenetration of disciplinary epistemologies. Cooperation in this case leads to a clustering of disciplinary rooted problem-solving and creates a transdisciplinary homogenized theory or model pool.
>
> (Gibbons et al., 1994, p. 29)

As a consequence, this form combines both tacit/practitioner understandings with those of academics and celebrates a collective interdisciplinary approach to the production of knowledge. It also recognizes the transitory nature of the knowledge that is produced and values the importance of understanding the particular as well as the general. From this perspective, knowledge is produced and exploited almost simultaneously and as a consequence, becomes shared much more widely between a variety of stakeholders – not simply business, but also a wider community.

From this more complex perspective, some argue that management might even be seen more in terms of 'a performance' (in the colloquial sense) than the application of economic logic, where managers need to create and work within an 'organizational landscape' consisting of people, things and structures whose continued existence within the organization requires argument and justification (Shotter, 1993). Here managers are not simply the overseers, instructors or conduits of enlightened vision, but in addition, practical authors who have to persuade others to enlist in the joint production of outcomes (Holman and Thorpe, 2003, p. 7). The knowledge being taught in many business schools today fails to convey business life in such terms because it still tends to avoid an appreciation of the ethnographic, personal and rhetorical nature of these persuasive skills (Ghoshal, 2005).

From the foregoing discussion, we would conclude that while there are signs of the potential for Mode 2 transdisciplinary research in performance management, the evidence of the studies in this volume points to a predominantly Mode 1 approach, albeit with growing experiences of fruitful multidisciplinary working. One of the key aspects of Mode 2 knowledge production is that it occurs as a result of the *interaction* that takes place between theory and practice. This interaction with practice – in business and other organizations – is also largely missing in business schools. Recognizing 'management students', their sponsoring organizations and CPD clients as knowledgeable practitioners who are in a position to test theories in new contexts, evaluate models and challenge past interpretations should be a key to the competitive advantage possessed by educational institutions. Instead there remains a tendency for 'research' to be conceived and undertaken separately from developmental or educational engagements with managers (very much in the mode of normal science, looking in on the world of management as detached observers). Clearly some research questions in the performance management field can be addressed at arm's length, through surveys and quantitative models following the Mode 1 tradition. But given the complexity and sensitivity of most performance problems, this seems unsustainable if research is to have at least some element of practical relevance as well as leading to robust and interesting theories.

To reiterate, and as earlier chapters in this book have indicated, there are often considerable disjunctions between, for example, 'effective practice' as elicited and explained through academic research and the routine practice of managers. To understand the basis for management actions and decisions more fully requires a lot more and better research. Focusing more sharply on performance management, in the next section we will identify a small number of key questions that remain unanswered in this book and form part of a longer-term research agenda.

Items for the performance management research agenda

In Chapter 18 we were confident enough, based on the collected wisdoms of the discipline and sector specialists in Part II, to provide a small number of firm recommendations for performance managers:

- Draw on as wide a range of information sources as possible;
- Engage the commitment of senior managers;
- Ensure that key staff at all levels make a contribution; and
- Be process led and let the identification of measures emerge in contrast to having a preconceived view of what the measures should be.

These are, of course, fairly standard components of 'good management' in general, but if they can contribute directly to better *performance* management that will be no bad thing! But one important aspect of most of the research reported here is that it is predominantly based on experiences in the UK. Increasing the international dimension in future research will be important if we are to gain clearer understanding of contextual influences such as culture, stakeholder power relationships and performance within networks and global supply chains.

We also identified and discussed the following common themes emerging from the 'data' in the chapters in Part II and reflected again in Table 19.1:

- Simple unitary measures (being supplanted by suites of measures reflecting key performance drivers);
- Efficiency and effectiveness (the dominant dimensions even in sectors where social values take precedence over the financial 'bottom line');

- Embracing soft and more strategic aspects of performance (essential, but with major implications for the design and choice of performance management techniques for given contexts); and
- The importance of process and change (which should not just be left up to the HR function!).

Each of these themes may be familiar territory to researchers in some disciplines, while their importance is only just dawning on others, so we would include them near the top of the agenda for new multidisciplinary performance management research programmes. They could represent fruitful areas for interdisciplinary research projects that, for example, test the robustness of performance management tools or theoretical models in new contexts.

Earlier in this chapter, three questions were posed arising out of the summary in Table 19.1, each of which also deserves to be promoted as part of our future research agenda. First we commented on the relative lack of explicit theoretical underpinnings for much performance management practice. This is also a feature of a lot of published PM research, with major international journals emphasizing empirical work. There are areas in which existing theories find relatively frequent application in PM (various strands in strategic management, psychological aspects of OB, HRM and marketing, mathematical theorems applied in OR models, and economic theories of incentives applied to employee and customer behaviour, for instance). But few if any theoretical explanations for market, organizational, group or individual performance do not depend on pre-existing bodies of theory.

One option would be to extend the range of theoretical sources to dilute the influence of psychology and economics, bringing in more sociology, anthropology, geography, for example, as well as insights from beyond the social sciences. Research in the fields of business ethics and corporate social responsibility, sustainable development and risk and uncertainty are already making creative use of humanities and physical sciences so this option holds considerable promise.

There is a lively argument to be had within the management research community about whether there can, and should, be such a thing as 'management theory' – newly minted especially for application in relation to management, and not owing its existence to any social science forebears. But waiting for this debate is a luxury that most performance management researchers cannot afford – our colleagues, clients and students deserve the relative (if often short-lived) certainty that our 'findings' can be explained at least in part by theories, or can be used to improve existing theories. One gets the feeling that the theory is 'bubbling under' in some of the more extensively researched areas of performance management, and ought now to be put explicitly on the agenda.

We also asked a slightly provocative question about whether a return on the investment in research–industry partnerships could yet be discerned. Although some activities are virtuous in their own right, we would argue that where resources are very constrained it is appropriate to evaluate the impact of activities that are, at least in part, undertaken in response to external policy drivers rather than having an intrinsic academic rationale.

That said, clearly we have also argued in favour of collaborative research, and co-production of knowledge, because most performance management research questions are of limited significance in the abstract – we are not striving for a unified theory of PM that can be demonstrated through pure logic alone! Indeed it might be far more appropriate to pursue performance management theory development in Mode 2 transdisciplinary terms: '...a continuous linking and relinking, in specific clusterings and configurations of knowledge which is brought together on a temporary basis in specific contexts of application. Thus, it is strongly oriented towards and driven by problem-solving. Its theoretical–methodological core, while cross-cutting through well-established disciplinary cores, is often locally driven and locally constituted, thus any such core is highly sensitive to further local mutations depending on the context of application' (Gibbons et al., 1994, p. 29). Those authors who have called for more contingent approaches should find much to reassure them here.

Emerging conclusions

The nature of this book, arising as it has from a sustained shared interest in performance management on the part of a diverse group of mainly UK-based researchers and some practitioner collaborators, makes drawing definitive conclusions impossible. But we can emphasize where we have arrived at so far in terms of some key elements of our continuing journey towards a better understanding of performance management practices and their impacts.

In terms of perhaps the most important research question that all our disciplines ask from time to time – 'What impact, if any, does performance management action have on performance?' – there remains a long distance to be travelled (collectively as well as in our 'discipline silos'). There are many derivative questions relating to: the level at which impacts may be found; over what timescale; with what degree of clarity in causal relationships; and even in terms of direction of those causal links. Good outcomes may arise by 'chance' in the presence of PM systems, which in turn take on a role that is only indirectly related to performance, for example. Unwanted effects can, and often do, arise from PM systems; they will not go away just because it is impolite to ask research questions about them. Performance management researchers pursuing the agenda set out above need to reflect on these fundamental themes of causation and dysfunction when selecting more bounded problems to investigate.

Furthermore, this family of questions around the impact of PM can only be addressed through excellent access to practice contexts, and with a willingness on the part of practitioners to hear the results – another aspect of the 'trade off' in practice-relevant research. If what 'they' are doing (albeit often in response to management educators' advice) does not work very well, it will probably only be possible to understand why through systematic research. Complex PM interventions may need longer-term research in a range of contexts in order to identify relevant dependent and independent variables. This book has illustrated a willingness on the part of many management academics to engage with the 'practice relevant teaching and research' debates. We have also shown relatively high levels of practitioner involvement (especially when compared to other fields of management research), a promising stage to have reached.

In this final chapter, we have found the need to question the intrinsic desirability of inter/transdisciplinary and multidisciplinary collaboration in PM research, having observed how strong the ties were to discipline roots and territories in most of the earlier chapters. This need was alluded to in Chapter 4 when Carmel de Nahlik asked: 'Can such different disciplines be expected to see performance management as "the same thing", and develop a shared language for understanding it, given their wide differences in level of focus and interest?' At this point we would probably admit that there is a long way to go in terms of a shared language – not least because there are perfectly sound reasons for the same terms to have particular meanings within discipline contexts. But there are also many examples in this book of comfortable partnerships between two or three disciplines – multidisciplinarity (in Gibbons et al.'s terms) is having some beneficial effects. Expanding those groupings to include more, less closely related disciplines may well prove fruitful in terms of generating new explanations for old problems, and tackling new and unexplored territories. Research funders could play a part in encouraging this, perhaps by supporting interdisciplinary groups in identifying competing or hidden assumptions, so that collaboration does not founder on the rocks of paradigm wars and territorial claims for common terms.

Finally, in Chapter 4 the following question was also posed

> Can all the disciplinary perspectives contribute to a harmonious and systemic 'unified theory' of performance management or will knowledge advance more swiftly through competing explanations, stakeholder worldviews and the juxtaposition of micro and macro levels of analysis?

Although those of a consensual disposition may find the harmonious path more attractive, on the basis of the contents of this book we feel obliged to opt for the more fragmented route. Indeed a serious challenge awaits if true 'Mode 2 transdisciplinarity' becomes the goal, as this would represent a shift in the opposite direction from the search for a unified 'discipline' with its accompanying theoretical and methodological certainties, legacies and aspirations for an 'evidence base', towards a temporary and continually evolving body of knowledge focused on the problems in hand.

But we would also argue that at this stage, 'diversity is strength'. Performance, and its management, are territories that are currently too large to be tackled whole. Systemic approaches are essential, but systems are human constructs and their boundaries need to be drawn where it is most appropriate for the questions under examination. Rather than seek a holy grail of unified theory, we would argue in favour of more and better multidisciplinary and multi-stakeholder research, effective collaboration and improved communication so that PM researchers are more aware of each other's work. Inter or transdisciplinarity may increasingly come to characterize research on the performance of projects, networks and sectors, but important contributions will also come from those disciplines that naturally focus at the micro level provided that ways are found to build a better picture of the whole as well as understanding the parts.

Bibliography

Ackoff, R. *The Art of Problem Solving* (New York: John Wiley & Sons, 1978), 179–200.

Adams, J. S. 'Toward an understanding of inequity', *Journal of Abnormal and Social Psychology*, 67 (1963) 422–36.

Aglietta, M. *A Theory of Capitalist Regulation* (London: New Left Books, 1979).

Alatrista, J. and Arrowsmith, J. 'Managing employee commitment in the not-for-profit sector', *Personnel Review*, Vol. 33, No. 5 (2004) 536–48.

Aldrich, H. *Organizations Evolving* (London: Sage, 1999).

Alford, J. *Performance in government; Working paper* (Melbourne: Graduate School of Management, University of Melbourne, 1992).

Amey, L. 'Tomkins on Residual Income', *Journal of Business Finance and Accounting*, Spring (1975) 55–68.

Amit, R. and Schoemaker, P. J. H. 'Strategic Assets and Organizational Rent', *Strategic Management Journal*, Vol. 14, No. 1 (1993) 33–46.

Anderson, H., Cobbold, I. and Lawrie, G. 'Balanced Scorecard Implementation in SMEs: Reflection', in *Literature and Practice* (SME Conference, Copenhagen, Denmark, 2001).

Andrews, R., Boyne, G. A., Law, J. and Walker, R. M. 'Myths, Measures and Modernisation: A Comparative Analysis of Local Authority Performance in England and Wales', *Local Government Studies*, Vol. 29, No. 4 (2003) 54–78.

Andrews, R., Boyne, G. A., Law, J. and Walker, R. M. 'External Constraints on Local Service Standards: The Case of Comprehensive performance Assessment in English Local Government', *Public Administration*, Vol. 83, No. 3 (2005) 639–56.

Anonymous. *Is it any wonder some heads cheat?* (London: The Guardian, 14 May 2002).

Anthony, P. D. *The Ideology of Work* (London: Tavistock, 1977).

Anthony, R. N. *Planning and control systems: a framework for analysis* (Cambridge, MA: Harvard University Press, 1965).

APM, *Project Management Body of Knowledge*, 4th edn (High Wycombe: Association for Project Management, 2000).

Applebaum, E., Bailey, T., Berg, P. and Kalleberg, A. L. *Manufacturing Advantage: The effects of High Performance Work Systems on Plant performance and Company Outcome* (Ithaca, NY: Cornell University Press, 2000).

Argyris, C. *Integrating the Individual and the Organisation* (New York: Wiley, 1964).

Argyris, C. and Schön, D. A. *Organizational learning: a theory of action perspective* (Reading, MA: Addison-Wesley, 1978).

Aristigueta, M. P. *Managing for results in state government* (Connecticut: Quorum, 1999).

Armstrong, M. 'Human resources management: a case of the emperor's new clothes?' *Personnel Management*, Vol. 19, No. 8 (1987) 30–5.

Armstrong, M. *Employee Reward*, 3rd edn (London: Chartered Institute of Personnel and Development, 2002).

Armstrong, M. and Baron, A. *Performance Management, the New Realities* (London: Chartered Institute of Personnel and Development, 1998).

Armstrong, P. 'Science, enterprise and profit: ideology in the knowledge-driven economy', *Economy and Society*, Vol. 30, No. 4 (2001) 524–52.

Arnold, J., Silvester, J., Patterson, F., Robertson, I. T., Cooper, C. L. and Burnes, B. *Work Psychology: Understanding Human Behaviour in the Workplace*, 4th edn (London: FT Prentice Hall, 2004).

Arthur, J. B. 'The link between business strategy and industrial relations in American steel mini mills', *Industrial Relations Review*, Vol. 45, No. 3 (1992).

Arthur, J. B. 'Effects of human resource systems on manufacturing performance and turnover', *Academy of Management Journal*, Vol. 37, No. 3 (1994) 670–87.

Atkinson, R. 'Project management: cost, time and quality, two best guesses and a phenomenon, it's time to accept other success criteria', *International Journal of Project Management*, Vol. 17, No. 6 (1999) 337–43.

Audit Commission, *Performance Review: a Handbook* (London: HMSO, 1986).

Audit Commission, *The Citizen's Charter – Local Authority Performance Indicators* (London: HMSO, 1992).

Audit Commission, *Best Value and the Audit Commission* (London: TSO, 1999).

Audit Commission, *Comprehensive Performance Assessment* (London: Audit Commission, 2002).

Austin, R. D. *Measuring and Managing Performance in Organizations* (New York: Dorset House Publishing, 1996).

Baccarini, D. 'The Logical Framework Method for Defining Project Success', *Project Management Journal*, Vol. 30, No. 4 (1999) 25–32.

Bach, S. and Sisson, K. *Personnel Management – A Comprehensive Guide to the Theory and Practice* (Blackwell Business: Oxford, 2000).

Bailey, C. 'The Liverpool Dockworkers' Strike 1995–98 and the Internet', paper presented at *International Conference on Global Companies – Global Unions, Global Research – Global Campaigns* (New York: Cornell Global Labor Institute, February 2006), www.geocities.com/unionsonline/bailey.htm accessed 04/08/07.

Bailey, T. 'Organisational innovation in the Apparel industry', *Industrial Relations*, Vol. 32 (1993) 30–48.

Bain & Co. *Management Tools: Annual Survey of Senior Executives* (London: Bain & Co., 2001).

Barlow, G. 'Deficiencies and the perpetuation of power: latent functions in performance appraisal', *Journal of Management Studies*, September (1989) 449–517.

Barney, J. B. 'Firm Resources and Sustained Competitive Advantage', *Journal of Management*, Vol. 17, No. 1 (1991) 99–120.

Bart, C. K. and Tabone, J. C. 'Mission statement rationales and organisational alignment in the not-for-profit health care sector', *Health Care Management Review*, Vol. 23, No. 4 (1998) 54–81.

Bartlett, C. A. and Ghoshal, S. 'Beyond the M-Form: Toward a Managerial Theory of the Firm', *Strategic Management Journal*, Vol. 14 (1993) 23–46.

Bartlett, W., Roberts, J. A. and Le Grand, J. *A Revolution in Social Policy: Quasi-market Reforms in the 1990s* (Bristol: The Policy Press, 1998).

Baritz, L. *The servants of power: A history of the use of social science in American industry* (NY: John Wiley, 1960).

Batsleer, J. 'Management and organisation' in Smith, J. S., Rochester, C. and Hedley, R. (eds) *An introduction to the voluntary sector* (London: Routledge, 1995).

Baum, J. R. and Locke, E. A. 'The relationship of entrepreneurial traits, skill and motivation to subsequent venture growth', *Journal of Applied Psychology*, Vol. 89, No. 4 (2004) 587–98.

Baum, J. R., Locke, E. A. and Kirkpatrick, S. A. 'A longitudinal study of the relation of vision and vision communication to venture growth and performance', *Journal of Applied Psychology*, Vol. 83, No. 1 (1998) 43–54.

Baumol, W. J. *Business Behaviour, Values and Growth* (New York: Macmillan, 1959).

Beardwell, I., Holden, N. and Clayton, L. *Human Resource Management – a Contemporary Approach*, 4th edn (London: FT Prentice Hall, 2004).

Beaver, G., Lashley, C. and Stewart, J. 'Management development', in Thomas, R. (ed.) *The Management of Small Tourism and Hospitality Firms* (London: Cassell, 1998).

Becher, A. *Academic Tribes and Territories: Intellectual Enquiry and the Cultures of Disciplines* (Milton Keynes: The Society for Research into Higher Education and the Open University Press, 1989).

Beer, S. *Decision and Control: The Meaning of Operational Research and Management Cybernetics* (London: John Wiley & Sons, 1966).

Beer, M., Spector, B., Lawrence, P., Quinn Mills, D. and Walton, R. *Human Resource Management: a general manager's perspective* (Free Press USA, 1985).

Ben-Ner, A. 'Co-operation, conflict and control in organisations', in Bowles, S., Gintis, H. and Gustafson, B. (eds) *Markets and Democracy: Participation, Accountability and Efficiency* (Cambridge, UK: Cambridge University Press, 1993).

Bennis, W. and O' Toole, T. 'How Business Schools lost their way', *Harvard Business Review*, Vol. 83 (2005) 96–104.

Berger, P. L. and Luckmann, T. *The Social Construction of Reality* (London: Penguin Press, 1967).

Bernard, S. 'The Drug Drought', *Pharmaceutical Executive* 1 November (2002), www.pharmexec.com/pharmexec/article/articleDetail.jsp?id=50753, accessed 06/08/07.

Bevan, G. and Hood, C. 'What's measured is what matters: targets and gaming in the English public health care system', *Public Administration*, Vol. 84, No. 3 (2006) 517–38.

Biglan, A. 'The characteristics of subject matter in different academic areas', *Journal of Applied Psychology*, Vol. 57, No. 3 (1973a) 195–203.

Biglan, A. 'Relationships between subject matter characteristics and the structure and output of university departments', *Journal of Applied Psychology*, Vol. 57, No. 3 (1973b) 204–13.

Birch, D. *Job Generation in America: How our Small Companies Put the Most People to Work* (New York: Free Press, 1987).

Birley, S. and Westhead, P. 'Growth and performance contrasts between "types" of small firms', *Cranfield School of Management Working paper*, 6/90 (1990a).

Birley, S. and Westhead, P. 'Growth and performance contrasts between "types" of small firms', *Strategic Management Journal*, Vol. 11, No. 7, Nov/Dec. (1990b) 535–57.

Blackmore, A. 'The reform of public services: the role of the voluntary sector' (with Bush, H. and Bhutta, M.) (London: NCVO, June 2005), available at www.ncvo-vol.org.uk/publications. accessed 06/08/07.

Blair, M. M. and Wallman, S. M. H. *Unseen Wealth* (Boston: Brookings Institution Press, 2001).

Blau, P. M. *The Dynamics of Bureaucracy: A Study of Interpersonal Relations in Two Government Agencies* (Chicago: University of Chicago Press, 1963).

Boardman, A. E., Greenberg, D. H., Vining, A. R. and Weimer, D. L. *Cost Benefit Analysis: Concepts and Practice*, 3rd edn (Upper Saddle River, NJ: Prentice Hall, 2006).

Boehm B. W. and Ross, R. 'Theory-W Software Project Management: Principles and Examples', *IEEE Transactions on Software Engineering*, Vol. 15, No. 7 (1989) 902–16.

Boonstra, A. and de Vries, J. 'Analyzing inter-organizational systems from a power and interest perspective', *International Journal of Information Management*, Vol. 25, No. 6, December (2005) 485–501.

Boseley, S. 'The selling of a wonder drug', *Guardian* (29 March 2006).

Boston, J., Martin, J., Pallot, J. and Walsh, P. *Reshaping the state; New Zealand's Bureaucratic Revolution* (Auckland: Oxford University Press, 1991).

Bourne, M., Mills, J., Wilcox, M., Neely, A. and Platts, K. 'Designing, implementing and updating performance measurement systems', *International Journal of Operations and Production Management*, Vol. 20, No. 7 (2000) 754–71.

Bovaird, T. 'Managing urban economic development: learning to change or the marketing of failure?', *Urban Studies*, Vol. 31, No. 4/5 (1994) 573–603.

Bovaird, T. 'The political economy of performance indicators' in Bouckaert, G. and Halachmi, A. (eds) *Organisational Performance and Measurement in the Public Sector* (Westport: Greenwood, 1996), pp. 145–166.

Bovaird, T. 'Public sector performance measurement' in Kempf-Leonard, K. (ed.) *Encyclopaedia of Social Measurement* (San Diego, CA: Elsevier Science, 2004).

Bovaird, T., Gregory, D. and Martin, S. 'Performance measurement in urban economic development', *Public Money and Management*, Vol. 8, No. 4 (1988) 17–22.

Bowey, A. M., Thorpe, R., with Hellier, P. *Payment Systems and Productivity*, (Basingstoke: Macmillan, 1986).

Boyd, B. K., Dess, G. G. and Rasheed, A. M. A. 'Divergence Between Archival and Perceptional Measures of the Environment: Causes and Consequences', *Academy of Management Review*, Vol. 18, No. 2 (1993) 204–26.

Boyle, D. *The Sum of Our Discontent: Why Numbers Make Us Irrational* (New York: Texere, 2001).

Boyne, G. 'Bureaucratic theory meets reality. Public choice and contracting out in US local government', *Public Administration Review*, Vol. 58 (1998) 474–84.

Boyne, G. 'Sources of public service improvement: A critical review and research agenda', *Journal of Public Administration Research and Theory*, Vol. 13 (2003) 367–94.

Boyne, G. A. 'Scale, Performance and the New Public Management: An Empirical Analysis of Local Authority Services', *Journal of Management Studies*, Vol. 33, No. 6 (1996) 809–26.

Boyne, G. A. 'Comparing the Performance of Local Authorities: An Analysis of the Audit Commission Indicators', *Local Government Studies*, Vol. 23, No. 4 (1997) 17–43.

Boyne, G. A. 'Planning, Performance and Public Services', *Public Administration*, Vol. 79, No. 1 (2001) 73–88.

Boyne, G. A. 'Concepts and Indicators of Local Authority Performance: An Evaluation of the Statutory Frameworks in England and Wales', *Public Money and Management*, Vol. 22, No. 2 (2002) 17–24.

Bramwell, R. and Cooper, C. 'VDUs in the workplace: Psychological and health implications', in Cooper, C. L. and Robertson, I. T. (eds) *International Review of Industrial and Organizational Psychology*, Vol. 10 (Chichester: Wiley, 1995) 213–27.

Braverman, H. *Labour and Monopoly Capital: The Degradation of Work in the Twentieth Century* (New York: Monthly Review Press, 1974).

Bray, T. *The New Public Relations*. (2005). www.tbray.org/ongoing/When/200x/2005/07/11/New-Public-Relations, accessed 06/08/07.

Bridgewater, B. (and eight additional authors), 'Surgeon specific mortality in adult cardiac surgery: Comparison between crude and risk stratified data', *British Medical Journal*, Vol. 327, No. 7405 (5 July 2003) 13–7.

Briers, M. and Chua, W. F. 'The role of actor networks and boundary objects in management accounting change: a field study of an implementation of activity based costing', *Accounting, Organizations and Society*, Vol. 26 (2001) 237–69.

Brignall, S. and Modell, S. 'An institutional perspective on performance measurement and management in the "new public sector"', *Management Accounting Research*, Vol. 11, No. 3 (2000) 281–306.

Brignall, S., Fitzgerald, L., Johnston R. and Markou, E. *Improving Service Performance: A Study of Step-change versus Continuous Improvement* (London: CIMA, 1999).

Brignall, T. J. 'Performance Measurement and Change in Local Government: A General Case and a Childcare Application', *Public Money and Management*, October–December (1993) 23–30.

Brignall, T. J. 'A Contingent Rationale for Cost System Design in Services', *Management Accounting Research*, Vol. 8 (1997) 325–46.

Brignall, T. J. 'The UnBalanced Scorecard: A Social and Environmental Critique', in Neely, A., Walters A. and Austin, R. (eds) *Performance Measurement and Management: Research and Action* (Cranfield, UK: Centre for Business Performance, Cranfield School of Management, 2002).

Brignall, T. J. and Ballantine, J. A. 'Performance Measurement in Service Businesses Revisited', *International Journal of Service Industry Management*, Vol. 7, No. 1 (1996a) 6–31.

Brignall, T. J. and Ballantine, J. A. *Interactions and Trade-Offs in Multi-Dimensional Performance Management* (University of Alberta, Edmonton, Canada: Strategic Management Accounting Conference, 10–11 May, 1996b).

Brignall, T. J. S. and Ballantine J. A. 'Strategic Enterprise Management Systems: New Directions for Research', *Management Accounting Research*, Vol. 15, No. 2, June (2004) 225–40.

British Quality Foundation, *The Excellence Model Description* (2007) www.bqf.org.uk/ex_description.htm, accessed 06/08/07.

Brockhaus, R. H. 'The psychology of the entrepreneur', in Kent, C. A., Sexton, D. L. and Vesper, K. H. (eds) *Encyclopædia of Entrepreneurship* (Englewood Cliffs, NJ: Prentice Hall, 1982).

BSI, *BS 6079-2:2000 Project Management – Part 2: Vocabulary* (London: British Standard Institution, 2000).

BSI, *BS EN ISO 1006: Quality Management and Guidelines to Quality in Project Management* (London: British Standard Institution, 1995).

BSI, *BS EN ISO 9000:2000 Quality Management Systems – Fundamentals and Vocabulary* (London: British Standard Institution, 2000).

Burawoy, M. *Manufacturing consent: changes in the labor process under monopoly capitalism* (Chicago, Ill: University of Chicago Press, 1979).

Burgoyne, J. 'Management learning: form history and perspectives', *Emerging Fields in Management: Connecting Learning and Critique* (Leeds: Leeds University working paper series, Leeds Business School, 2000).

Burns, J. and Baldvinsdottir, G. 'An institutional perspective of accountants' new roles – the interplay of contradictions and praxis', *European Accounting Review*, Vol. 14, No. 4 (2005) 725–57.

Burns, T. and Stalker, G. *The Management of Innovation* (London: Tavistock, 1966).

Burrell, G. and Morgan, G. *Sociological Paradigms and Organisational Analysis* (London: Heinemann Educational Books, 1979).

Burt, R. S. 'Structural Holes', in *The Social Structure of Competition* (Cambridge, MA: Harvard University Press, 1992).

Cabinet Office, 'Private action, public benefit: a review of charities and the wider not-for-profit sector', in *Strategy Unit Report* (London: Cabinet Office, September 2002).

Campbell, N. R. *An Account of the Principles of Measurement and Calculation*, (London: Longmans, 1928).

Carr, P. and Beaver, G. 'The enterprise culture: understanding a misunderstood concept', *Strategic Change*, Vol. 11, No. 2 (2002) 105–13.

Carroll, J. D. 'The Rhetoric and Political Reality in the National Performance Review', *Public Administration Review*, Vol. 55 (1995) 302–12.

Carroll, G. R. and Hannan, M. T. *The Demography of Corporations and Industries* (Princeton: Princeton University Press, 2000).

Carter, C., Clegg, S., Hogan, J. and Kornberger, M. 'The Polyphonic Spree: The Case of the Liverpool Dockers', *Industrial Relations Journal*, Vol. 34, No. 4 (2003) 290–304.

Carter, N., Klein, R. and Day, P. *How organisations measure success: the use of performance indicators in government* (London: Routledge, 1992).

Cascio, W. F. *Applied Psychology in Human Resource Management*, 5th (International) edn (London: Prentice Hall, 1998).

Castells, M. *The Rise of the Network Society: The Information Age: Economy Society and Culture Vol. I* (Oxford: Blackwells, 1996).

Castells, M. *The Power of Identity: Economy Society and Culture Vol. II* (Oxford: Blackwells, 1997).

Castells, M. *End of Millennium: The Information age: Economy Society and Culture Vol. II*, 2nd edn (Oxford: Blackwells, 2000).

Caws, P. 'Definition and Measurement in Physics', in Churchman, C. W. and Ratoosh, P. *Measurement: Definition and Theories* (New York: John Wiley & Sons, 1959).

CEML, 'Joining Entrepreneurs in their World', *Council for Excellence in Management and Leadership* (London, 2002).

Centre for Voluntary Action Research (CVAR), *The adoption and use of quality systems in the voluntary sector* (London: Quality Standards Task Group/Charities Evaluation Services, 2004).

Chandler, A. D. *Strategy and Structure* (Cambridge, MA: MIT Press, 1962).

Charity Commission, *Reporting charities' performance and achievements*, www. charitycommission.gov.uk, October 2004, accessed 12/07/05.

Charnes, A., Cooper, W. W., Lewin, A. Y. and Seiford, L. M. *Data Envelopment Analysis: Theory, Methodology and Applications* (Boston: Kluwer, 1995).

Checkland, P. 'Achieving "desirable and feasible" change: an application of Soft System Methodology', *Journal of Operational Research Society*, Vol. 36 (1985) 821–31.

Checkland, P. and Holwell, S. *Information, Systems, and Information Systems.* (Chichester: John Wiley & Sons, 1998).

Chell, E. 'Towards researching the "opportunistic entrepreneur": A social constructionist approach and research agenda', *European Journal of Occupational and Organisational Psychology*, Vol. 9, No. 1 (2000) 63–80.

Child, J. 'Organizational structure, environment and performance; the role of strategic choice', *Sociology*, Vol. 6 (1972) 1–22.

Christensen, T. and Lægreid, P. *New Public Management: The Transformation of Ideas and Practice* (Aldershot: Ashgate, 2002).

Clarke, J. Thorpe, R., Anderson, L. and Gold, J. 'It's all action, it's all learning: Action Learning in SMEs', *Journal of European Industrial Training*, Vol. 30, No. 6 (Emerald Pubs, 2006) 441–55.

Clarkson, G. P. and Hodgkinson, G. P. 'Sensemaking on the front line: The key implications for call centre performance', in Neely, A., Kennerley, M. and Walters, A. (eds) *Fourth International Conference on Performance Measurement and Management: Public and Private,* July, Edinburgh (Cranfield, UK: Centre for Business Performance, 2004), pp. 251–8.

Cleland, D. I. 'Project Stakeholder Management', *Project Management Journal*, Vol. 17, No. 4 (1986) 36–44.

Coad, A. 'Strategic control', in Berry, A. J., Broadbent, J. and Otley D. (eds) *Management control: theories, issues and practices* (London: Macmillan, 1995).

Cobbold, I. and Lawrie, G. 'The Development of Balanced Scorecard as a Strategic Management Tool', in Neely, A. (ed.) *Proceedings of the Performance Management Association Conference*, Boston, USA (Cranfield, UK: Centre for Business Performance, 2002).

Conner, K. R. 'A Historical Comparison of the Resource-Based Theory and Five Schools of Thought Within Industrial Organization Economics: Do We Have a New Theory of the Firm?', *Journal of Management*, Vol. 17, No. 1 (1991) 121–54.

Connolly, C. and Hyndman, N. 'Charity accounting: An empirical analysis of the impact of recent changes', *British Accounting Review*, Vol. 32 (2000) 77–100.

Connolly, C. and Hyndman, N. 'A comparative study on the impact of revised SORP 2 on British and Irish Charities', *Financial Accountability and Management*, February, Vol. 17, No. 1 (2001) 73–97.

Connor, S. 'Glaxo chief: Our drugs do not work on most patients', *Independent* (8 December 2003).

Constable, C. and McCormick, R. 'The Making of British Managers', A Report for the BIM and CBI into Management Training, Education and Development, *British Institute of Management* and *Confederation of British Industry*, London (1987).

Conway, N. and Briner, R. B. *Understanding Psychological Contracts at Work: A Critical Evaluation of Theory and Research* (Oxford: Oxford University Press, 2005).

Cooke-Davies, T. 'The "real" success factors on projects', *International Journal of Project Management*, Vol. 20, No. 3 (2002) 185–90.

Cooper, C. *Individual Differences,* 2nd edn (London: Arnold, 2002).

Cooper, R. 'Does your company need a new cost system?', *Journal of Cost Management*, Spring (1987) 45–9.

Cooper, R. and Kaplan, R. S. 'Measure costs right: make the right decisions', *Harvard Business Review*, September–October (1988) 96–103.

Cooper, T. *The responsible administrator: An approach to ethics for the administration role* (San Francisco: Jossey Bass, 1990).

Cope, J. 'Toward a dynamic learning perspective of entrepreneurship', *Entrepreneurship, Theory and Practice*, Vol. 29, No. 4 (2005) 373–97.

Cope, J. and Watts, G. 'Learning by doing: An exploration of experience, critical incidents and reflection in entrepreneurial learning', *International Journal of Entrepreneurial Behaviour and Research*, Vol. 6, No. 3 (2000) 104–24.

Corvellec, H. 'For a narrative criticism of organisational performance', Paper presented at *New Directions in Organisational Performance Conference*, Morpeth, 28–29 March (2001).

Coulson, A. 'Value for Money in PFI Proposals: A Commentary on the 2004 UK Treasury Guidelines for Public Sector Comparators', University of Birmingham: Institute of Local Government Studies (INLOGOV) Working Paper (2006).

Courtney, R. *Managing voluntary organisations: new approaches* (Hemel Hempstead: ICSA Publishing, 1996).

Cowen, P. J. 'Review: Panorama: "The Secrets of Seroxat" ', *British Medical Journal* Vol. 325 (19 October 2002) 910.

Crockett, F. 'Revitalizing executive information systems', *Sloan Management Review*, Summer (1992).

Cunningham, I. 'Human resource management in the voluntary sector: Challenges and opportunities', *Public money and management*, April–June (1999) 19–25.

Currie, R. M. *Work Study*. (London: Pitman International, 1959).

Dale, B. G., Boaden, R. J. and Lascalles, D. M. 'Total Quality Management', in Dale, B. G. (ed.) *Managing Quality*, 2nd edn (Hemel Hempstead: Prentice-Hall, 1994), pp. 3–13.

Daniel, R. D. 'Management Information Crisis', *Harvard Business Review,* Vol. 39, No. 5 (1961) 111–21.

Daniels, K., Harris, C. and Briner, R. B. 'Understanding the risks of stress: A cognitive approach', *Health & Safety Executive*, Contract Research Report 427/2002 (Norwich: HMSO, 2002).

Dasgupta, P. 'Economics of Social Capital', *The Economic Record*, Vol. 81, Supplement 1, August (2005) S2–S21.

David, R. J. and Han, S.-K. 'A systematic assessment of the empirical support for transaction cost economics', *Strategic Management Journal*, Vol. 25, No. 1 (2003) 39–58.

Davidsson, P. and Delmar, F. 'Some important observations concerning job creation by firm size and age', in Pleitner, H. J. (ed.) *Renaissance der KMU in einer globalisierten Wirtschaft* (St Gallen: KMU Vlg HSG, 1997).

Davidsson, P., Achtenhagen, L. and Naldi, L. 'Research on Small Firm Growth: A Review', A paper presented at the *34th European Institute of Small Business Conference* (Turku, Finland, 2004).

Davies, H., Nutley, S. and Smith, P. (eds) *What Works? Evidence-based Policy and Practice in Public Services* (Bristol: Policy Press, 2000).

Davis, J. H., Schoorman, F. D. and Donaldson, L. 'Toward a new stewardship theory of management', *Academy of Management Review*, Vol. 22, No. 1 (1997) 20–47.

Day, P. and Klein, R. *Accountabilities: five public services* (London: Tavistock, 1987).

De Alessi, L. 'The economics of property rights: a review of the evidence', *Research in Law and Economics*, Vol. 2 (1980) 1–47.

de Nahlik C. F. and Holloway, J. A. 'The tender trap? The network and the firm – support system or spider's web?', *unpublished paper presented at meeting of Management Control Association*, 25 November 2005 (Milton Keynes: Open University, 2005).

De Wit, A. 'Measurement of Project Management Success', *International Journal of Project Management*, Vol. 6, No. 3 (1988) 164–70.

Delbridge, R. and Lowe, J. 'Managing human resources for business success: a review of the issues', *The International Journal of Human Resource Management*, Vol. 8 (1997) 857–73.

Deming, W. E. 'Quality, productivity and competitive position', *MIT Centre for Advanced Engineering Study* (Cambridge, MA, 1982).

Deming, W. E. *Out of the Crisis* (Cambridge, MA: Cambridge Press, 1986).

Denzin, N. K. and Lincoln, Y. S. (eds) *The Sage Handbook of Qualitative Research*, 3rd edn (Thousand Oaks: Sage, 2005).

Department of Health, *The NHS Plan: A Plan for Investment, A Plan for Reform* (London: TSO, 2000).

Department of Health, *The Performance Measurement Framework* (London: Department of Health, 2001).

Department of Trade and Industry (DTI), *Our Competitive Future: Building the Knowledge Driven Economy* (London: UK Government White Paper, 1998).

Dess, C. and Robinson, R. 'Measuring Organizational Performance in the Absence of Objective Measures: The Case of the Privately Held Firm and Conglomerate Business Unit', *Strategic Management Journal*, Vol. 5, No. 3 (1984) 265–73.

DETR, *Best Value and Audit Commission Performance Indicators 2000/2001* (Department of the Environment Transport and the Regions, London: TSO, 1999).

DETR, *KPI report for the Minister for Construction by the KPI Working Group* (Department of the Environment, Transport and the Regions, 2000), http://www.dti.gov.uk/files/file16441.pdf, accessed 04/08/07

Dicken, P. *Global Shift: transforming the world's economy*, 3rd edn (London: Paul Chapman, 1998).

Dickie-Clark, H. P. *The Marginal Situation* (London: Routledge, 1966).

Dillman, D. A. *Mail and Internet Surveys: The Tailored Design Method* (New York: Wiley, 1999).

Di Maggio, P. J. and Powell, W. W. 'The Iron Cage Revisited: Institutional Isomorphism and Collective Rationality in Organizational fields', *American Sociological Review*, Vol. 48, April (1983) 147–60.

Di Maggio, P. and Powell, W. 'Introduction', in Powell, W. and Di Maggio, P. (eds) *The New Institutionalism in Organisational Analysis* (Chicago, III: University of Chicago Press, 1991).

Dixon, J. R., Nanni A. J. and Vollmann, T. E. *The New Performance Challenge: Measuring Operations for World-Class Competition* (Homewood, Il: Dow Jones-Irwin, 1990).

Douglas, R. *Unfinished Business* (Auckland: Random House, 1993).

Downs, G. and Larkey, P. *The Quest for Government Efficiency* (New York: Temple Smith, 1986).

Doyle, P. 'Setting business objectives and measuring performance', *European Management Journal*, Vol. 12, No. 2 (1994) 123–32.

Drucker, P. *The Practice of Management* (London: Pan, 1968).

Drucker, P. *Managing the nonprofit organisation – Principles and practices* (New York: HarperCollins, 1990).

DTI, *Innovation Report – Competing in the Global Economy: the Innovation Challenge* (London, UK: Government White Paper, 2003).

DTI, *Critical Success Factors: Creating Value From Your Intangibles* (London: Department of Trade and Industry, 2004).

Duncan, B. 'Characteristics of Organizational Environments and Perceived Environmental Uncertainty', *Administrative Sciences Quarterly*, Vol. 17 (1972) 313–27.

Dunleavy, P. *Democracy, Bureaucracy and Public Choice; Economic Explanations in Political Science* (Hemel Hempstead: Harvester Wheatsheaf, 1991).

Dunleavy, P. and Hood, C. 'From Old Public Administration to New Public Management', *Public Money and Management*, Vol. 14, No. 3 (1994) 9–16.

Dunleavy, P. and O' Leary, B. *Theories of the State* (Basingstoke: Macmillan, 1987).

Dunn, B. and Mathews, S. 'The pursuit of excellence is not optional in the voluntary sector, it is essential', *International Journal of Health Care Quality Assurance*, Vol. 14, No. 3 (2001) 121–5.

Dyson, R. 'Strategy, performance and operational research', *Journal of Operational Research Society*, Vol. 51 (2000) 5–11.

Easterby-Smith, M. 'Disciplines of organizational learning: contributions and critiques', *Human Relations*, Vol. 50, No. 9 (1997) 1085–113.

Eccles, R. and Pyburn, P. 'Creating a Comprehensive System to Measure Performance', *Management Accounting* (US), October (1992) 41–4.

Eccles, R. G. 'The performance measurement manifesto', *Harvard Business Review*, January/February (1991) 131–7.

Economic and Social Research Council, *Building Partnerships: Enhancing the Quality of Management Research* (The Bain Report) (Swindon: ESRC, 1994).

Edwards, J., Kay, J. and Mayer, C. *The Economic Analysis of Accounting Profitability* (Oxford University Press, 1987).

Egan, J. *Rethinking Construction* (Department of the Environment, Transport and the Regions, London: HMSO, 1998).

Eliassen, K. and Kooiman, J. *Managing Public Organisations* (London: Sage, 1993).

Emmanuel, C. and Otley, D. *Accounting for Management Control* (Chapman and Hall, 1985).

e-reward.co.uk 'What is Happening in Performance Management Today', *E-reward.co.uk Research Report* 32, April (2005).

European Foundation for Quality Management, *Self-assessment Guidelines* (Brussels: EFQM, 1998).

European Foundation for Quality Management, *The EFQM Excellence Model: Public and Voluntary Sector Version* (Brussels: EFQM, 2000).

European Foundation for Quality Management, *Business Excellence Model* (Brussels: EFQM, 2001), available at: www.efqm.org.

Etzioni, A. 'The Third Sector and Domestic Missions', *Public Administration Review*, Vol. 33, No. 4 (July–August) (1973) 314–23.

Ezzamel, M., Hoskin, K. and Macve, R. 'Managing it all by Numbers: A Review of Johnson and Kaplan's "Relevance Lost"', *Accounting and Business Research*, Vol. 20, No. 78 (1990) 153–66.

Fahey, L. and Narayanan, V. *Macroenvironmental Analysis for Strategic Management* (St Paul, MN: West Publishing Company, 1986).

Farnham, D. and Horton, S. *Managing the New Public Services*, 2nd edn (Hants: Macmillan, 1996).

Fayol, H. *General and Industrial Administration* (London: Pitman, 1949).

Fearfull, A. and Kamenou, N. 'How do you account for it? A critical exploration of career opportunities for and experiences of ethnic minority women', *Critical Perspectives on Accounting*, Vol. 17, No. 7 (2006) 883–901.

Feldwick, P. 'What is Brand equity anyway, and how do you measure it?' *Journal of the Market Research Society*, Vol. 38, No. 2 (April 1996).

Ferlie, E., Ashburner, L., Fitzgerald, L. and Pettigrew, A. *The new public management in action* (Oxford, UK: Oxford University Press, 1996).

Ferlie, E., Hartley, J. F. and Martin, S. 'Changing public service organizations: current perspectives and future prospects', *British Journal of Management*, Vol. 14 (2003) S1–14.

Ferreira, A. and Otley, D. 'The design and use of management control systems: an extended framework for analysis', unpublished paper (2004).

Fincham, R. 'Natural workgroups and the process of job design', *Employee Relations*, Vol. 11 (1989) 17–22.

Fischer, J. 'Contingency-based research on management control systems', *Journal of Accounting Literature*, Vol. 14 (1995) 24–53.

Fitzgerald, L. and Moon, P. 'Performance measurement: case study evidence from the UK', *Management Accounting annual conference, University of Aston*, September (1996a).

Fitzgerald, L. and Moon, P. *Performance Measurement in Service Industries: Making it Work* (London: CIMA, 1996b).

Fitzgerald, L., Johnston, R., Brignall, T. J., Silvestro, R. and Voss, C. *Performance Measurement in Service Businesses* (London: Chartered Institute of Management Accountants (CIMA), 1991).

Fleming, Q. W. and Koppelman, J. M. *Earned Value Project Management* (Newtown Square, Pennsylvania: Project Management Institute, 2000).

Fletcher, C. *Appraisal Routes to Improved Performance* (London: Institute of Personnel and Development, 1993).

Fombrun, C., Tichy, N. and Devanna M. (eds). *Strategic Human Resource Management* (New York: John Wiley & Sons, 1984).

Forbes, D. 'Cognitive approaches to new venture creation', *International Journal of Management Reviews*, Vol. 1, No. 4 (1999) 415–39.

Foucault, M. *Discipline and Punish: the birth of the prison* (London: Penguin, 1977).

Fowler, A. 'Performance management: the MBO of the 1990's?', *Personnel Management*, July (1990) 47–54.

Fowler, A. 'Assessing NGO performance: difficulties, dilemmas and a way ahead' in Edwards, M. and Hulme, D. (eds) *Non-governmental organisations – Performance and Accountability: Beyond the magic bullet* (London: Earthscan publications Ltd, 1998), 143–56.

Francis, G. and Holloway, J. 'What have we learned? Themes from the literature on best-practice benchmarking', *International Journal of Management Reviews*, Vol. 9, No. 3 (2007) 171–89.

Fraser, R. and Hope, J. *Beyond budgeting* (Boston, MA: Harvard Business School Press, 2003).

Freeman, R. E. *Strategic Management: A Stakeholder Approach* (London: Pitman, 1984).

Fryer, D. and Payne, R. 'Being unemployed: A review of the literature on the psychological experience of unemployment', in Cooper, C. L. and Robertson, I. (eds) *International Review of Industrial and Organizational Psychology* (Chichester: Wiley, 1986), pp. 235–78.

Fulop, L. and Linstead, S. 'Motivation and meaning', in Linstead, S., Fulop, L. and Lilley, S. (eds) *Management and Organisation: A Critical Text* (Basingstoke: Palgrave, 2004), pp. 280–323.

Gardiner, J. P. 'Robust and lean designs with state of the art automotive and aircraft examples', in Freeman, C. (ed.) *Design, Innovation and Long cycles in Economic Development* (London: Frances Pinter, 1986).

Gardiner, P. D. and Stewart, K. 'Revisiting the golden triangle of cost, time and Quality: the role of NPV in project control, success and failure', *International Journal of Project Management*, Vol. 18, No. 4 (2000) 251–56.

Garengo, P., Biazzo, S. and Bititci, U. S. 'Performance measurement systems in SMEs: A review for a research agenda', *International Journal of Management Reviews*, Vol. 7, No. 1 (2005) 25–47.

Ghalayini, A. G. and Noble, J. S. 'The changing basis of performance Measurement', *International Journal of Operations & Production Management*, Vol. 16, No. 8 (1996) 63–80.

Ghoshal, S. 'Bad management theories are destroying good management practices', *Academy of Management Learning and Education*, Vol. 4 (2005) 75–91.

Gibb, A. 'In pursuit of a new "enterprise" and "entrepreneurship" paradigm for learning: creative destruction, new values, new ways of doing things and new combinations of knowledge', *International Journal of Management Reviews*, Vol. 4, No. 3 (2002) 233–69.

Gibbons, M., Limoges, C., Nowotny, H., Schwartzman, S., Scott, P. and Trow, M. *The New Production of Knowledge: the Dynamics of Science and Research in Contemporary Societies* (London: Sage, 1994).

Giddens, A. *The constitution of society* (Cambridge: Polity Press, 1984).

Giddens, A. *The third way: the renewal of social democracy* (Cambridge: Polity Press, 1999).

Gilbert, N., Pyka, A. and Ahrweiler, P. 'Innovation Networks – A Simulation Approach', *Journal of Artificial Societies and Social Simulation*, Vol. 4, No. 3 (2001) www.soc.surrey.ac.uk/JASSS/4/3/8.html, accessed 06/08/07.

Goldstein, H. *Multilevel Statistical Models* (London: Edward Arnold, 1995).

Goldstein, H. and Spiegelhalter, D. J. 'League tables and their limitations: statistical issues in comparisons of institutional performance', *Journal of the Royal Statistical Society* A, Vol. 159 (1996) 385–443.

Gooday, G. J. N. *The Morals of Measurement: Accuracy, Irony, and Trust in Late Victorian Electrical Practice* (Cambridge: Cambridge University Press, 2004).

Goodyear, M. 'Divided by a common language: diversity and deception in the world of global marketing', *Journal of the Market Research Society*, Vol. 38, No. 2 (April 1996).

Goold, M. and Campbell, A. *Strategies and Styles: The Role of the Centre in Managing Diversified Corporations* (Blackwell, 1987).

Gordon, J. and Lockyer, K. *Project Management and Project Planning* (FT Prentice Hall, 2005).

Gore, A. 'From Red Tape to Results: Creating a Government that Works Better and Costs Less', *Report of the National Performance Review* (Washington, DC: US Government Printing Office, 1993).

Goss, D. and Jones, R. 'Organisation structure and SME training provision', *International Small Business Journal*, Vol. 10, No. 4 (1997) 13–25.

Gough, I. *The Political Economy of the Welfare State* (London: Macmillan, 1979).

Government Performance and Results Act, *Public Law 103–62* (Washington DC: Congress, 1993).

Grant, R. M. 'The Resource-Based Theory of Competitive Advantage: Implications for Strategy Formulation', *California Management Review*, Vol. 33, No. 3 (1991) 114–35.

Grant, R. M. 'Toward a Knowledge-Based Theory of the Firm', *Strategic Management Journal*, Vol. 17, Winter Special Issue (1996) 109–22.

Gray, A. *Business-like but not like a business: the challenge for public management* (London: CIPFA (Chartered Institute of Public Finance Accountancy), 1998).

Gray, C. 'Growth orientation and the small firm', in Caley, K., Chell, E., Chittenden, F. and Mason, L. (eds) *Small Enterprise Development* (London: Paul Chapman Publishing, 1992).

Gray, C. *Formality, Intentionality and Planning: Features of Successful Entrepreneurial SMEs in the Future?* (Brisbane, Australia: paper presented at the ICSB World Conference, June 2000).

Greenberg, J. 'A Taxonomy of Organizational Justice Theories', *The Academy of Management Review*, Vol. 12, No. 1 (1987) 9–22.

Greenwood, R. and Hinings, C. R. 'Understanding Radical Organizational Change: Bringing Together the Old and the New Institutionalism', *Academy of Management Review*, Vol. 21, No. 4 (1996) 1022–54.

Greiling, D. 'Performance measurement – a driver for increasing the efficiency of public services?', *Paper given at EGPA – European Group of Public Administration Study Group 2: Productivity and Quality in the Public Sector* (2005). soc.kuleuven.be/io/egpa/qual/bern/Greiling.pdf, accessed 06/08/07.

Greve, H. R. 'Market niche entry decisions: Competition, learning, and strategy in Tokyo banking, 1894–1936', *Academy of Management Journal*, Vol. 43, No. 5, (2000) 816–36.

Grieco, M., Little, S. and Macdonald, K. 'The Silent Revolution: Electronic Data Interchange, Metadata and Metagovernance', *European Spatial Research and Policy*, Vol. 10, No. 2 (2003) 5–7.

Griffin, P. 'Wiring the Union: Scottish "devolution", informatisation and metagovernance', *European Spatial Research and Policy – Special Issue on Metagovernance,* Issue 2 (2003) 59–88.

Guest, D. 'Human Resource Management and Industrial Relations', *Journal of Management Studies*, Vol. 24, No. 5 (1987) 503–21.

Guest, D. 'Personnel and Human Resource Management: can you tell the difference?' *Personnel Management*, January (1989).

Guest, D. 'Is the psychological contract worth taking seriously?' *Journal of Organisational Behaviour*, Vol. 19 (1998) 649–64.

Guest, D. and Hoque, K. 'Human Resource management and the new industrial relations', in Beardwell, I. J. (ed.) *Contemporary Industrial Relations* (Oxford University Press, 1996).

Guzzo, R. A. and Dickson, M. W. 'Teams in organizations: Recent research on performance and effectiveness', *Annual Review of Psychology*, Vol. 47 (1996) 307–38.

Haas, M. D. and Kleingeld, A. 'Multilevel design of performance measurement systems: enhancing strategic dialogue through the organization', *Management Accounting Research*, Vol. 10 (1998) 223–61.

Hackman, J. R. and Oldham, G. R. 'Development of the job diagnostic survey', *Journal of Applied Psychology*, Vol. 60 (1975) 159–70.

Halfpenny, P. and Reid, M. 'Research on the voluntary sector: an overview', *Policy and Politics*, Vol. 30, No. 4 (2002) 533–50.

Hamel, G. and Prahalad, C. K. 'Managing strategic responsibility in the MNC', *Strategic Management Journal*, Vol. 4 (1983) 341–51.

Hammer, M. 'Re-engineering Work: Don't Automate, Obliterate', *Harvard Business Review*, July–August (1990).

Hammer, M. and Champy, J. *Re-engineering the Corporation: A Manifesto for Business Revolution* (USA: HarperCollins Publishers, 1993).

Hansen, S. C., Otley, D. T. and Van der Stede, W. A. 'Practice developments in budgeting: an overview and research perspective', *Journal of Management Accounting Research*, Vol. 15 (2003) 95–116.

Hansmann, H. B. 'The Role of Nonprofit Enterprise', *Yale Law Journal*, Vol. 8 (1980) 835–98.

Hart, O. and Moore, J. 'Foundations of Incomplete Contracts', *Review of Economic Studies*, Vol. 66 (1999) 115–38.

Hartle, F. *Re-engineer your Performance Management Process* (London: Kogan Page, 1995).

Hartley, J. 'Organizational change and development'. in Warr, P. (ed.) *Psychology at work*. 5th edn (Harmondsworth: Penguin, 2002).

Hawawini, G., Subramanian, V. and Verdin, P. 'Is Performance driven by Industry- or Firm-specific factors? A new Look at the Evidence', *Strategic Management Journal*, Vol. 24, No. 1 (2003) 1–16.

Hayes, R. H. and Abernathy, W. J. 'Managing our way to economic decline', *Harvard Business Review*, July–August (1980) 67–77.

Hayes, J. and Nutman, P. *Understanding the Unemployed: The Psychological Effects of Unemployment* (London: Tavistock, 1981).

Hayes, R. H. and Clark, K. B. 'Why some factories are more productive than others', *Harvard Business Review*, September–October (1986) 66–73.

Headrick, D. R. *The Tools of Empire: Technology and European Imperialism in the Nineteenth Century* (Oxford: Oxford University Press, 1981).

Hendry, C. and Pettigrew, A. 'The Practice of Strategic Human Resource Management', *Personnel Review*, Vol. 15, No. 5 (1986) 3–8.

Hendry, C. and Pettigrew, A. 'Human Resource Management: an agenda for the 1990s', *International Journal of Human Resource Management*, Vol. 1, No. 1 (1990) 17–43.

Herbig, P., Golden, J. and Dunphy, S. 'The relationship of structure to entrepreneurial and innovative success', *Marketing and Intelligence and Planning*, Vol. 12, No. 9 (1994) 37–48.

Herman, N. and Brignall, S. *Financial shared services centres and the role of the accountant* (Gothenburg, Sweden: EAA Annual Congress, May 2005).

Heron, J. and Reason, P. 'The practice of cooperative inquiry: research "with" rather than "on" people', *Handbook of Action Research: Participant Inquiry and Practice* (London: Sage, 2001), Ch. 16.

Herriot, P. *The Employment Relationship: A Psychological Perspective* (London: Routledge, 2001).

Herzberg, F. *Work and the nature of man* (London: Staples Press, 1966).

Herzberg, F. 'One more time: How do you motivate employees?', *Harvard Business Review*, Vol. 46 (1968) 109–31.

Heseltine, M. *Where there's a will* (London: Arrow, 1987).

Hicks, P. E. *Introduction to Industrial Engineering and Management Science* (London: McGraw-Hill, 1977).

Hind, A. *The governance and management of charities* (High Barnet: Voluntary Sector Press, 1995).

Hirshleifer, J. 'On the Economics of Transfer Pricing', *Journal of Business*, July (1956) 172–84.

HM Government, 'Efficiency and Effectiveness in the Civil Service', *Cmmd 8499* (London: HMSO, 1982).

HM Government, *Measuring Up: Performance Indicators in Further Education* (London: HMSO, 1990).

HM Government, 'Financial Statement and Budget Report', *HC 968* (London: The Stationery Office, 2006), http://www.hm-treasury.gov.uk./media/B/3/bud06_completereport_2320.pdf, accessed 04/08/07.

HM Treasury, Public Service Agreements (2007) http://www.hm-treasury.gov.uk/documents/public_spending_reporting/public_service_performance/public_service_performance_index.cfm, accessed 04/08/07.

Hockey, R. 'Human performance in the working environment', in Warr, P. (ed.), *Psychology at Work*, 5th edn (London: Penguin, 2002), pp. 26–50.

Hodgson, P. *The first step in restoring public trust in statistics* (London: Financial Times, 1 December 2005).

Hofstede, G. *The game of budget control* (London: Tavistock, 1968).

Hollingsworth, B., Dawson P. J. and Maniadakis, N. 'Efficiency measurement of health care: a review of non-parametric methods and applications', *Health Care Management Science*, Vol. 2 (1999) 161–72.

Holloway, J. 'Managing performance', in Rose, A. and Lawton, A. (eds) *Public Services Management* (London: Prentice Hall, 1999), pp. 238–59.

Holloway, J. 'Investigating the impact of performance measurement', in Neely, A. (ed.) *Performance Measurement – Past, Present and Future* (Cambridge: Judge Institute, University of Cambridge, 2000), pp. 234–41.

Holloway, J. A. 'Investigating the impact of performance measurement', *International Journal of Business Performance Management*, Vol. 3, No. 2/3/4 (2002) 167–80.

Holloway, J., Hinton, C. M., Francis, G. A. and Mayle, D. T. *Identifying best practice in benchmarking* (London: CIMA, 1999).

Holman, D. and Thorpe, R. *Management and Language* (London: Sage, 2003).

Holmes, L. and Grieco M. 'The power of transparency: the Internet, e-mail, and the Malaysian political crisis', *Asia Pacific Business Review*, Vol. 8, No. 2, Winter (2001).

Holmes, L., Hosking, D. M. and Grieco, M. *Organising in the information age* (Aldershot: Ashgate, 2002).

Holström, B. *On Incentives and Control in Organizations*, unpublished PhD thesis (Stanford: Stanford University, 1977).

Hood, C. 'A public management for all seasons?', *Public Administration*, Vol. 69, Spring (1991) 3–19.

Hood, C. 'The "New Public Management" in the 1980s: variations on a theme'. *Accounting Organisations and Society*, Vol. 20, No. 2/3 (1995) 93–109.

Hood, C. *The Art of the State: Culture, Rhetoric, and Public Management* (Oxford, UK: Oxford University Press, 1998).

Hope, J. and Fraser, R. 'Beyond Budgeting', *Management Accounting*, January (1999).

Hopwood, A. 'An Empirical Study of the Role of Accounting Data in Performance Evaluation', *Empirical Research in Accounting: Supplement to Journal of Accounting Research* (1972) 156–82.

Hopwood, A. 'If only there were simple solutions, but there aren't: some reflections on Zimmerman's critique of empirical management accounting research', *European Accounting Review*, Vol. 11, No. 4 (2002) 777–86.

Houldsworth, E. and Jirasinghe, D. *Managing and Measuring Employee Performance: Lessons from Research into HR Practice*, (London: Kogan Page, 2006).

House of Commons, 'On Target? Government by Measurement', Public Administration Select Committee, Fifth Report, *HC62-1* (London: The Stationery Office, 2003).

Howard, M. interviewed on *Today* (BBC Radio 4, 10 August 2004).

Hudson, M. *Managing without profit – The art of managing third-sector organisations*, 2nd edn (London: Directory of Social Change, 2004).

Hughes, O. *Public Management and Administration* (Basingstoke: Palgrave, 2003).

Humble, J. *Management by Objectives* (London: Management Publications, 1972).

Huse, M. and Landstrom, H. 'European entrepreneurship and small business research: methodological openness and contextual differences', *International Studies of Management and Organisation*, Vol. 27, No. 3 (1997) 3–12.

Huselid, M. 'The Impact of HRM practices on turnover, productivity and corporate financial performance', *Academy of Management Journal*, Vol. 38, No. 3 (1995) 635–72.

Huselid, M., Jackson, S. and Schuler, R. 'Technical and strategic human resource management effectiveness as determinants of firm performance', *Academy of Management Journal*, Vol. 40, No. 1 (1997).

Hutton, Lord *Report of the inquiry into the circumstances surrounding the death of Dr David Kelly* (London: House of Commons, 2004). www.the-hutton-inquiry.org.uk/content/rulings.htm, accessed 06/08/07.

Iezzoni, L. *Risk Adjustment for Measuring Healthcare Outcomes*, 2nd edn (Chicago: Health Administration Press, 1997).

Ingham, H. and Harrington, L. T. *Interfirm Comparison* (London: William Heinemann, 1980).

IRS, 'Employment Trends', *IRS Employment Review*, 781, August (2003).

Ittner, C. D. and Larcker, D. F. 'Empirical managerial accounting research: are we just describing management accounting practice?', *European Accounting Review*, Vol. 11, No. 4 (2002) 787–94.

Iyer, K. C. and Jha, K. N. 'Factors affecting cost performance: evidence from Indian construction projects', *International Journal of Project Management*, Vol. 23, No. 4 (2005) 283–95.

Jackall, R. J. *Moral Mazes: The world of corporate managers* (New York, OUP, York and Oxford, 1988).

Jackson, P. and Palmer, B. *First steps in measuring performance for the public sector: a management guide* (London: Public Finance Foundation, 1989).

Jacobs, R. 'Alternative methods to measure hospital efficiency: data envelopment analysis and stochastic frontier analysis', *Health Care Management Science*, Vol. 4 (2001) 103–15.

Jahoda, M. *Employment and Unemployment: A Social Psychological Analysis* (Cambridge: Cambridge University Press, 1982).

Jensen, M. C. and Meckling, W. H. 'Theory of the firm: managerial behaviour, agency costs and ownership structure', *Journal of Financial Economics*, 3 October (1976) 305–60.

Johnsen, A. 'What does 25 years of experience tell us about the state of performance measurement in public policy and management?' *Public Money and Management*, Vol. 25, No. 1 (2005) 9–19.

Johnson, G. *Strategic Change and the Management Process* (Oxford: Blackwell, 1987).

Johnson, G. and Scholes, K. *Exploring Corporate Strategy* (Harlow: FT Prentice-Hall, 2002).

Johnson, H. T. and Kaplan, R. S. *Relevance Lost: The Rise and Fall of Management Accounting* (Harvard Business School Press, 1987).

Johnson, H. T. 'Managing by Remote Control: Recent Management Accounting Practice in Historical Perspective', in Temin, P. (ed.) *Inside the Business Enterprise: Historical Perspectives on the Use of Information* (The University of Chicago Press, 1991).

Johnson, H. T. *Relevance Regained: From Top-Down Control to Bottom-Up Empowerment* (The Free Press, 1992).

Johnson, L. *Presidential Papers, Vol. 1* (Washington DC: Library of Congress, 1968).

Johnston, R. and Clark, G. *Services Operations Management*, 2nd edn (Essex: Pearson Education Ltd, 2005).

Johnston, R., Fitzgerald, L. and Brignall, T. J. S. 'The involvement of management accountants in operational process change', *International Journal of Operations and Production Management*, Vol. 22, No. 12 (2002) 1325–38.

Jones, F. and Fletcher, B. C. 'Job control and health', in Schabracq, M. J., Winnubst, J. A. M. and Cooper, C. L. (eds) *Handbook of Work and Health Psychology* (Chichester: Wiley, 1996), pp. 33–50.

Juran, J. and Gryna, F. M. *Quality planning and analysis* (New York: McGraw-Hill, 1980).

Kaplan, R. S. 'Devising a Balanced Scorecard Matched to Business Strategy', *Planning Review*, September/October (1994) 15–17, 19, 48.

Kaplan, R. S. and Norton, D. P. 'The balanced scorecard: measures that drive performance', *Harvard Business Review*, Vol. 70, No. 1 (1992) 71–9.

Kaplan, R. S. and Norton, D. P. 'Putting the Balanced Scorecard to Work', *Harvard Business Review*, September–October (1993) 134–47.

Kaplan, R. S. and Norton, D. P. 'Using the balanced scorecard as a strategic management system', *Harvard Business Review*, Vol. 74, No. 1 (1996a) 75–85.

Kaplan, R. S. and Norton, D. P. *The balanced scorecard* (Boston, MA: Harvard Business School Press, 1996b).

Kaplan, R. S. and Norton, D. P. 'Having trouble with your strategy? Then map it', *Harvard Business Review*, September–October (2000) 167–76.

Kaplan, R. S. and Norton, D. P. *The strategy focused organization* (Boston, MA: Harvard Business School Press, 2001).

Karlins, M. (ed.) *Psychology in the Service of Man* (New York: John Wiley, 1973).

Katznelson, I. *Marxism and the City* (Oxford: Clarendon Press, 1992).

Kay, J. 'Accountants, too, could be happy in a golden age', *Oxford Economic Papers*, Vol. 17 (1976) 66–80.

Kay, J. *How Measurement in Organisations Has Changed* (Conference speech, 2000), available at www.johnkay.com/society/181, accessed 06/08/07.

Kearns, K. K. *Managing for accountability – Preserving the public trust in public and nonprofit organisations* (San Francisco: Jossey-Bass, 1996).

Keenoy, T. 'Human Resource Management: rhetoric, reality and contradiction', *International Journal of Human Resource Management*, Vol. 1, No. 3 (1990) 363–84.

Keenoy, T. 'HRM as Hologram: a polemic', *Journal of Management Studies*, Vol. 36, No. 1 (1999) 1–23.

Kellock Hay, G., Beattie, R., Livingstone, R. and Munro, P. 'Change, HRM and the voluntary sector', *Employee Relations*, Vol. 23, No. 3 (2001) 240–56.

Kemp, N. J., Wall, T. D., Clegg, C. W. and Cordery, J. L. 'Autonomous work groups in a greenfield site: A comparative study', *Journal of Occupational Psychology*, Vol. 56 (1983) 271–88.

Kendall, J. and Knapp, M. 'The voluntary sector in the UK', *Johns Hopkins Nonprofit Sector*, series 8 (Manchester: Manchester University Press, 1996).

Kendall, J. *The voluntary sector* (London: Routledge, 2003).

Kendall, J. and Knapp, M. 'Measuring the performance of voluntary organisations', *Public Management*, Vol. 2, No. 1 (2000) 105–32.

Kerzner, H. 'Systems project management: A case study at the IRS', *Systems Project Management*, Vol. 40, No. 1 (1989) 7–9.

Kerzner, H. *In search of Excellence in Project Management* (New York: Van Nostrand Reinhold, 1998).

Kessler, I. and Purcell, J. 'Performance Related Pay: Objectives and Application', *Human Resource Management Journal*, Vol. 2, No. 3, Spring (1992) 16–33.

Ketokivi, M. A. and Schroeder, R. G. 'Perceptual Measures of Performance: Fact or Fiction?', *Journal of Operations Management*, Vol. 22, No. 3 (2004) 247–64.

Kharif, O. 'An Epidemic of "Viral Marketing"', *Business Week Online* (30 August 2000) at www.businessweek.com/bwdaily/dnflash/aug2000/nf20000830_601.htm, accessed 06/08/07.

Kim, W. C. and Mauborgne, R. A. 'A Procedural Justice Model of Strategic Decision Making: Strategy Content Implications in the Multinational', *Organization Science*, Vol. 6, No. 1 (1995) 44–61.

Klein, J. *A critique of competitive advantage* (Manchester: a paper presented at the Critical Management Studies Conference, 2001).

Klein, N. *No Logo* (London: HarperCollins, 2000).

Klein, R. *The new politics of the NHS* (Harlow: Longman, 2001).

Kogut, B. 'The Network as Knowledge: Generative Rules and the Emergence of Structure', *Strategic Management Journal*, Vol. 21 (2000) 405–25.

Kogut, B. and Zander, U. 'Knowledge of the Firm, Combinative Capabilities, and the Replication of Technology', *Organization Science*, Vol. 3, No. 3 (1992) 383–97.

Kotter, J. 'Leading Change: why transformation efforts fail', *Harvard Business Review*, March–April, Vol. 73, No. 2 (1995) 59–67.

Kris, A. and Fahy, M. J. *Shared service centres: delivering value from more effective finance and business processes* (London: FT Prentice Hall, Pearson Education, 2003).

Kuhn, T. S. *The Structure of Scientific Revolutions* (Chicago: University of Chicago Press, 1962).

Lancaster, K .J. 'A new approach to consumer theory', *Journal of Political Economy*, Vol. 74 (1966) 132–57.

Landry, C., Morley, D., Southwood, R. and Wright, P. *What a way to run a railroad* (London: Camedia, 1985).

Langfield-Smith, K. 'Management control systems and strategy: a critical review', *Accounting, Organizations and Society*, Vol. 22 (1997) 207–32.

Latham, M. *Constructing the team* (London: HMSO, 1994).

Laughlin, R. 'Empirical research in accounting: alternative approaches and a case for "middle-range" thinking', *Accounting, Auditing & Accountability Journal*, Vol. 8, No. 1 (1995).

Lawler, E. E. and Bullock, R. J. 'Pay and Organisational Change', *The Personnel Administrator,* May (1978).

Leat, D. 'Accountability' in Bruce, I. (ed.) *Charity talks on successful development*, VOLPROF, Centre for the Voluntary Sector and Not for Profit Management (London: City University Business School, 1993).

Lebas, M. J. 'Performance Measurement and Performance Management', *International Journal of Production Economics*, Vol. 41, No. 1 (1995) 23–35.

Lee, J. Y. 'How to Make Financial and Non-financial Data Add Up', *Journal of Accountancy*, September (1992) 62–6.

Legge, K. *Power, Innovation, and Problem-solving in Personnel Management* (London: McGraw-Hill, 1978).

Legge, K. 'Human Resource Management: a critical analysis', in Storey, J. (ed.) *New Perspectives on Human Resource Management* (London: Routledge, 1989).

Legge, K. 'Rhetoric, reality and hidden agendas', in Storey, J. (ed.), *Human Resource Management: A Critical Text* (London: Routledge, 1995a), pp. 33–59.

Legge. K. *HRM: Rhetorics and Realities* (Basingstoke: Macmillan Business, 1995b).

Lehn, K. and Makhija, A. 'EVA® & MVA as Performance Measures and Signals for Strategic Change', *Strategy and Leadership*, Vol. 24, No. 3, May/Jun (1996) 34–8.

Lenin, V. I. *What Is To Be Done?* (English translation edited by Utrechin, S. V.) (Oxford: Clarendon Press, 1902, translated 1963).

Lev, B. 'Intangibles at a Crossroads: What's Next?', *Financial Executive*, Vol. 18, No. 2 (2002) 35–9.

Levinthal, D. A. 'Adaptation on rugged landscapes', *Management Science*, Vol. 43, No. 7 (1997) 934–50.

Lewin, A. Y. 'Perspective', *Organization Science*, Vol. 8, No. 4 (1997) 351.

Lewin, A. Y. and Volberda, H. W. 'Prolegomena on Coevolution: A Framework for Research on Strategy and New Organizational Forms', *Organization Science*, Vol. 10, No. 5 (1999) 519–34.

Lewin, A. Y., Long, C. P. and Carroll, T. N. 'The Coevolution of New Organizational Forms', *Organization Science*, Vol. 10, No. 5 (1999) 535–50.

Lewin, K. in Cartwright, D. *Field theory in social science: selected theoretical papers* (New York: Harper and Row, 1951).

Likierman, A. 'Performance indicators: 20 early lessons from managerial use', *Public Money & Management*, Vol. 13 (1993) 15–22.

Lindblom, C. 'The Science of Muddling Through'. *Public Administration Review*, Vol. 19 (1959) 78–88.

Lipietz, A. *Towards a New Economic Order: Postfordism, Ecology and Democracy* (Cambridge: Polity Press, 1992).

Lippman S. A. and Rumelt, R. P. 'The payments perspective: micro-foundations of resource analysis', *Strategic Management Journal*, Vol. 24, No. 10 (2003) 903–27.

Little, S. 'Globalisation, Europeanisation and metagovernance: society, space and technology', *European Spatial Research and Policy – Special Issue on Metagovernance*, Vol. 10, No. 2 (2003) 9–24.

Little, S. and Clegg, S. 'Recovering experience, confirming identity, voicing resistance: the Braceros, the internet and counter-coordination', *Critical Perspectives on International Business*, Vol. 1, No. 2/3 (2005).

Little, S. E. *Design and determination: the role of information technology in redressing regional inequities in the development process* (Aldershot: Ashgate, 2004).

Little, S. E. and Grieco, M. S. 'Electronic Stepping Stones: a mosaic metaphor for the production and re-distribution of communicative skill in an electronic mode', in Clegg, S. and Kornberger, M. (eds) *Space, Organization and Management* (Stockholm: Copenhagen Business School Press/Liber, 2004).

Little, S. E. and Grieco, M. S. 'Big Pharma, social movements, international labour and the internet: critical perspectives on coordination', *European Journal of Industrial Relations* (Special issue on 'Imagined Solidarities: Labour and the Information Age' 2008, Forthcoming).

Little, S. E., Holmes, L. and Grieco, M. S. 'Island histories, open cultures?: the electronic transformation of adjacency', *Southern African Business*, Review Vol. 4, No. 2 (2000).

Lock, R. S. 'The regulatory role of the Charity Commission', *Managerial Auditing Journal*, Vol. 13, No. 7 (1998) 403–10.

Locke, E. A. 'The ideas of Frederick W. Taylor: an evaluation', *Academy of Management Review*, Vol. 7, No. 1 (1982) 14–24.

Luft, J. and Shields, M. 'Zimmerman's contentious conjectures: describing the present and prescribing the future of empirical management accounting research', *European Accounting Review*, Vol. 11, No. 4 (2002) 795–804.

Lukka, K. and Mouritsen, J. 'Homogeneity or heterogeneity of research in management accounting?', *European Accounting Review*, Vol. 11, No. 4 (2002) 805–12.

Lycett, M., Rassau, A. and Danson, J. 'Programme management: a critical review', *International Journal of Project Management*, Vol. 22, No. 4 (2004) 289–99.

Lynch, R. L. and Cross, K. F. *Measure Up! Yardsticks for Continuous Improvement* (Blackwell, 1991).

Lynch, R. L. and Cross, K. F. *Measure up!* (2nd edn) (Cambridge, MA: Blackwell, 1995).

Lyotard, F. 'The Postmodern Condition: A Report on Knowledge' (translated by Bennington, G. et al). (Minneapolis: University of Minnesota, 1984)

Machin, J. L. 'Management control systems: whence and whither?', in Lowe, E. A. and Machin, J. L. (eds) *New perspectives in management control* (London: Macmillan, 1983), 22–42.

Macnamara, T., D'Silva, K. and Morton, S. A. 'Evaluation of the Strategic Grants programme: Preferred outcomes and flagship approaches', *Report commissioned by the Community Fund* (London: South Bank University, October 2004).

Maltz, A. C., Shenhar A. J. and Reilly, R. R. 'Beyond the Balanced Scorecard: Refining the Search for Organizational Success Measures', *Long Range Planning*, Vol. 36 (2003) 187–204.

Mancebon, M. and Molinero, C. 'Performance in primary schools', *Journal of Operational Research Society*, Vol. 51 (2000) 843–54.

March, J. G. 'Exploration and Exploitation in Organizational Learning', *Organization Science*, Vol. 2, No. 1 (1991) 71–87.

March, J. G. 'The Evolution of Evolution', in Baum, J. A. C. and. Singh, J. V. (eds) *Evolutionary Dynamics of Organizations* (1994) 3–20.

Marketing Leadership Council, *Measuring Marketing Performance* (Washington DC: Corporate Executive Board, August 2001).

Marketing Leadership Council, *Stewarding the Brand for Profitable Growth* (Washington DC: Corporate Executive Board, December 2001).

Marr, B. *Strategic performance management: leveraging and measuring your intangible value drivers* (Oxford: Butterworth-Heinemann, 2006).

Marris, R. L. *The Economic Theory of 'Managerial' Capitalism* (London: Macmillan, 1964).

Martin, S. 'The Modernisation of UK Local Government: Markets, Managers, Monitors and Mixed Fortunes', *Public Management Review*, Vol. 4 (2002) 3.

Maslow, A. H. 'A theory of human motivation', *Psychological Review*, Vol. 40 (1943) 370–96.

Maslow, A. *Motivation and personality* (New York: Harper and Row, 1954).

Mason, R. O. and Swanson, E. B. 'Measurement for Management Decision: A Perspective', in Mason, R. O., Swanson, E. B. *Measurement for Management Decision* (Reading, MA: Addison-Wesley, 1981) pp. 10–25.

Matlack, C., Holmes, S. and Balfour, F. 'Airbus May Hit An Air Pocket Over China', *Business Week Online* (13 April 2006).

Matlay, H. 'Contemporary training initiatives in Britain: a small business perspective', *Journal of Small Business and Enterprise Development*, Vol. 11, No. 4 (2004) 4504–13.

Maxwell, R. J. 'Quality assessment in health', *British Medical Journal*, Vol. 288, 12 May (1984) pp. 1470–2.

Maylor, H. 'Beyond the Gantt chart: project management moving on', *European Management Journal*, Vol. 19, No. 2 (2001) 92–100.

McClelland, D. *The Achieving Society* (Princeton: Van Norstrand, 1961).

McClelland, D. 'Testing for competence rather than for intelligence', *American Psychologist*, Vol. 28 (1973) 1–14.

McClelland, D. and Burnham, D. H. 'Power is the great motivator', *Harvard Business Review*, Vol. 54 (1976) 100–10.

McConnell, J. V. 'Criminals can be brainwashed – now', in Karlins, M. (ed.) *Psychology in the Service of Man* (New York: Wiley, 1973), pp. 102–10.

McDuffie, J. P. 'Human Resource bundles and manufacturing performance: organisational logic and flexible production systems in the World Auto industry', *Industrial and Labour Relations Review*, Vol. 48 (1995) 197–221.

McGill, I. and Beaty, L. *Action Learning* (London: Kogan Page, 1995).

McGregor, D. *The human side of enterprise* (New York: McGraw-Hill, 1960).

McLaughlin, K. 'Towards a "modernised" voluntary and community Sector? Emerging lessons from government-voluntary and community sector relationships in the UK', *Public Management Review*, Vol. 6, No. 4 (2004) 555–62.

McLaughlin, K., Osborne, S. and Ferlie, E. *The new public management: Current trends and future prospects* (London: Routledge, 2002).

Medawar, C. and Herxheimer, A. 'A comparison of adverse drug reaction reports form professionals and users, relating to risk of dependence and suicidal behaviour with paroxetine', *International Journal of Risk and Safety in Medicine*, Vol. 16 (2003/4) 5–19, www.socialaudit.org.uk/YELLOW%20CARD%20REVIEW.pdf, accessed 06/08/07.

Melnyk, S. A., Stewart, D. M. and Swink, M. 'Metrics and performance measurement in operations management: dealing with the metrics maze', *Journal of Operations Management*, Vol. 22, No. 3 (2004) 209–18.

Merchant, K. 'How and why firms disregard the controllability principle', in Bruns, W. and Kaplan, R. (eds) *Accounting and management: field study perspectives.* (Harvard Business School Press, 1987) 316–38.

Metcalf, L. and Richards, S. *Improving Public Management* (London: Sage, 1987).

Meyer, J. W. and Rowan, B. 'Institutionalized Organizations: Formal Structure as Myth and Ceremony', *American Journal of Sociology*, Vol. 83, No. 2 (1977) 340–63.

Meyer, M. W. *Rethinking Performance Measurement – Beyond the Balanced Scorecard* (Cambridge: Cambridge University Press, 2002).

Midwinter, A, 'New Labour and the modernisation of British local government: A critique', *Financial Accountability and Management*, Vol. 17, No. 4 (2001) 311–20.

Might R. J. and Fischer, W. A. 'The role of structural factors in determining project management success', *IEEE Transactions on Engineering Management*, Vol. 32, No. 2 (1985) 71–7.

Milgrom, P. and Roberts, J. 'The efficiency of equity in organizational decision-processes', *American Economic Review*, Vol. 80 (1990a) 154–9.

Milgrom, P. and Roberts, J. 'The economics of modern manufacturing: technology, strategy and organization', *American Economic Review*, Vol. 80 (1990b) 511–29.

Milgrom, P. and Roberts, J. *Economics, Organization and Management* (Englewood Cliffs, NJ: Prentice Hall, 1992).

Milgrom, P. and Roberts, J. 'Complementarities and Fit: Strategy, Structure and Organisational Change in Manufacturing', *Journal of Accounting and Economics*, Vol. 19, No. 2 (1995) 179–208.

Mintzberg, H. 'Planning on the left side, managing on the right', *Harvard Business Review*, Vol. 54 (1976) 49–58.

Mintzberg, H. 'A Note on that Dirty Word "Efficiency" ', *Interfaces*, Vol. 12, October (1982) pp. 101–5.

Mintzberg, H. *Power in and around organizations* (Englewood Cliffs, NJ: Prentice Hall, 1983).

Mintzberg, H. *Managers not MBAs: A hard look at the soft practices of managing and management development* (San Francisco CA: Berrett-Koehler, 2004)

Mitchell, W. 'Dual Clocks: entry order influences on incumbent and new market share and survival when specialised assets retain their value', *Strategic Management Journal*, Vol. 12, No. 2 (1991) 85–100.

Modell, S. 'Performance measurement myths in the public sector: a research note'. *Financial Accountability and Management*, Vol. 20, No. 1 (2004) 39–55.

Molnar, M. J. 'Executive Views on Intangible Assets: Insights From the Accenture/Economist Intelligence Unit Survey', *Accenture Research Note 'Intangible Assets and Future Value'*, Issue One, April (2004).

Moore, M. H. *Creating Public Value: Strategic Management in Government* (Cambridge, MA: Harvard University Press, 1995).

Morris P. W. G. and Hough, G. H. *The Anatomy of Major Projects, A Study of the Reality of Project Management* (Chichester: John Wiley, 1987).

Morrison Paul, C. J. *Cost Structure and the Measurement of Economic Performance: Productivity, Utilization, Cost Economies, and Related Performance Indicators* (Boston: Kluwer, 1999).

Mouritsen, J. 'Five aspects of accounting departments' work', *Management Accounting Research*, 1996, Vol. 7, No. 3 (1996) 283–303.

Moynihan, D. and Ingraham, P. 'When does performance information contribute to performance information use?' *Maxwell School of Management Working Paper*, (New York State: Syracuse IO University, 2001).

MPAF, *A Study of the Major Projects Agreement on the BAA Terminal 5 Programme*, (Major Projects Agreement Forum (MPAF), August 2005), http://www.mpaforum.org.uk, website accessed 04/08/07.

Mueller, D. *Public Choice 11: A Revised Edition* (Cambridge: Cambridge University Press, 1989).

Mueller, D. *Public Choice III* (Cambridge: Cambridge University Press, 2003).

Murray, E. and Richardson, P. 'Measuring strategic performance: are we measuring the right things? – right?', in Neely, A. (ed.) *Performance Measurement – Past, Present and Future* (Cambridge: Judge Institute, University of Cambridge, 2000) 411–26.

Nanni, A. J., Dixon, J. R. and Vollmann, T. E. 'Strategic Control and Performance Measurement', *Journal of Cost Management*, Summer (1990) 33–42.

Nathan, Lord, *Report of the committee on the law and practice relating to charitable trusts*, Cmd. 8710 (London: HMSO, 1952).

Nathan, Lord, 'Effectiveness and the voluntary sector', *Report of a working party established by NCVO* (London: NCVO, April 1990).

NCVO. 'Improving our Performance: Quality', *Background paper 41* (2004) www.ncvo-vol.org.uk, accessed 31/07/07.

NCVO. *Financial benchmarking* (2005a) www.ncvo-vol.org.uk, accessed 31/07/07.

NCVO. *Improving our Performance: a strategy for the voluntary and community sector* (2005b), www.ncvo-vol.org.uk, accessed 31/07/07.

NCVO. *Measuring performance* (2005c) www.ncvo-vol.org.uk, accessed 31/07/07.

NCVO. *Outcomes and impact* (2005d) www.ncvo-vol.org.uk, accessed 31/07/07.

NCVO. *Performance reporting* (2005e) www.ncvo-vol.org.uk, accessed 31/07/07.

Needham, P. 'The myth of the self-regulating work group', *Personnel Management*, August (1982) 39–41.

Neely, A. 'The performance measurement revolution: why now and what next?', *International Journal of Operations and Production Management*, Vol. 19, No. 2 (1999) 205–29.

Neely, A. and Austin, R. 'Measuring operations performance – past present and future', *Proceedings of the second International Conference on Performance Measurement, Cambridge, Cranfield School of Management*, 19–21 July, Neely, A. (ed.), (2000) 419–26.

Neely, A., Gregory, M. and Platts, K. 'Performance measurement system design: a literature review and research agenda', *International Journal of Operations and Production Management*, Vol. 15, No. 4 (1995) 80–116.

Neely, A., Richards, H., Mills, J., Platts, K. and Bourne, M. 'Designing performance measures: a structured approach', *International Journal of Operations and Production Management*, Vol. 17, No. 11 (1997) 1131–52.

Neely, A. D. *Measuring business performance* (London: Economist Books, 1998).

Neely, A. D. 'Performance measurement – past, present and future', *Preface, Proceedings of the second International Conference on Performance Measurement, Cambridge, Cranfield School of Management*, 19–21 July, Neely, A. (ed.) (Cranfield: Centre for Business Performance, 2000).

Neely, A. D. and Waggoner, D. B. 'Performance measurement – theory and practice', *Conference Proceedings* (Cambridge: Preface, Centre for Business Performance, 1998).

Neely, A. D., Adams, C. and Kennerley, M. *The performance prism: the scorecard for measuring and managing stakeholder relationships* (London: Financial Times/Prentice Hall, 2002).

Nelson, R. R. 'Bringing institutions into evolutionary growth theory', *Journal of Evolutionary Economics*, Vol. 12 (2002) 17–28.

Newton, T. and Findlay, P. 'Playing god? The Performance of Appraisal', *Human Resource Management Journal*, (1996) 42–58.

NHS Executive, *The New NHS: A National Framework for Assessing Performance* (London: Department of Health, 1998).

Nicholas, J. 'Successful Project Management: A Force-Field Analysis', *Journal of Systems Management*, Vol. 40, No. 1 (1989) 24–30, 36.

Niskanen, W. A. *Bureaucracy and Representative Government* (Chicago: Aldine-Atherton, 1971).

Nonaka, I. and Takeuchi, H. *The Knowledge-Creating Company: How Japanese Companies Create the Dynamics of Innovation* (New York: Oxford University Press, 1995).

Nørreklit H. 'The balance on the balanced scorecard – a critical analysis of some of its assumptions', *Management Accounting Research*, Vol. 11 (2000) 65–88.

Nørreklit, H. 'The Balanced Scorecard: what is the score?, A rhetorical analysis of the Balanced Scorecard', *Accounting, Organisations and Society*, Vol. 28 (2003) 591–619.

North, D. C. *Institutions, Institutional Change and Performance* (Cambridge, UK: Cambridge University Press, 1990).

Norton, D. and SEM Product Management, *SAP Strategic Enterprise Management: Translating Strategy into Action: The Balanced Scorecard* (SAP AG, 1999).

Nutley, S. M., Walter, I. and Davies, H. T. O. *Using evidence. How research can inform public services* (Bristol: The Policy Press, 2007).

O'Hanlon, J. and Peasnell, K. 'Wall Street's contribution to management accounting: the Stern Stewart EVA® financial management system', *Management Accounting Research*, Vol. 9, No. 4 (1998) 421–44.

OECD, *Public Management Developments: 1991* (and various other years) (Paris: Organization for Economic Cooperation and Development, 1991).

OECD, *Performance Management in Government* (Paris: Organization for Economic Cooperation and Development, 1996).

OFWAT, *Future Water and Sewerage Charges 2000–05; Draft Determinations* (London: Office of Water Trading, 1999).

OGC, *Managing Successful Projects with PRINCE2* (London: Office of Government and Commerce, TSO, 2002).

OGC, *Managing successful programmes* (London: Office of Government and Commerce, TSO, 2007).

Ohmae, K. *The End of the Nation State: The rise of regional economics* (New York: Free Press, 1995).

Olve, N. G. and Wetter, J. R. *Performance Drivers: A Practical Guide to Using the Balanced Scorecard* (Chichester: Wiley, 2000).

Omisakin, I. 'Value-for-money in the voluntary sector', *Management Accounting*, March (1997).

OPSR, *Improving Programme and Project Delivery (IPPD)* (Office of Public Services Reform, 2003); archive.cabinetoffice.gov.uk/opsr/documents/pdf/ippdfinal03.pdf, accessed 04/08/07.

Ormerod, R. J. 'The role of OR in shaping the future: smart bits, helpful ways and things that matter', *Journal of Operational Research Society*, Vol. 48 (1997) 1045–56.

Osborne, D. and Gaebler, T. *Reinventing Government: How the Entrepreneurial Spirit is Transforming the Public Sector* (Reading, MA: Addison-Wesley, 1992).

Osborne, S. P. 'Introduction: managing in the voluntary and nonprofit sector' in Osborne, S. P. (ed.) *Managing in the voluntary sector. A handbook for managers in charitable and nonprofit organisations* (London: International Thomson Business Press, 2006a), pp. 1–4.

Osborne, S. P. 'Performance and quality management in VNPOs', in Osborne, S. P. (ed.) *Managing in the voluntary sector. A handbook for managers in charitable and nonprofit organisations* (London: International Thomson Business Press, 2006b), pp. 217–36.

Osborne, S. P. 'What is "voluntary" about the voluntary and non-profit sector?' in Osborne, S. P. (ed.) *Managing in the voluntary sector. A handbook for managers in charitable and nonprofit organisations*, (London, International Thomson Business Press, 2006c), pp. 5–17.

Otley, D. 'The contingency theory of management accounting: achievement and prognosis', *Accounting, Organizations and Society*, Vol. 5 (1980) 194–208 and 413–28.

Otley, D. 'Issues in accountability and control: some observations from a study of colliery accountability in the British Coal Corporation', *Management accounting research*, Vol. 1 (1990) 101–23.

Otley, D. 'Management control in contemporary organisations: towards a wider framework', *Management Accounting Research*, Vol. 5 (1994) 289–99.

Otley, D. 'Performance management: a framework for management control systems research', *Management Accounting Research*, Vol. 10 (1999) 363–82.

Ouchi, W. G. 'A conceptual framework for the design of optimal control mechanisms', *Management Science*, Vol. 25 (1979) 833–49.

Palmer, P. *External regulation and internal control in the charity sector*, unpublished PhD thesis (London: Centre for Internal Auditing, City University, February 1995).

Palmer, P. 'Foreword', in Courtney, R. *Managing voluntary organisations: new approaches* (Hemel Hempstead: ICSA Publishing, 1996).

Palmer, P., Isaacs, M. and D' Silva, K. 'Charity SORP compliance – findings of a research study', *Managerial Auditing Journal*, Vol. 16, No. 5 (2001) 255–62.

Parker, D., 'Is the private sector more efficient? A study in the public v. private debate', *Public Administration Bulletin*, Vol. 48 (1985) 2–23.

Parker, S. K. 'Designing jobs to enhance well-being and performance', in Warr, P. (ed.) *Psychology at Work*, 5th edn (London: Penguin, 2002), pp. 276–99.

Parker, S. K., Wall, T. D. and Cordery, J. L. 'Future work design research and practice: Towards an elaborated model of work design', *Journal of Occupational and Organizational Psychology*, Vol. 74 (2001) 413–40.

Pascale, R. T. *Managing on the edge: companies that use conflict to stay ahead* (New York: Simon & Schuster, and Viking: London, 1990)

Patterson, M., West, M., Lawthom, R. and Nickell, S. *Impact of People management Practices on Business Performance* (London: Institute of Personnel and Development, 1997).

Peasnell, K. V. 'Some formal connections between economic values and yields and accounting numbers', *Journal of Business Finance and Accounting*, Vol. 9 (1982) 361–81.

Pellegrinelli, S. 'Programme management: organising project-based change', *International Journal of Project Management*, Vol. 15, No. 3 (1997) 141–9.

Performance and Innovation Unit (PIU), *Workforce Development Project, Analysis Paper* (London: Cabinet Office, 2001).

Pettigrew, A. (1997) 'The double hurdles for management research', in Clarke, T. (ed.) *Advancement in organisational behaviour: essays in honour of D.S. Pugh*, 277–96. London: Dartmouth Press.

Pettigrew, A. and Whipp, R. 'Understanding the Environment', in Mabey, C. and Mayon-White, B. (eds) *Managing Change*, 2nd edn (London: The Open University/Paul Chapman Publishing, 1993).

Pfeffer, J. *The Human Equation: Building Profits by Putting People First* (Boston, MA: Harvard Business School Press, 1998).

Pfeffer, J. and Fong, C. T. 'The end of Business Schools? Less success than meets the eye', *Academy of Management Executive* (2002) 78–95.

Pfeffer, J. and Salancik, G. *The External Control of Organizations: A resource dependence perspective* (New York: Harper and Row, 1978).

Pfeffer, J. and Sutton, R. I. *Hard facts, dangerous half truths and total nonsense: profiting from evidence-based management* (Boston, MA: Harvard Business School Press, 2006a).

Pfeffer, J. and Sutton, R. I. 'Evidence-based management', *Harvard Business Review*, Vol. 84, No. 1 (2006b) 62–74.

Pidd, M. 'Perversity in Public Service Performance Measurement', *International Journal of Productivity and Performance Management*, Vol. 54, No. 5 (2005) 482–93.

Pinto, J. K. and Prescott, J. E. 'Planning and Tactical Factors in the Project Implementation Process', *Journal of Management Studies*, Vol. 3 (1990) 305–27.

Pinto J. K. and Slevin, D. P. 'Critical factors in successful project management', *IEEE Transactions on Engineering Management*, Vol. 34, No. 1 (1987) 22–7.

Pinto, J. K. and Slevin, D. P. 'Project Success: Definitions and Measurement Techniques', *Project Management Journal*, Vol. 19, No. 1 (1988) 67–71.

Pinto, M. B. and Pinto, J. K. 'Determinants of Cross-Functional Cooperation in the Project Implementation Process', *Project Management Journal*, Vol. 20, No. 4 (1991) 13–20.

Plachy. 'The point factor job evaluation system: a step by step guide', *Compensation and benefits review*, September–October (1987) 12–27.

Pollitt, C. 'Beyond the managerial model: the case for broadening performance assessment in government and the public services', *Financial Accountability and Management*, Vol. 2, No. 3, Autumn (1986) 155–70.

Pollitt, C. *Managerialism and the public services: the Anglo-American experience* (Oxford, England: Basil Blackwell, 1990).

Pollitt, C. *Integrating Financial Management and Performance Management* (Paris: OECD, 1999).

Pollitt, C. 'Clarifying Convergence', *Public Management Review*, Vol. 4, No. 1 (2001) 471–92.

Pollitt, C. *The Essential Public Manager* (Philadelphia: Open University Press, 2003).

Pollitt, C. *Performance Information for democracy – the missing link?* (Berlin: European Evaluation Society, 2004).

Pollitt, C. 'Performance Management in Practice: A comparative study of Executive agencies', *Journal of Public Administration Research and Theory*, Vol.16, No. 1 (2006) 25–44.

Pollitt, C. and Bouckaert, G. *Public Management Reform* (Oxford: Oxford UP, 2000).

Porter, M. E. *Competitive Strategy: Techniques for Analysing Industries and Competitors* (New York: The Free Press and Basingstoke: Macmillan, 1980).

Porter, M. E. *Competitive Advantage: Creating and Sustaining Superior Performance* (New York: The Free Press, 1985).

Porter, M. E. *The Competitive Advantage of Nations* (London: Macmillan, 1990).

Porter, T. M. *Trust in Numbers: The Pursuit of Objectivity in Science and Public Life* (Princeton: Princeton University Press, 1995).

Prahalad, C. K. and Hamel, G. 'The core competence of the corporation', *Harvard Business Review*, Vol. 68, May–June (1990) 79–91.

Print, C. F. 'People Value – There's No Accounting for People'. *Henley Centre for Value Improvement, Henley Discussion*, Paper 8 (2004). www.henleymc.ac.uk /hcvi, accessed 06/08/07.

Provan, K. G., Beyer, J. M. and Kruytbosch, C. 'Environmental linkages and power in resource-dependence relations between organizations', *Administrative Science Quarterly*, Vol. 25, No. 2 (1980) 200–25.

Public Services Productivity Panel, *Public Services Productivity: Meeting the challenge* (London, HM Treasury, 2000), p. 25.

Purcell, J. 'Mapping management style in employee relations', *Journal of Management Studies*, Vol. 24, No. 5 (1987) 533–48.

Purcell, J. and Sisson, K. 'Strategies and practice management of industrial relations', in Bain, G. (ed.) *Industrial Relations in Britain* (Oxford: Blackwell, 1983).

Purcell, J., Kinnie, N., Hutchinson, S., Rayton, B. and Swart, J. *Understanding the People and Performance Link: Unlocking the black box* (Research report, CIPD, 2002).

Quality Standards Task Group (QSTG). *Improving our performance: a strategy for the voluntary and community sector* (London: NCVO, 2004).

Raby, M. 'Project Management Earned Value', *Work Study*, Vol. 49, No. 1 (2000) 6–9.

Radin, B. A. 'The Government Performance and Results Act (GPRA): Hydra-headed Monster or Flexible Management Tool?', *Public Administration Review*, Vol. 58 (1998) 307–17.

Radnor, Z., unpublished teaching material (UK: University of Warwick, 2005).

Radnor, Z. J. 'Hitting the target and missing the point: Developing an understanding of Organisational Gaming', in Van Dooren, W. and Van de Walle, S. (eds) *Utilising Public Sector Performance Information*, Kernaghan, K. and van der Donk, W. (series eds) *Governance and Public Management* (Palgrave Macmillan, 2008).

Radnor, Z. J. and Lovell, B. 'Success factors for Implementation of the Balanced Scorecard in a NHS Multi-agency setting', *International Journal of Health Care and Quality Assurance*, Vol. 16, No. 2 (2003) 99–108.

Rappaport, A. 'Linking Competitive Strategy and Shareholder Value Analysis', *Journal of Business Strategy*, Vol. 7, No. 4, Spring (1987) 58–67.

Rashid, N. *Managing Performance in Local Government* (London: Kogan Page, 1999).

Raymond, E. S. *The Cathedral and the Bazaar: musings on Linux and Open source by an accidental revolutionary*, revised ed. (Sebastopol, CA: O'Reilly, 2001).

Reason, P. and Bradley, M. (eds) *Handbook of Action Research: Participative Inquiry in Action* (London: Wiley, 2000).

Reason, P. and Rowan, J. *Human Inquiry: A Sourcebook of New Paradigm Research* (London: Wiley, 1981).

Reed, J., Jones, D. and Irvine, J. 'Appreciating impact: Evaluating small voluntary organisations in the United Kingdom', *Voluntas: International Journal of Voluntary and Nonprofit organisation*, Vol. 16, No. 2 (2005) 123–41.

Reporters Without Borders, *Freedom of the Press Worldwide*, www.rsf.org/IMG/pdf/report.pdf, 2006, accessed 04/08/07.

Ridgway, V. F. 'Dysfunctional Consequences of Performance Measurements', *Administrative Science Quarterly*, Vol. 1, No. 2 (1956) 240–7.

Robertson, I., Bartram, D. and Callinan, M. 'Personnel selection and assessment', in Warr, P. (ed.) *Psychology at Work,* 5th edn (London: Penguin, 2002), pp. 100–52.

Rockart, J. F. 'Chief executives define their own data needs', *Harvard Business Review*, Vol. 57, No. 2 (1979) 81–93.

Roethlisberger, F. J. and Dickson, W. J. *Management and the worker* (Cambridge, MA: Harvard University Press, 1939).

Rogers, S. *Performance Management in Local Government* (London: Longman, 1990).

Rosenberg, M. J. 'New ways to reduce distrust between the U.S. and Russia', in Karlins, M. (ed.) *Psychology in the Service of Man* (New York: Wiley, 1973), 200–12.

Rosenfelt, R. H. 'The elderly mystique', in Karlins, M. (ed.) *Psychology in the Service of Man* (New York: Wiley, 1973), 294–301.

Rosenhead, J. (ed.) *Rational Analysis for a Problematic World*. (Chichester: John Wiley & Sons, 1989).

Ross, S. A. 'The Economic Theory of Agency: The Principal's Problem', *The American Economic Review*, Vol. 63, No. 2 (1973) 134–9.

Rousseau, D. M. *Psychological Contracts in Organizations: Understanding Written and Unwritten Agreements* (Thousand Oaks: Sage, 1995).

Rousseau, D. M. 'Psychological contracts in the workplace: Understanding the ties that motivate', *The Academy of Management Executive*, Vol. 18 (2004) 120–27.

Rousseau, D. M. 'Is there such a thing as "evidence-based management"?', *Academy of Management Review*, Vol. 31, No. 2 (2006) 256–69.

Rousseau, D. M. and McCarthy, S. 'Educating managers from an evidence-based perspective', *Academy of Management Learning and Education*, Vol. 6, No. 1 (2007) 84–101.

Rousseau, D. M. and Wade-Benzoni, K. A. 'Changing individual-organization attachments: A two-way street', in Howard, A. (ed.), *The Changing Nature of Work* (San Francisco, CA: Jossey-Bass, 1995), 290–322.

Royal Statistical Society, *Performance Indicators: Good, Bad, and Ugly* (London: RSS Working Party on Performance Monitoring in the Public Services, 2003).

Rucci, A. J., Kirn, S. P. and Quinn, R. T. 'The employee-customer-profit chain at Sears', *Harvard Business Review*, Vol. 76 (1998) 82–98.

Russ-Eft, D. and Preskill, H. *Evaluation in Organization – a Systematic Approach to Enhancing Learning, Performance, and Change* (Cambridge, MA: Perseus, 2001).

Sabbagh, K. *21st Century Jet: the making of the Boeing 777* (Basingstoke: Macmillan, 1995).

Saint Martin, D. *Building the new managerialist state* (Oxford: Oxford UP, 2000).

Salamon, J. and Anheier, H. 'The non-profit sector cross-nationally – Patterns and types', in CAF, *Researching the Voluntary Sector*, 2nd edn (Tonbridge: Charities Aid Foundation, 1994).

Sanderson, I. 'Performance management, evaluation and learning in "modern" local government', *Public Administration*, Vol. 79, No. 2 (2001) 297–313.

Scapens, R. W. and Jazayeri, M. 'ERP systems and management accounting change, opportunities and impacts: a research note', *European Accounting Review*, Vol. 12, No. 1 (2003) 201–33.

Scapens, R. W. and Macintosh, N. 'Structuration Theory in Management Accounting', *Accounting, Organizations and Society*, Vol. 15, No. 5 (1990) 455–77.

Scarbrough, H. and Swan, J. A. 'Discourses of knowledge management and the learning organization: their production and consumption', in Easterby-Smith, M. and Lyles, M. A. (eds) *Handbook of Organizational Learning and Knowledge Management* (London: Blackwell, 2003) 495–512.

Scase, R. and Goffee, R. *The Real World of the Small Business Owner* (London: Cromm Helm, 1980).

Schedler, K. 'Performance Measurement Challenges in Switzerland: Lessons from Implementation', *International Public Management Review* (2000).

Schmidt, F. L. and Hunter, J. E. 'The validity and utility of selection methods in personnel psychology: Practical and theoretical implications of 85 years of research findings', *Psychological Bulletin*, Vol. 124 (1998) 262–74.

Selznick, P. 'Institutionalism "Old" and "New" ', *Administrative Science Quarterly*, Vol. 41 (1996) 270–7.

Shenhar, A. J., Dvir, D. and Maltz, A. C. 'Project Success: A Multidimensional Strategic Concept', *Long Range Planning*, Vol. 34 (2001) 699–725.

Shenhar, A. J., Levy, O. and Dvir, D. 'Mapping the Dimensions of Project Success', *International Journal of Project Management*, Vol. 28, No. 2 (1997) 5–13.

Sheridan, T. 'A new frame for financial management', *Management Accounting*, London, Vol. 72, No. 1 (1994) 42–3.

Shewhart, W. A. *Economic Control of Quality of Manufactured Product*, reissue edn (Originally published in 1931) (American Society for Quality, 1980).

Shipman Enquiry, Report of an Enquiry by Dame Janet Smith (2007). www.the-shipman-inquiry.org.uk/, accessed 06/08/07.

Shore, L. and Coyle-Shapiro, J. A.-M. 'New developments in the employee-organization relationship', *Journal of Organizational Behaviour*, Vol. 24 (Special Issue), (2003) 443–50.

Shotter, J. *Conversational Realities: Constructing Life Through Language* (London: Sage, 1993).

Simmonds, K. 'Strategic Management Accounting' in Fanning, D. (ed.) *Handbook of Management Accounting* (Gower, 1983) 25–8.

Simons, R. *Levers of control* (Cambridge, MA: Harvard Business School Press, 1995).

Simons, R. *Performance measurement and control systems for implementing strategy* (Englewood Cliffs, NJ: Prentice Hall, 2000).

Skinner, D. O., Tagg, C. and Holloway, J. A. 'Managers and research: the pros and cons of qualitative approaches', *Management Learning*, Vol. 31, No. 2 (2000) 163–79.

Slack, N., Chambers, S., Johnston, R. and Betts, A. *Operations and Process Management* (FT Prentice Hall, 2005).

Sloan, A. P. *My Years with General Motors* (New York: Doubleday, 1964).

Smith, A. *An inquiry into the wealth of nations* (London: Strahan and Cadell, 1776).

Smith, P. 'The use of performance indicators in the public sector', *Journal of the Royal Statistical Society. Series A (Statistics in Society)* Vol. 153 (1990) 53–72.

Smith, P. 'On the unintended consequences of publishing performance data in the public sector', *International Journal of Public Administration*, Vol. 18 (1995) 277–310.

Smith, P. (ed.) *Measuring Outcome in the Public Sector* (London: Taylor and Francis, 1996).

Smith, P. C. and Goddard, M. 'Performance management and Operational Research: a marriage made in heaven?' *Journal of the Operational Research Society*, Vol. 53 (2002) 247–55.

Solomons, D. *Divisional Performance: Measurement and Control* (Irwin, 1963).

Sparks, K., Faragher, B. and Cooper, C. L. 'Well-being and occupational health in the 21st century workplace', *Journal of Occupational and Organizational Psychology*, Vol. 74 (2001) 489–509.

Sparrow, P. 'New organisational forms, processes, jobs and psychological contracts', in Sparrow, P. R. and Marchington, M. (eds) *Human Resource Management: The New Agenda* (Harlow: Pearson Education, 1998), 117–41.

Sparrow, P. and Marchington, M. *Human Resource Management: The New Agenda* (Harlow: Pearson Education, 1998).

Sparrow, P. R. and Cooper, C. L. *The Employment Relationship: Key Challenges for HR* (London: Butterworth Heinemann, 2003).

Spender, J. C. *Industry Recipes: The nature and sources of management judgement* (Oxford: Basil Blackwell,1989).

Spender, J. C. 'Making Knowledge the Basis of a Dynamic Theory of the Firm', *Strategic Management Journal*, Vol. 17, Special Issues (1996) 45–62.

Spottiswood, C. *Improving Police Performance: A New Approach to Measuring Police Efficiency*. Public Services Productivity Panel (London: HM Treasury, 2000).

Srikanth, M. L. 'For Performance Think Non-traditional', *Industry Week*, July (1992) 49–52.

Stainton-Rogers, R., Stenner P., Gleeson, K. and Stainton Rogers, W. *Social Psychology: A Critical Agenda* (Cambridge: Polity Press, 1995).

Standish Group International, *The CHAOS Report* (Standish Group International, 1994), www.standishgroup.com, accessed 04/08/07.

Stanworth, M. J. K. and Curran, J. *Management Motivation in the Smaller Business* (London: Gower, 1973).

Starkey, K. and Madan, P. 'Bridging the relevance gap: aligning stakeholders in the future of management research', *British Journal of Management*, Vol. 12 (Special Issue, 2001) S3–S26.

Starkey, K. and Tiratsoo, N. *Business Schools and the Bottom Line* (Cambridge University Press, 2007).

Steele, R. and Albright, C. 'Games Managers Play at Budget Time', *MIT Sloan Management Review*, Vol. 45, No. 3 (Spring 2004) 81–4.

Stern, J. M., Stewart, G. B. III and Chew, D. H., Jr. 'The EVA® Financial System', *Journal of Applied Corporate Finance*, Vol. 8, No. 2 (summer 1995) 32–46.

Stewart, J. and Beaver, G. (eds) *HRD in Small Organisations: Research and Practice* (Routledge: London, 2004).

Stoker, G. 'Creating a local government for a post-Fordist society: the Thatcher project?' in Stewart, J. and Stoker, G. (eds) *The Future of Local Government* (Basingstoke: Macmillan, 1989).

Storey, J. 'Developments in human resource management: an interim report', *Warwick papers in industrial relations* (Coventry: University of Warwick, 1987) No. 17.

Storey, J. *New Perspectives on the Management of Human Resources* (Routledge, 1989).

Storey, J. *Developments in the Management of Human resources: An analytical Review* (London: Blackwell, 1992).

Storey, J. (ed.), *Human Resource Management: A Critical Text* (1st edn) (London: Routledge, 1995).

Storey, J. (ed.) *Human Resource Management: A Critical Text* (2nd edn) (London: Thomson Learning, 2001).

Strack, R. and Villis, U. 'RAVE: Integrated value management for customer, human, supplier and invested capital', *European Management Journal*, Vol. 20, No. 2 (2002) 147–58.

Sugarman, C. 'US produce standards focus more on appearance than quality', *The Pittsburgh Press* (August 5, 1990) p. E1.

Taylor, F. W. *The Principles of Scientific Management* (New York: Harper, 1911).

Taylor, J. and McAdam, R. 'A longitudinal study of business improvement models: cross purposes or congruity?', *Managing Service Quality*, Vol. 13, No. 5 (2003) 382–97.

Taylor, P., Mulvey, G., Hyman, J. and Bain, P. 'Work organization, control and the experience of work in call centres', *Work, Employment and Society*, Vol. 16 (2002) 133–50.

Teece, D. J., Pisano, G. and Shuen, A. 'Dynamic capabilities and strategic management', *Strategic Management Journal*, Vol. 18, No. 7 (1997) 509–33.

Theuvsen, L. 'Doing better while doing good: Motivational aspects of pay-for-performance effectiveness in nonprofit organisations', *Voluntas: International Journal of Voluntary and Nonprofit Organisation*, Vol. 15, No. 2 (2004) 117–36.

Thomas, A. L. 'The FASB and the Allocation Fallacy', *The Journal of Accountancy*, November (1975) 65–8.

Thompson, G. F. *Between hierarchies and markets: the logic and limits of network forms of organization* (Oxford University Press, 2003).

Thompson, J. N. *The Co-evolutionary Process*, 1st edn (Chicago: Chicago Press, 1994).

Thompson, J. R. 'Reinventing as Reform: Assessing the National Performance Review', *Public Administration Review*, Vol. 60 (2000) 508–21.

Thompson, M. and Richardson, R. *The impact of People Management Practices – A review of the literature* (IPD, 1999).

Thorpe, R. 'Designing and Implementation of Remuneration Systems', in Thorpe, R. and Homan, G. *Strategic Reward Systems* (Financial Times-Prentice Hall, 2000), Ch. 7.

Thorpe, R. and Beasley, T. 'The characteristics of performance management research. Implications and challenges', *International Journal of Productivity and Performance Management*, Vol. 53, No. 4 (2004) 334–44.

Thorpe, R., Clarke, J., Gold, J. and Anderson, L. *Using performance measurement in the strategic development of Small Firms: the case for GVA* (Paper presented at the British Academy of Management Conference, Oxford, 2005a).

Thorpe, R., Holt, R., Macpherson, A. and Pittaway, L. 'Using knowledge within small and medium-sized firms: A systematic review of the evidence', *International Journal of Management Reviews*, Vol. 7, No. 4 (2005b) 257–81.

Thorpe, R., Jones, O., Macpherson, A. and Holt, R. 'The Evolution of Business Knowledge in Smaller Firms', in Scarbrough, H. *The Evolution of Business Knowledge* (Oxford University Press, 2008), Ch. 2.

Tomkins, C. 'Residual Income: a rebuttal of Professor Amey's arguments', *Journal of Business Finance and Accounting*, Summer (1975) 161–8.

Townley, B. 'Foucault, Power/Knowledge, and its Relevance for Human Resource Management', *Academy of Management Review*, July (1993) 518–45.

Townley, B. *Reframing Human Resource Management: Power, Ethics and the Subject at Work* (London: Sage Publications, London, 1994)

Tranfield, D. and Starkey, K. 'The nature, social organization and promotion of management research: towards policy', *British Journal of Management*, Vol. 9 (1998) 341–53.

Trist, E. L. and Bamforth, K. W. 'Some sociological and psychological consequences of the longwall method of coal-getting: An examination of the psychological situation and defences of a work group in relation to the social structure and the technological content of the work system', *Human Relations*, Vol. 1 (1951) 3–38.

Truss, C. 'Complexities and controversies in linking HRM with organisational outcomes', *Journal of Management Studies*, Vol. 38, No. 8 (2001) 1121–48.

Truss, C., Gratton, L., Hope-Hailey V., McGovern, P. and Stiles, P. 'Soft and Hard Models of HRM: A Reappraisal', *Journal of Management Studies*, Vol. 34, No. 1, January (1997), 53–73.

Tukel, O. I. and Rom, W. O. 'An empirical investigation of project evaluation Criteria', *International Journal of Operations and Production Management*, Vol. 21, No. 3 (2001) 400–16.

Tuman, J. *Models for Achieving Success through Team-building and Stakeholder Management*, in Dinsmore, P. G. (ed.) (US: AMACOM: 1993) 207–23.

Turney, P. and Anderson, B. 'Accounting for Continuous Improvement', *Sloan Management Review*, Winter (1989) 37–47.

Tyson, S. and Fell, A. *Evaluating the Personnel Function* (London: Routledge, 1996).

Ulrich, D. 'A New Mandate for Human Resources', *Harvard Business Review*, Vol. 76, No. 1 (1998) 124–34.

US OECM DOE, 'Planning, Budgeting, Acquisition, and Management of Capital Assets', *Circular A-11, Part 7* (2003). oecm.doe.gov/Portals/2/s300.pdf, accessed 04/07/08.

Vecchio, R. P. *Organizational Behavior*, 3rd edn (Fort Worth: Harcourt Brace, 1995).

Venkatraman, N. and Ramanujam, V. 'Measurement of Business Economic Performance: An Examination of Method Convergence', *Journal of Management*, Vol. 13, No. 1 (1987) 109–12.

Vernon, R. 'The location of economic activity' in Dunning, J. H. (ed) *Economic Analysis and the Multinational Enterprise* (London: Allen & Unwin, 1974).

Vickers, J. and Yarrow G. *Privatisation: An Economic Analysis* (Cambridge, MA: The MIT Press, 1988).

Vigoda, E. 'Performance in the third sector: a micro-level framework and some lessons from Israel, *International Journal of Public Administration*, Vol. 24, No. 11, November (2001) 12–67.

Voss, C. A. 'Operations Management from Taylor to Toyota – and beyond?', *British Journal of Management*, Vol. 6 Special Issue, December (1995) S17–29.

Vroom, V. *Work and Motivation* (New York: Wiley, 1964).

Walsh, K. and Davis, H. *Competition and Service: The Impact of the Local Government Act 1988* (London: HMSO, 1993).

Walters, M. (ed.) *The Performance Management Handbook* (London: Institute of Personnel Development, 1995).

Wang, C. L. and Ahmed, P. K. 'Dynamic capabilities: A review and research agenda', *International Journal of Management Reviews*, Vol. 9, No. 1 (2007) 31–51.

Warr, P. *Work, Unemployment and Mental Health* (Oxford: Oxford Science Publications, 1987).

Warr, P. 'The study of well-being, behaviour and attitudes', in Warr, P. (ed) *Psychology at Work*, 5th edn (London: Penguin, 2002) 1–25.

Wateridge, J. 'How can IS/IT projects be measured for success?', *International Journal of Project Management*, Vol. 16, No. 1 (1998) 59–63.

Watson, T. *The Personnel Managers* (London: Routledge, 1997).

Webber, M. 'The urban place and the non-place urban realm', in Webber, M. M. Dyckman, J. W., Foley, D. L., Gutenberg, A. Z., Wheaton, W. L. C. and Wurster, C. B. (eds) *Explorations in Urban Structure* (Philadelphia: University of Pennsylvania, 1964).

Weick, K. E. *The Social Psychology of Organizing* (Reading, MA: Addison-Wesley, 1969).

Weisbrod, B. A. *The Nonprofit Economy* (Cambridge, MA: The Harvard University Press, 1988).

Welch, J. and Byrne, J. *Jack: Straight from the Gut* (Warner Business, 2003).

Wernerfelt, B. 'A Resource-based View of the Firm', *Strategic Management Journal*, Vol. 5 (1984) 171–80.

West Yorkshire Police Authority, 'Policing Strategy and Policing Plan' (2007). www.wypa.org, accessed 04/08/07.

Westerveld, E. 'The Project Excellence Model®: linking success criteria and critical success factors', *International Journal of Project Management*, Vol. 21, No. 6 (2003) 411–18.

White, D. and Fortune, J. 'Current practice in project management – An empirical study', *International Journal of Project Management*, Vol. 20, No. 1 (2002) 1–11.

Whittington, R., Pettigrew, A. M., Peck, S., Fenton, E. and Conyon, M. 'Change and Complementarities in the New Competitive Landscape', *Organization Science*, July (1999).

Wickes, M. *An explorative study into the utility of visual reporting systems in project and programme management environments* (Cranfield University, PhD Thesis, 2005).

Wilding, R. 'Enhancing value by effective supply chain collaboration: creating designer relationships', *Proceedings of EUROLOG 2006: Logistics in the value chain: Designer or Performer?* Palais des Congres de Strasbourg, Strasbourg, 21–22 June (Organised by ELA and Aslog, Paris, 2006).

Wilkes, M. and Dale, B. G. 'Attitudes to Self-Assessment and Quality Awards: A Study in Small and Medium Sized Companies', *Total Quality Management*, Vol. 9, No. 8 (1998) 731–9.

Williamson, O. E. *Markets and Hierarchies: Analysis and Anti-trust Implications* (New York: Free Press, 1975).

Williamson, O. E. *The Economic Institutions of Capitalism: Firms, Markets, Relational Contracting* (New York: Free Press, 1985).

Williamson, O. E. *The Mechanisms of Governance*, 1st edn (New York: Oxford University Press, 1996).

Wilson, J. Q. *Bureaucracy: what government agencies do and why they do it* (New York: Basic Books, 1989).

Wilson, J. Q. 'Reinventing public administration', *Political Science and Politics*, Vol. 27, No. 4 (1994) 667–73.

Winch, G., Usmani, A. and Edkins, A. 'Towards total project quality: a gap analysis approach', *Construction Management & Economics*, Vol. 16, No. 2 (1998) 193–207.

Winstanley, D. and Stuart-Smith, K. 'Policing performance: the ethics of performance management', *Personnel Review*, Vol. 25, No. 6 (1996) 66–84.

Winstanley, D., Sorabji, D. and Dawson, S. 'When the pieces don't fit: a stakeholder power matrix to analyse public sector restructuring', *Public Money and Management*, Vol. 15, No. 2 (1995) 19–26.

Wise, D. 'Performance measurement for charities', *Charities Management Services* (London: ICSA Publishing, 1995).

Wood, S. and De Menezes, L. 'High Commitment management in the UK', *Human Relations*, Vol. 51, No. 4 (1998) 485–515.

Woodward, D. G., Edwards, P. and Birkin, F. 'Organisational legitimacy and stakeholder information provision', *British Journal of Management*, Vol. 7, No. 4 (1996) 329–48.

Yin, K. *Case Study Research. Design and Methods (Applied Social Research Methods Series, Vol. 5)* (Newbury Park, CA: Sage, 2003).

Zifcak, S. *New Managerialism: Administrative Reform in Whitehall and Canberra.* (Buckingham, UK: Open University Press, 1994).

Zimmerman, J. L. 'The municipal accounting maze: an analysis of political incentives', *Journal of Accounting*, Vol. 15, No. 5 (1978) 107–55.

Zimmerman, J. L. 'Some conjectures regarding empirical management accounting research', *Journal of Accounting and Economics*, Vol. 32, Nos 1–3 (2001) 411–27.

Author Index

Subject Index

In this index tables; figures; appendices and notes are indicated in italics, enclosed in parenthesis, following the page number. E.g. game theory approach, 54(*n.1*).

Notes are indicated by *n*. Tables by *tab*. Figures by *fig*. Appendices by *app*.